HEROMAN 3

Original/Stan Lee + BONES TAMON OHTA

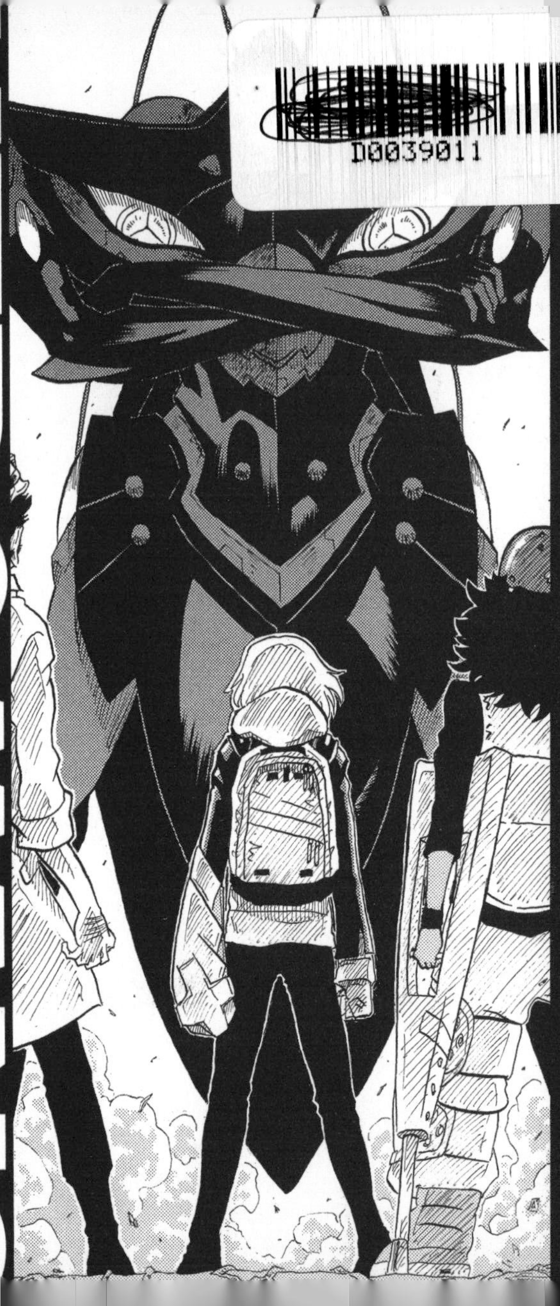

HEROMAN

03 ▸ contents

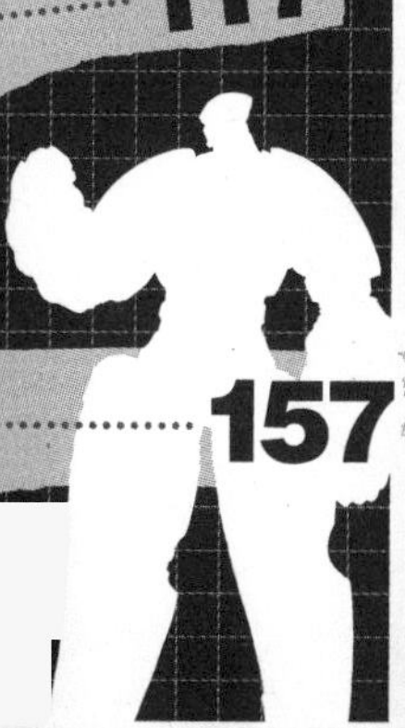

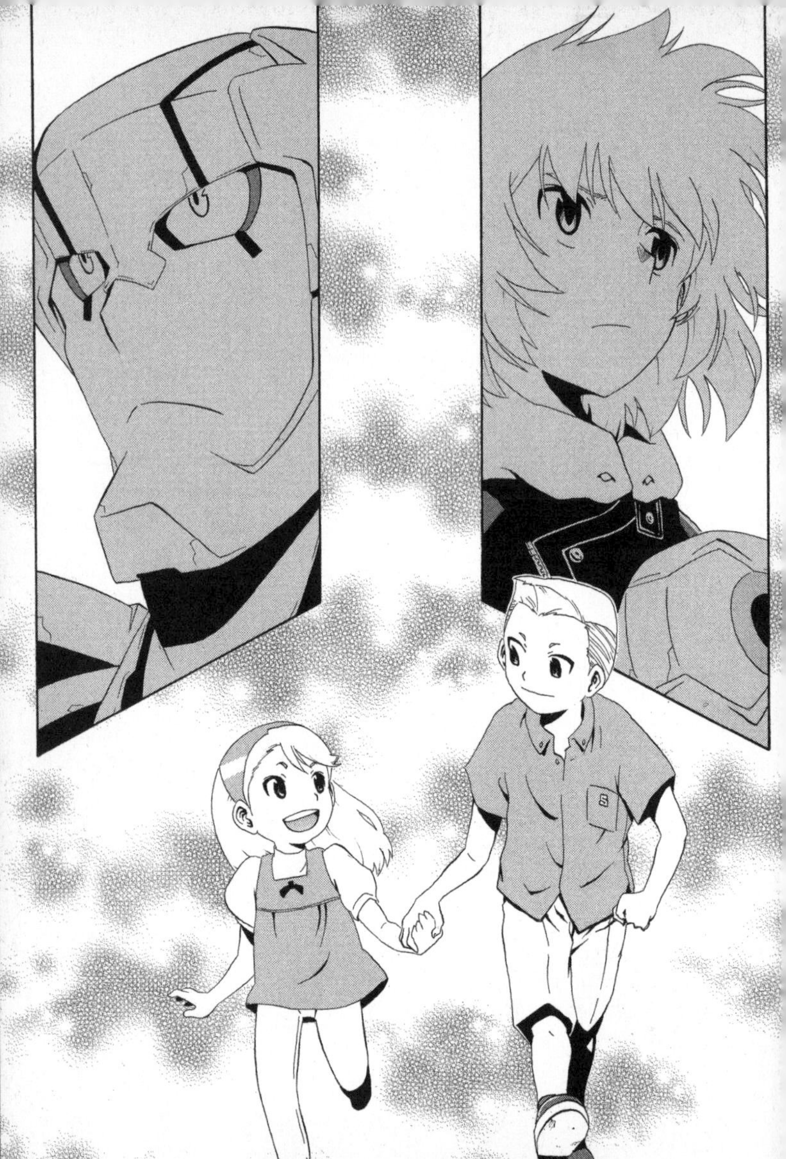

#10 BROTHER

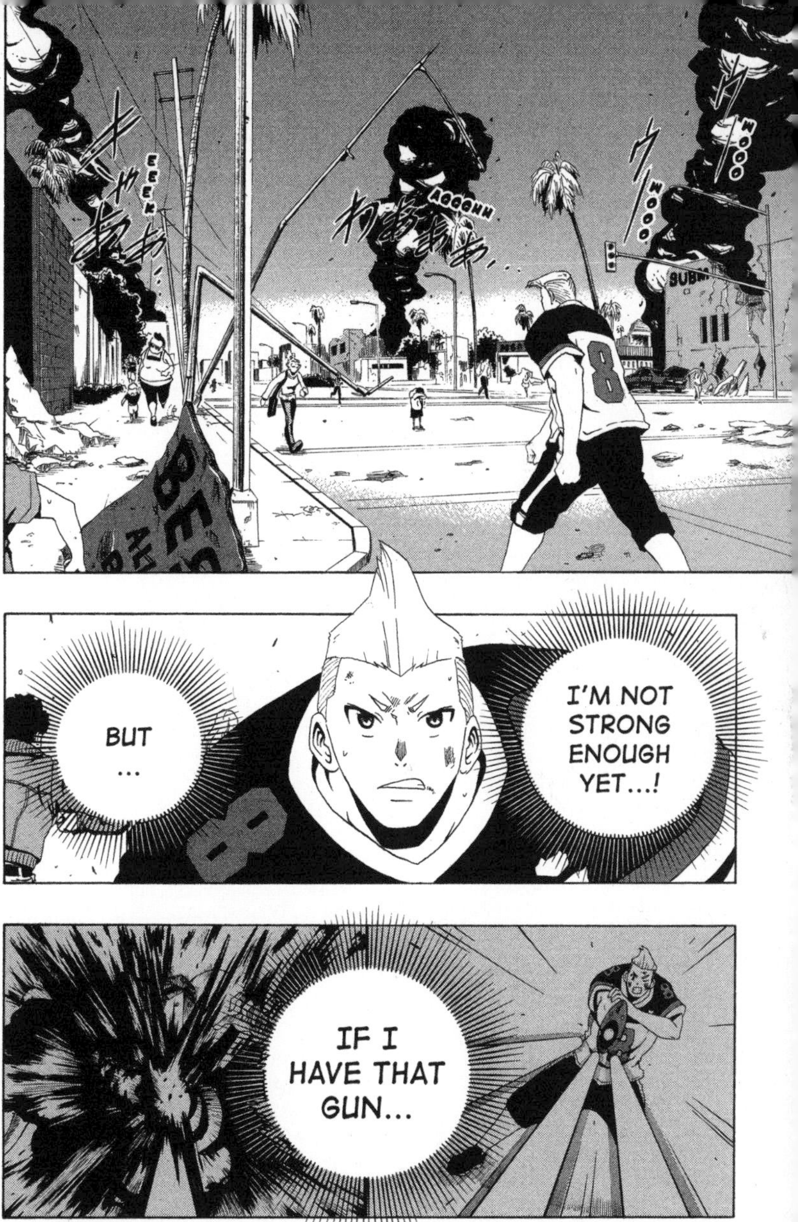
WOOOO
WOOOO
AOOOHH
EEEK
I'M NOT STRONG ENOUGH YET...!
BUT ...
IF I HAVE THAT GUN...

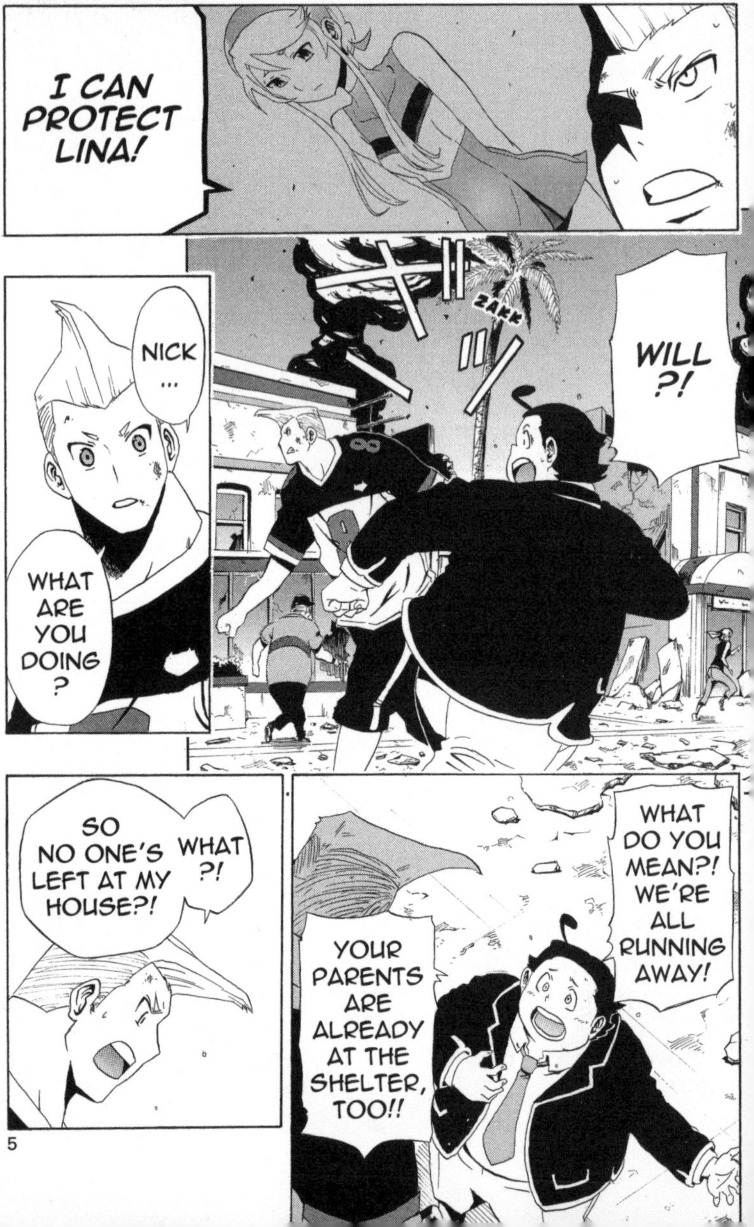
I CAN PROTECT LINA!
ZAKK
WILL?!
NICK...
WHAT ARE YOU DOING?
WHAT DO YOU MEAN?! WE'RE ALL RUNNING AWAY!
YOUR PARENTS ARE ALREADY AT THE SHELTER, TOO!!
WHAT?!
SO NO ONE'S LEFT AT MY HOUSE?!

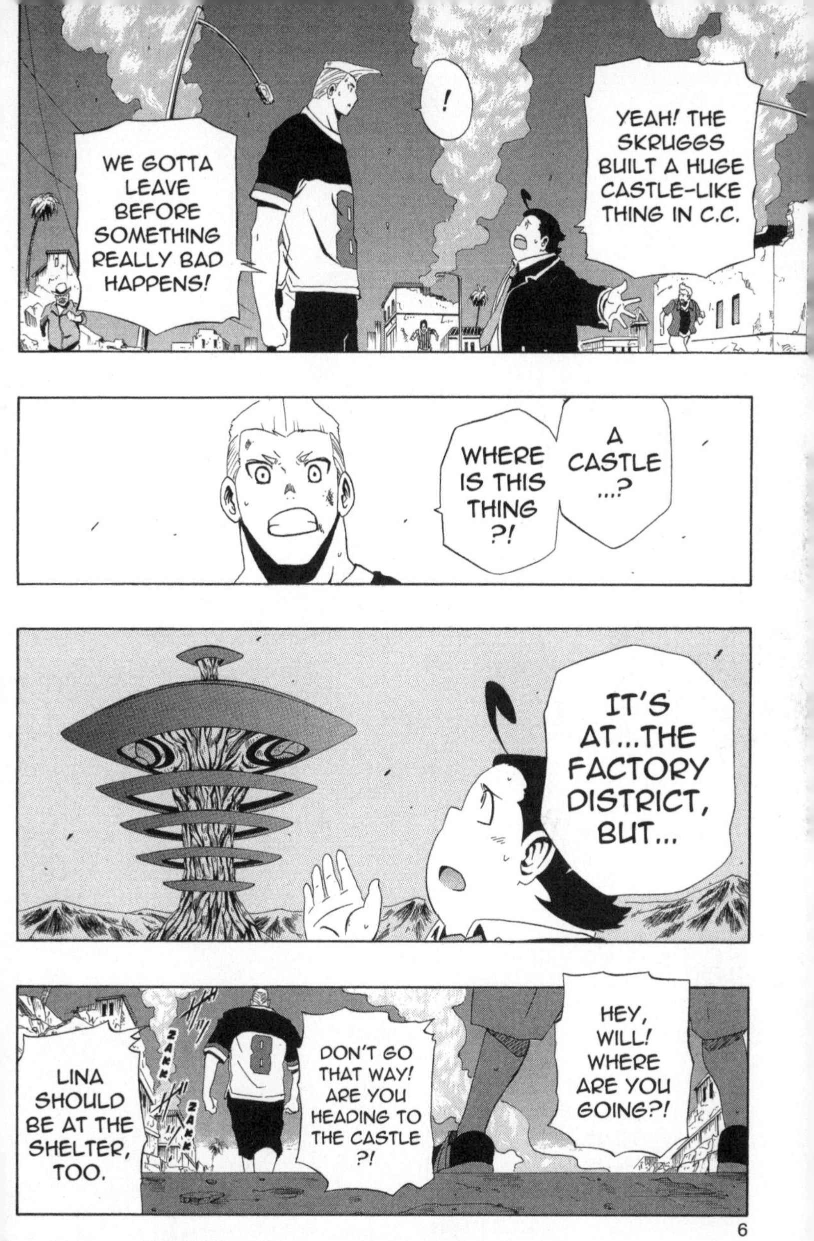
YEAH! THE SKRUGGS BUILT A HUGE CASTLE-LIKE THING IN C.C.
!
WE GOTTA LEAVE BEFORE SOMETHING REALLY BAD HAPPENS!
A CASTLE ...?
WHERE IS THIS THING ?!
IT'S AT...THE FACTORY DISTRICT, BUT...
HEY, WILL! WHERE ARE YOU GOING?!
DON'T GO THAT WAY! ARE YOU HEADING TO THE CASTLE ?!
ZAKK
ZAKK
LINA SHOULD BE AT THE SHELTER, TOO.

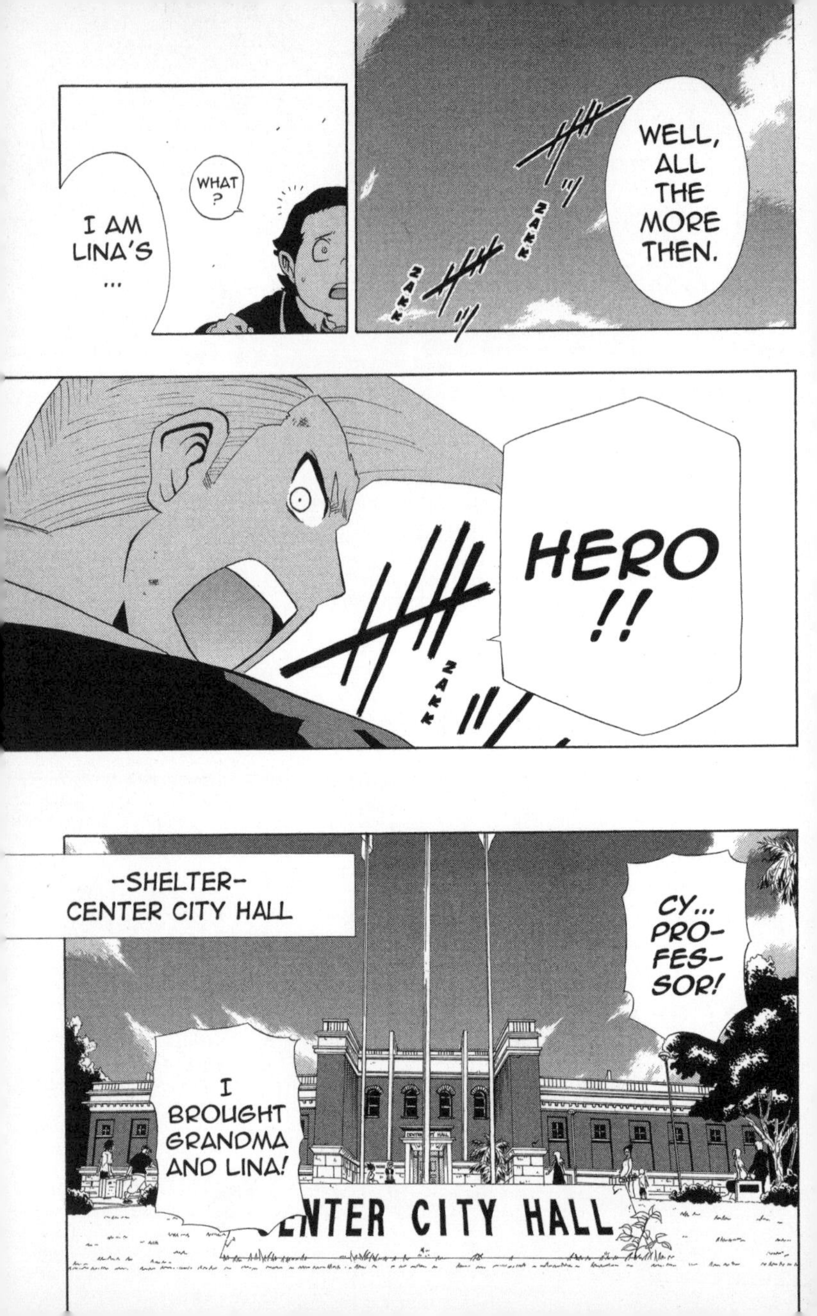
WELL, ALL THE MORE THEN.
ZAKK
ZAKK
WHAT?
I AM LINA'S ...
HERO!!
ZAKK
-SHELTER- CENTER CITY HALL
CY... PROFESSOR!
I BROUGHT GRANDMA AND LINA!
ENTER CITY HALL

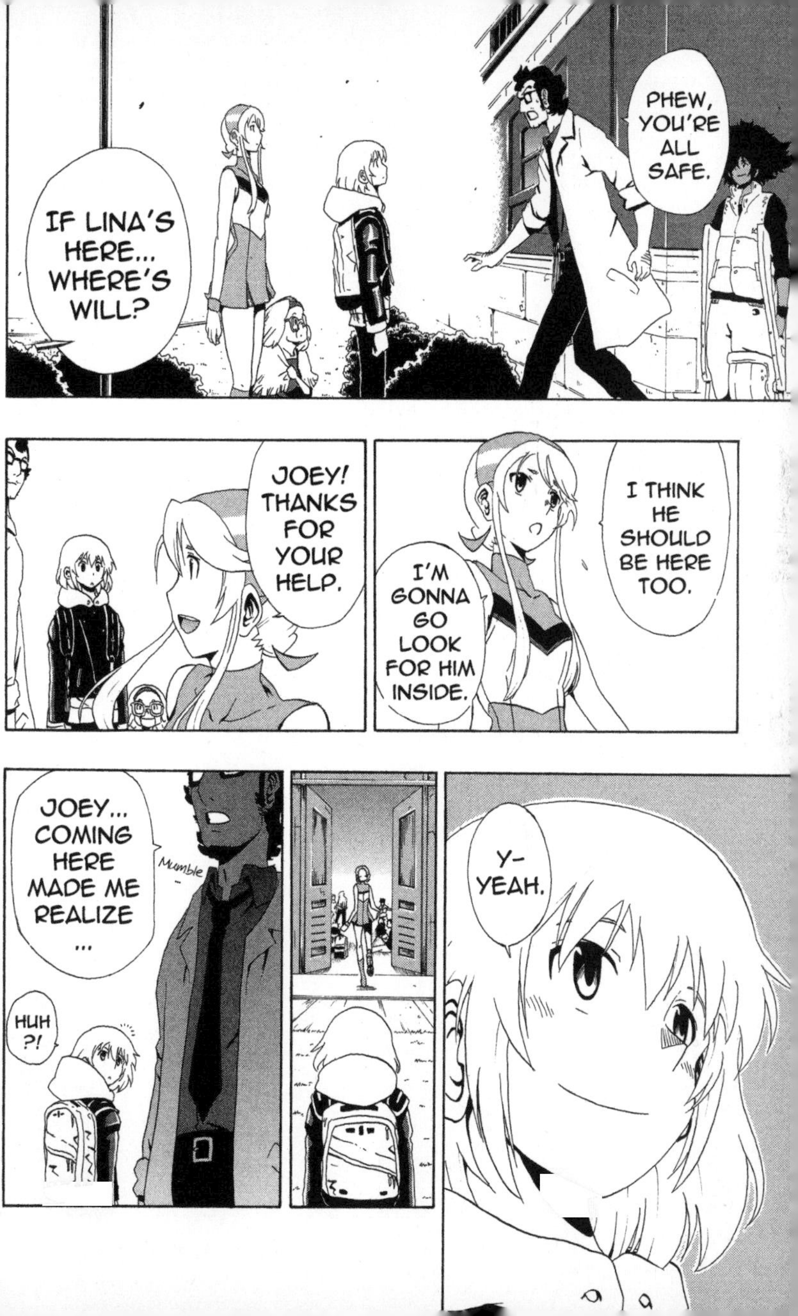
PHEW, YOU'RE ALL SAFE.
IF LINA'S HERE... WHERE'S WILL?
I THINK HE SHOULD BE HERE TOO.
I'M GONNA GO LOOK FOR HIM INSIDE.
JOEY! THANKS FOR YOUR HELP.
Y-YEAH.
JOEY... COMING HERE MADE ME REALIZE ...
Mumble
HUH ?!

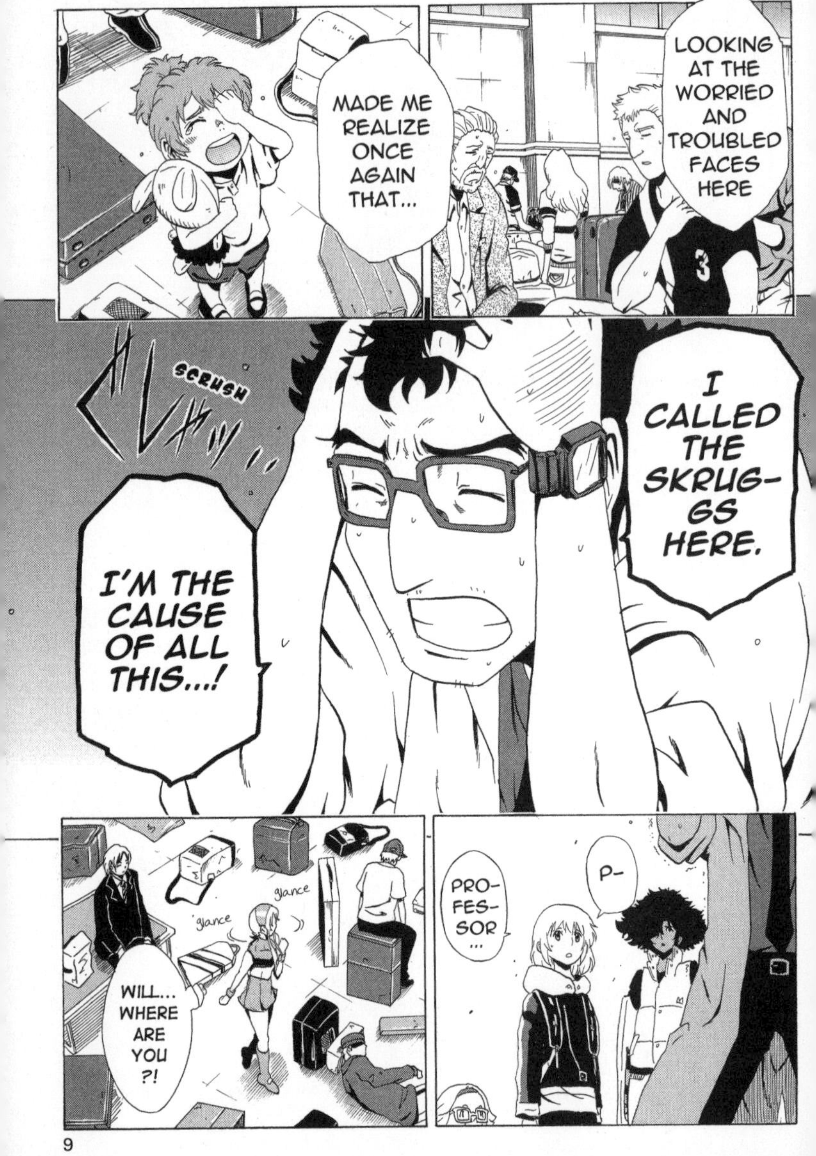
LOOKING AT THE WORRIED AND TROUBLED FACES HERE
MADE ME REALIZE ONCE AGAIN THAT...
I CALLED THE SKRUG-GS HERE.
SCRUSH
I'M THE CAUSE OF ALL THIS...!
P-
PRO-FES-SOR ...
glance
glance
WILL... WHERE ARE YOU ?!

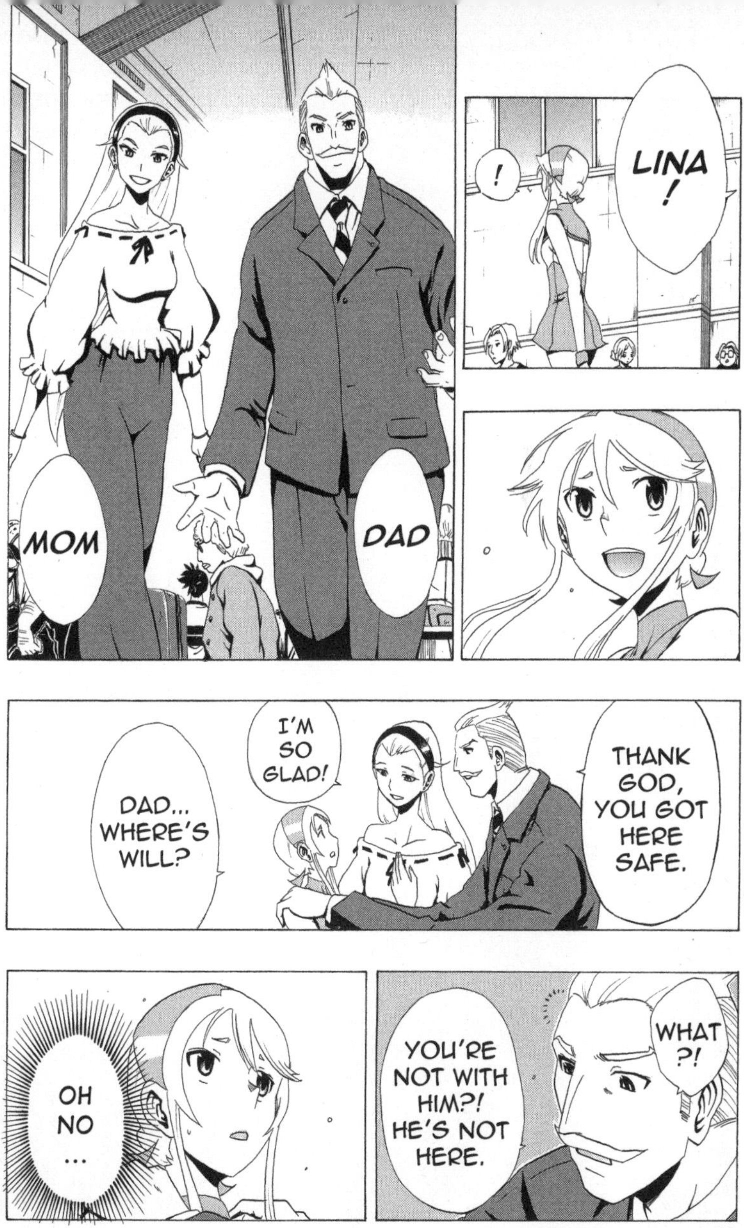
LINA!
!
DAD
MOM
THANK GOD, YOU GOT HERE SAFE.
I'M SO GLAD!
DAD... WHERE'S WILL?
WHAT?!
YOU'RE NOT WITH HIM?! HE'S NOT HERE.
OH NO ...

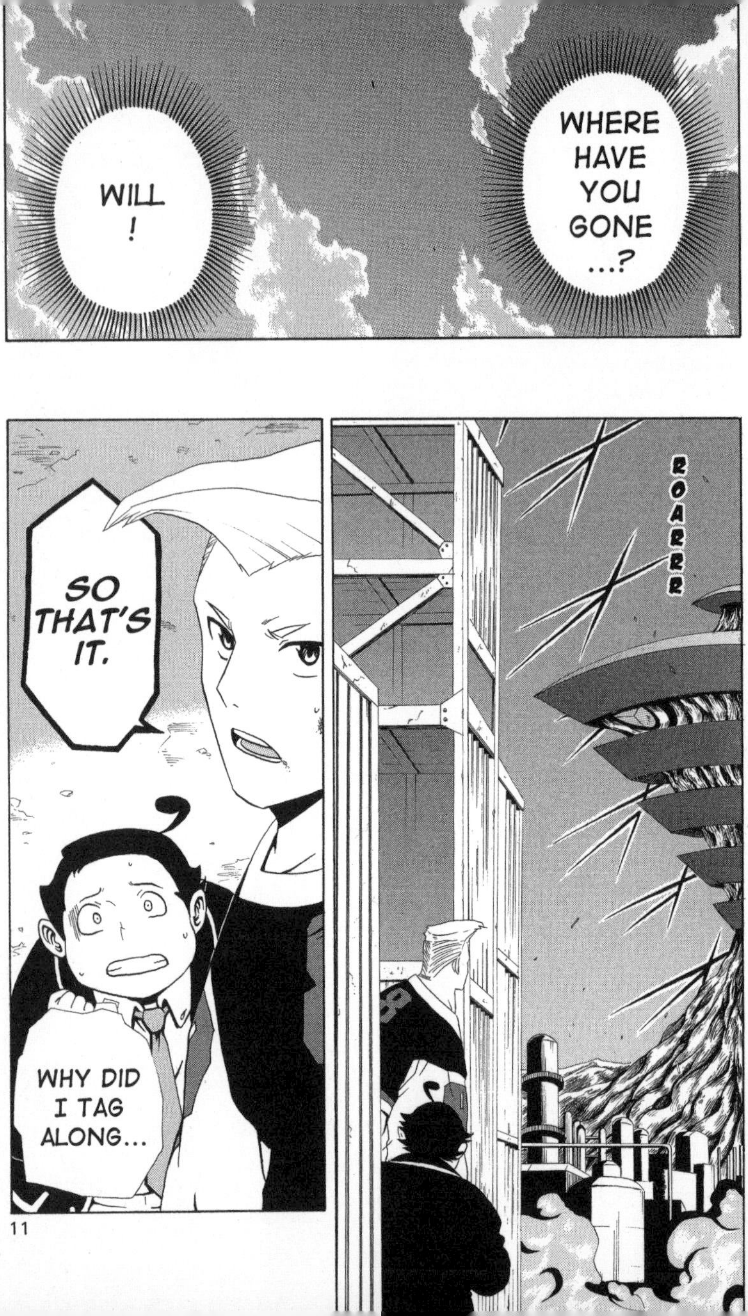
WHERE HAVE YOU GONE ...?
WILL !
ROARRR
SO THAT'S IT.
WHY DID I TAG ALONG...

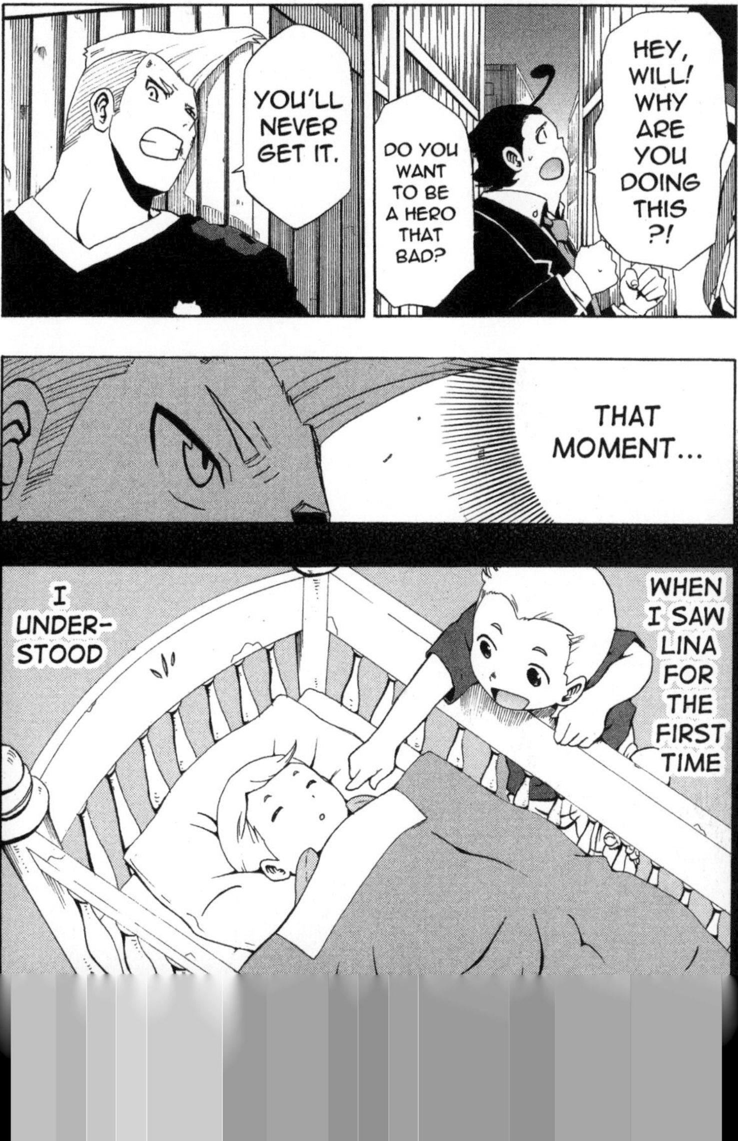
HEY, WILL! WHY ARE YOU DOING THIS?!
DO YOU WANT TO BE A HERO THAT BAD?
YOU'LL NEVER GET IT.
THAT MOMENT...
WHEN I SAW LINA FOR THE FIRST TIME
I UNDERSTOOD

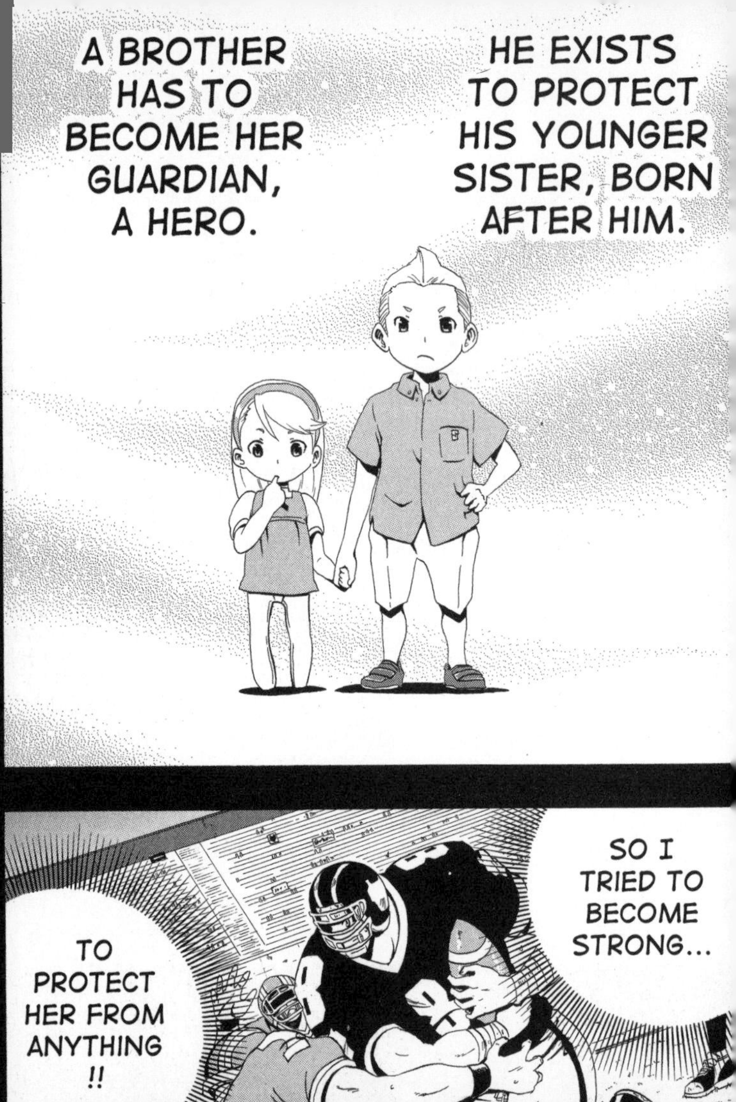
HE EXISTS TO PROTECT HIS YOUNGER SISTER, BORN AFTER HIM.
A BROTHER HAS TO BECOME HER GUARDIAN, A HERO.
SO I TRIED TO BECOME STRONG...
TO PROTECT HER FROM ANYTHING !!

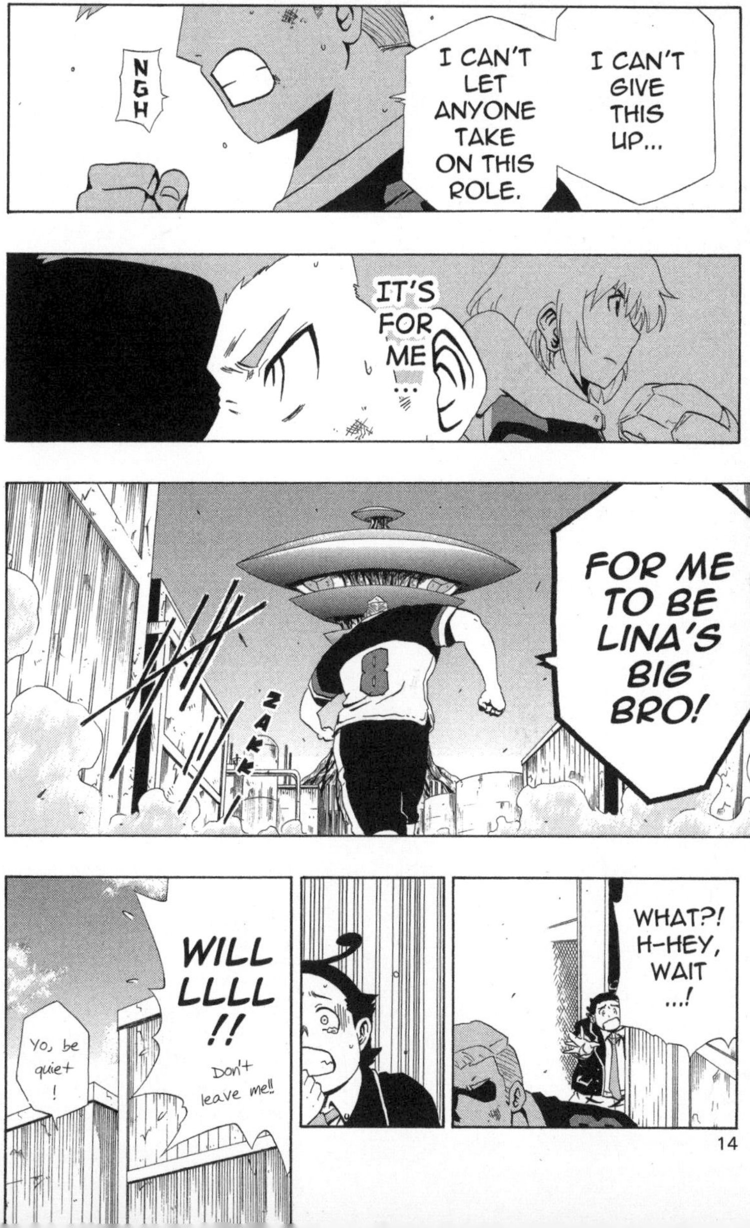
I CAN'T GIVE THIS UP...
I CAN'T LET ANYONE TAKE ON THIS ROLE.
NGH
IT'S FOR ME ...
FOR ME TO BE LINA'S BIG BRO!
ZAKK
WHAT?! H-HEY, WAIT ...!
WILL LLLL!!
Don't leave me!!
Yo, be quiet!

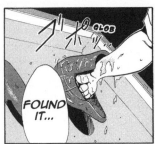

FOUND IT...

!

TH– THAT'S THE WEAPON ?!

YEAH! THIS IS ALL I NEED ...

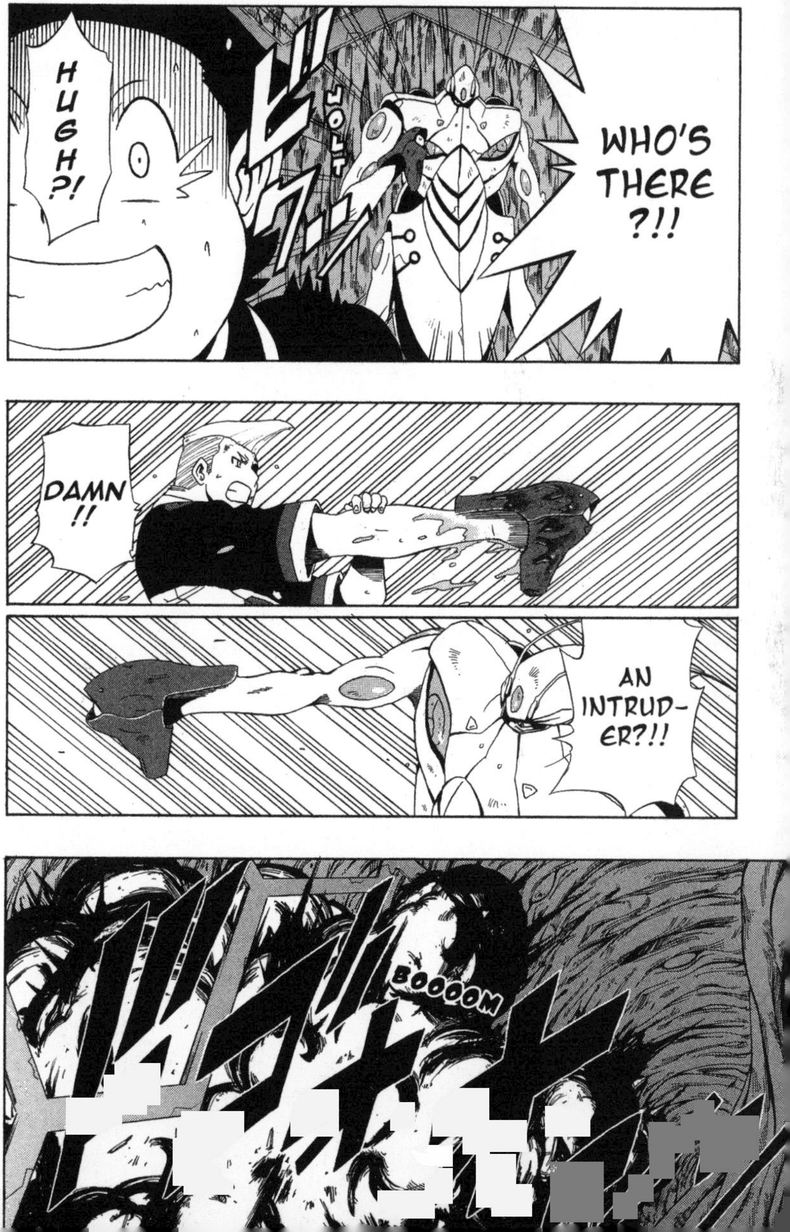
WHO'S THERE?!!
JOLT
HUGH?!
DAMN!!
AN INTRUDER?!!
BOOOOOM

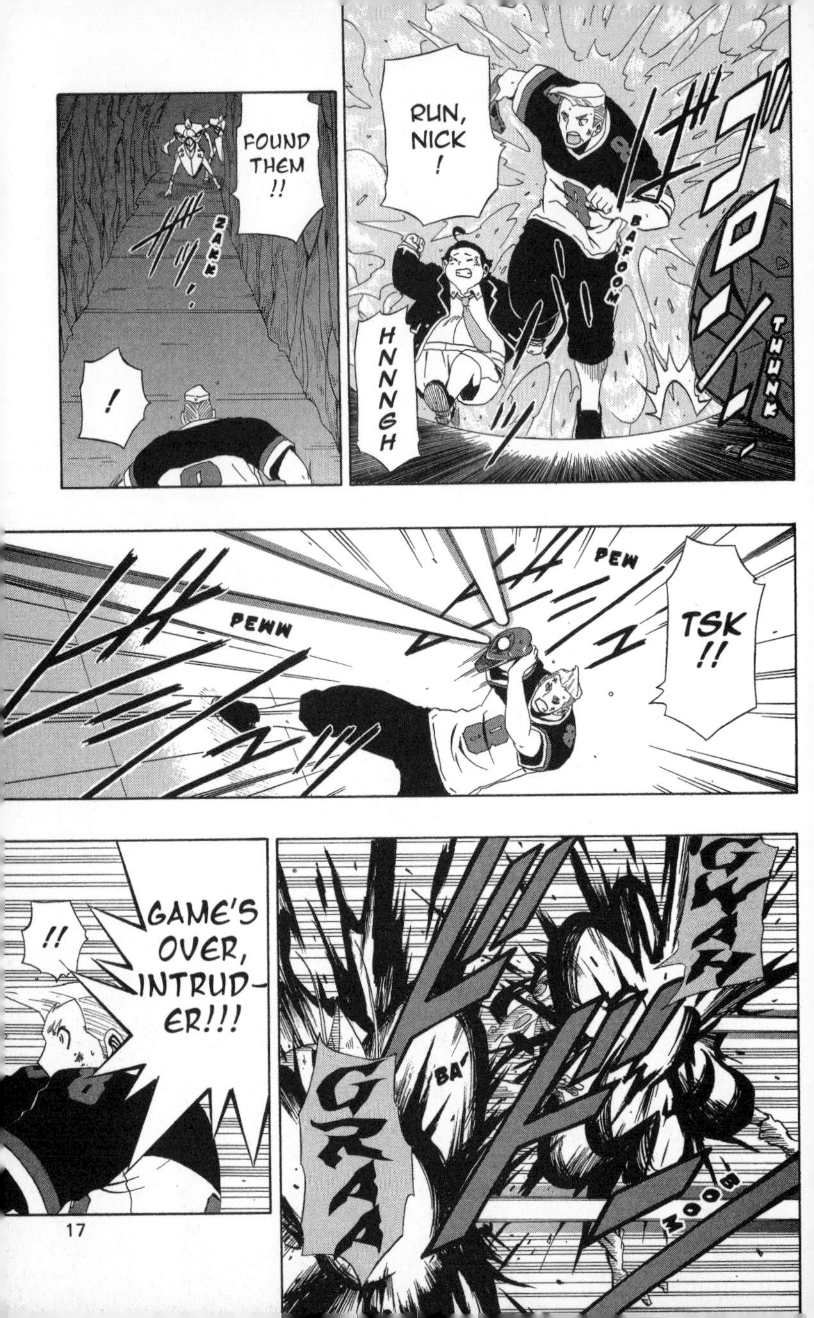
RUN, NICK!
BAFOOM
THUNK
HNNNGH
FOUND THEM!!
ZAKK
!
TSK!!
PEW
PEWW
GYAH
BOOM
BA'
GRAA
GAME'S OVER, INTRUDER!!!
!!

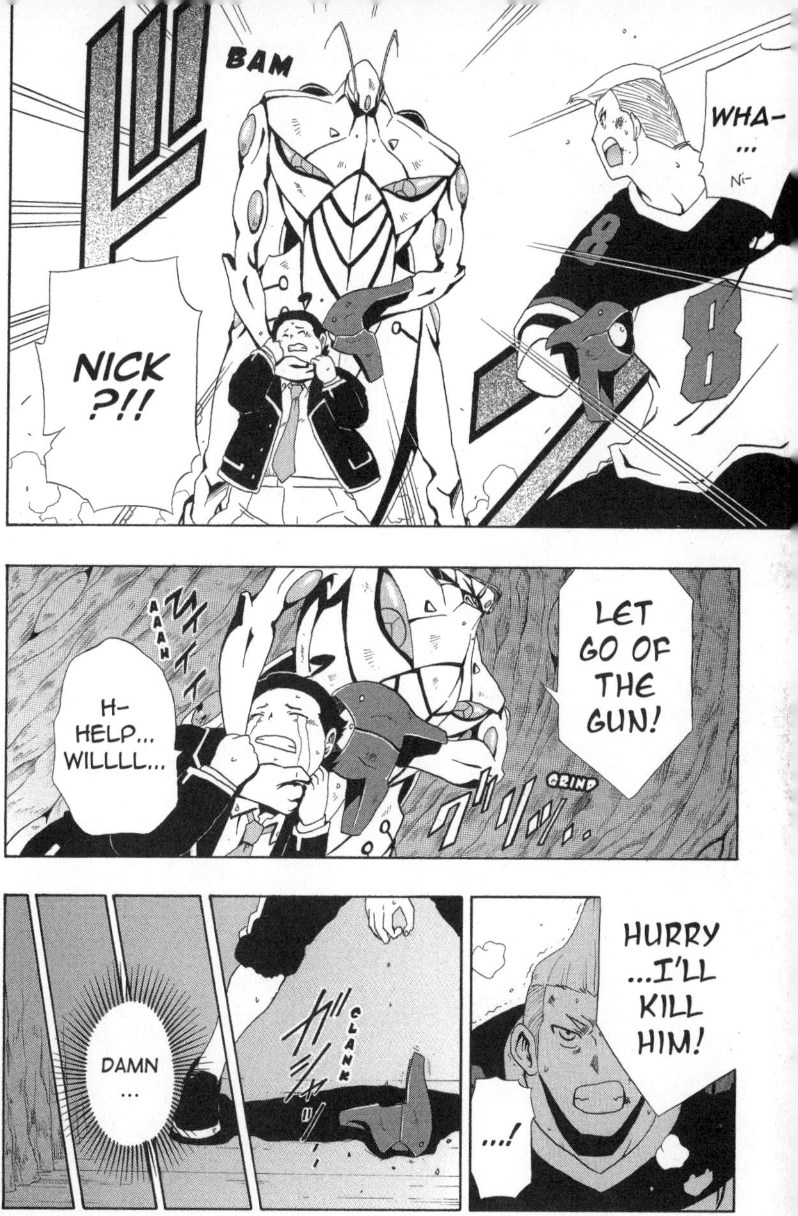
WHA-...
Ni-
BAM
NICK ?!!
LET GO OF THE GUN!
GRIND
AAAH
H-HELP... WILLLL...
HURRY ...I'LL KILL HIM!
...!
CLANK
DAMN ...

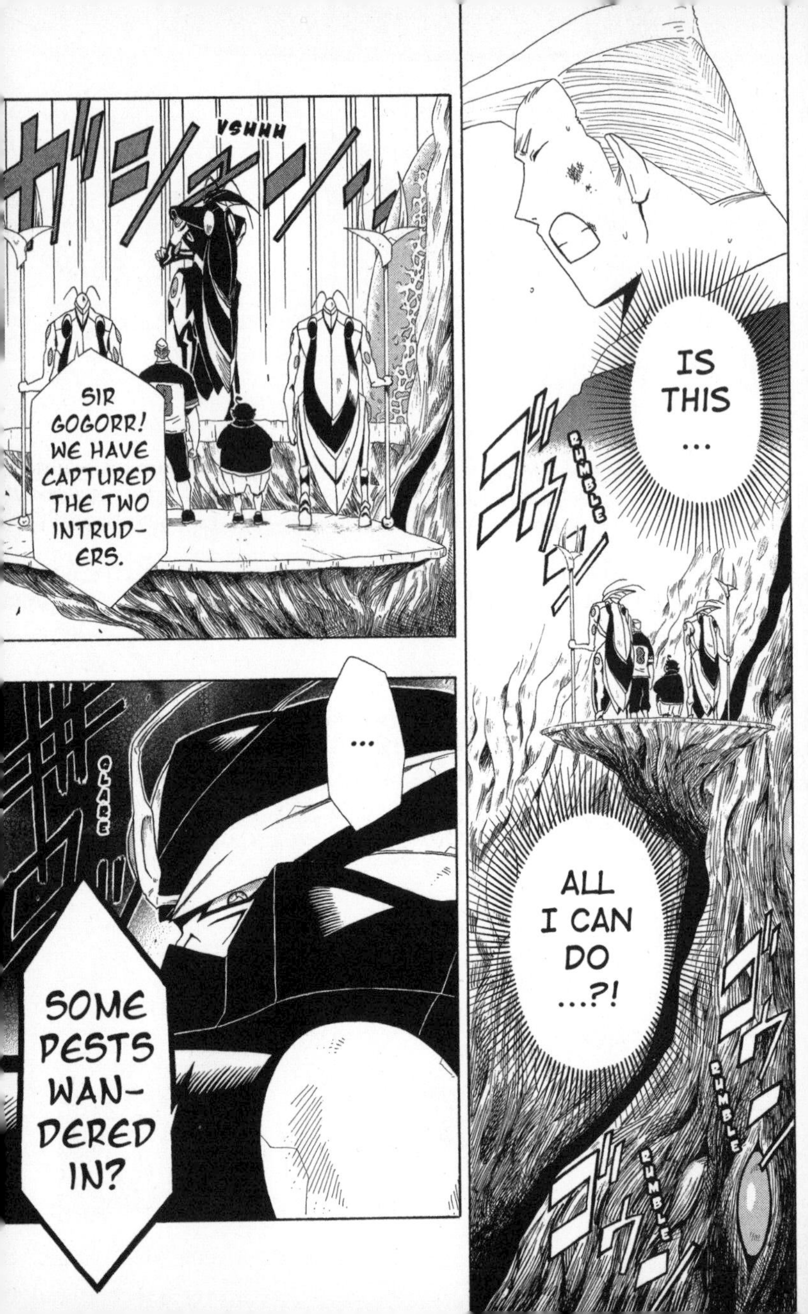
IS THIS ...
RUMBLE
ALL I CAN DO ...?!
RUMBLE
RUMBLE
VSHHH
SIR GOGORR! WE HAVE CAPTURED THE TWO INTRUD-ERS.
...
GLARE
SOME PESTS WAN-DERED IN?

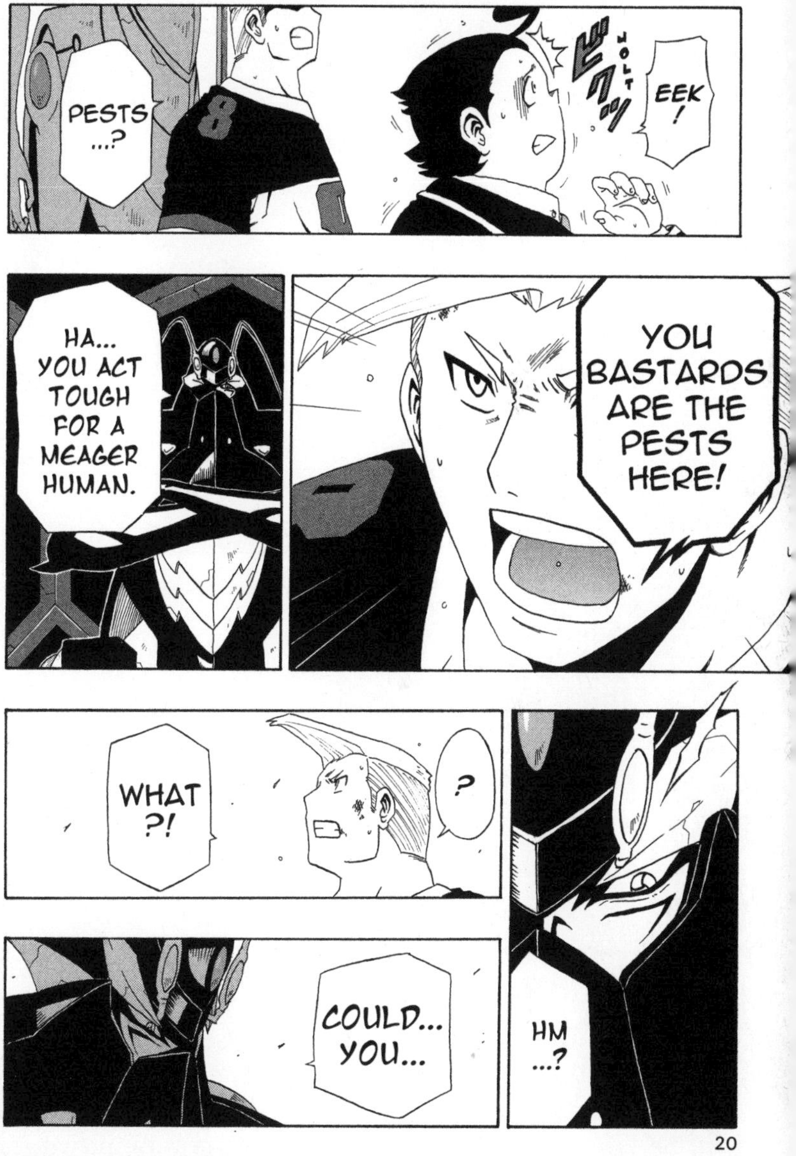
EEK!
JOLT
PESTS ...?
YOU BASTARDS ARE THE PESTS HERE!
HA... YOU ACT TOUGH FOR A MEAGER HUMAN.
HM ...?
?
WHAT ?!
COULD... YOU...

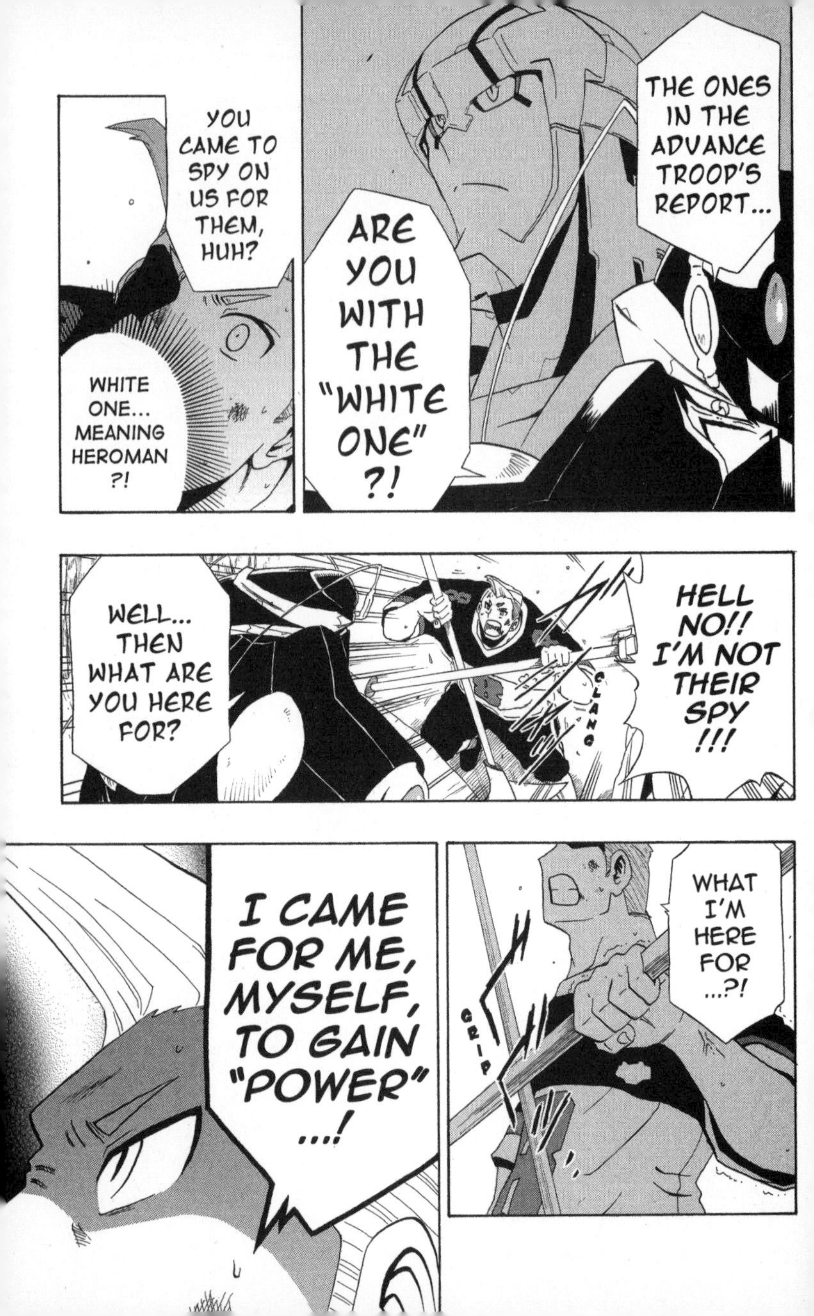
THE ONES IN THE ADVANCE TROOP'S REPORT...
ARE YOU WITH THE "WHITE ONE"?!
YOU CAME TO SPY ON US FOR THEM, HUH?
WHITE ONE... MEANING HEROMAN?!
HELL NO!! I'M NOT THEIR SPY!!!
CLANG
WELL... THEN WHAT ARE YOU HERE FOR?
WHAT I'M HERE FOR ...?!
GRIP
I CAME FOR ME, MYSELF, TO GAIN "POWER" ...!

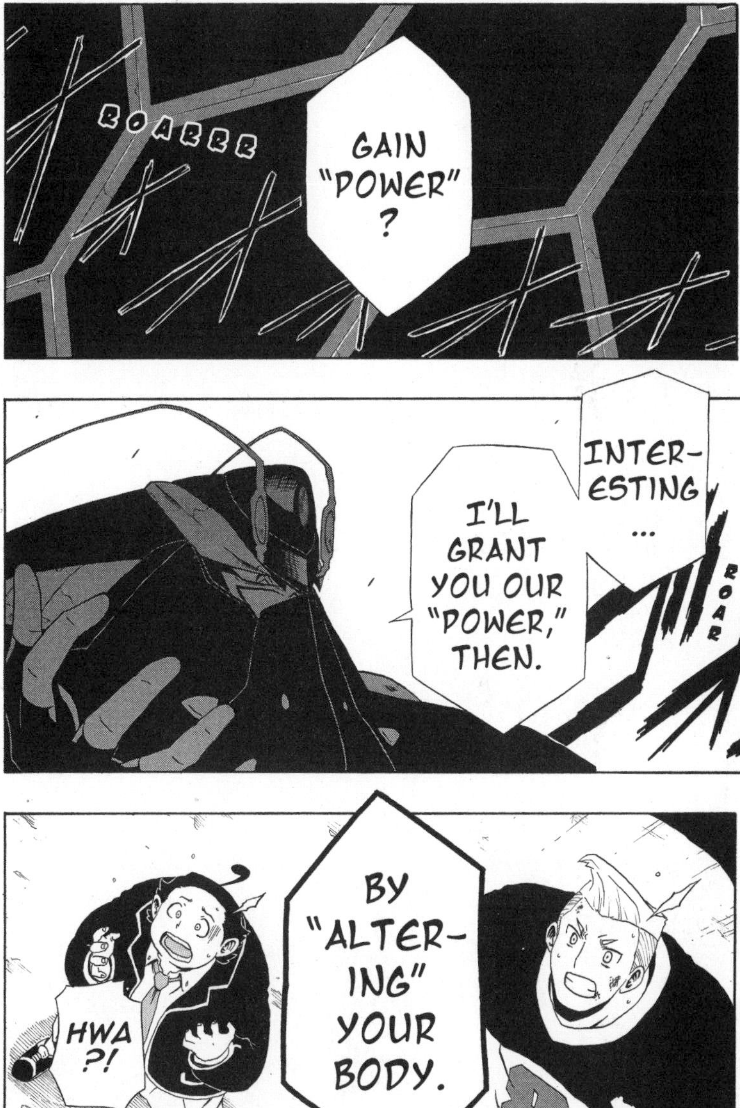
GAIN "POWER" ?
ROARRR
ROAR
INTER-ESTING ...
I'LL GRANT YOU OUR "POWER," THEN.
BY "ALTER-ING" YOUR BODY.
HWA ?!

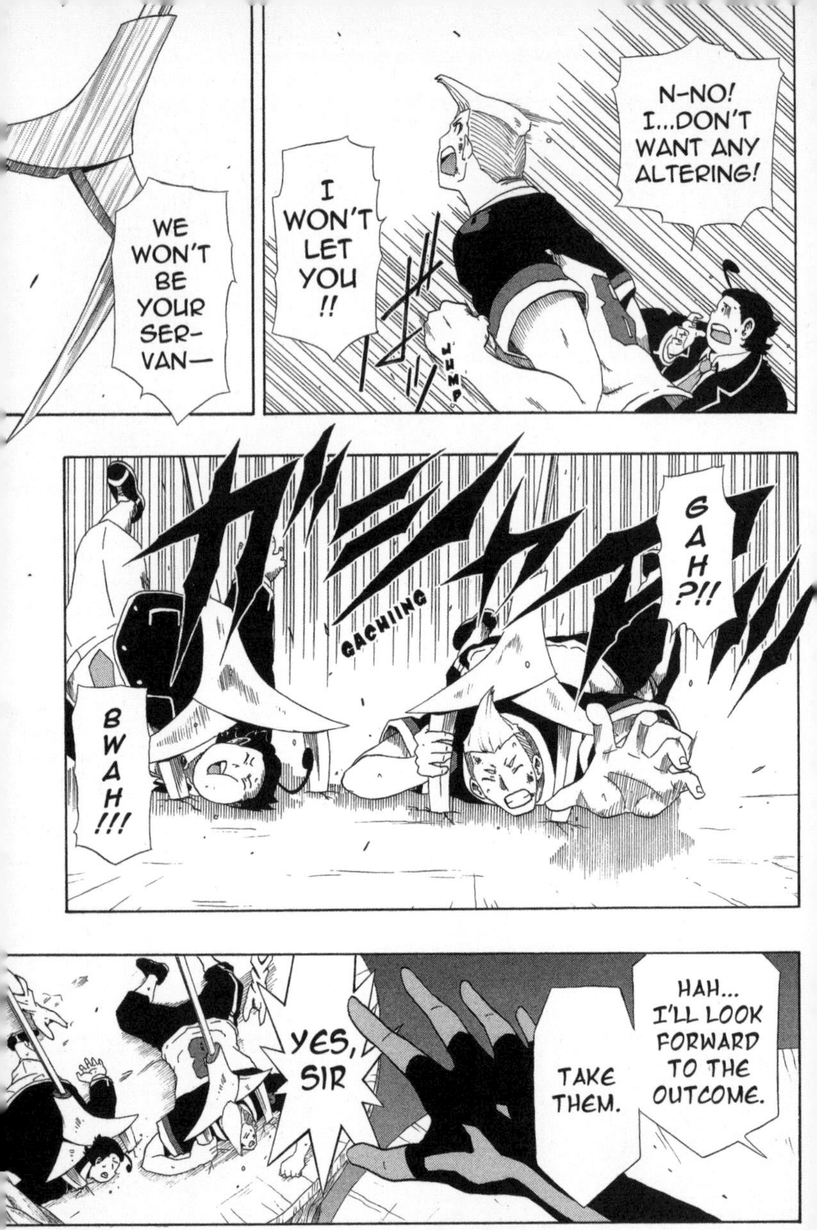
N-NO! I...DON'T WANT ANY ALTERING!
I WON'T LET YOU!!
JUMP
WE WON'T BE YOUR SER-VAN—
GAH?!!
GACHIING
BWAH!!!
HAH... I'LL LOOK FORWARD TO THE OUTCOME.
TAKE THEM.
YES, SIR

CAN'T I...

WHY DOES THIS HAPPEN ...?

DAMN IT...!

BE... YOUR HERO ...?

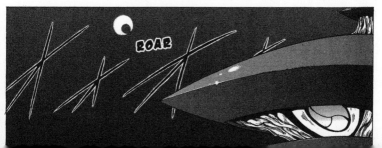

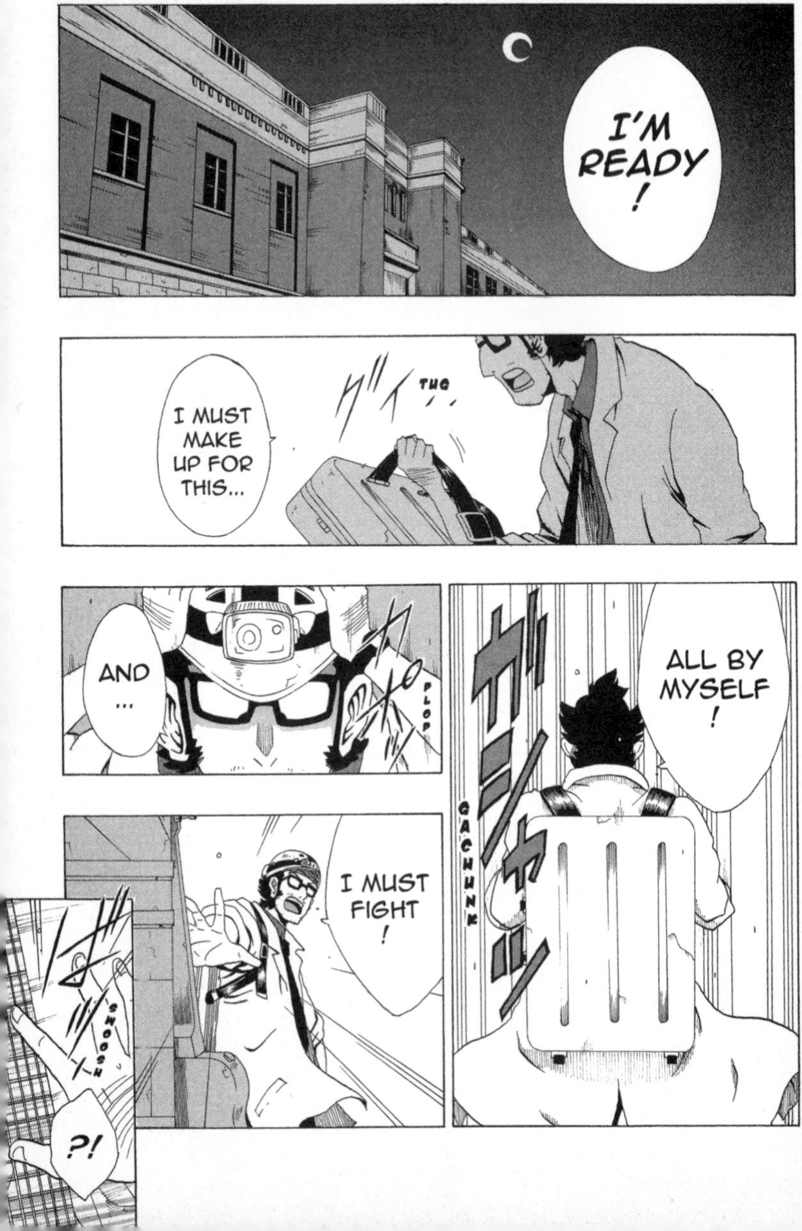
I'M READY!
TUG
I MUST MAKE UP FOR THIS...
ALL BY MYSELF!
GACHUNK
AND ...
PLOP
I MUST FIGHT!
SWOOSH
?!

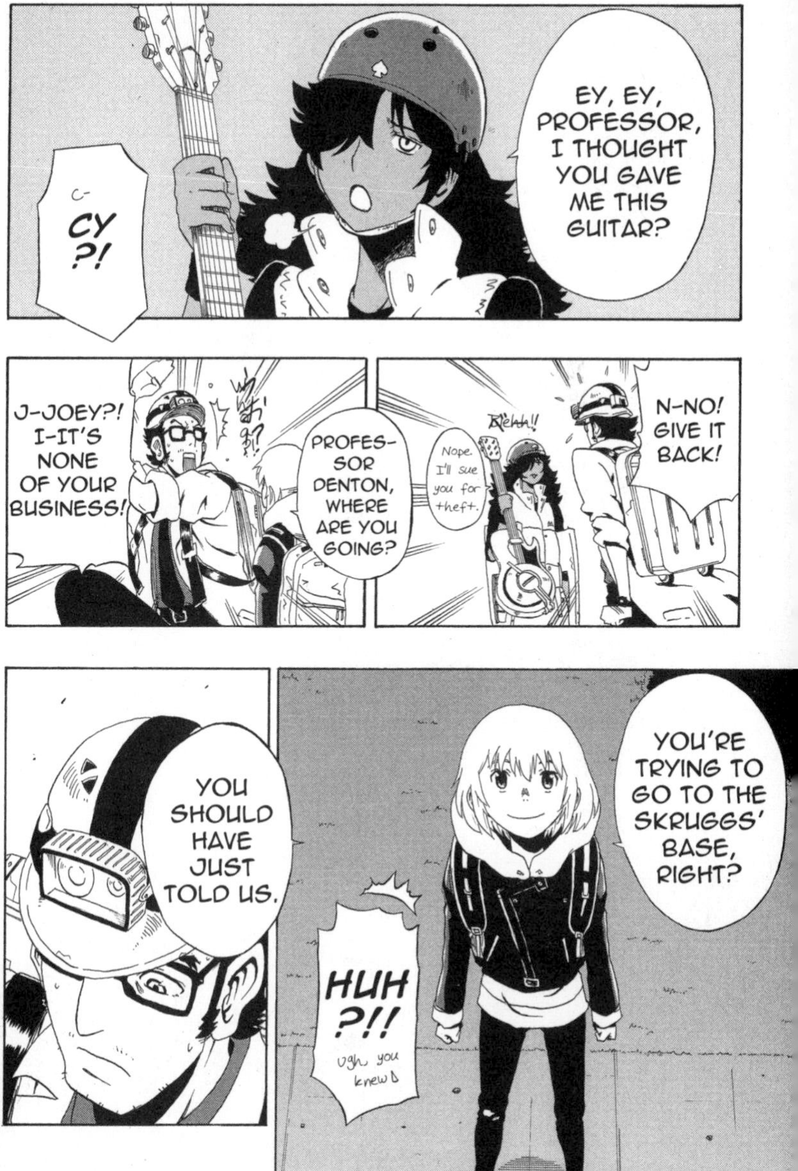
EY, EY, PROFESSOR, I THOUGHT YOU GAVE ME THIS GUITAR?
C- CY ?!
N-NO! GIVE IT BACK!
Blehh!!
Nope. I'll sue you for theft.
PROFES-SOR DENTON, WHERE ARE YOU GOING?
J-JOEY?! I-IT'S NONE OF YOUR BUSINESS!
YOU'RE TRYING TO GO TO THE SKRUGGS' BASE, RIGHT?
HUH ?!!
Ugh, you knew
YOU SHOULD HAVE JUST TOLD US.

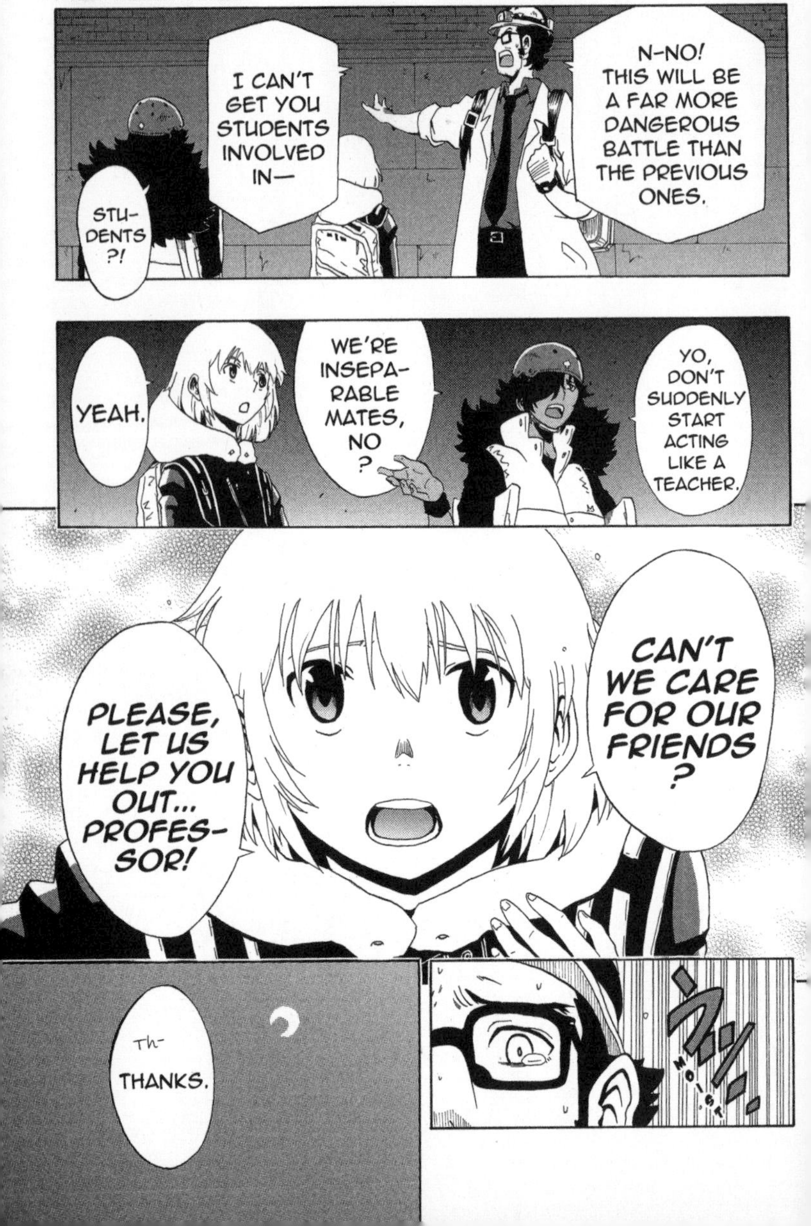
N-NO! THIS WILL BE A FAR MORE DANGEROUS BATTLE THAN THE PREVIOUS ONES.
I CAN'T GET YOU STUDENTS INVOLVED IN—
STU-DENTS?!
YO, DON'T SUDDENLY START ACTING LIKE A TEACHER.
WE'RE INSEPA-RABLE MATES, NO?
YEAH.
CAN'T WE CARE FOR OUR FRIENDS?
PLEASE, LET US HELP YOU OUT... PROFES-SOR!
MOIST
Th- THANKS.

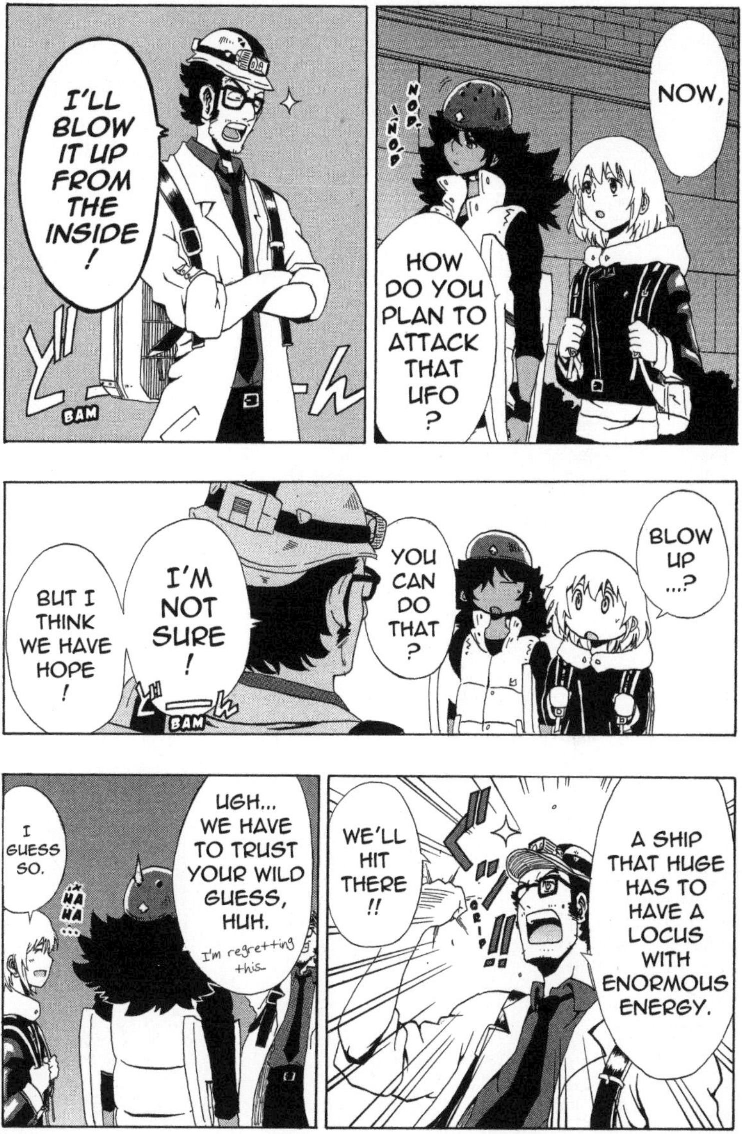
NOW,
HOW DO YOU PLAN TO ATTACK THAT UFO?
NOD, NOD
I'LL BLOW IT UP FROM THE INSIDE!
BAM
BLOW UP ...?
YOU CAN DO THAT?
I'M NOT SURE!
BUT I THINK WE HAVE HOPE!
BAM
A SHIP THAT HUGE HAS TO HAVE A LOCUS WITH ENORMOUS ENERGY.
WE'LL HIT THERE!!
GRIP
UGH... WE HAVE TO TRUST YOUR WILD GUESS, HUH.
I'm regretting this.
HA HA...
I GUESS SO.

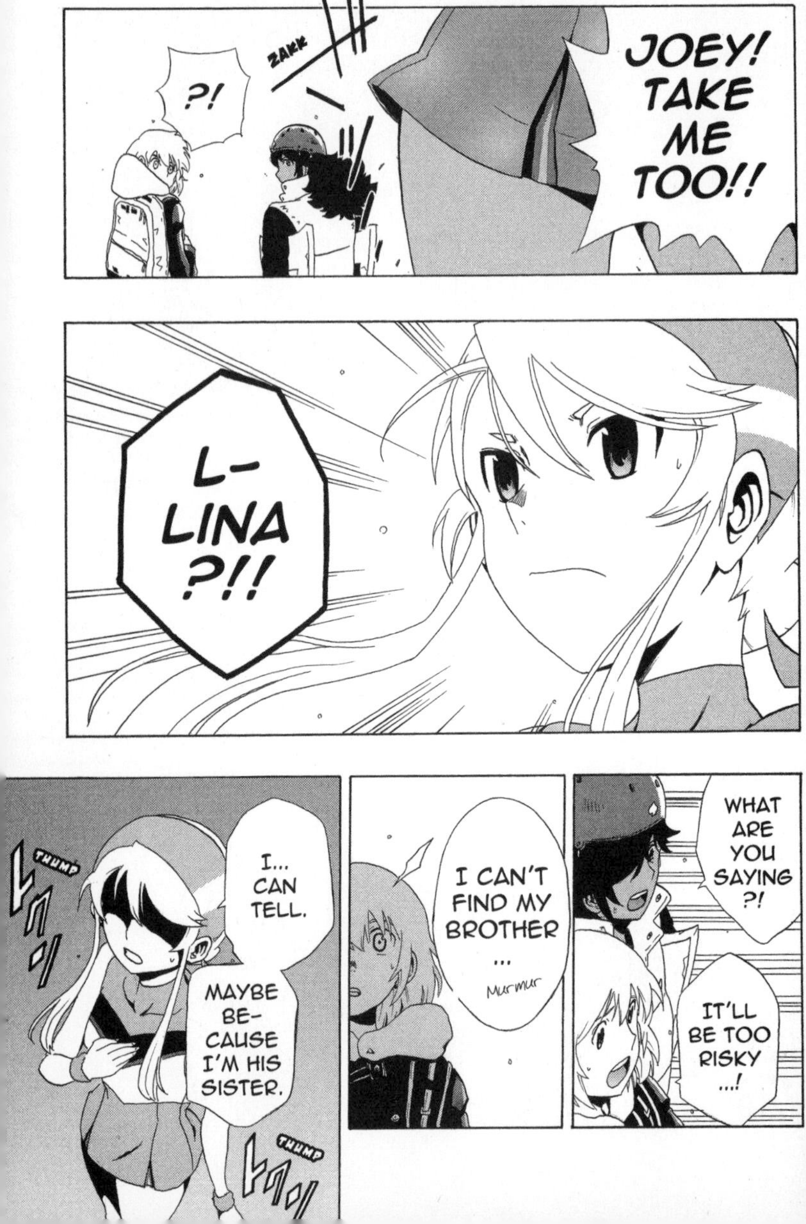
JOEY! TAKE ME TOO!!
ZAKK
?!
L-LINA?!!
WHAT ARE YOU SAYING?!
IT'LL BE TOO RISKY...!
I CAN'T FIND MY BROTHER...
Murmur
THUMP
I... CAN TELL.
MAYBE BE-CAUSE I'M HIS SISTER.
THUMP

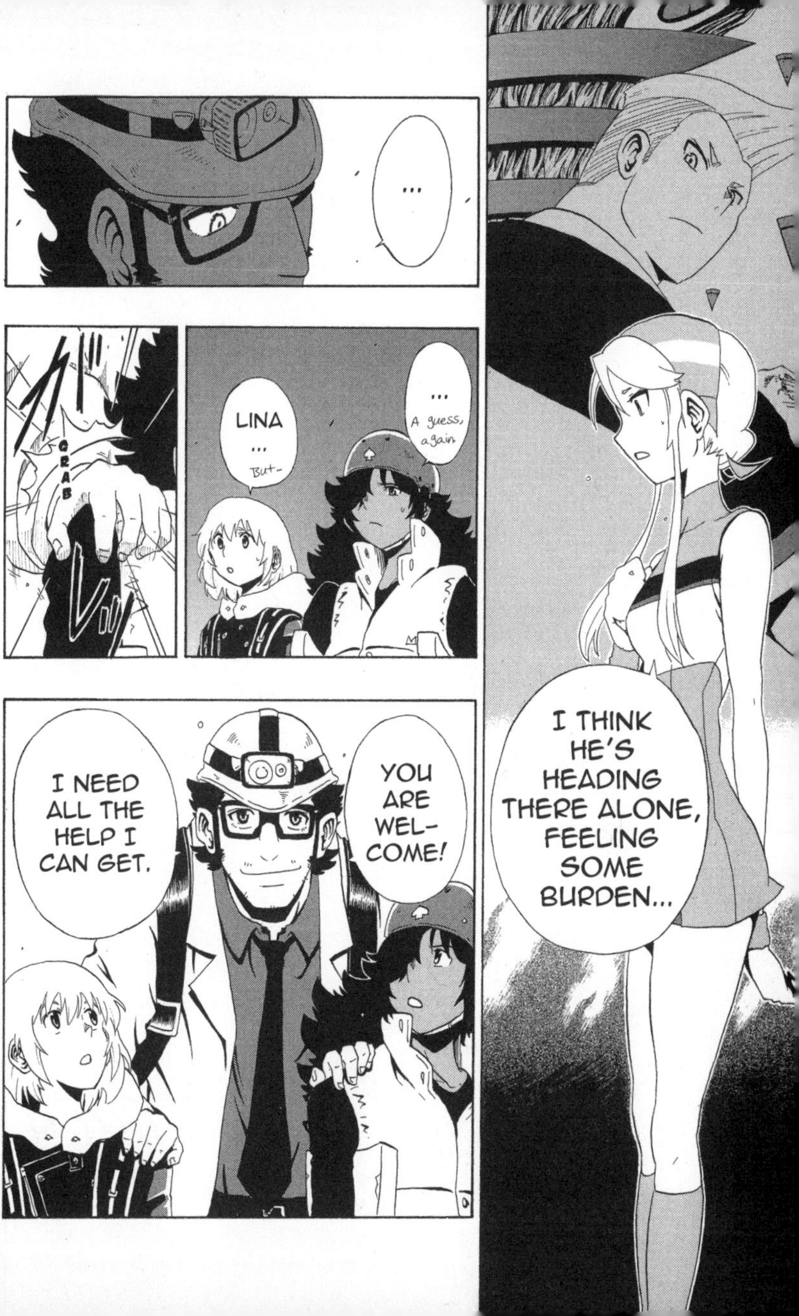
I THINK HE'S HEADING THERE ALONE, FEELING SOME BURDEN...
...
... A guess, again
LINA ... But...
GRAB
YOU ARE WEL- COME!
I NEED ALL THE HELP I CAN GET.

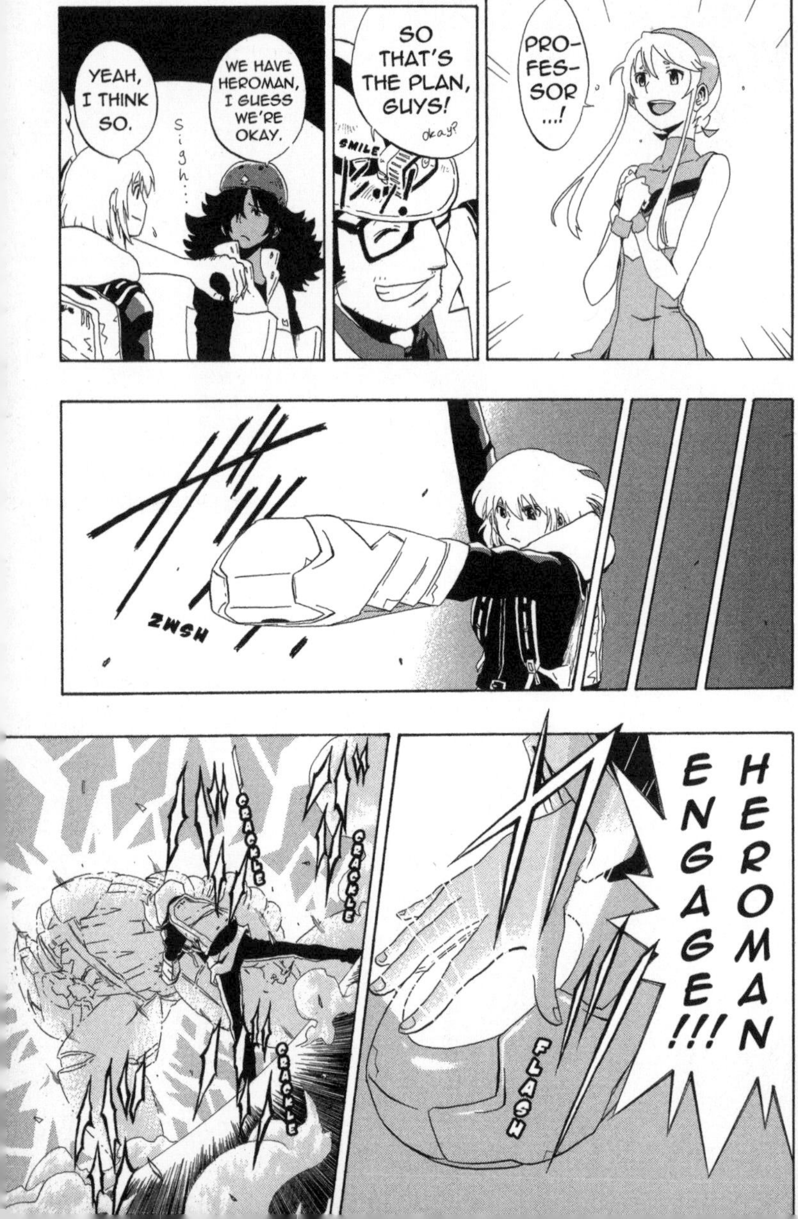
PRO-FES-SOR ...!
SO THAT'S THE PLAN, GUYS!
okay?
SMILE
WE HAVE HEROMAN, I GUESS WE'RE OKAY.
Sigh...
YEAH, I THINK SO.
ZWSH
HEROMAN ENGAGE!!!
FLASH
CRACKLE
CRACKLE
CRACKLE

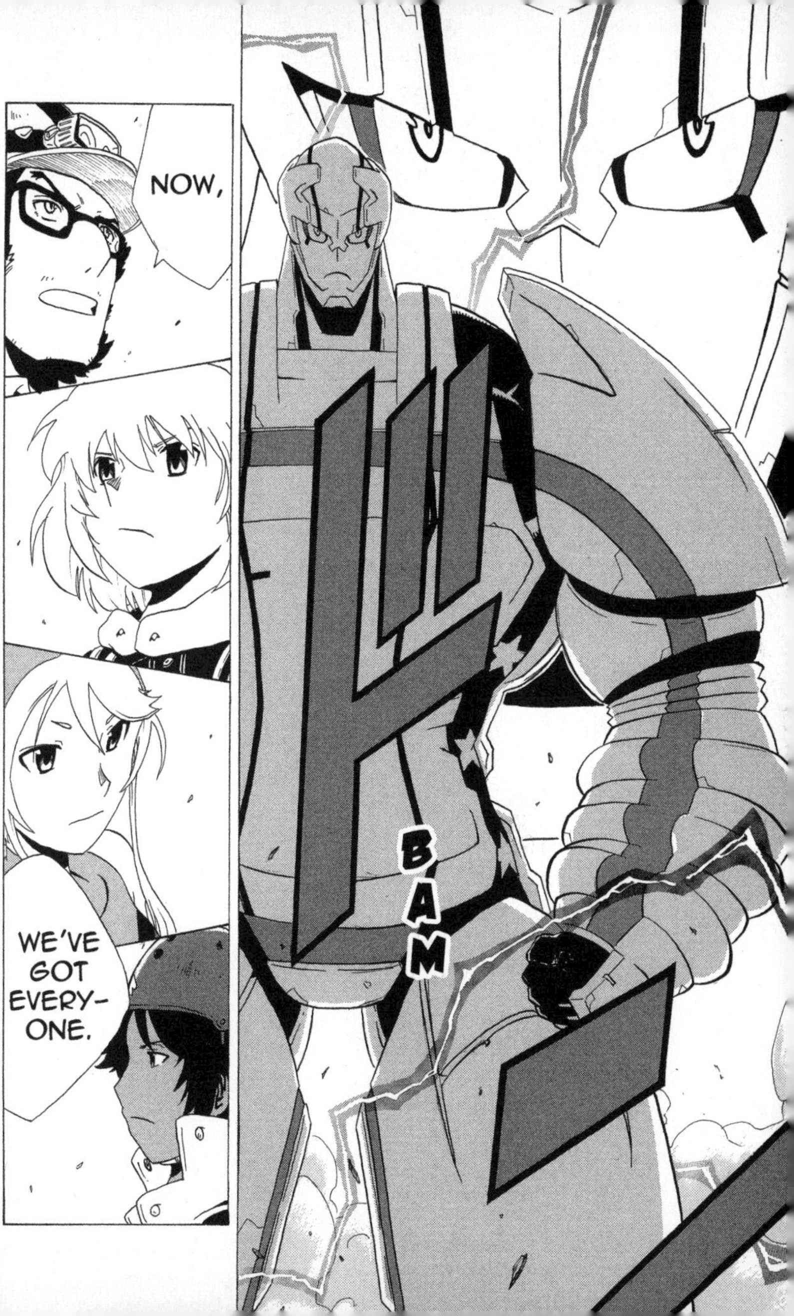
BAM
NOW,
WE'VE GOT EVERY-ONE.

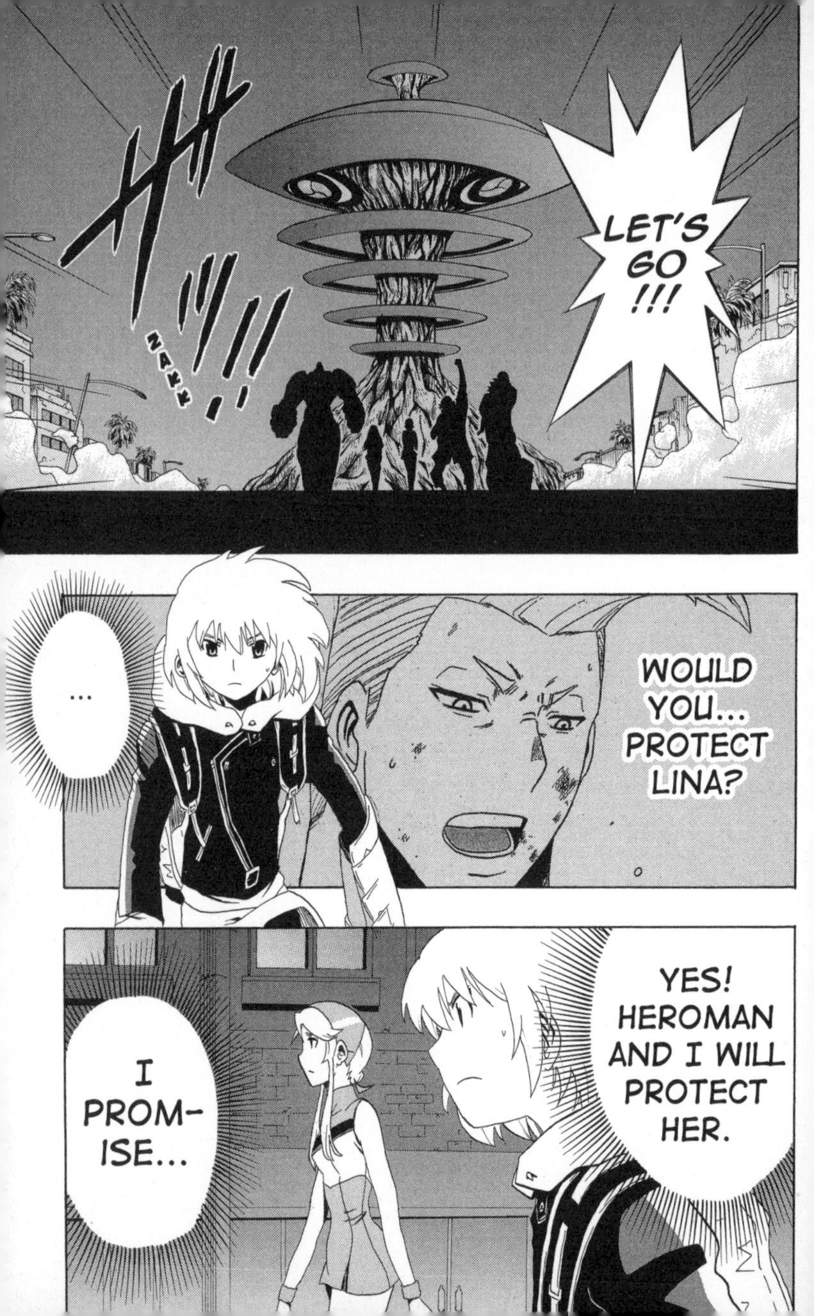
LET'S GO!!!
ZAKK
WOULD YOU... PROTECT LINA?
...
YES! HEROMAN AND I WILL PROTECT HER.
I PROM-ISE...

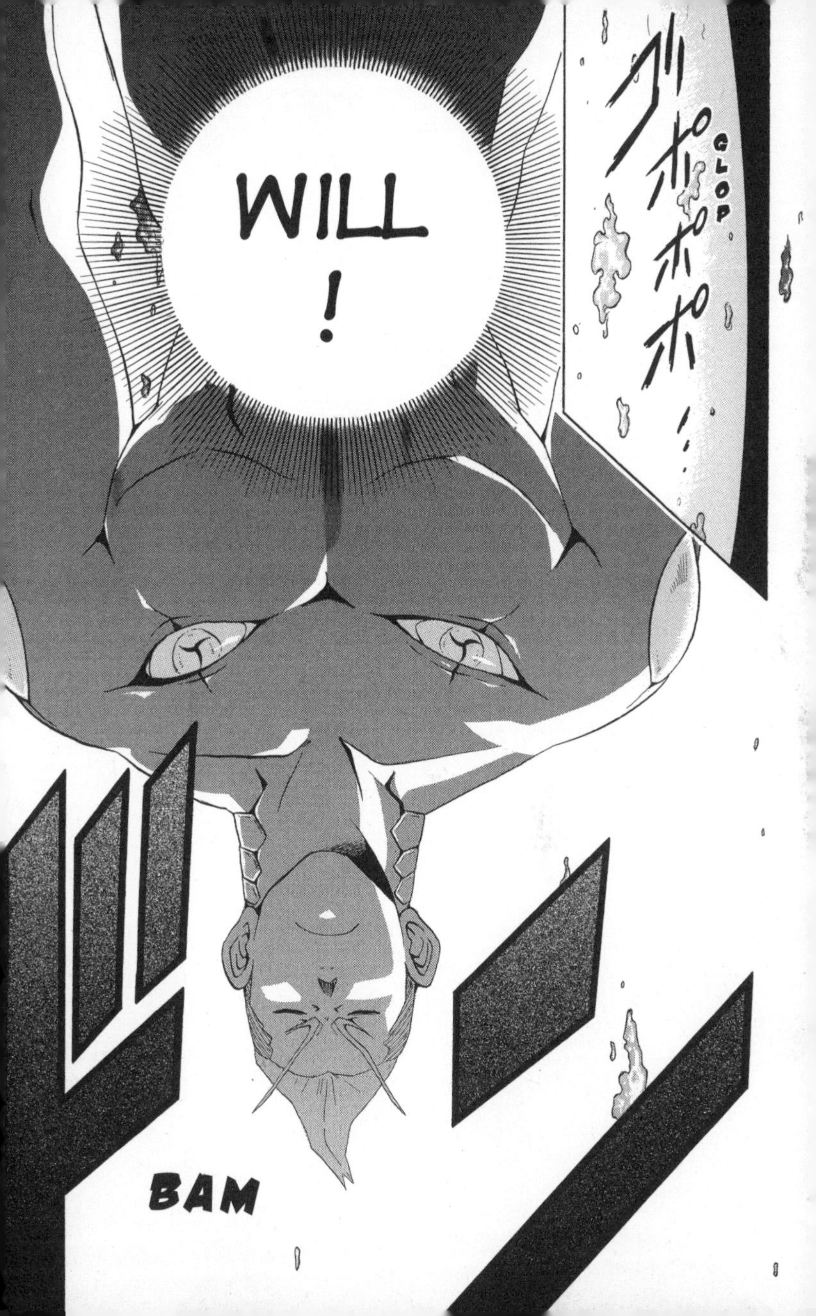
グポポポ!!
GLOP
WILL !
BAM

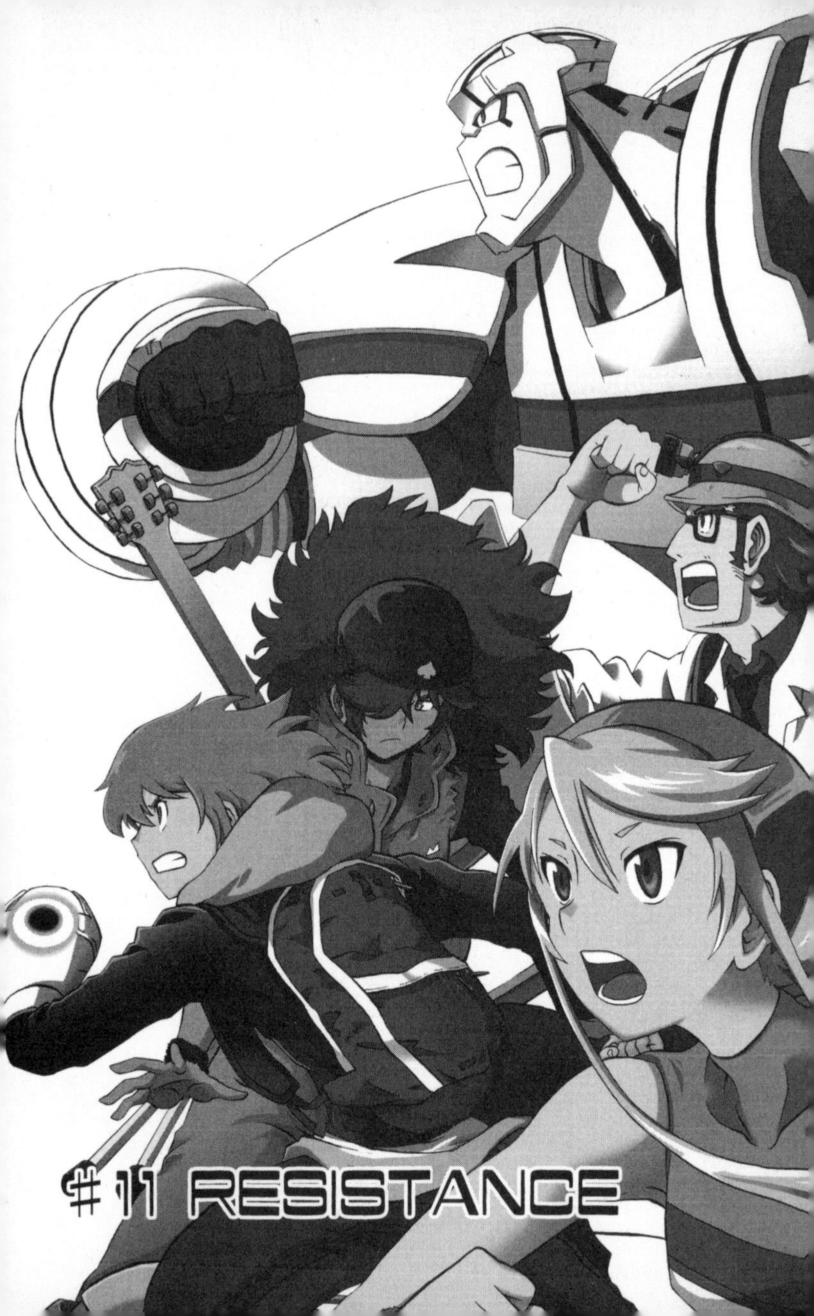

#11 RESISTANCE

HEROMAN

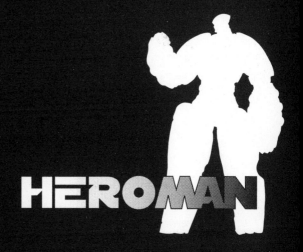

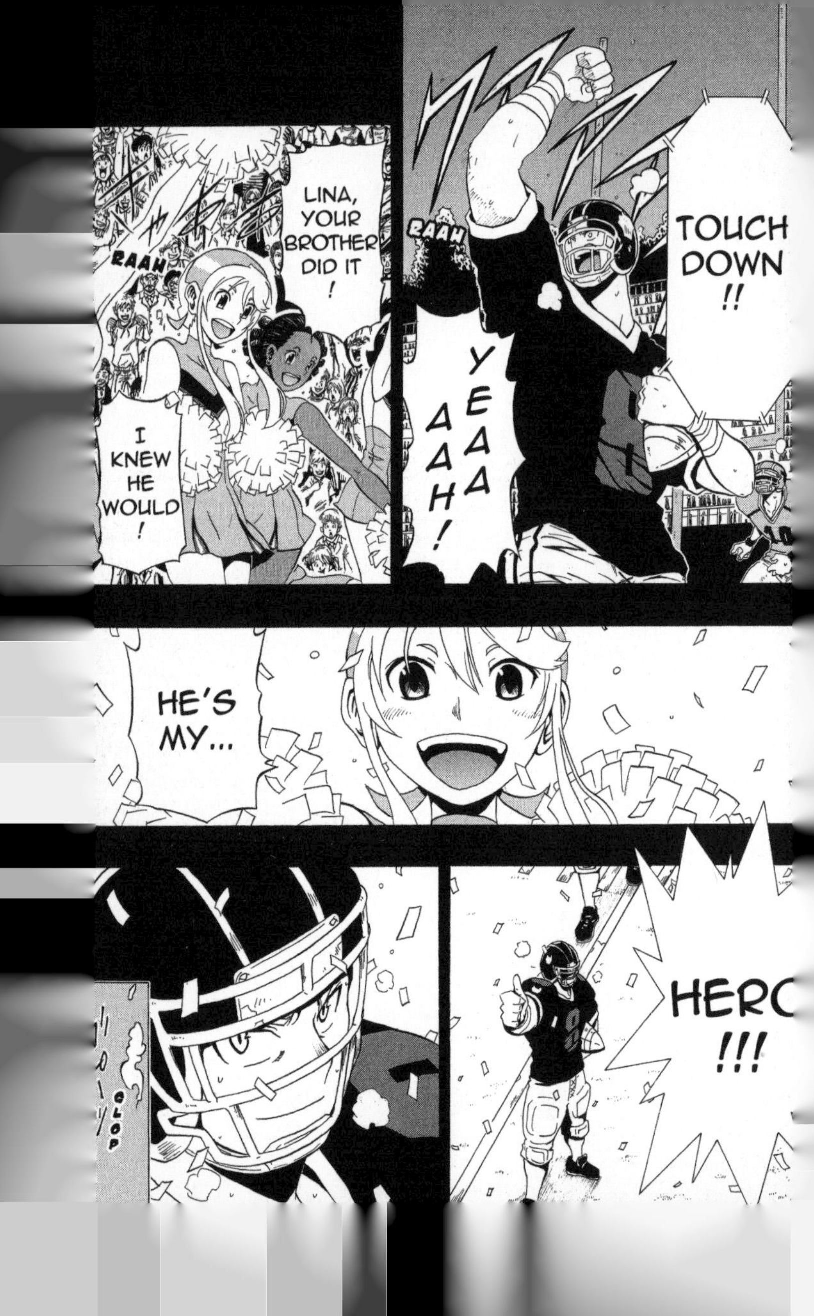
TOUCH DOWN !!
RAAH
YEAAAAAH!
LINA, YOUR BROTHER DID IT !
RAAH
I KNEW HE WOULD !
HE'S MY...
HERO !!!
CLOP

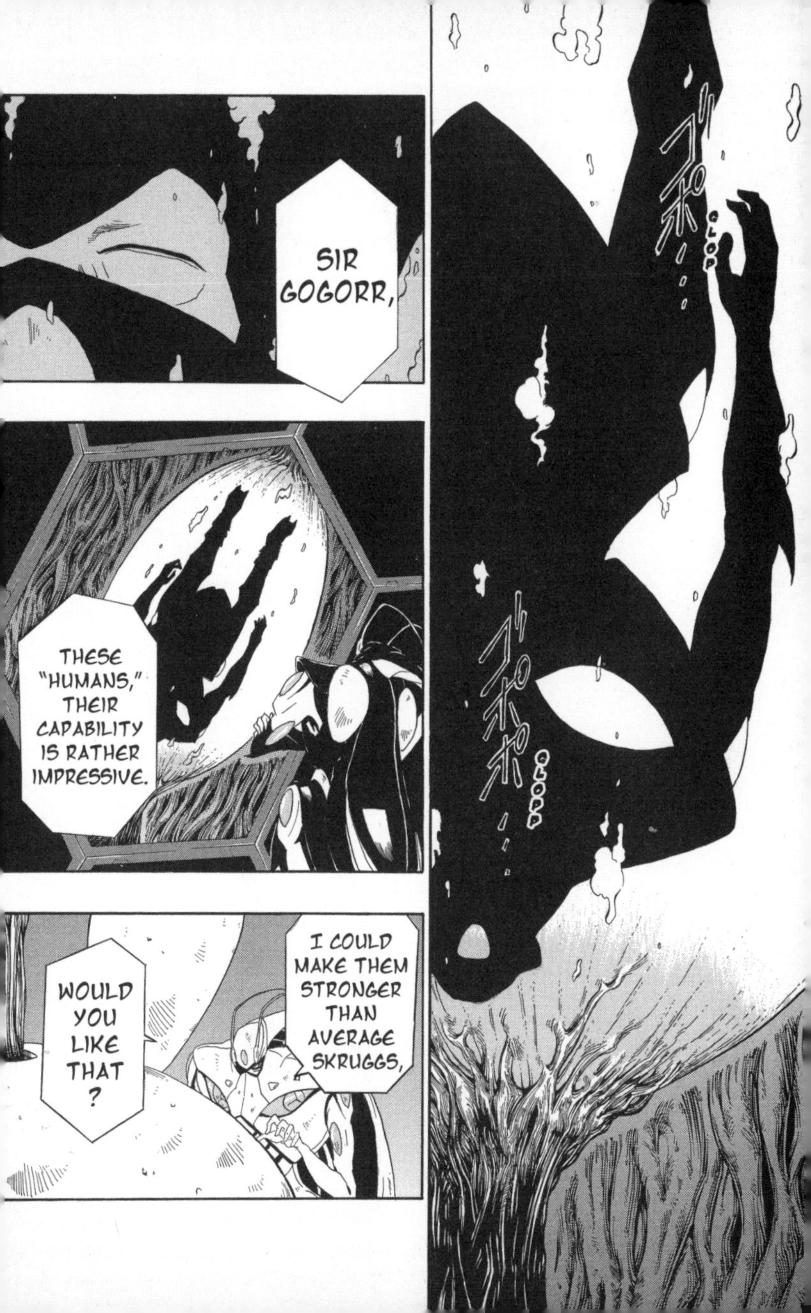
GLOP
GLOPP
SIR GOGORR,
THESE "HUMANS," THEIR CAPABILITY IS RATHER IMPRESSIVE.
I COULD MAKE THEM STRONGER THAN AVERAGE SKRUGGS,
WOULD YOU LIKE THAT?

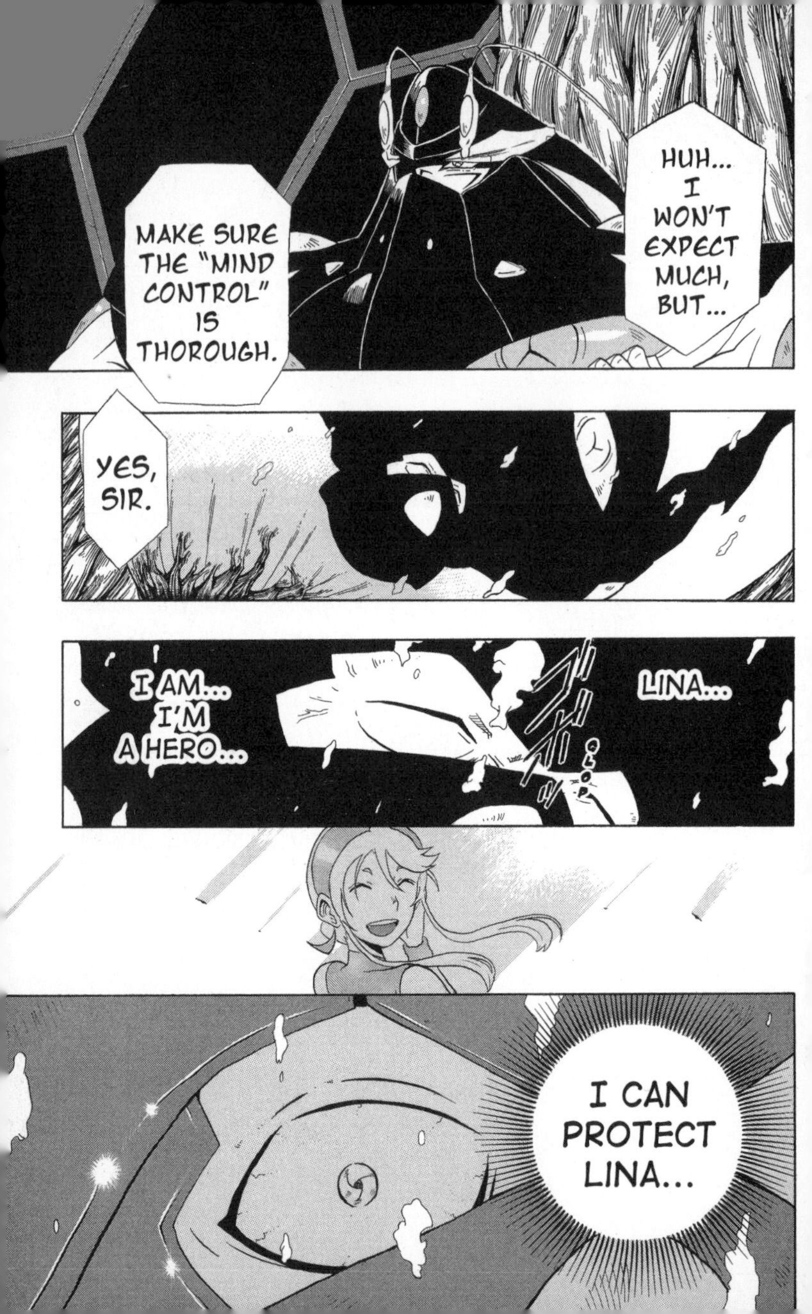
HUH... I WON'T EXPECT MUCH, BUT...
MAKE SURE THE "MIND CONTROL" IS THOROUGH.
YES, SIR.
LINA...
GLOP
I AM... I'M A HERO...
I CAN PROTECT LINA...

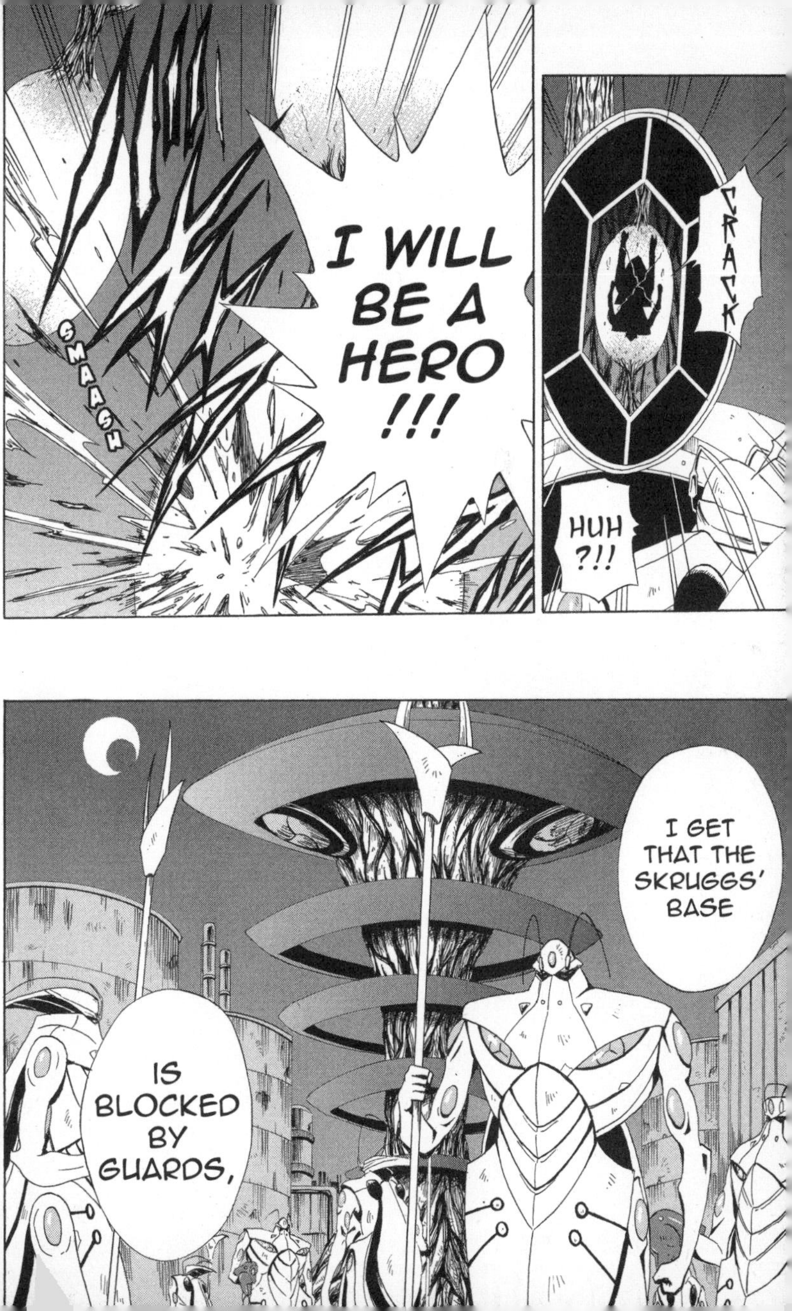
CRACK
HUH?!!
I WILL BE A HERO!!!
SMAASH
I GET THAT THE SKRUGGS' BASE
IS BLOCKED BY GUARDS,

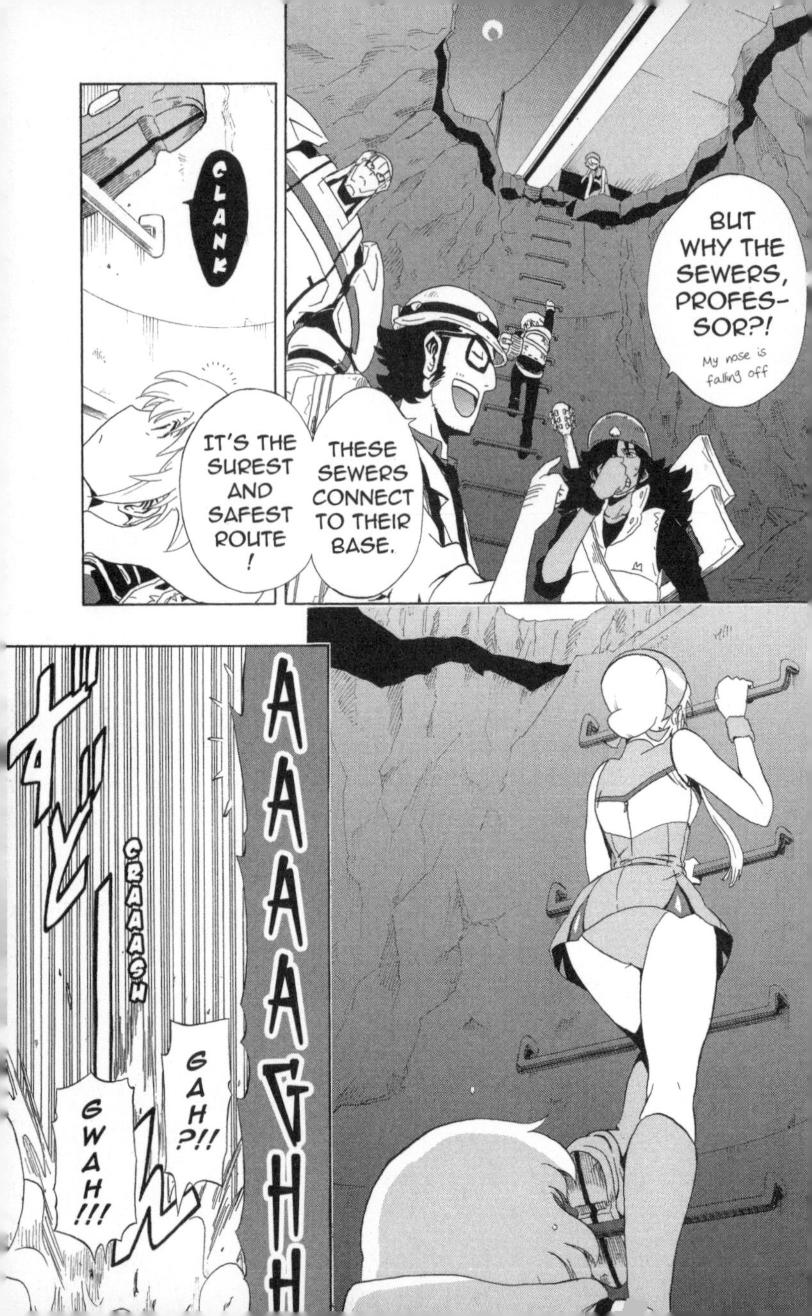
BUT WHY THE SEWERS, PROFESSOR?!
My nose is falling off
THESE SEWERS CONNECT TO THEIR BASE.
IT'S THE SUREST AND SAFEST ROUTE!
CLANK
AAAAGHH
GAH?!!
GWAH!!!
CRAAAASH

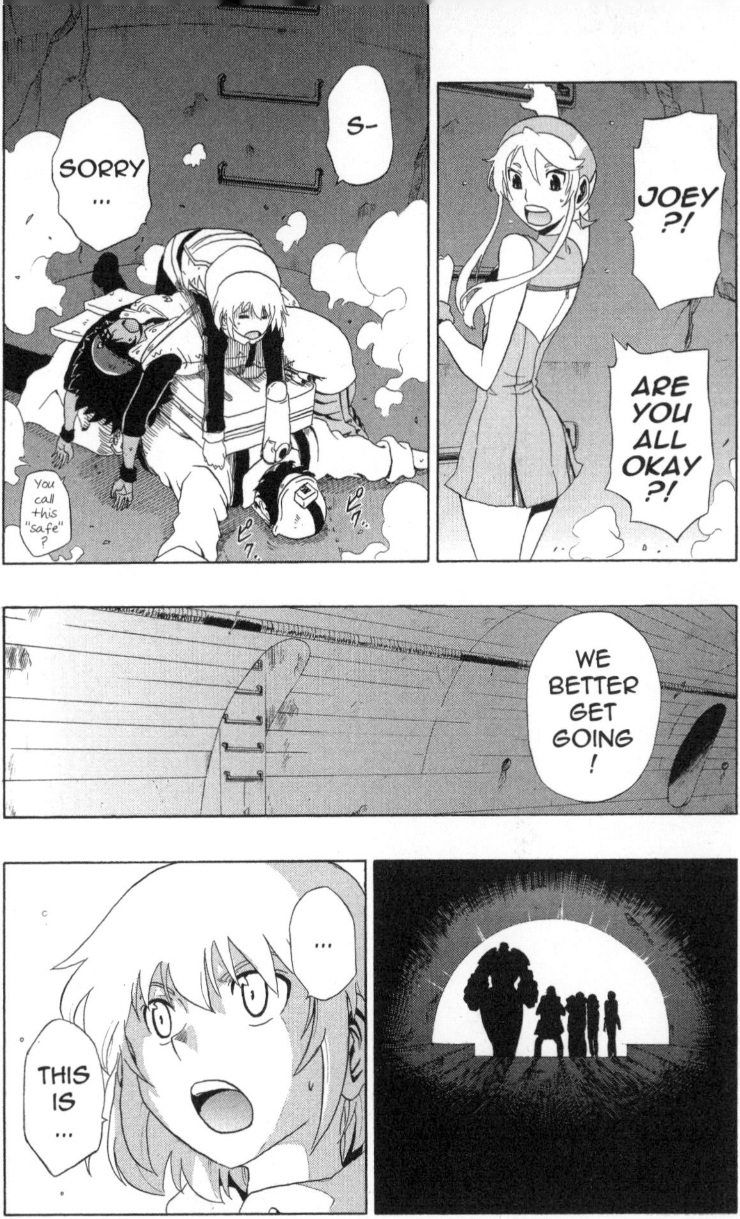
JOEY ?!
ARE YOU ALL OKAY ?!
S-
SORRY ...
You call this "safe" ?
WE BETTER GET GOING !
...
THIS IS ...

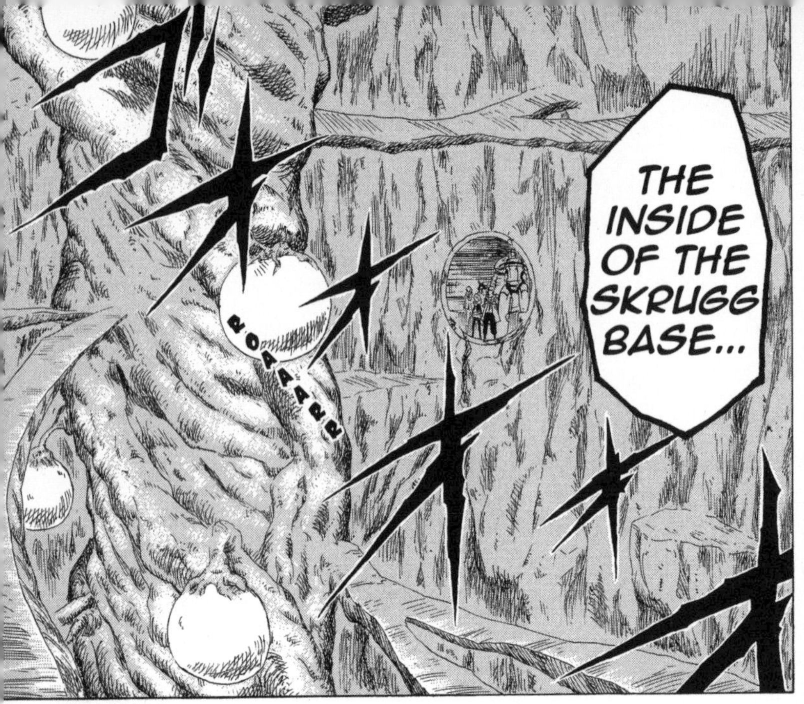
THE INSIDE OF THE SKRUGG BASE...
ROAAAARR

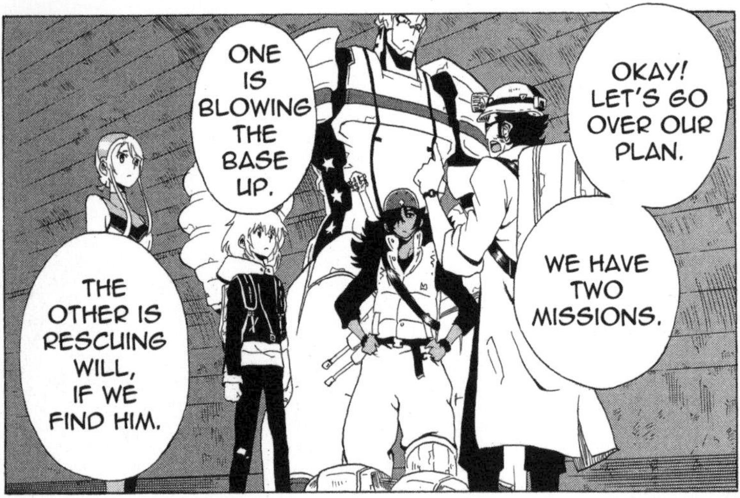
OKAY! LET'S GO OVER OUR PLAN.
WE HAVE TWO MISSIONS.
ONE IS BLOWING THE BASE UP.
THE OTHER IS RESCUING WILL, IF WE FIND HIM.

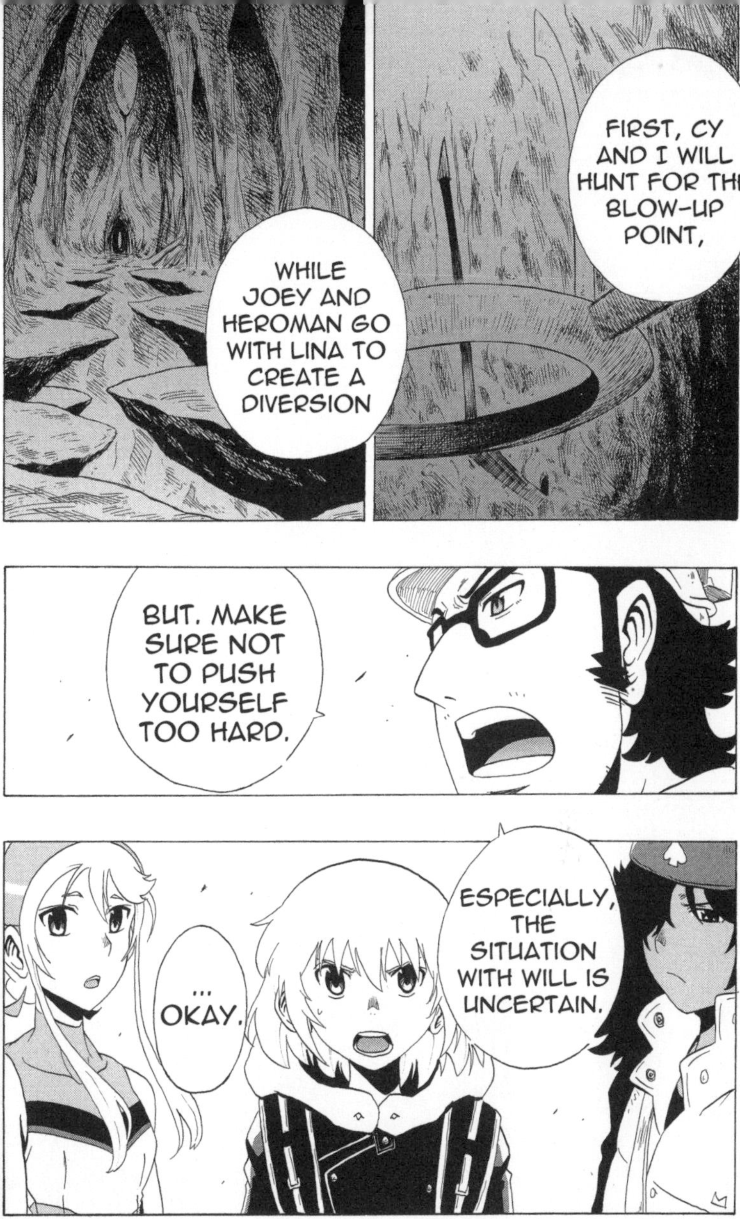
FIRST, CY AND I WILL HUNT FOR THE BLOW-UP POINT,
WHILE JOEY AND HEROMAN GO WITH LINA TO CREATE A DIVERSION
BUT. MAKE SURE NOT TO PUSH YOURSELF TOO HARD.
ESPECIALLY, THE SITUATION WITH WILL IS UNCERTAIN.
... OKAY.

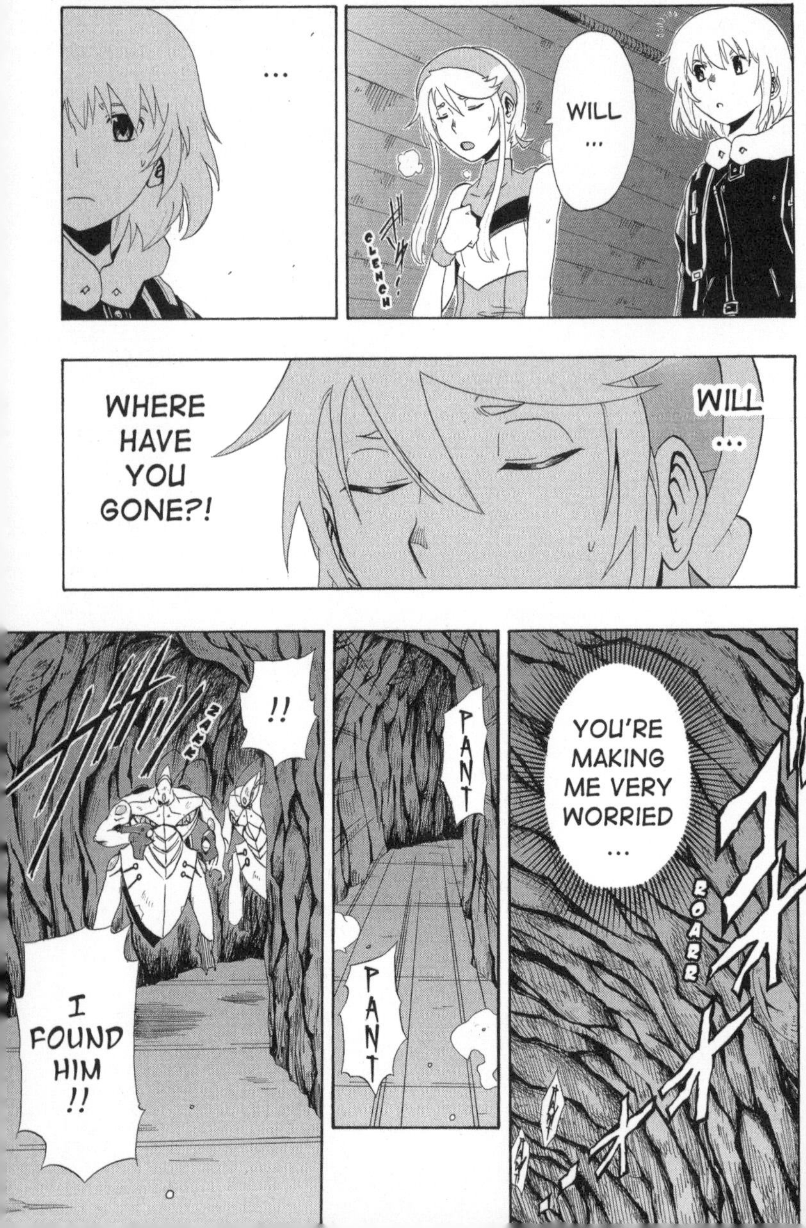
WILL ...
CLENCH
...
WILL ...
WHERE HAVE YOU GONE?!
YOU'RE MAKING ME VERY WORRIED ...
ROARR
PANT
PANT
ZAKK
!!
I FOUND HIM !!

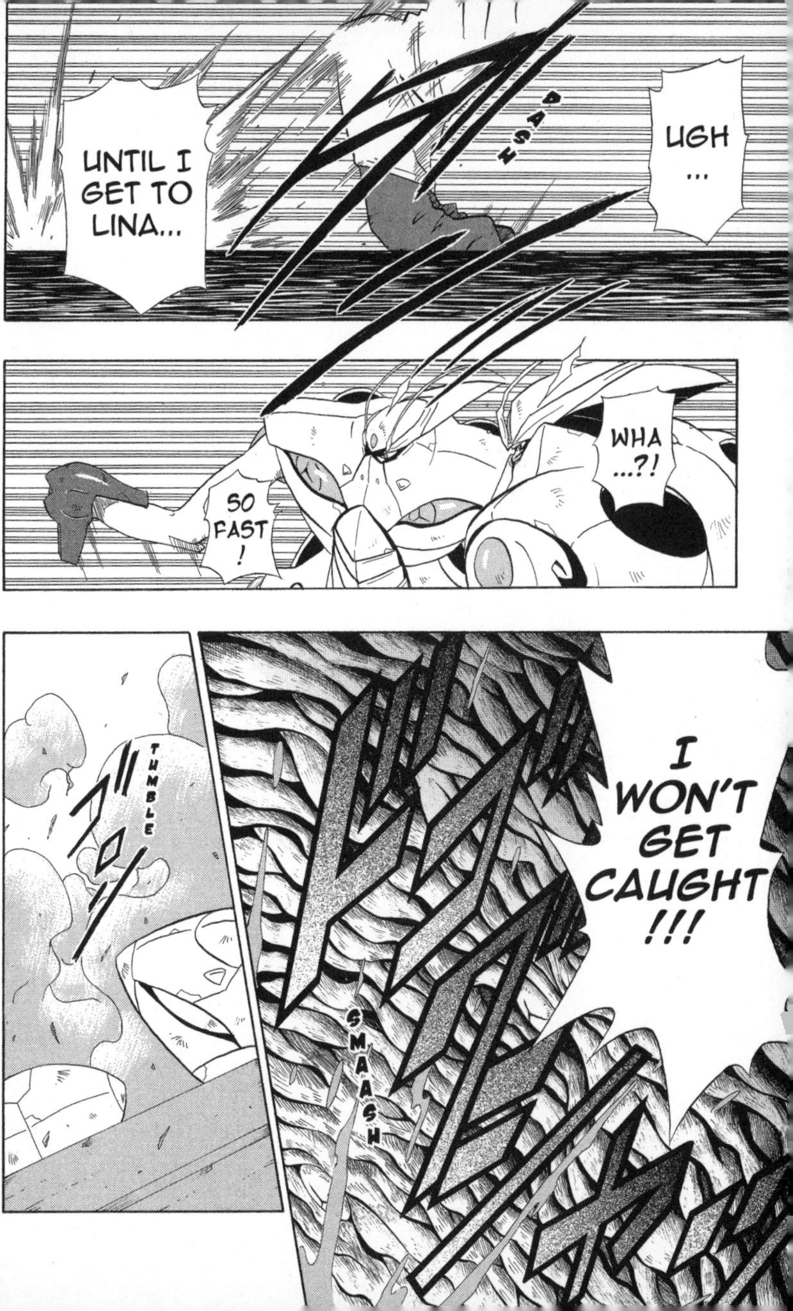
UGH ...
DASH
UNTIL I GET TO LINA...
WHA ...?!
SO FAST !
I WON'T GET CAUGHT !!!
SMAASH
TUMBLE

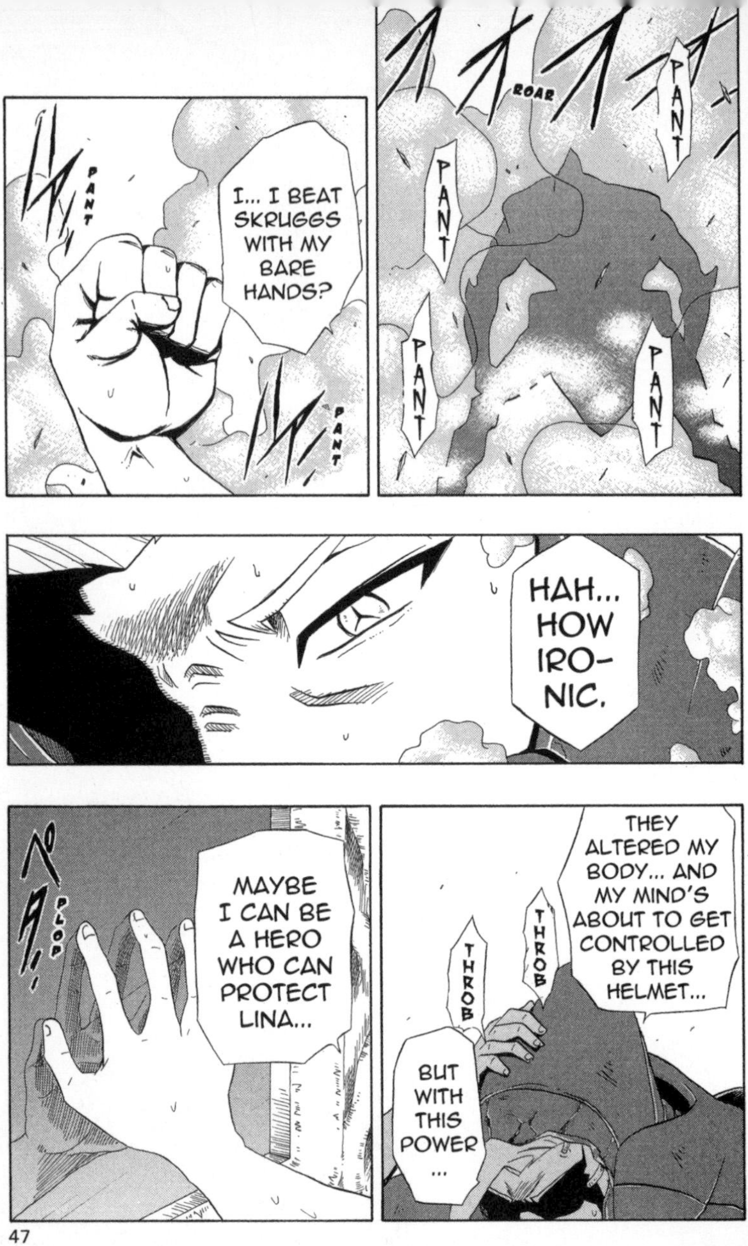
ROAR
PANT
PANT
PANT
PANT
PANT
I... I BEAT SKRUGGS WITH MY BARE HANDS?
PANT
HAH... HOW IRO-NIC.
THEY ALTERED MY BODY... AND MY MIND'S ABOUT TO GET CONTROLLED BY THIS HELMET...
THROB
THROB
BUT WITH THIS POWER...
PLOP
MAYBE I CAN BE A HERO WHO CAN PROTECT LINA...

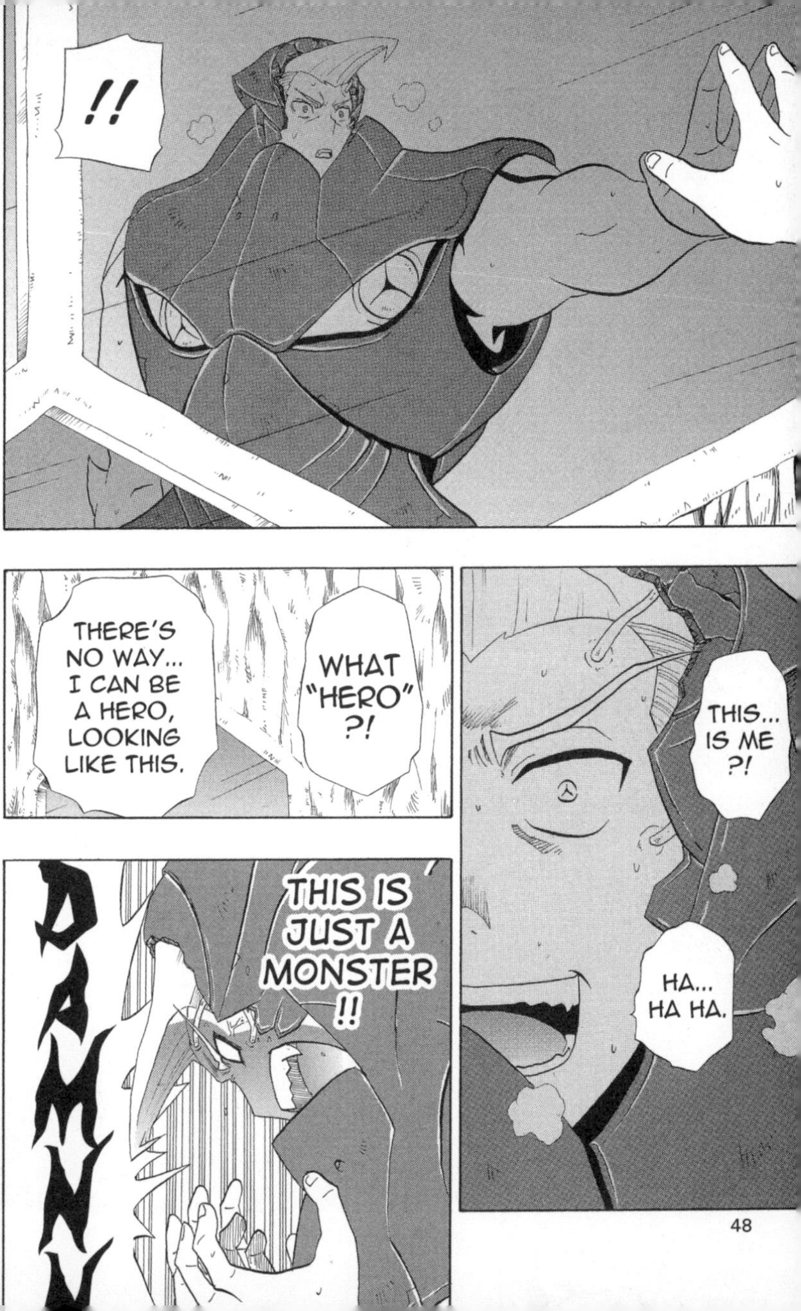
!!
THIS... IS ME ?!
HA... HA HA.
WHAT "HERO" ?!
THERE'S NO WAY... I CAN BE A HERO, LOOKING LIKE THIS.
THIS IS JUST A MONSTER !!
DAMN

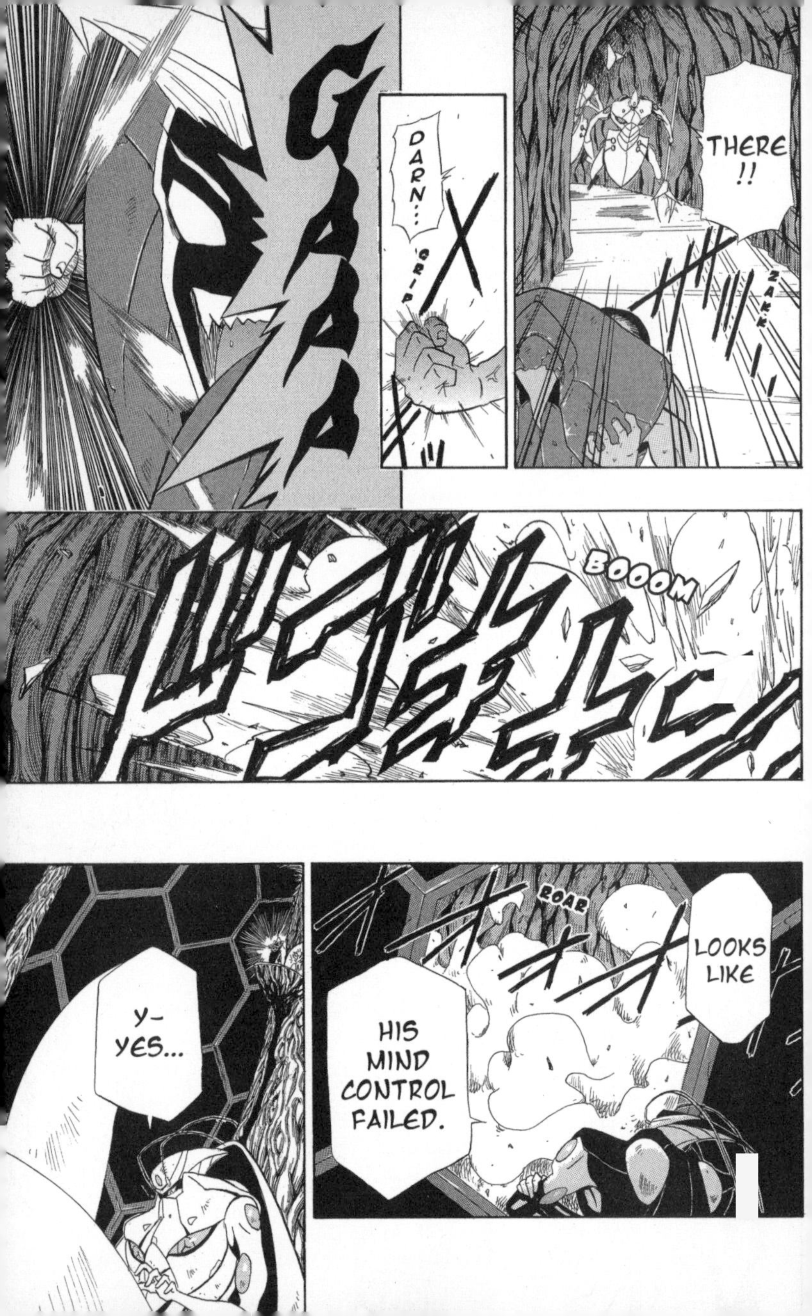
THERE!!
ZAKK
DARN...
GRIP
BOOOM
ROAR
LOOKS LIKE
HIS MIND CONTROL FAILED.
Y-YES...

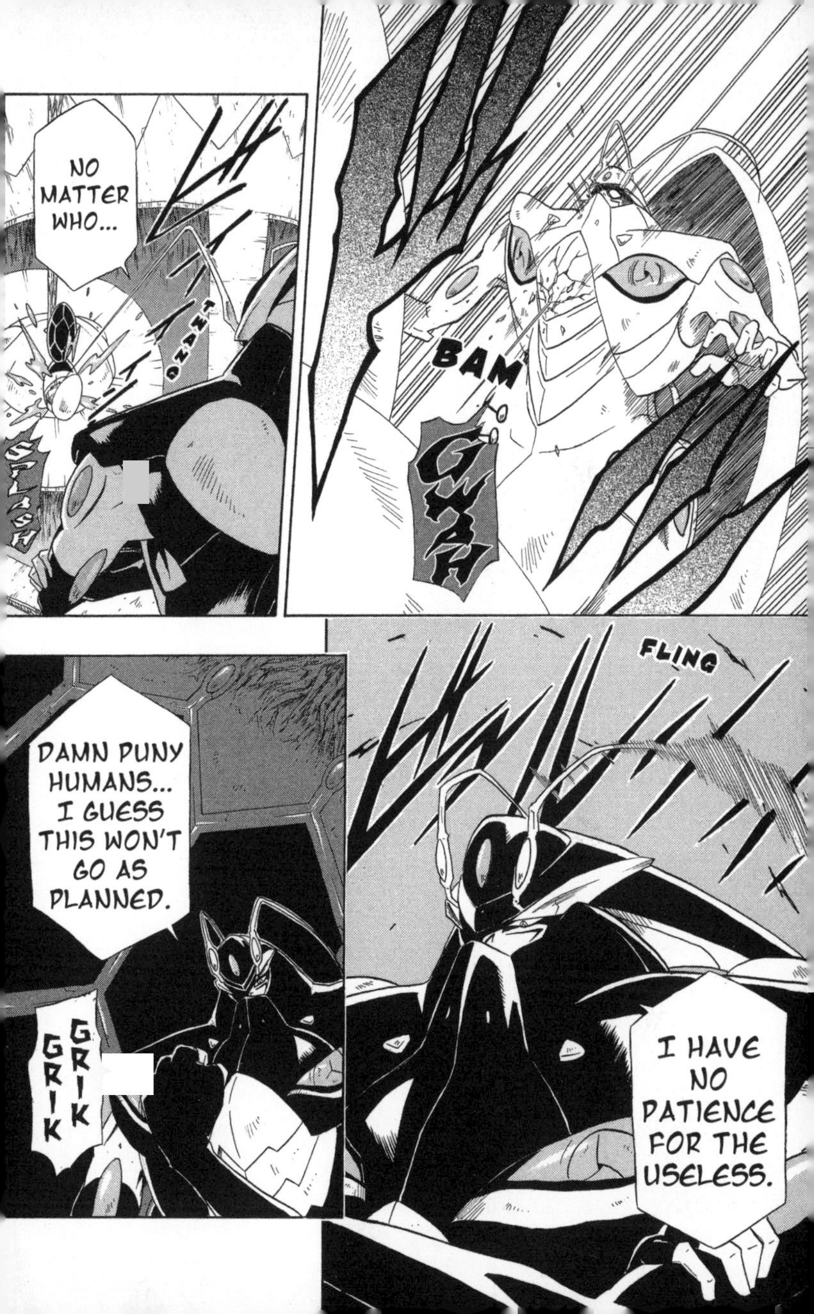
BAM
GWAH
NO MATTER WHO...
TWANG
SPLASH
FLING
I HAVE NO PATIENCE FOR THE USELESS.
DAMN PUNY HUMANS... I GUESS THIS WON'T GO AS PLANNED.
GRIK GRIK

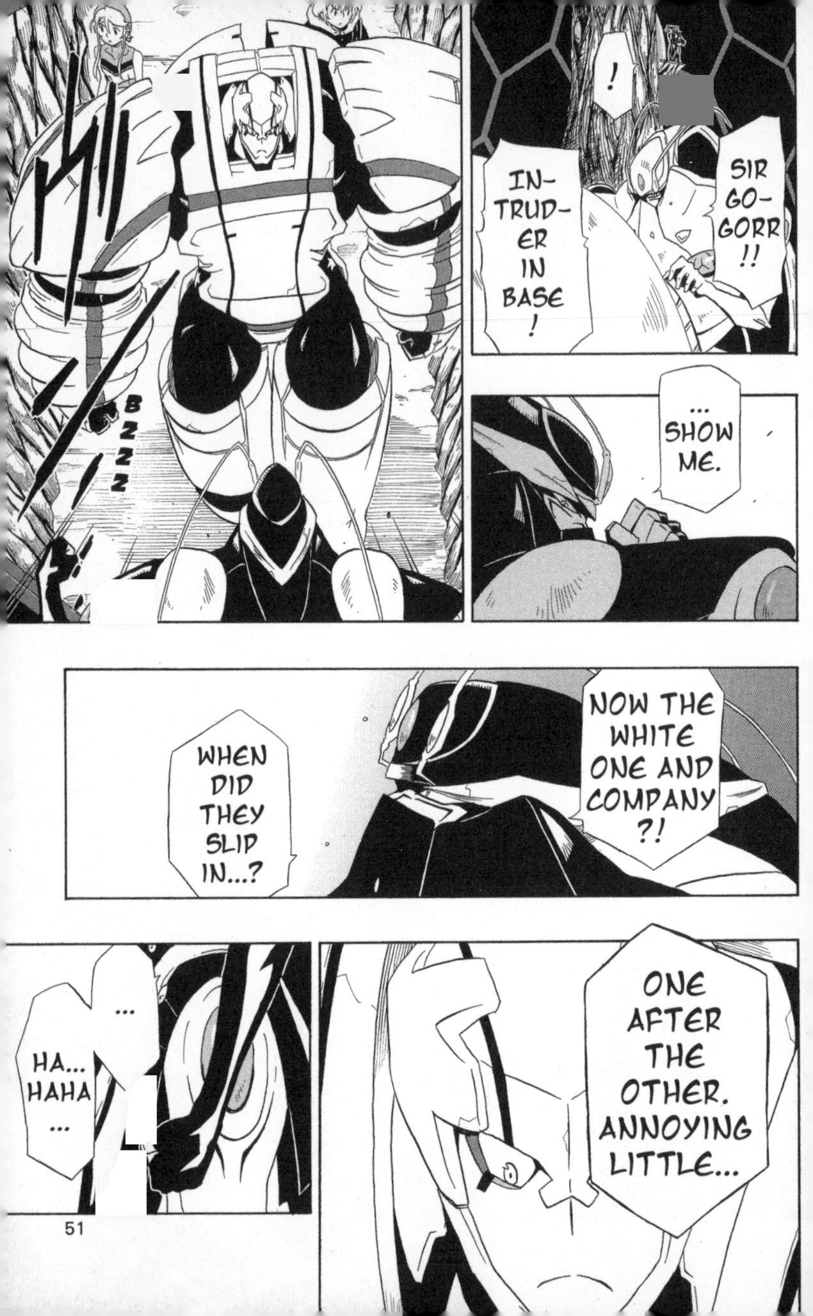
SIR GO-GORR!!
!
INTRUDER IN BASE!
...SHOW ME.
BZZZ
NOW THE WHITE ONE AND COMPANY?!
WHEN DID THEY SLIP IN...?
ONE AFTER THE OTHER. ANNOYING LITTLE...
...
HA... HAHA ...

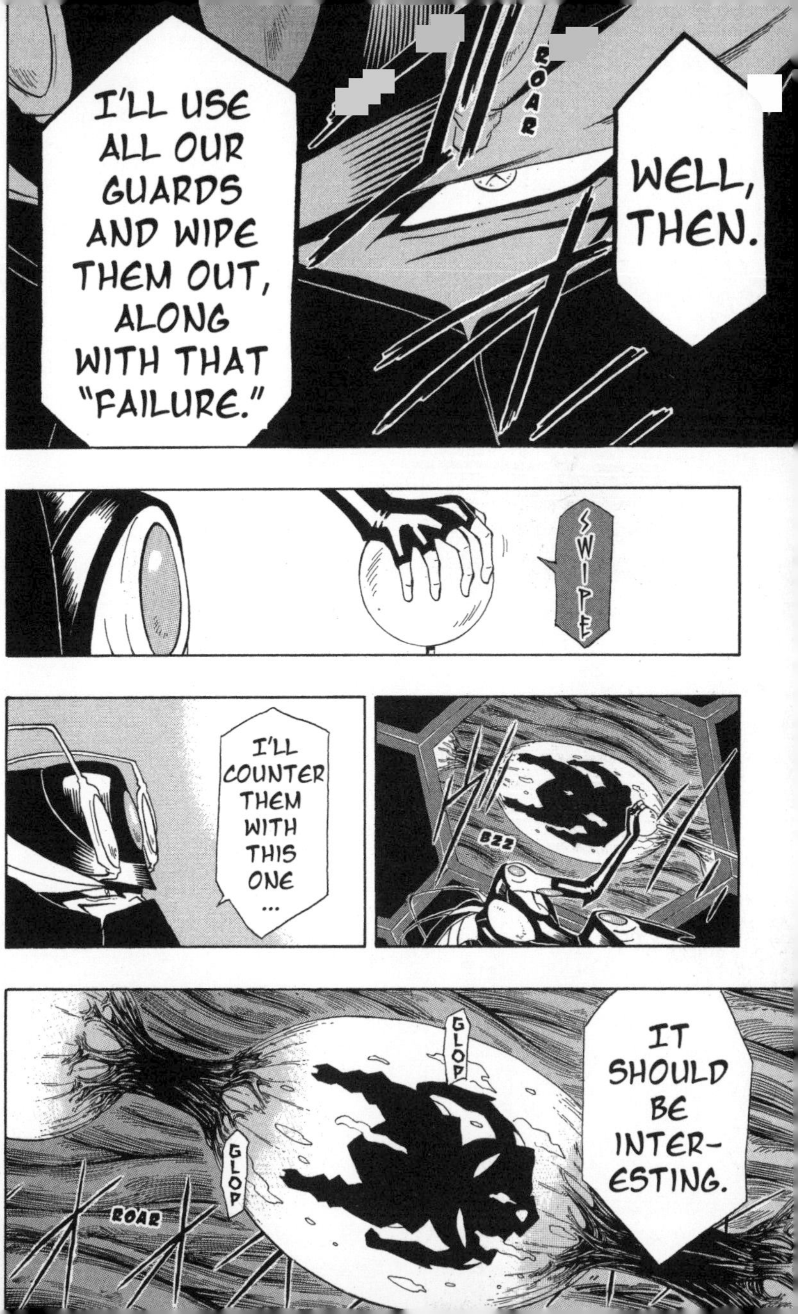
WELL, THEN.
ROAR
I'LL USE ALL OUR GUARDS AND WIPE THEM OUT, ALONG WITH THAT "FAILURE."
SWIPE
BZZ
I'LL COUNTER THEM WITH THIS ONE ...
IT SHOULD BE INTER-ESTING.
GLOP
GLOP
ROAR

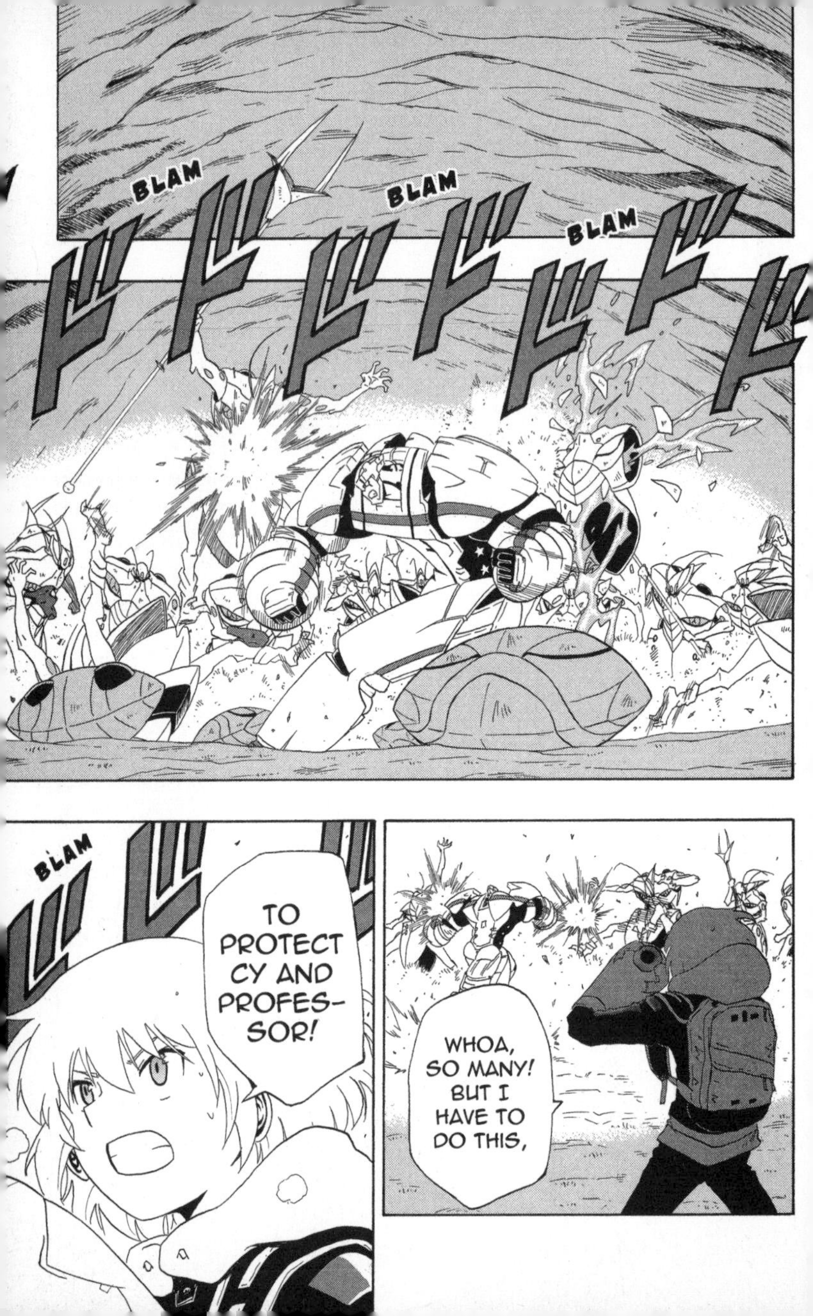
BLAM
BLAM
BLAM
WHOA, SO MANY! BUT I HAVE TO DO THIS,
BLAM
TO PROTECT CY AND PROFES-SOR!

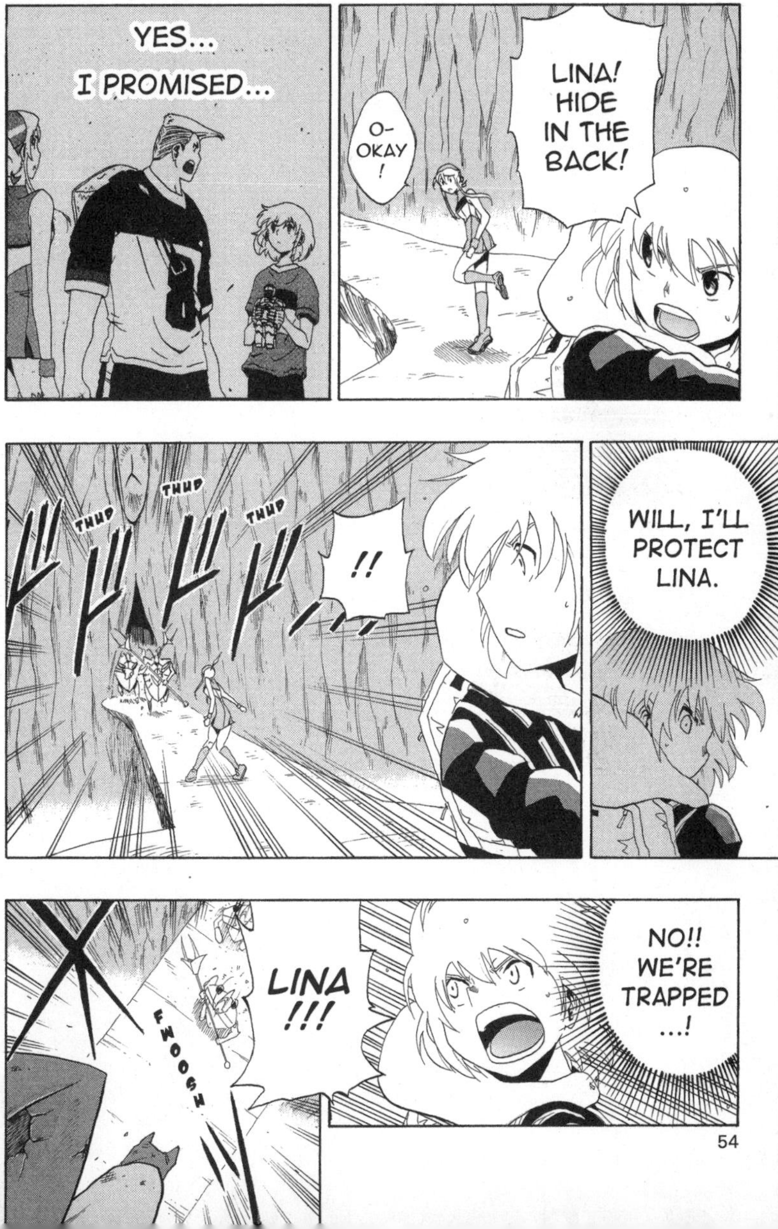
LINA! HIDE IN THE BACK!
O-OKAY!
YES... I PROMISED...
WILL, I'LL PROTECT LINA.
THUD
THUD
THUD
!!
NO!! WE'RE TRAPPED ...!
LINA !!!
FWOOSH

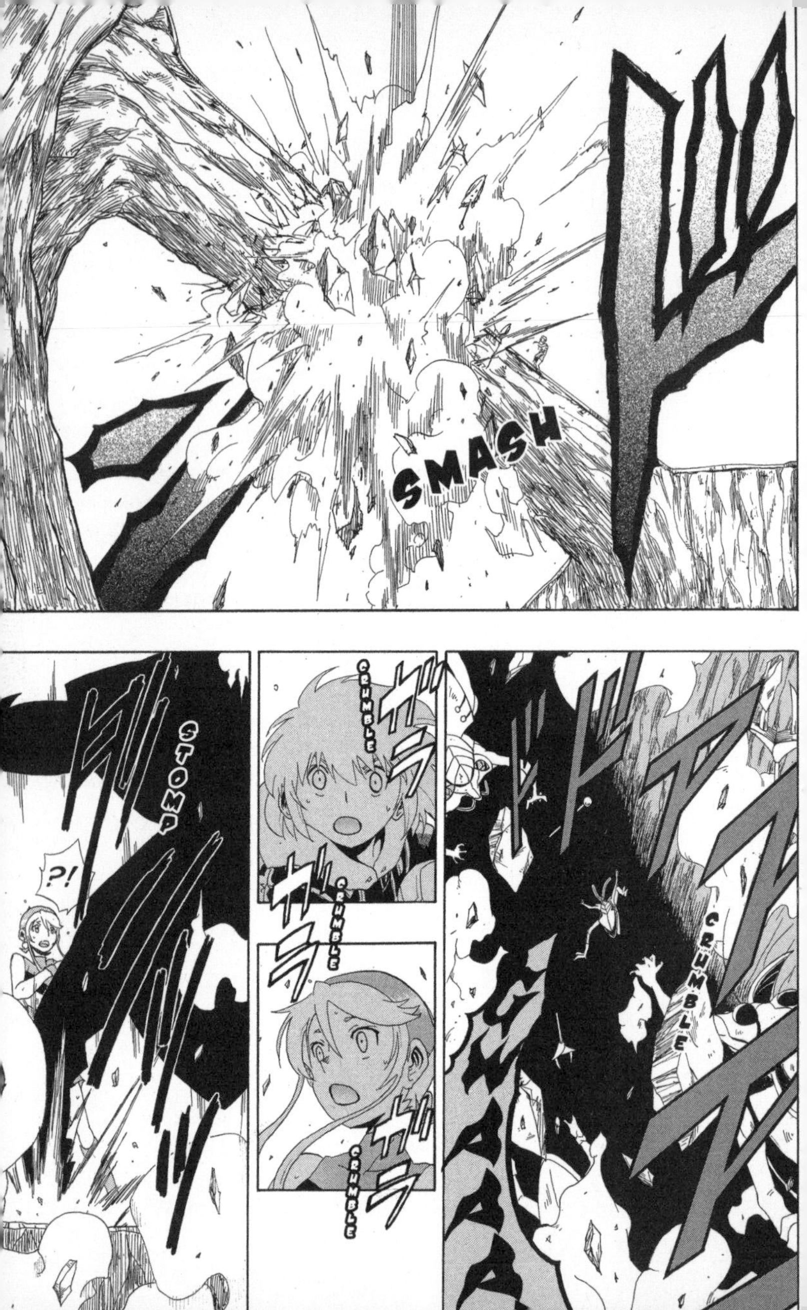
SMASH
CRUMBLE
CRUMBLE
CRUMBLE
CRUMBLE
STOMP
?!

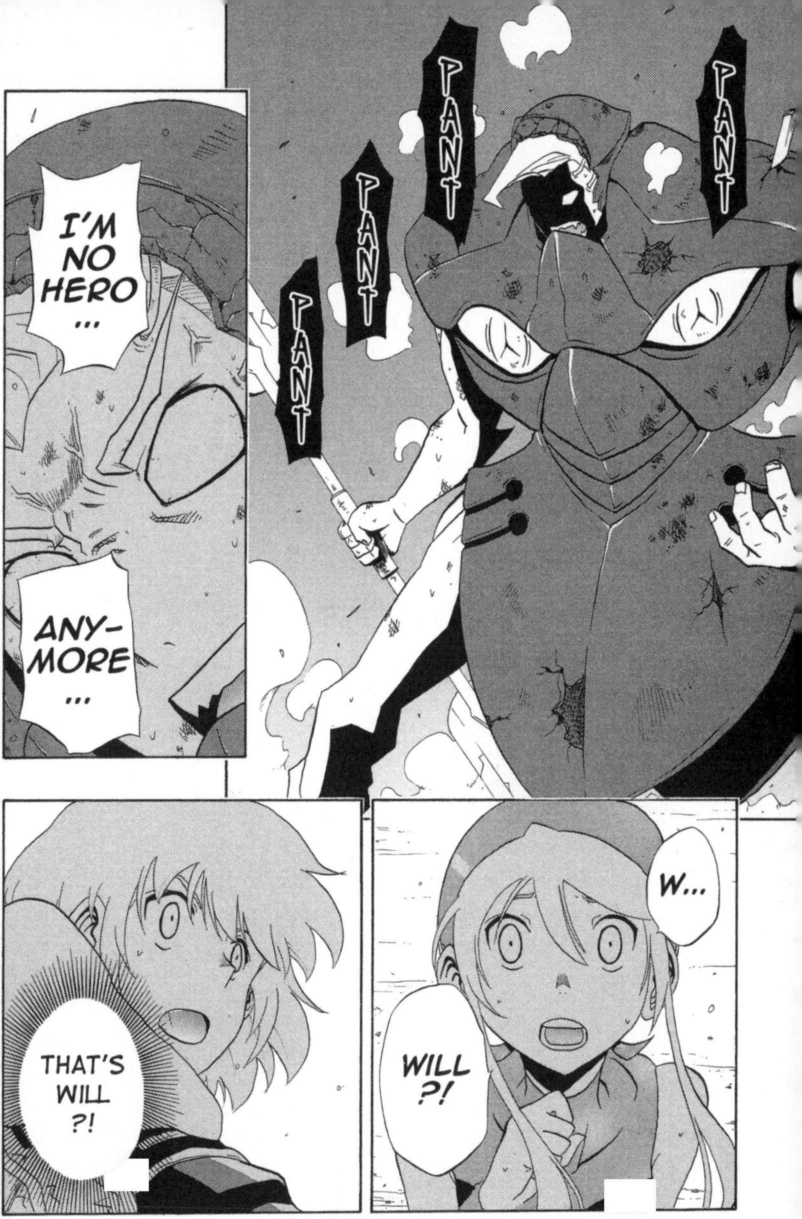
PANT
PANT
PANT
PANT
I'M NO HERO ...
ANY-MORE ...
W...
WILL ?!
THAT'S WILL ?!

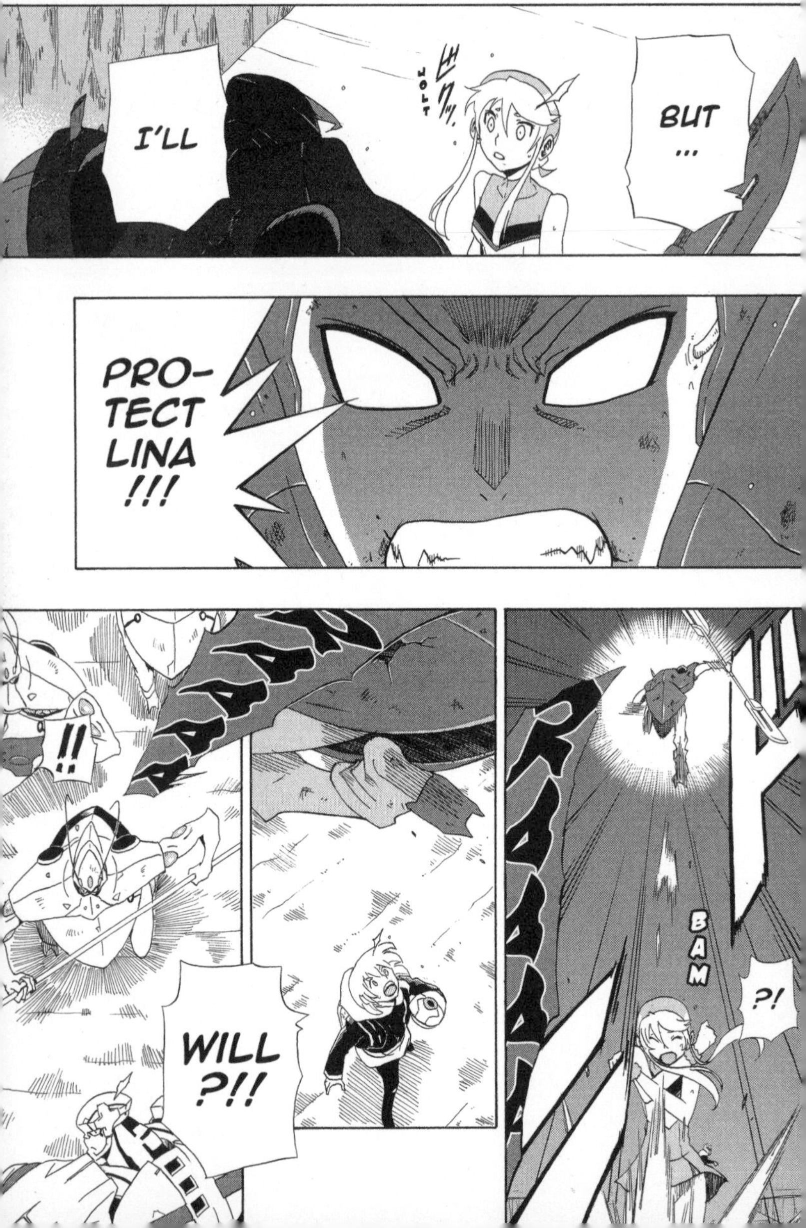
BUT ...
JOLT
I'LL
PRO-TECT LINA !!!
BAM
?!
WILL ?!!
!!

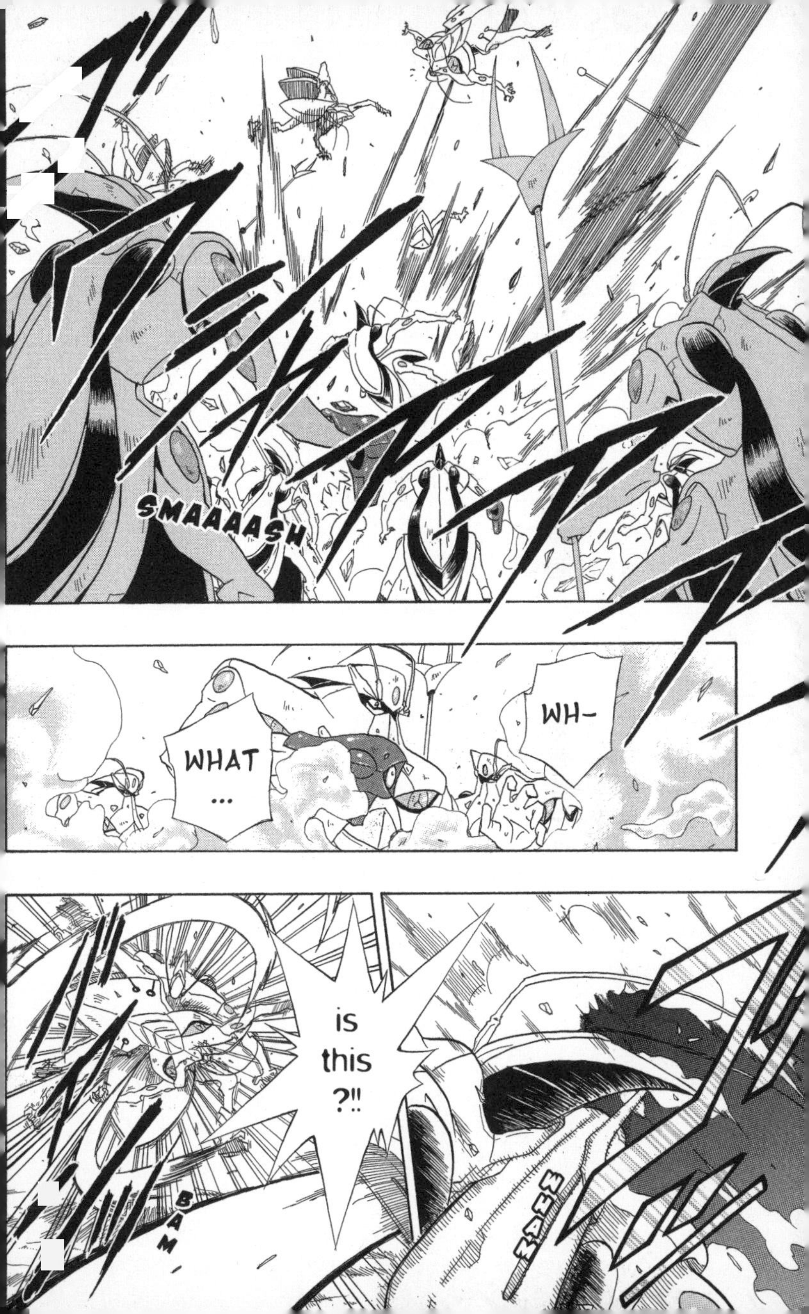
SMAAAASH
WH-
WHAT ...
WHAM
is this ?!!
BAM

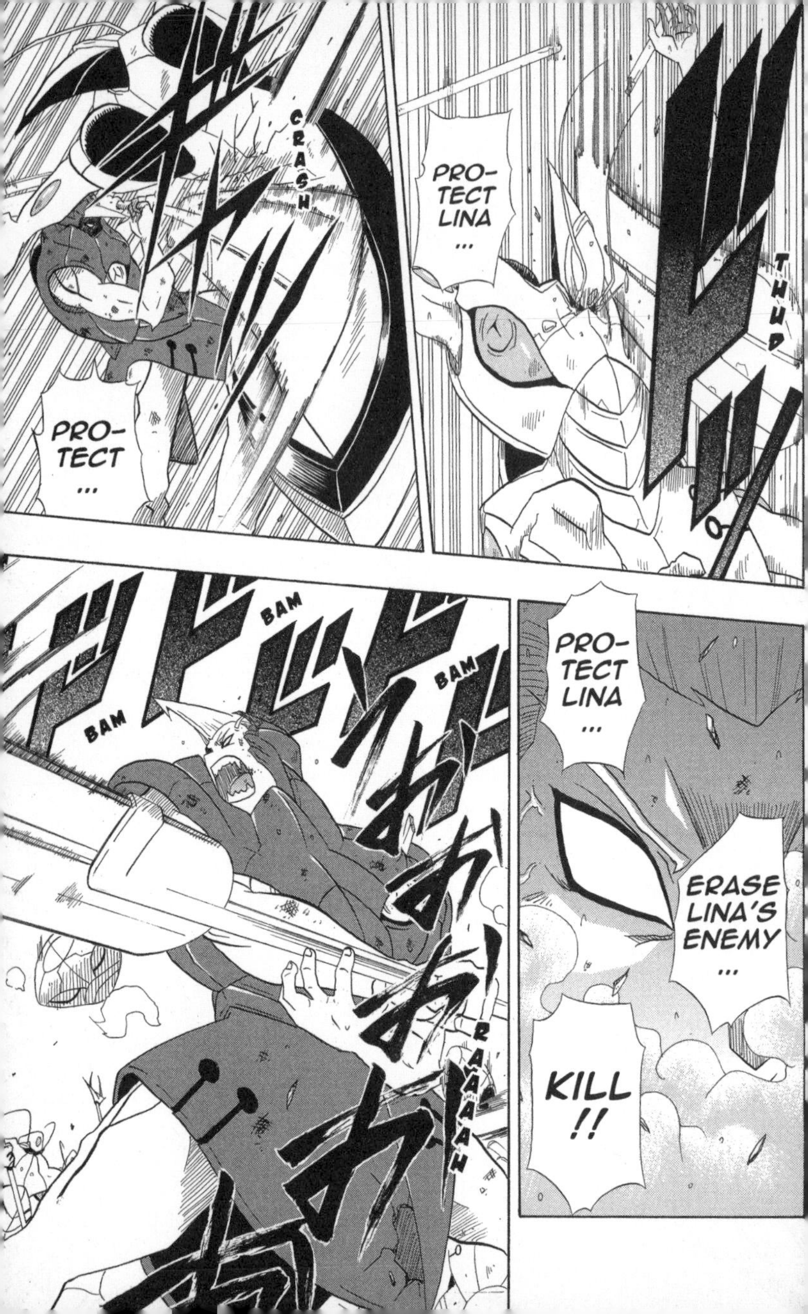
PRO-TECT LINA ...
THUD
CRASH
PRO-TECT ...
PRO-TECT LINA ...
ERASE LINA'S ENEMY ...
KILL !!
BAM
BAM
BAM
RAAAAAAH

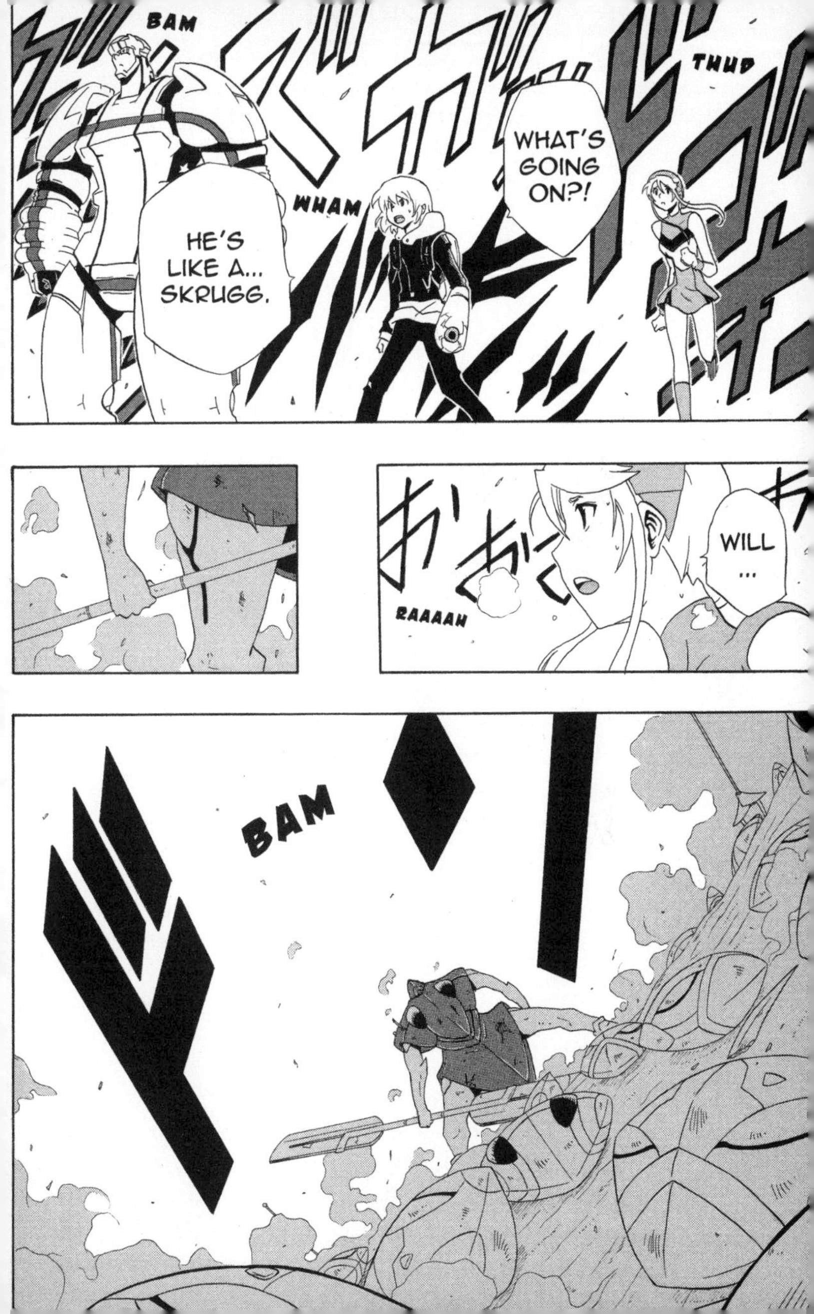
THUD
WHAT'S GOING ON?!
BAM
WHAM
HE'S LIKE A... SKRUGG.
WILL ...
RAAAAH
BAM

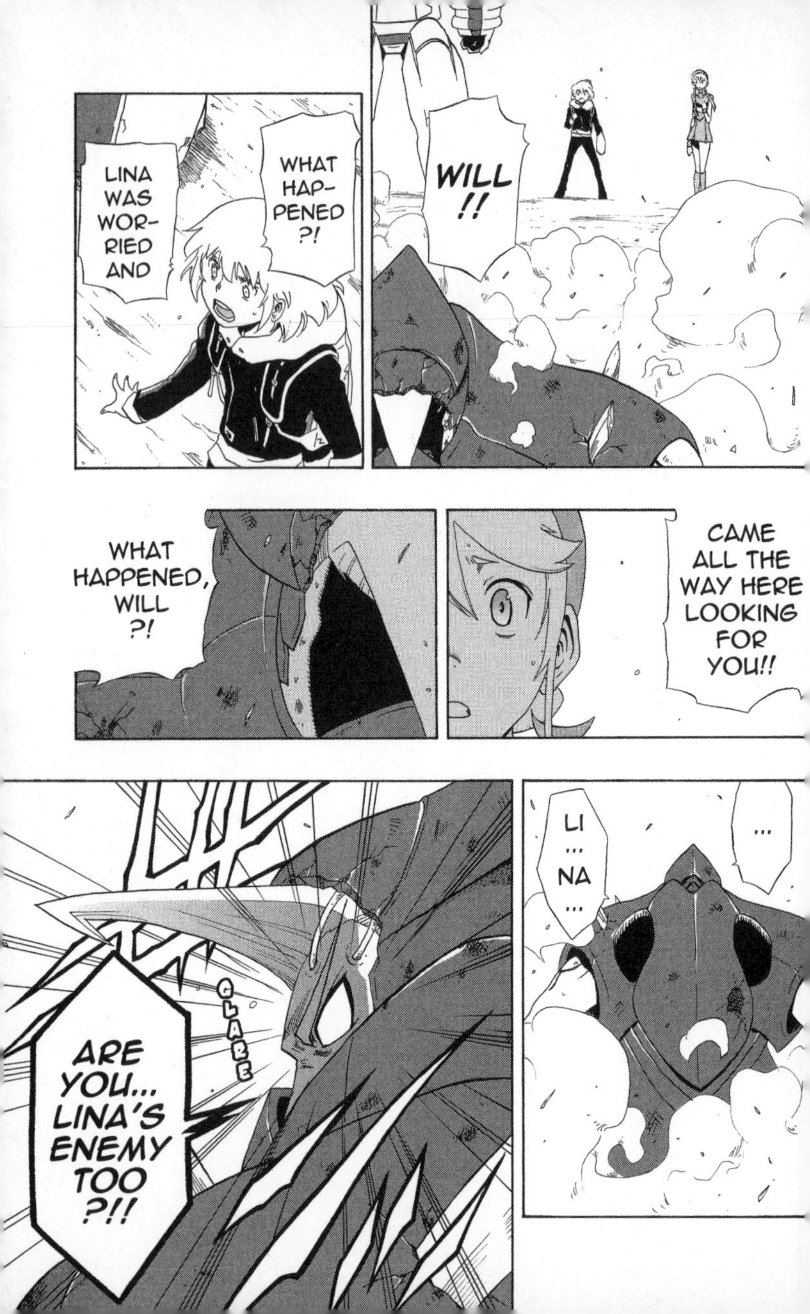
WILL!!
WHAT HAP-PENED?!
LINA WAS WOR-RIED AND
CAME ALL THE WAY HERE LOOKING FOR YOU!!
WHAT HAPPENED, WILL?!
...
LI... NA...
GLARE
ARE YOU... LINA'S ENEMY TOO?!!

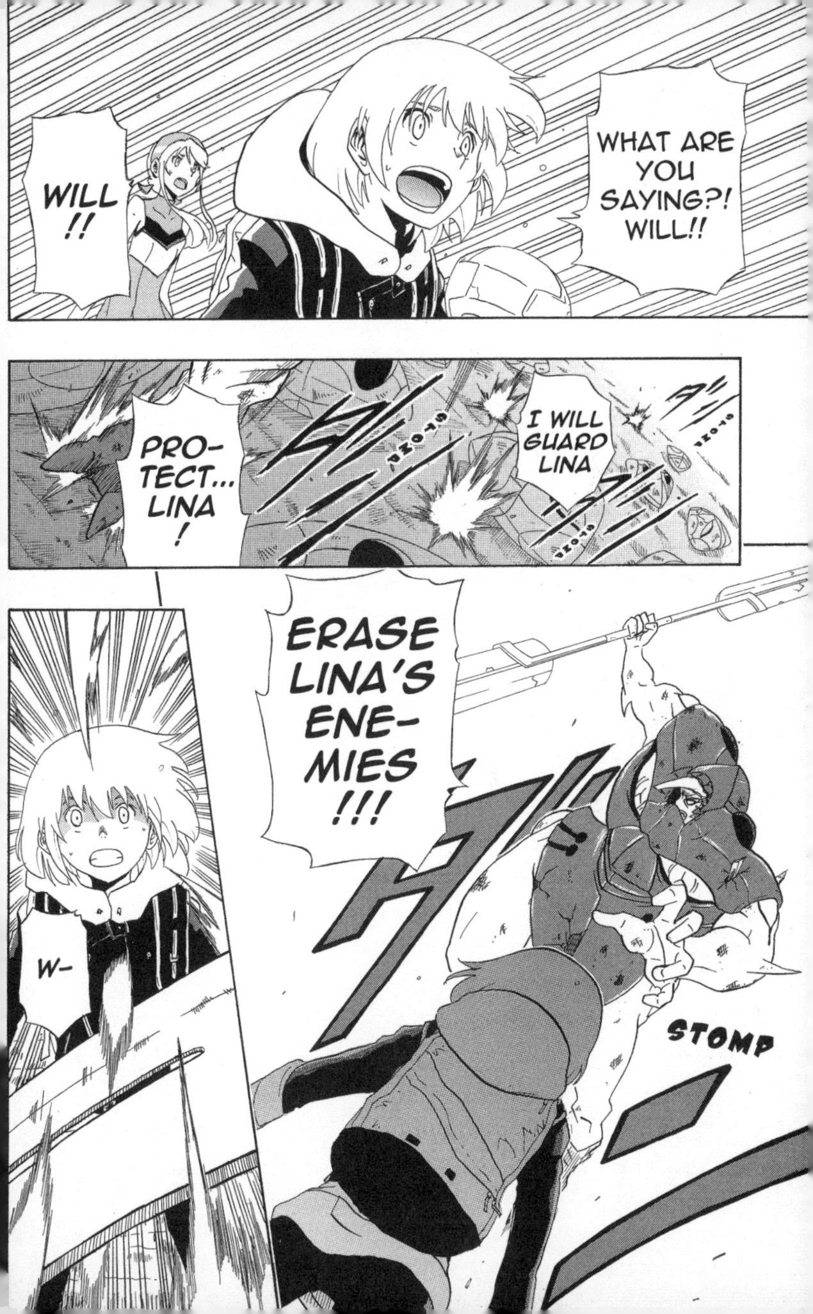
WHAT ARE YOU SAYING?! WILL!!
WILL !!
I WILL GUARD LINA
PRO-TECT... LINA !
ERASE LINA'S ENE-MIES !!!
STOMP
W-

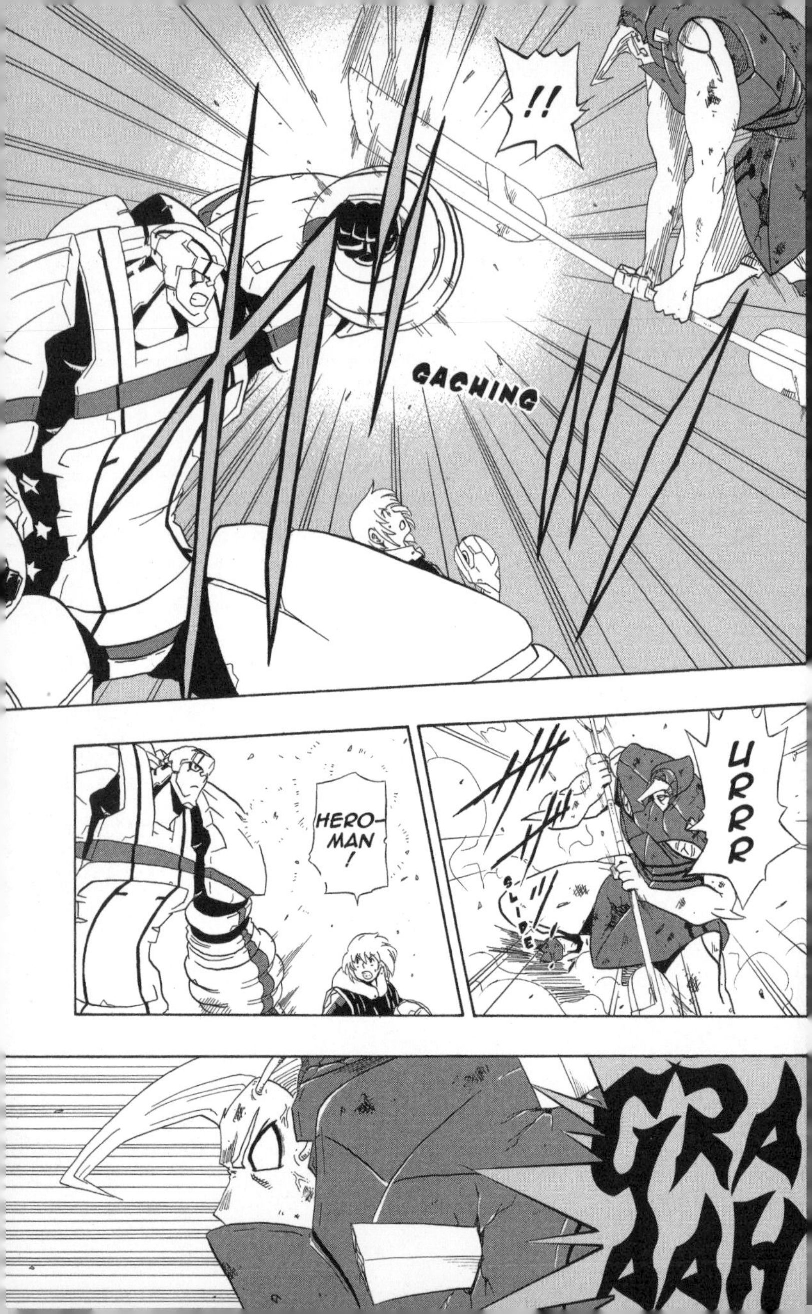
!!
GACHING
URRR
SLIDE
HERO-MAN!
GRAAAH

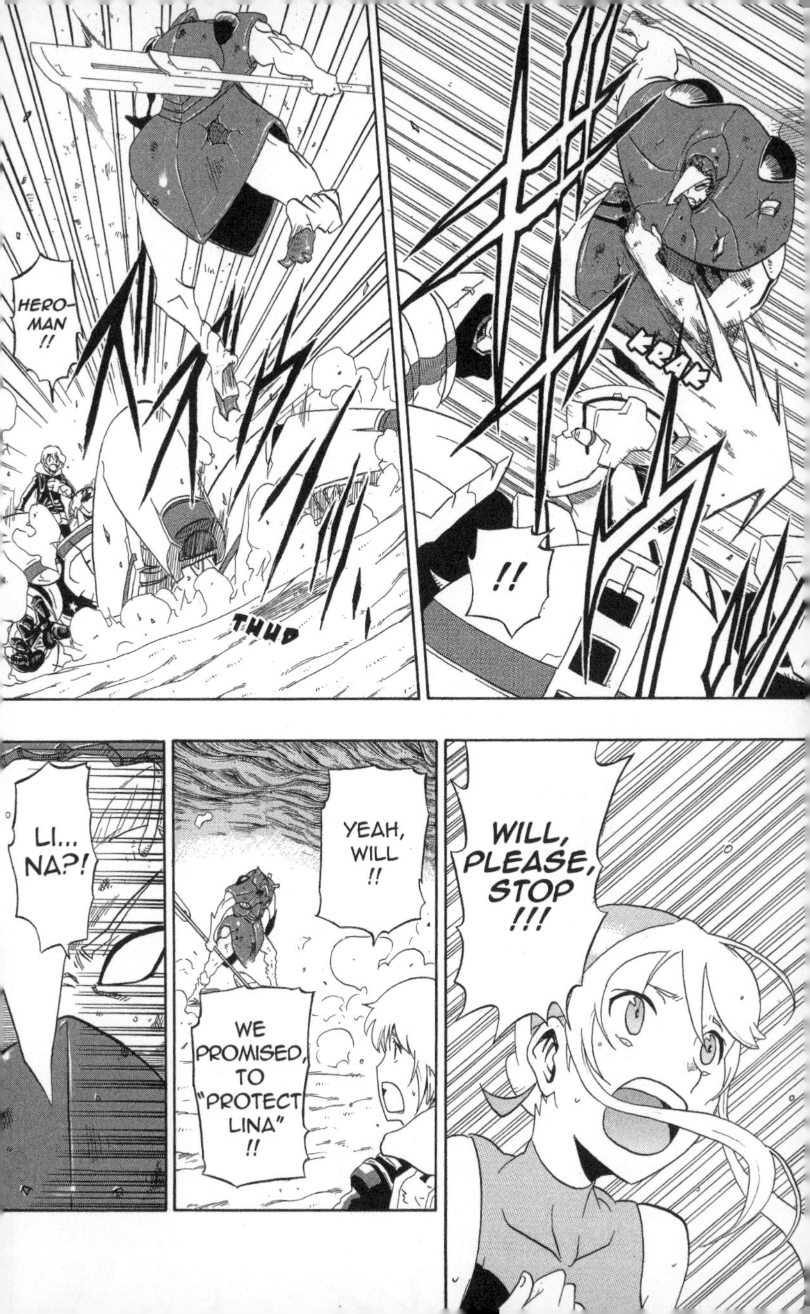
KRAK
!!
HERO-MAN !!
THUD
WILL, PLEASE, STOP !!!
YEAH, WILL !!
WE PROMISED, TO "PROTECT LINA" !!
LI... NA?!

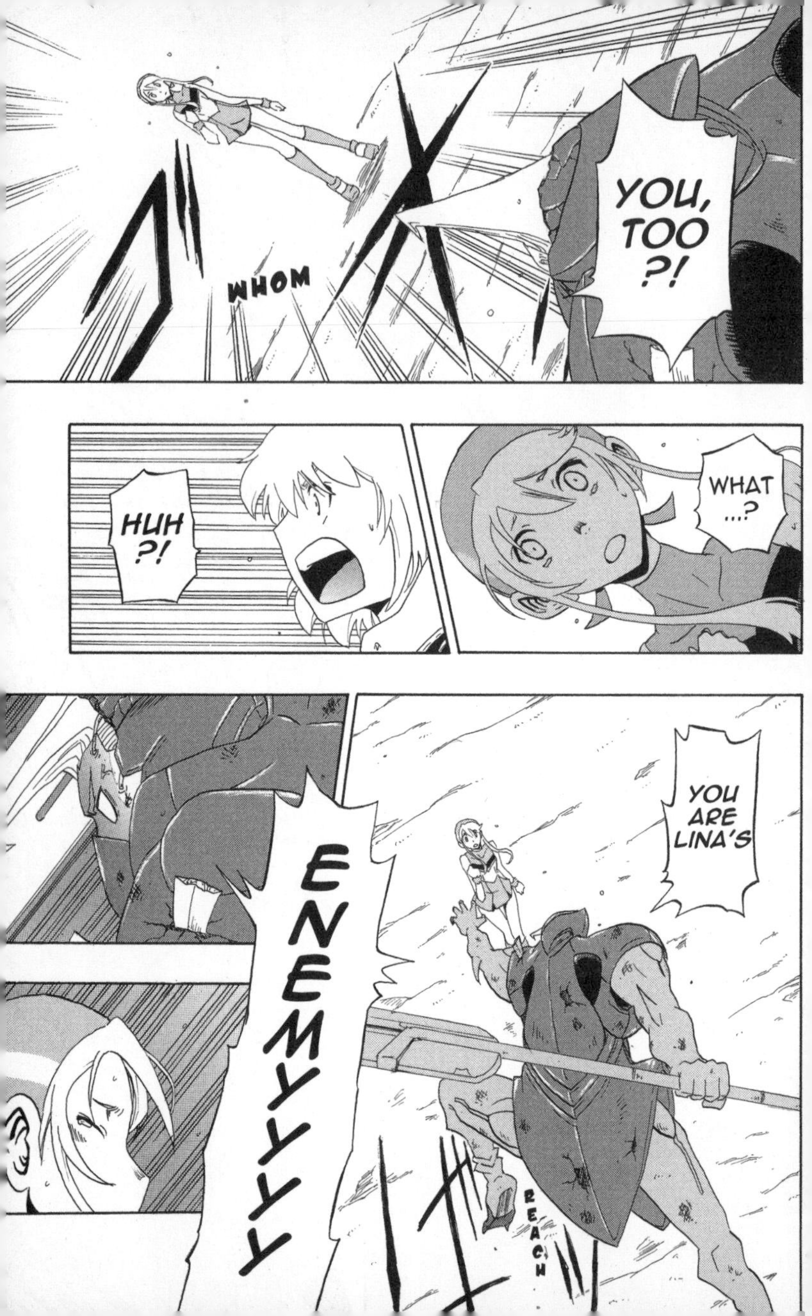
YOU, TOO ?!
WHOM
WHAT ...?
HUH ?!
YOU ARE LINA'S
ENEMYYYY
REACH

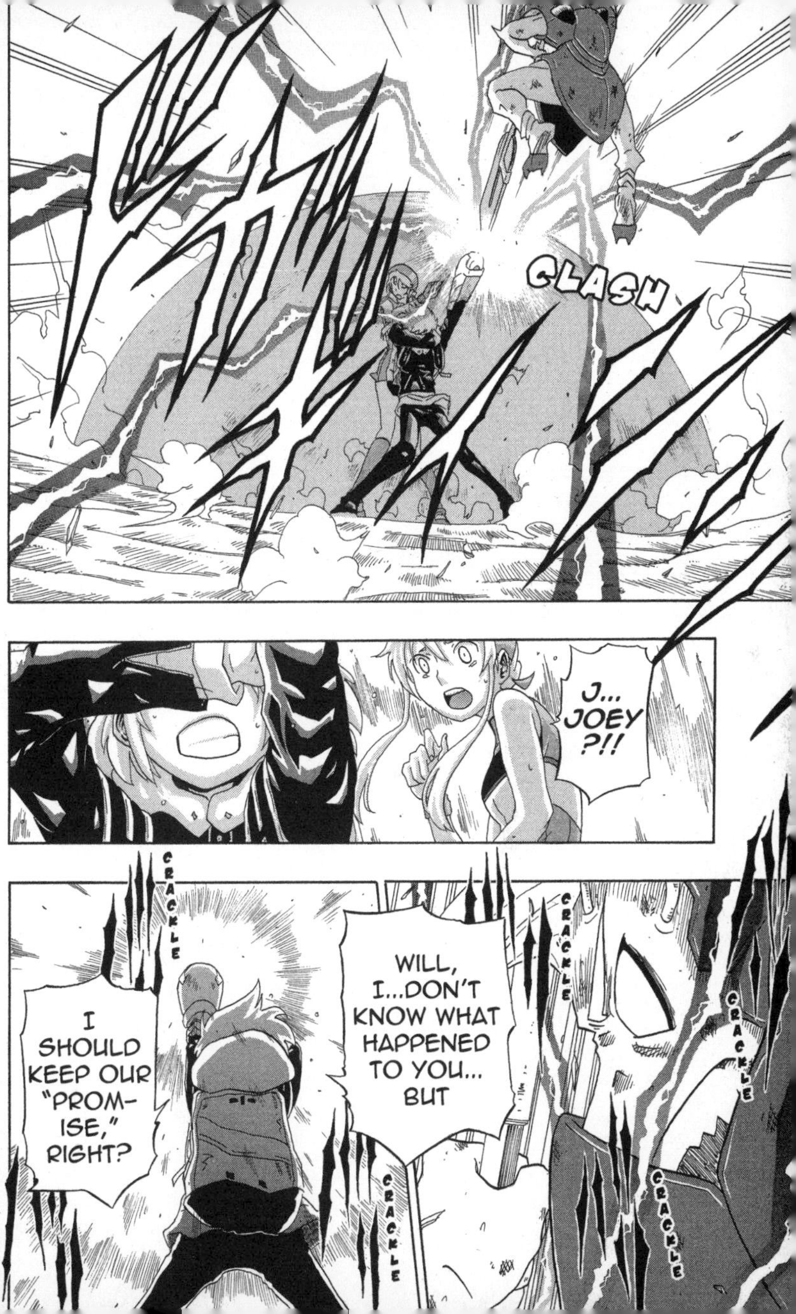
CLASH
J... JOEY ?!!
CRACKLE
CRACKLE
WILL, I...DON'T KNOW WHAT HAPPENED TO YOU... BUT
CRACKLE
I SHOULD KEEP OUR "PROMISE," RIGHT?
CRACKLE
CRACKLE

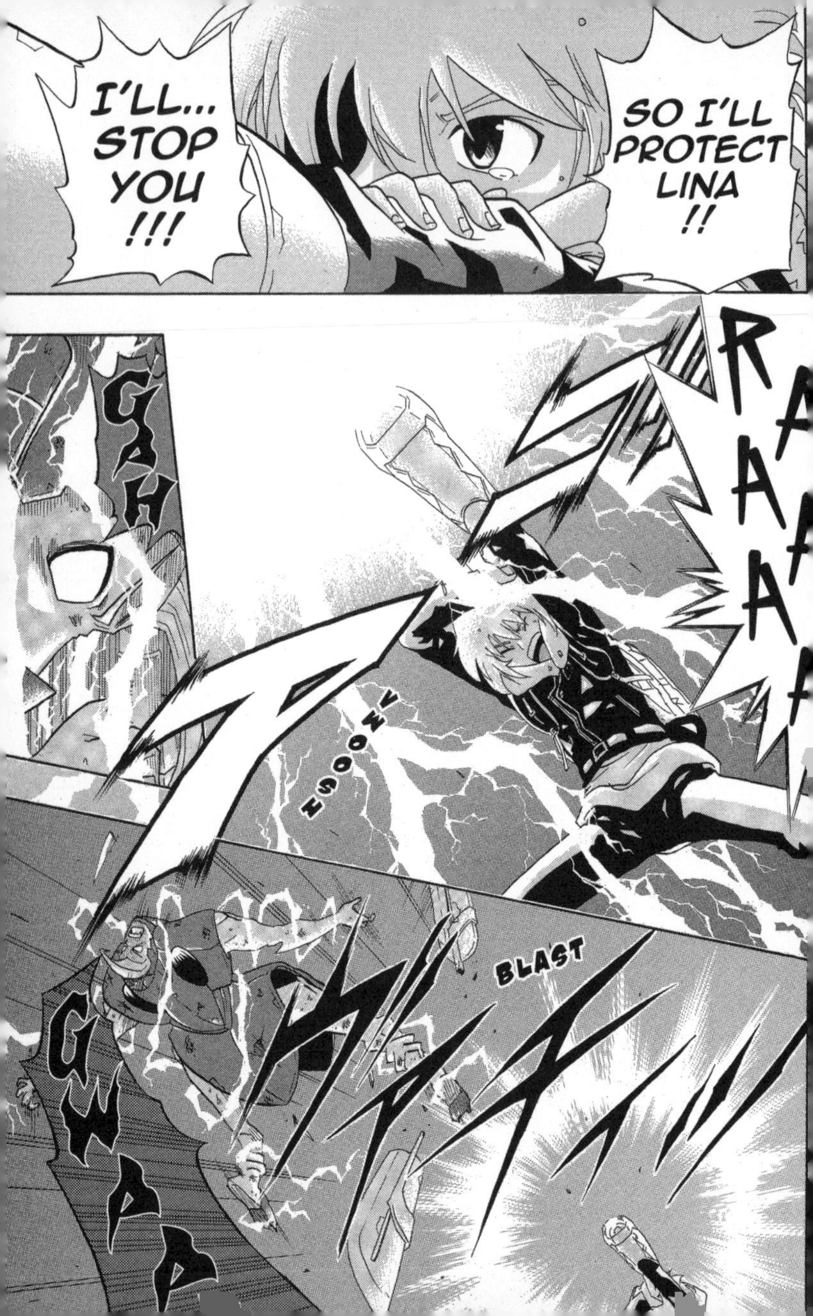
SO I'LL PROTECT LINA !!
I'LL... STOP YOU !!!
RAAAAA
GAH
VWOOSH
BLAST
GWAA

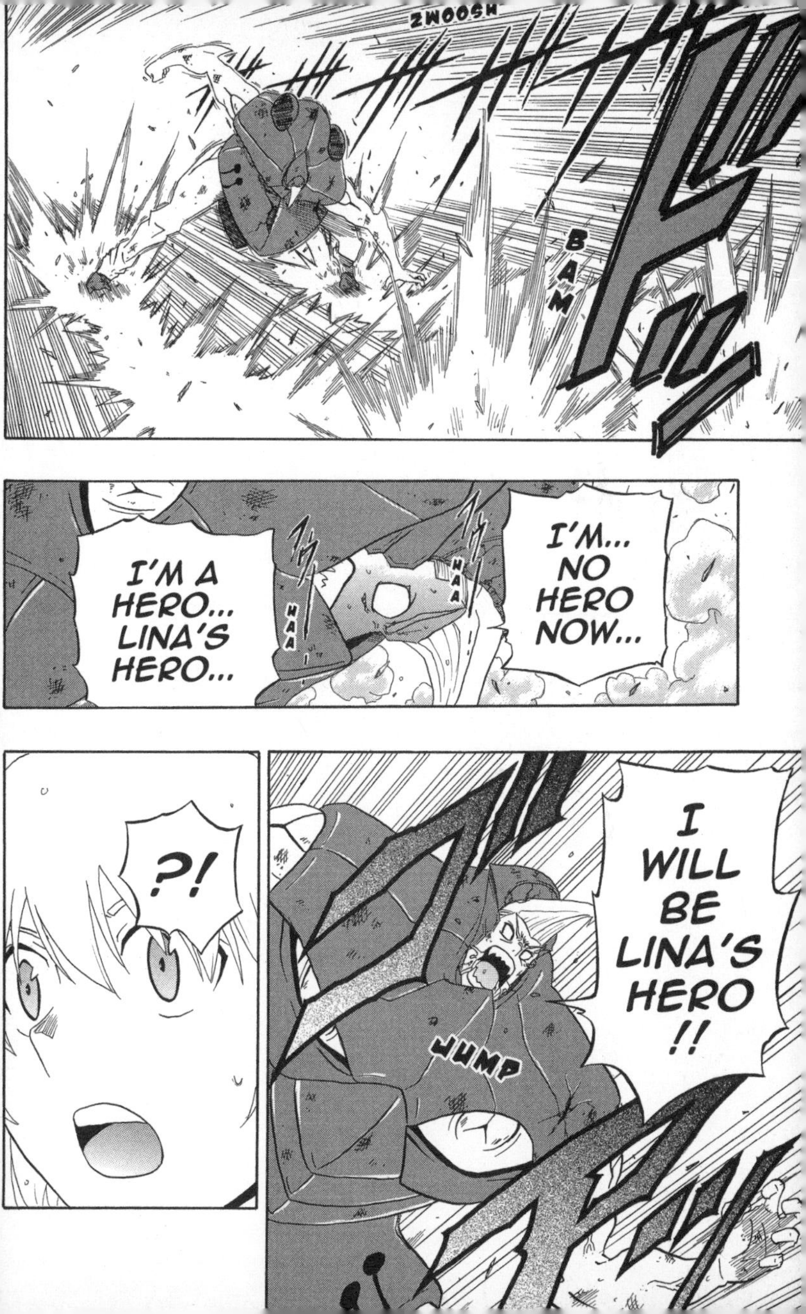
ZWOOSH
BAM
I'M... NO HERO NOW...
HAA
HAA
I'M A HERO... LINA'S HERO...
I WILL BE LINA'S HERO!!
JUMP
?!

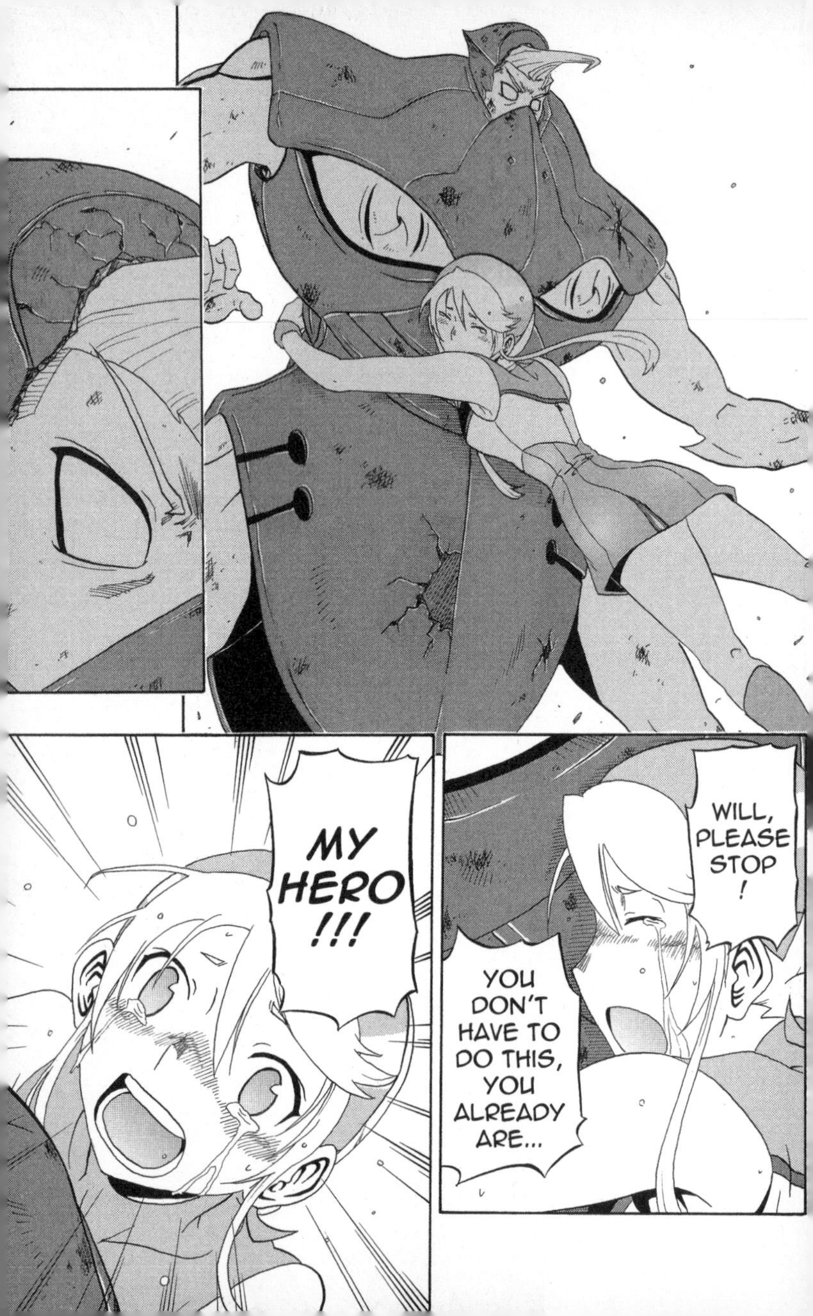
WILL, PLEASE STOP!
YOU DON'T HAVE TO DO THIS, YOU ALREADY ARE...
MY HERO!!!

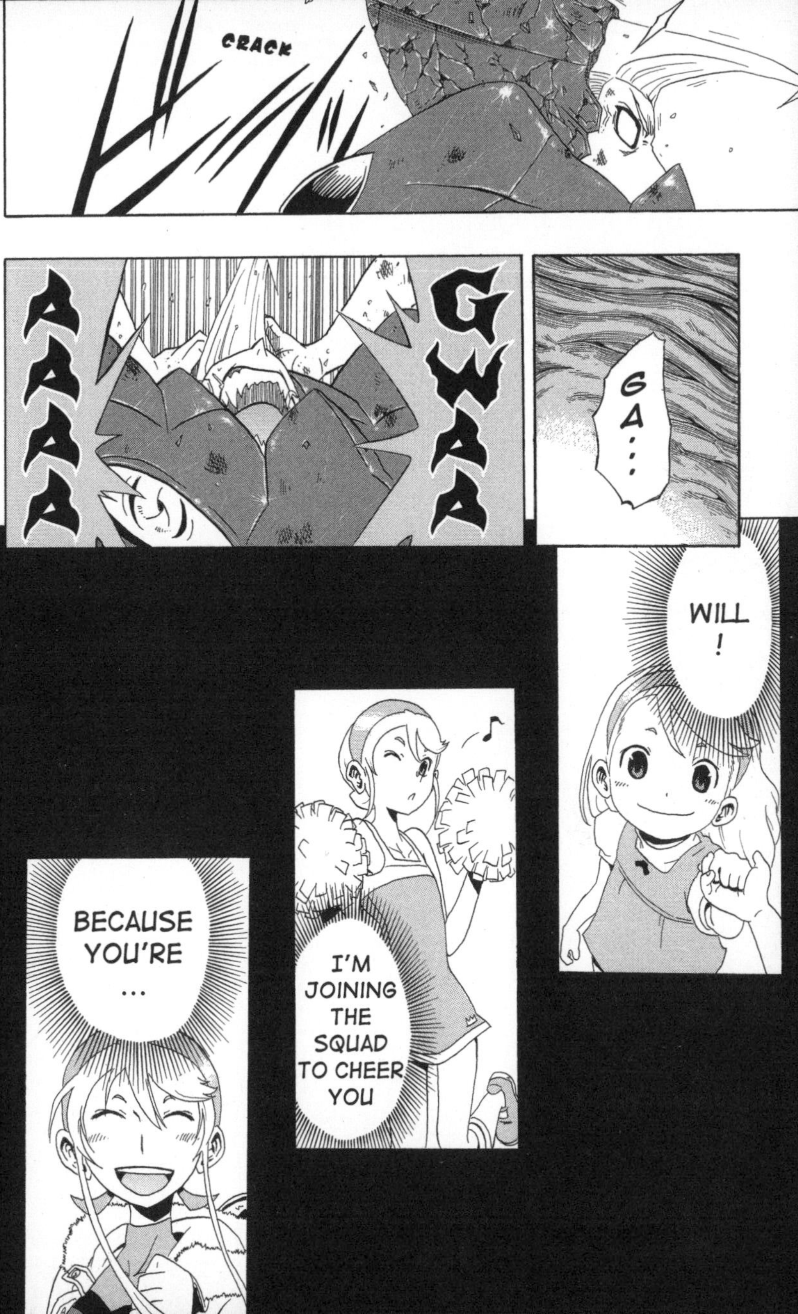
CRACK
GA...
GWAA
AAAA
WILL!
I'M JOINING THE SQUAD TO CHEER YOU
BECAUSE YOU'RE ...

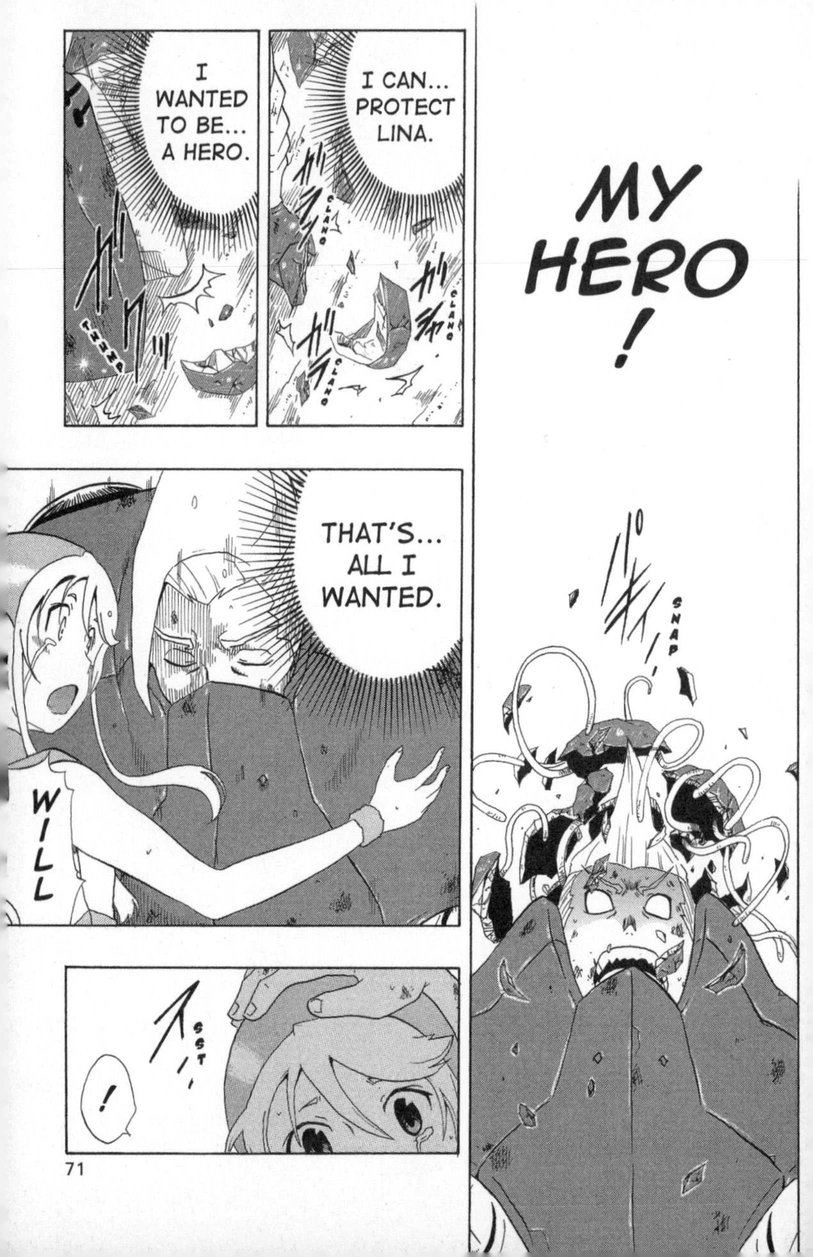
MY HERO!
SNAP
I CAN... PROTECT LINA.
CLANG
CLANG
CLANG
I WANTED TO BE... A HERO.
THUMP
THAT'S... ALL I WANTED.
WILL
SST
!

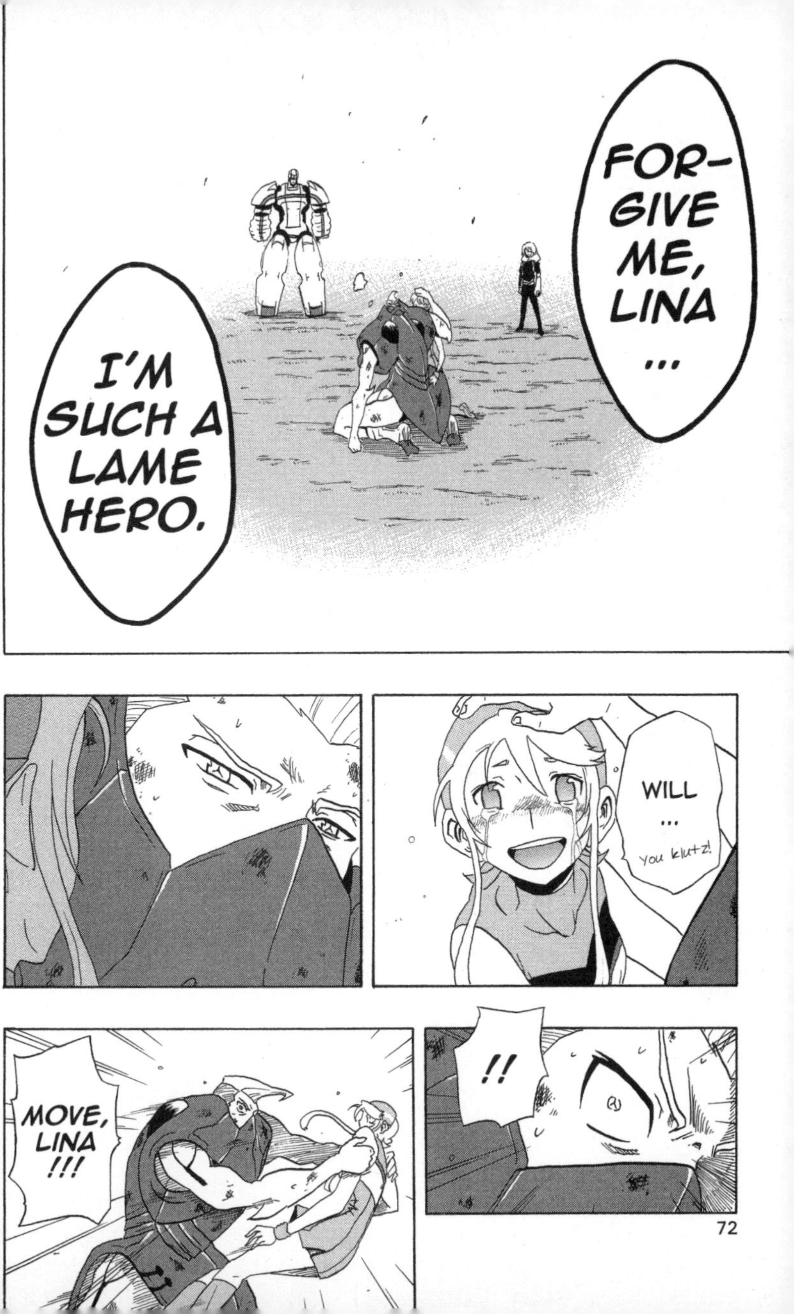
FOR-GIVE ME, LINA ...
I'M SUCH A LAME HERO.
WILL ...
YOU KLUTZ!
!!
MOVE, LINA !!!

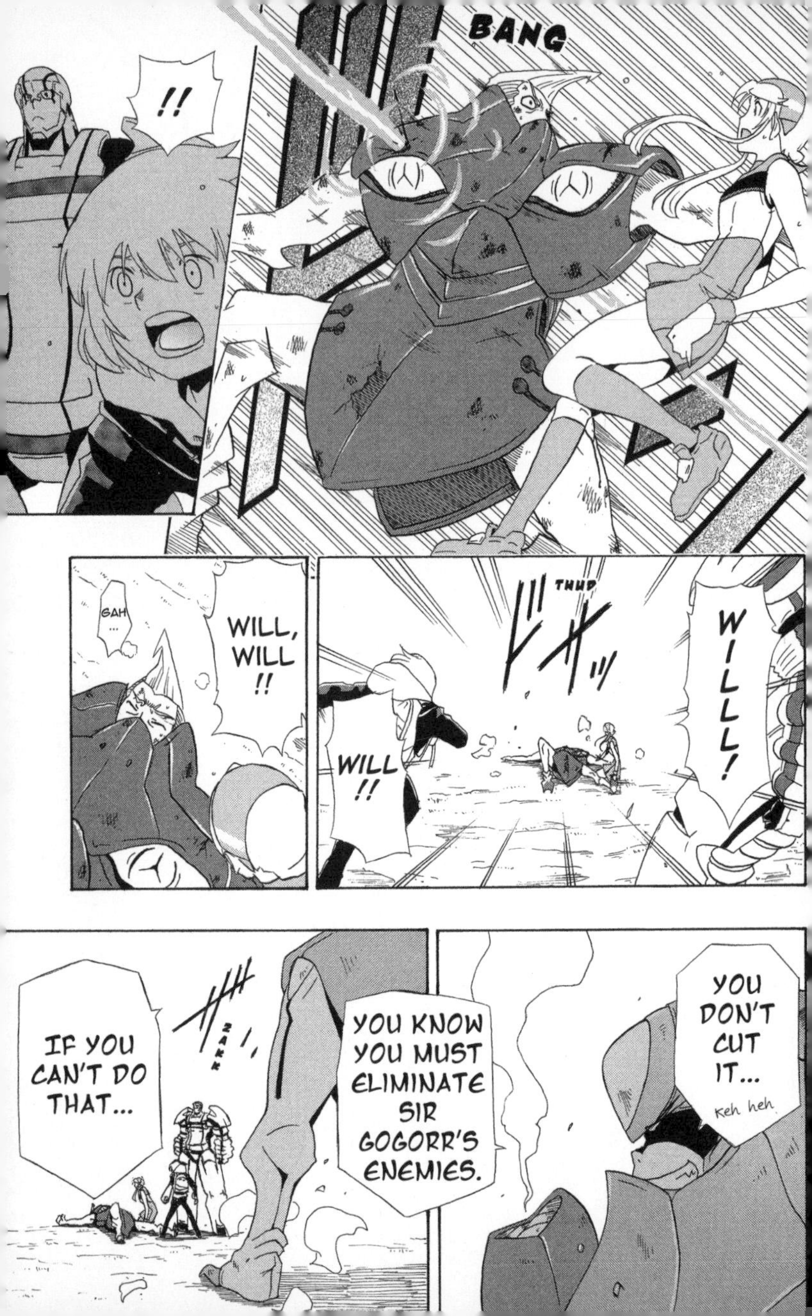
BANG
!!
WILLLL!
THUD
WILL !!
WILL, WILL !!
GAH...
YOU DON'T CUT IT...
keh heh
YOU KNOW YOU MUST ELIMINATE SIR GOGORR'S ENEMIES.
ZAKK
IF YOU CAN'T DO THAT...

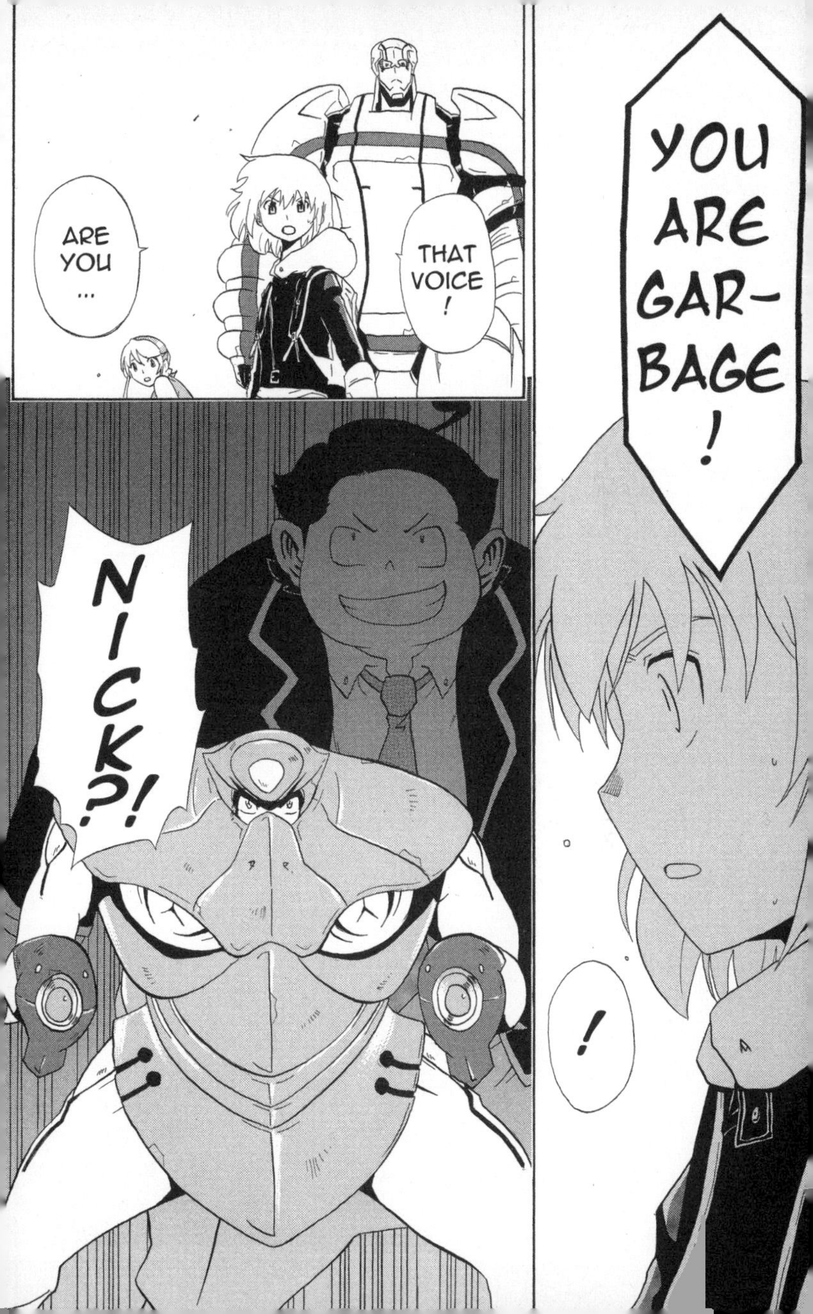
YOU ARE GAR-BAGE!
!
THAT VOICE!
ARE YOU ...
NICK?!

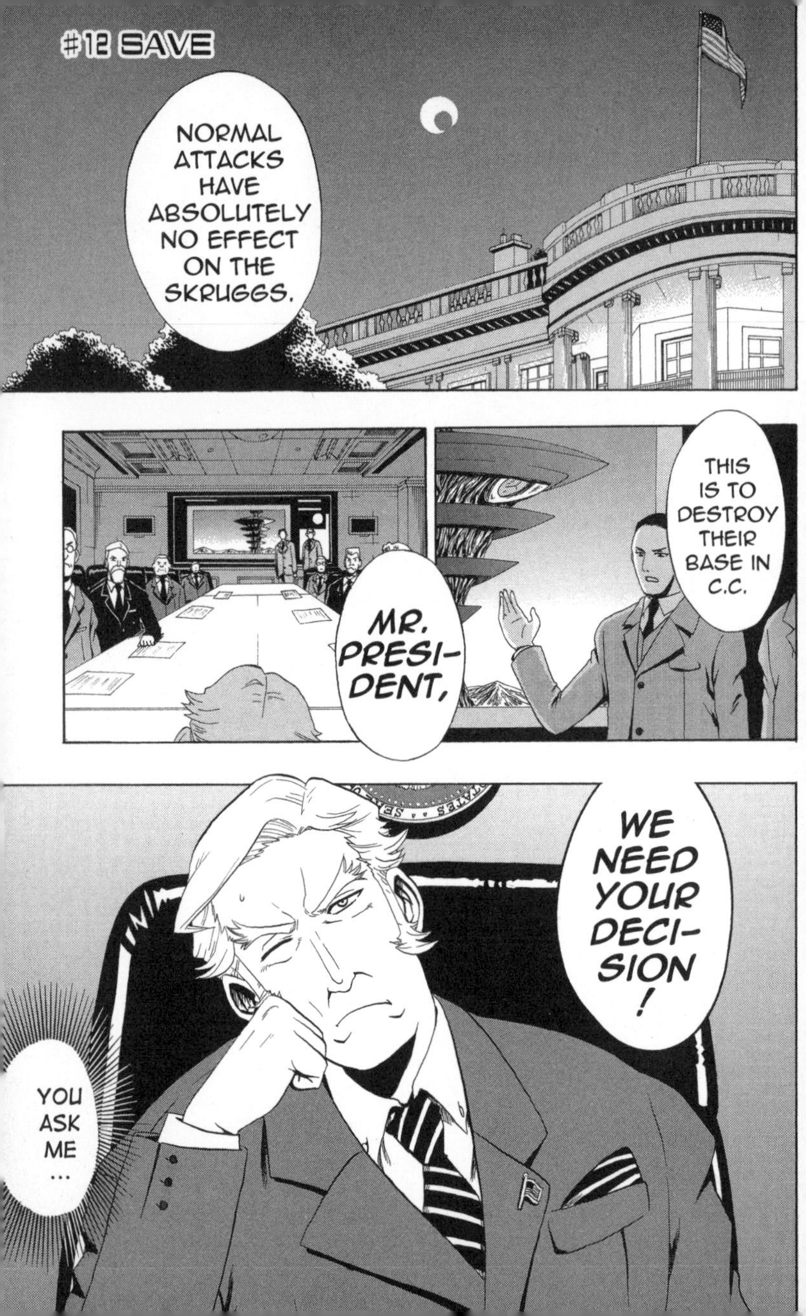
#12 SAVE
NORMAL ATTACKS HAVE ABSOLUTELY NO EFFECT ON THE SKRUGGS.
THIS IS TO DESTROY THEIR BASE IN C.C.
MR. PRESIDENT,
WE NEED YOUR DECISION!
YOU ASK ME ...

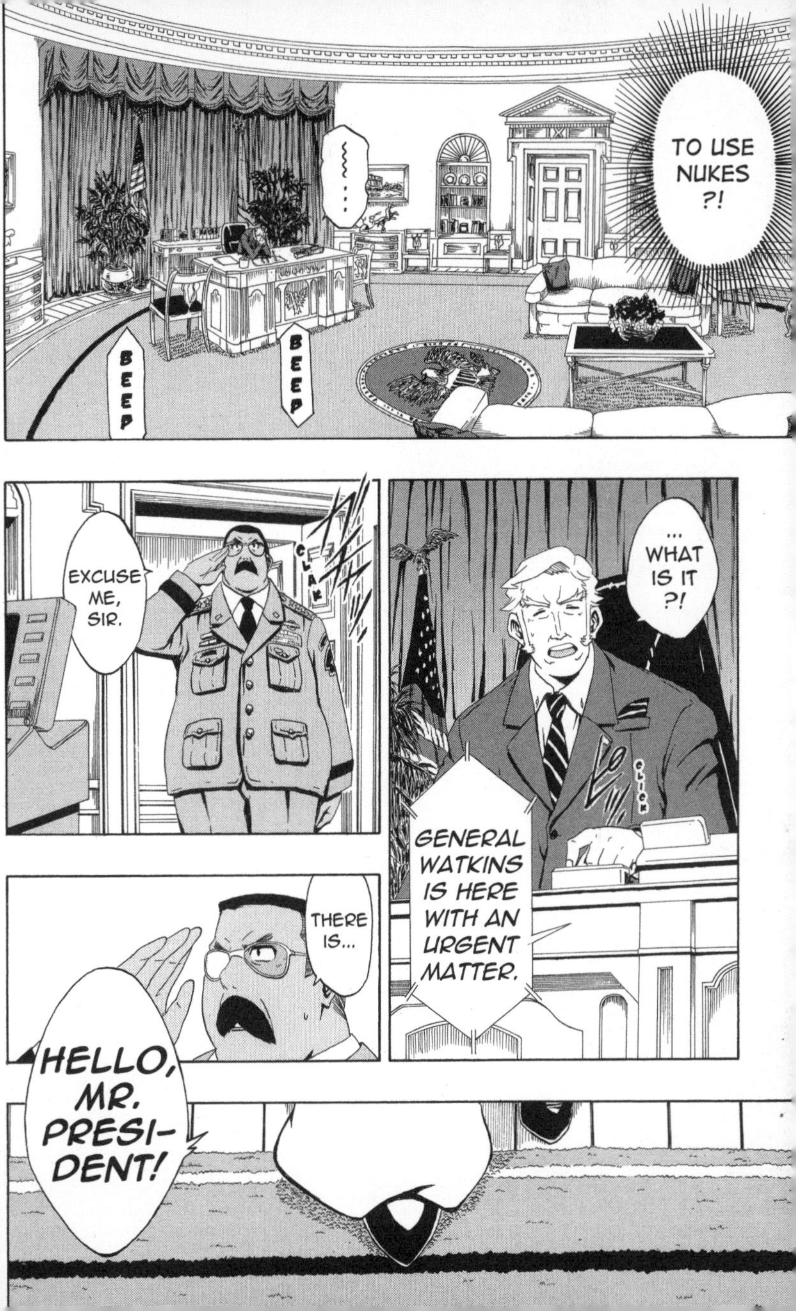
TO USE NUKES ?!
...
BEEP
BEEP
... WHAT IS IT ?!
CLICK
GENERAL WATKINS IS HERE WITH AN URGENT MATTER.
CLAK
EXCUSE ME, SIR.
THERE IS...
HELLO, MR. PRESIDENT!

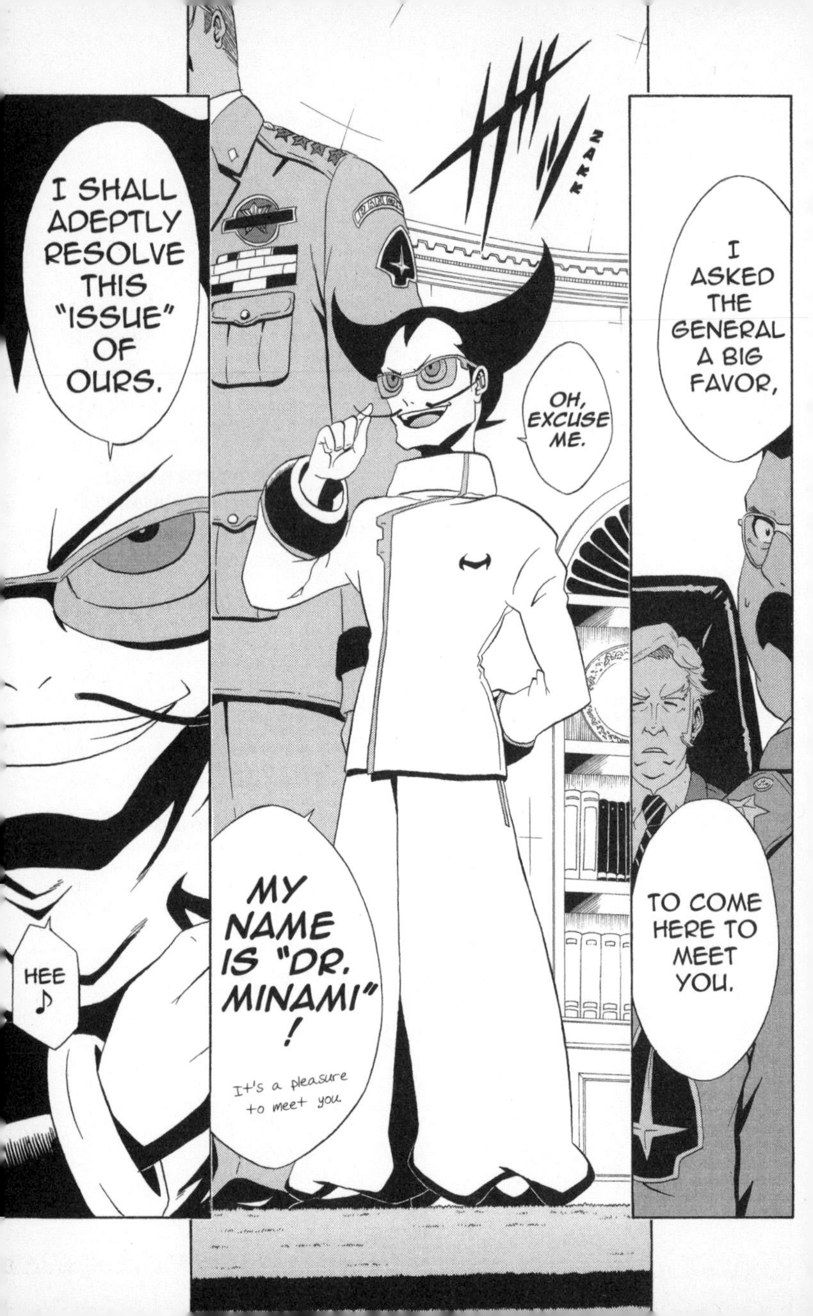
I ASKED THE GENERAL A BIG FAVOR,
TO COME HERE TO MEET YOU.
ZAKK
OH, EXCUSE ME.
MY NAME IS "DR. MINAMI"!
It's a pleasure to meet you.
I SHALL ADEPTLY RESOLVE THIS "ISSUE" OF OURS.
HEE ♪

#12 SAVE

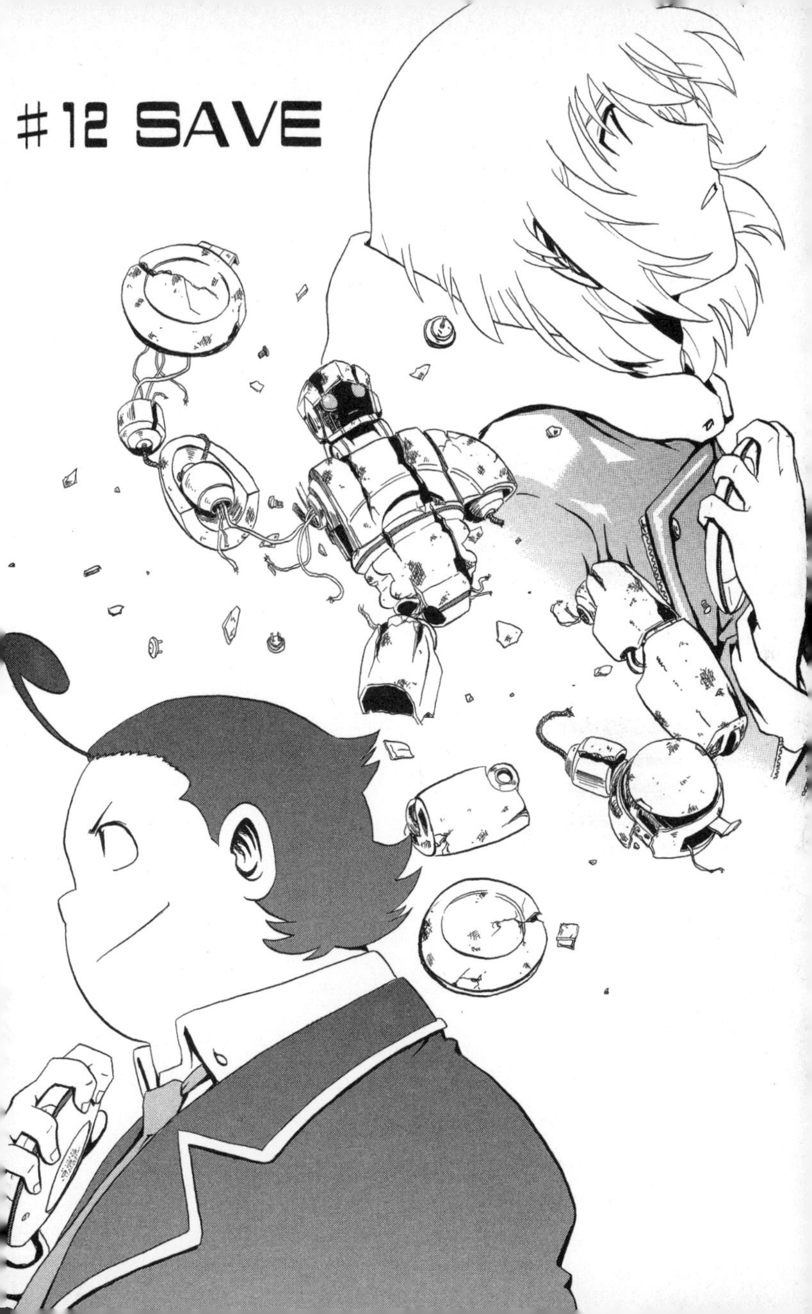

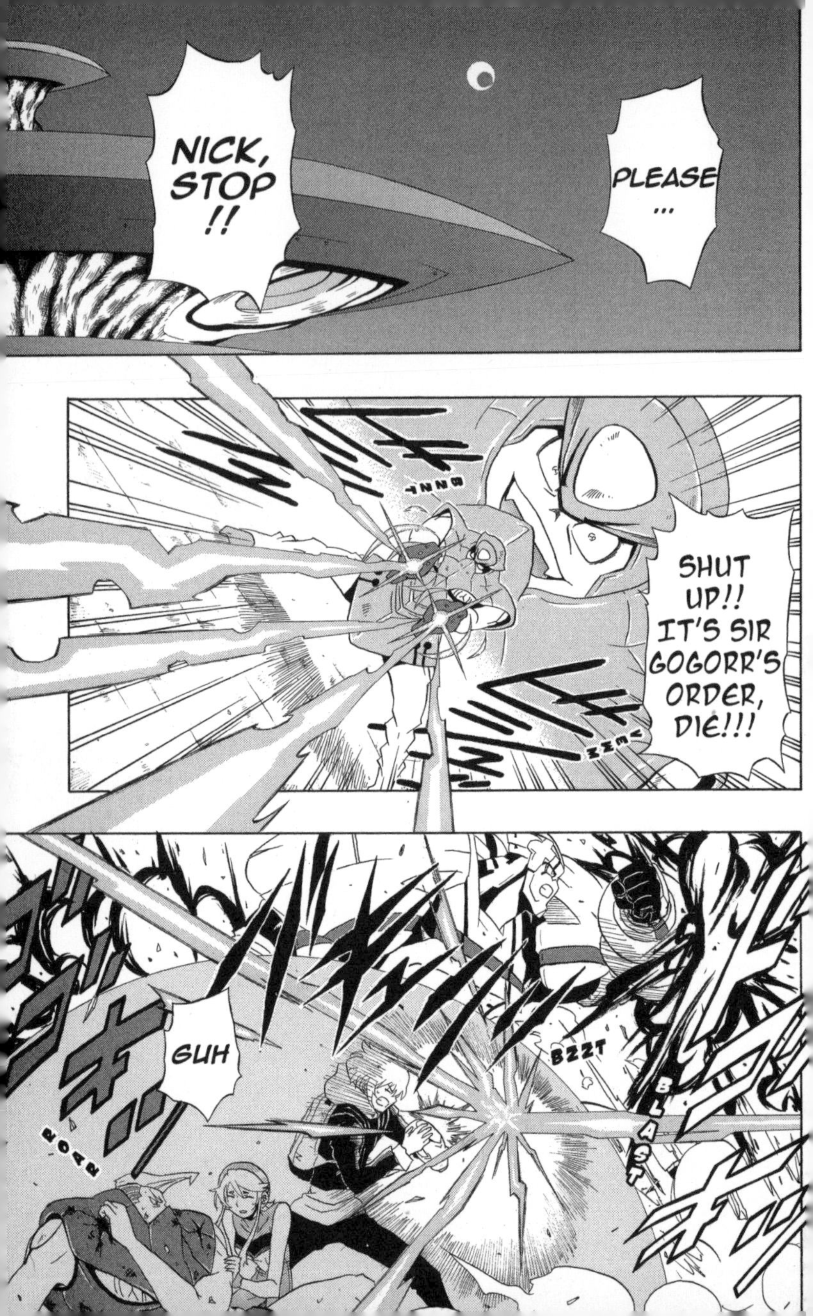
PLEASE ...
NICK, STOP !!
BNNT
SHUT UP!! IT'S SIR GOGORR'S ORDER, DIE!!!
VZZZ
BZZT
BLAST
GUH
ROAR

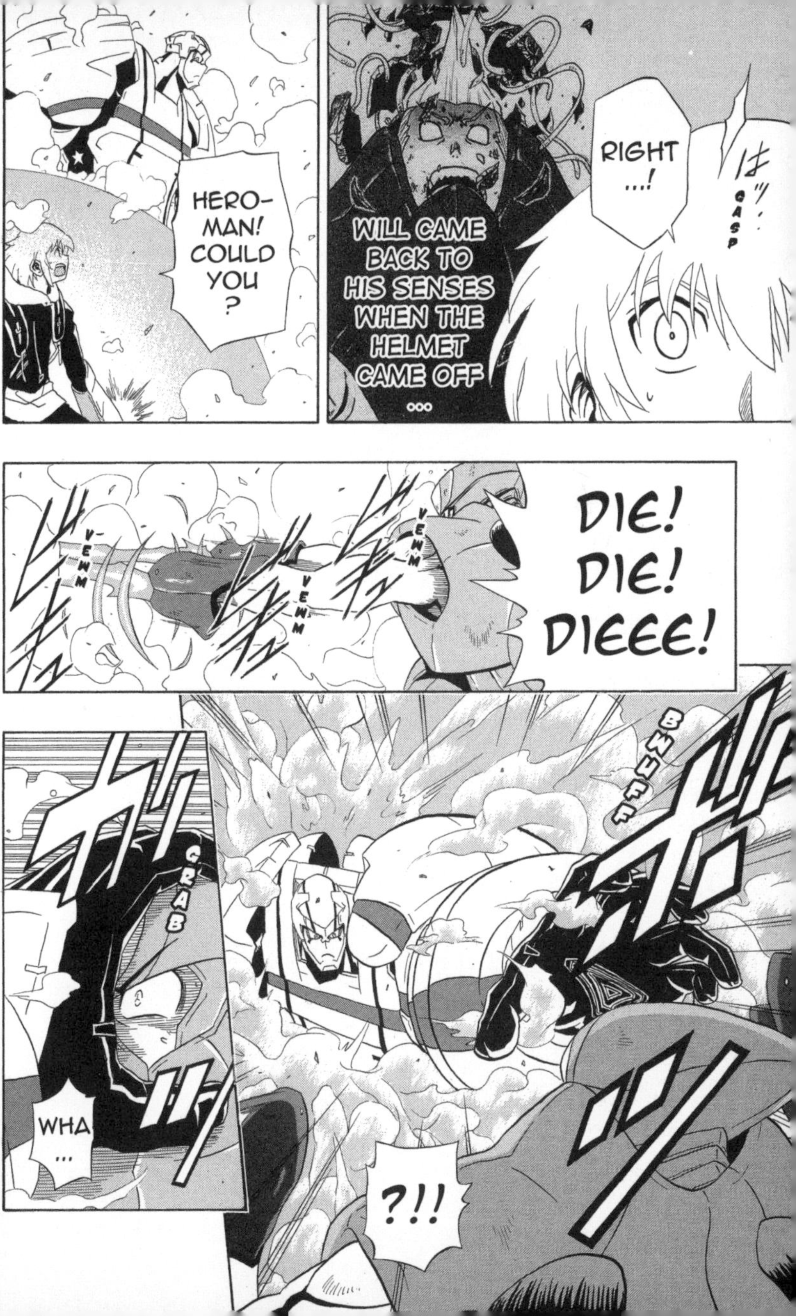
RIGHT ...!
はッ
GASP
WILL CAME BACK TO HIS SENSES WHEN THE HELMET CAME OFF ...
HERO-MAN! COULD YOU ?
DIE! DIE! DIEEE!
VEWM
VEWM
VEWM
BWUFF
?!!
GRAB
WHA ...

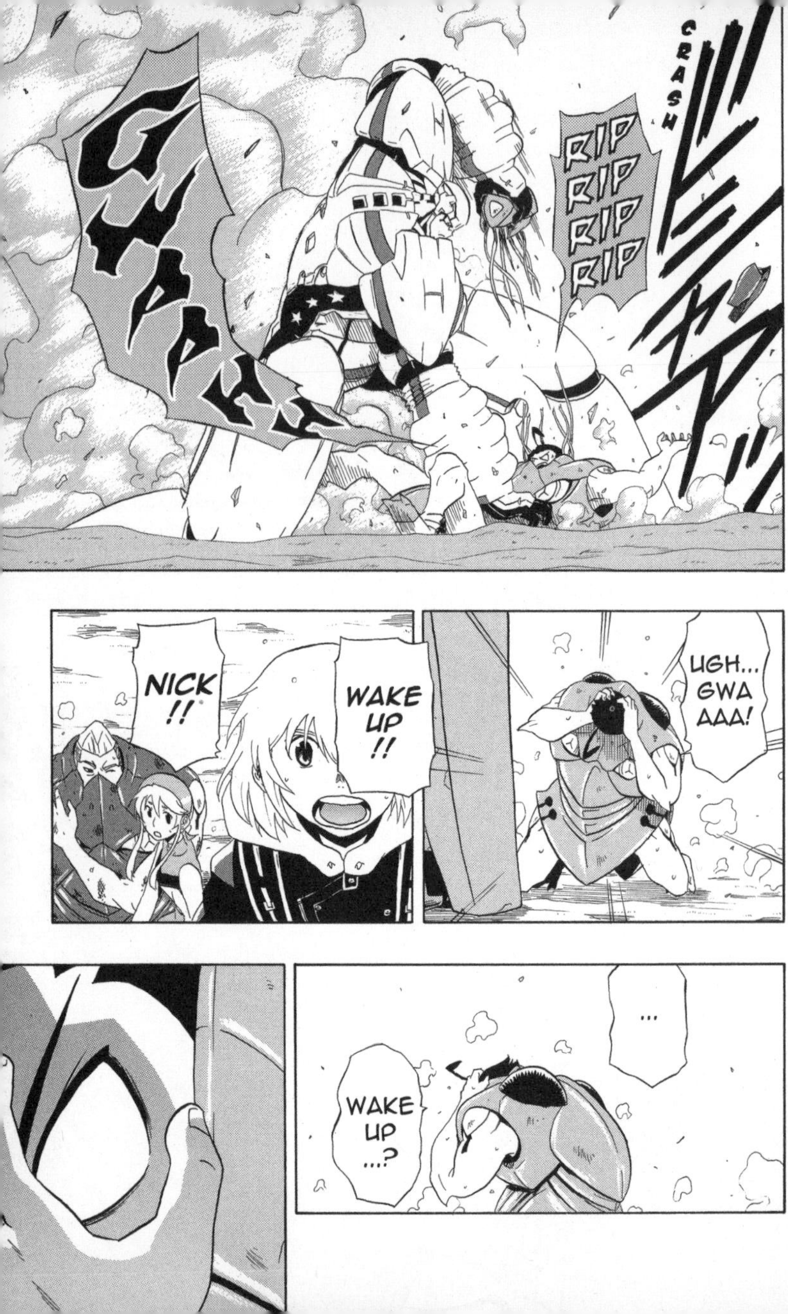
CRASH
RIP RIP RIP RIP
UGH... GWA AAA!
WAKE UP !!
NICK !!
...
WAKE UP ...?

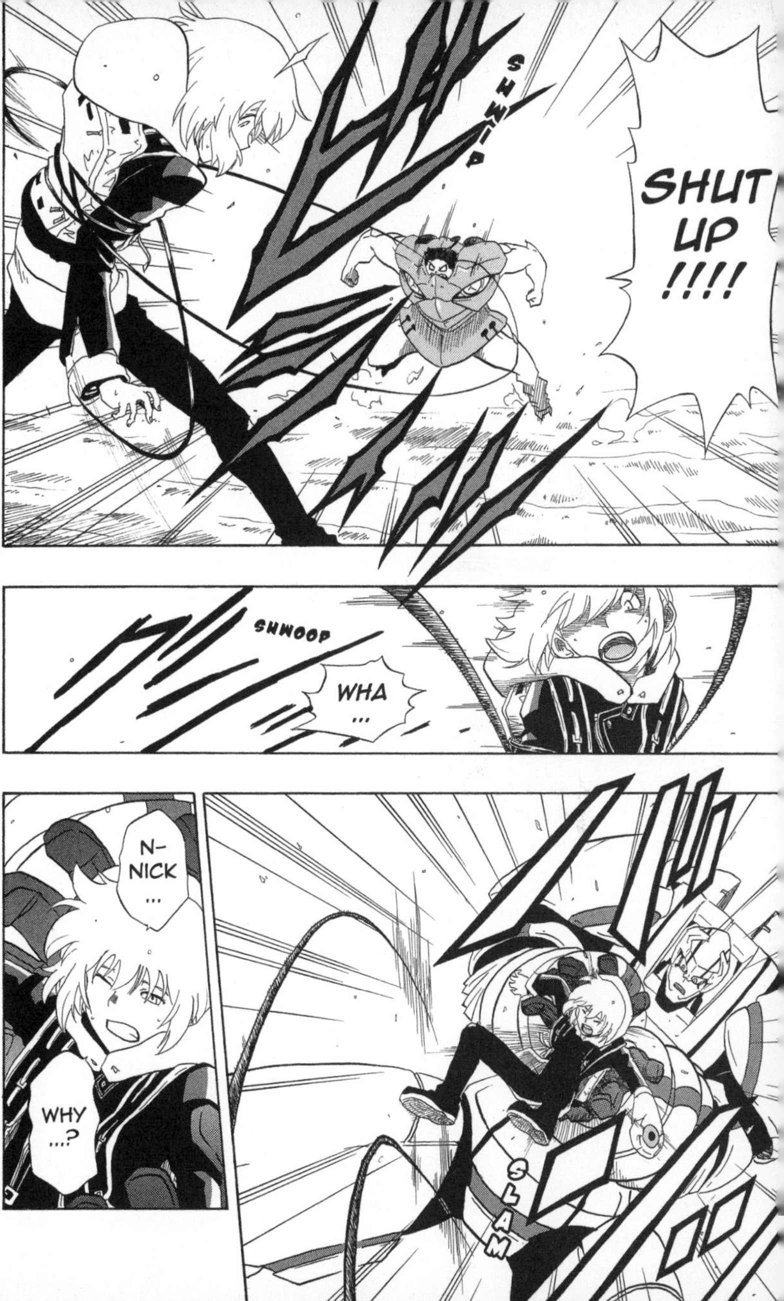
SHUT UP !!!!
SHWIP
SHWOOP
WHA ...
SLAM
N-NICK ...
WHY ...?

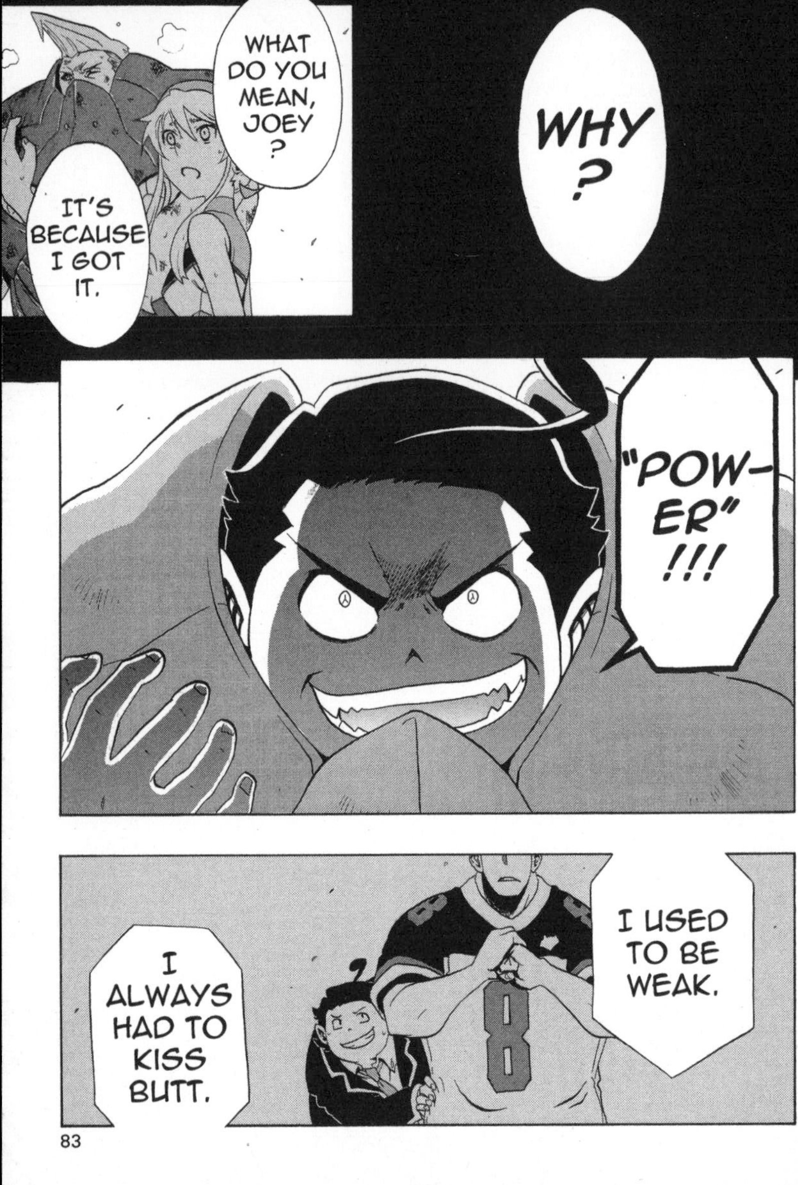
WHY?
WHAT DO YOU MEAN, JOEY?
IT'S BECAUSE I GOT IT.
"POW-ER"!!!
I USED TO BE WEAK.
I ALWAYS HAD TO KISS BUTT.

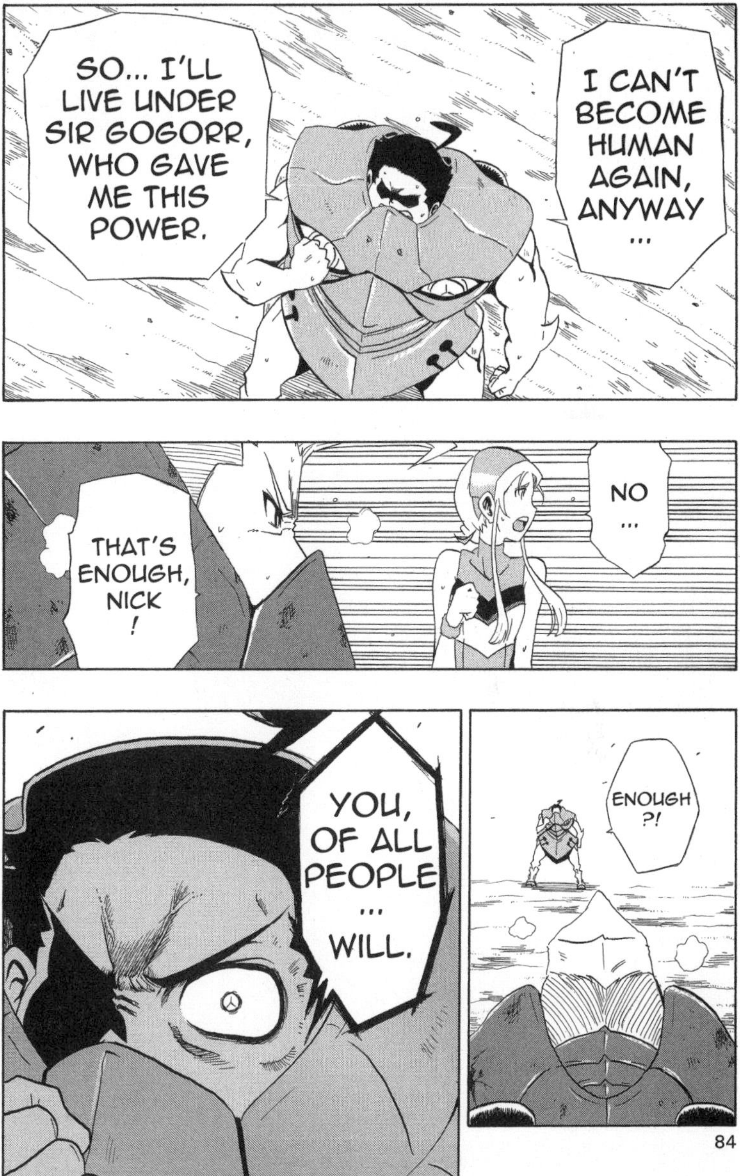
I CAN'T BECOME HUMAN AGAIN, ANYWAY...
SO... I'LL LIVE UNDER SIR GOGORR, WHO GAVE ME THIS POWER.
NO...
THAT'S ENOUGH, NICK!
ENOUGH?!
YOU, OF ALL PEOPLE... WILL.

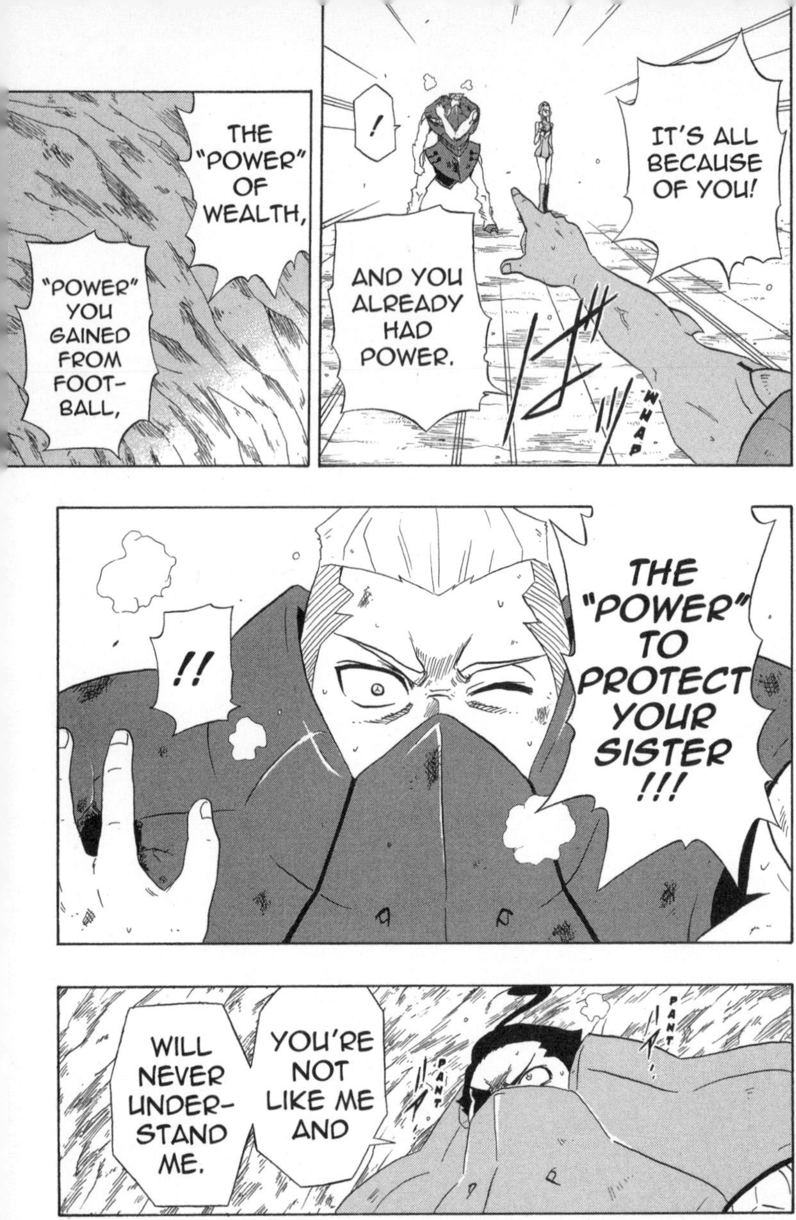
IT'S ALL BECAUSE OF YOU!
!
AND YOU ALREADY HAD POWER.
WHAP
THE "POWER" OF WEALTH,
"POWER" YOU GAINED FROM FOOT-BALL,
THE "POWER" TO PROTECT YOUR SISTER !!!
!!
PANT
PANT
YOU'RE NOT LIKE ME AND
WILL NEVER UNDER-STAND ME.

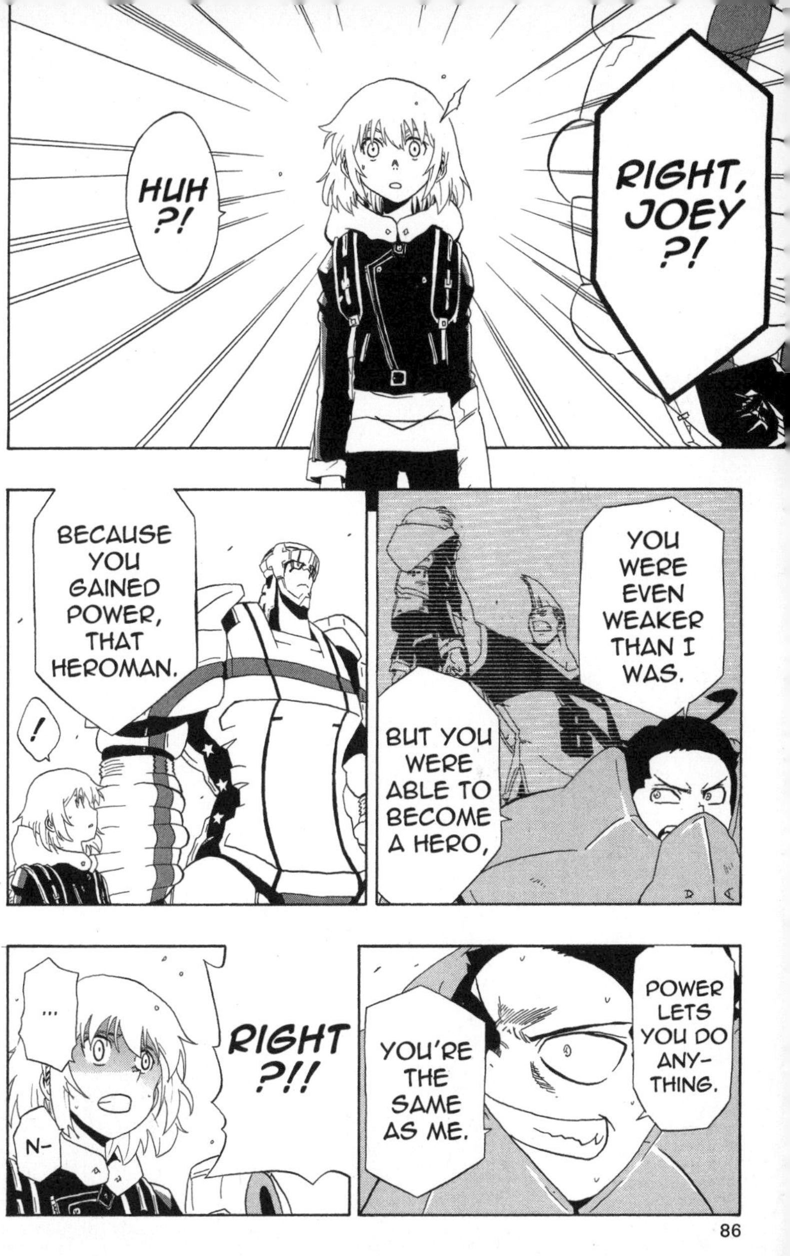
RIGHT, JOEY ?!
HUH ?!
YOU WERE EVEN WEAKER THAN I WAS.
BUT YOU WERE ABLE TO BECOME A HERO,
BECAUSE YOU GAINED POWER, THAT HEROMAN.
!
POWER LETS YOU DO ANY-THING.
YOU'RE THE SAME AS ME.
RIGHT ?!!
...
N-

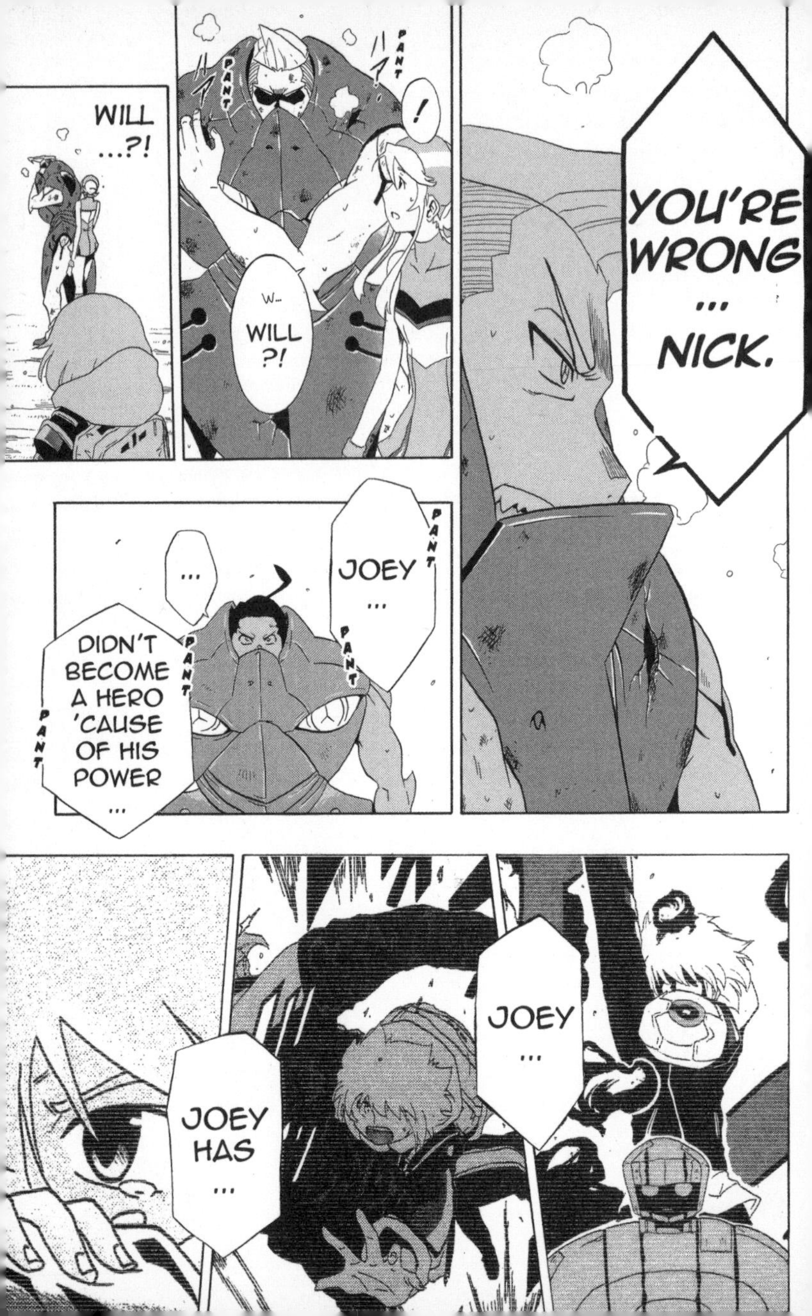
YOU'RE WRONG ... NICK.
PANT
PANT
!
W... WILL ?!
WILL ...?!
PANT
JOEY ...
PANT
...
PANT
DIDN'T BECOME A HERO 'CAUSE OF HIS POWER ...
PANT
JOEY ...
JOEY HAS ...

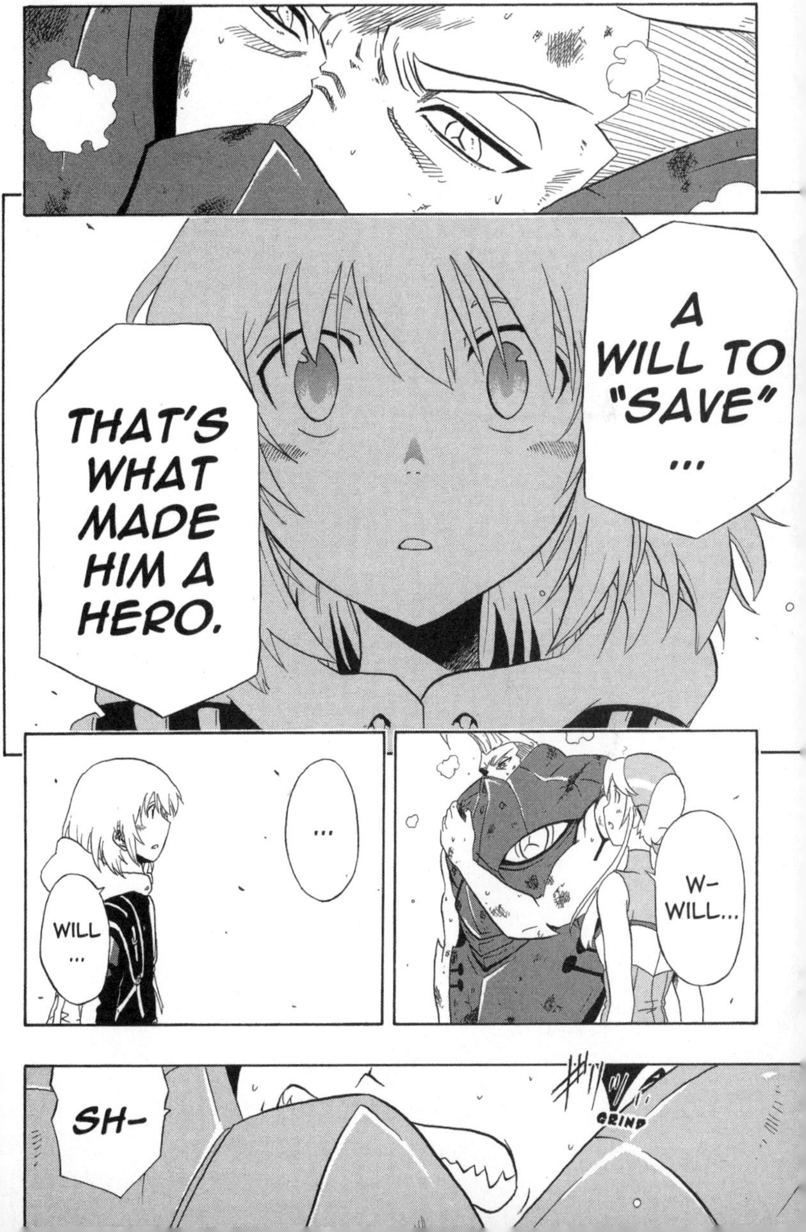
A WILL TO "SAVE"...
THAT'S WHAT MADE HIM A HERO.
W-WILL...
...
WILL...
GRIND
SH-

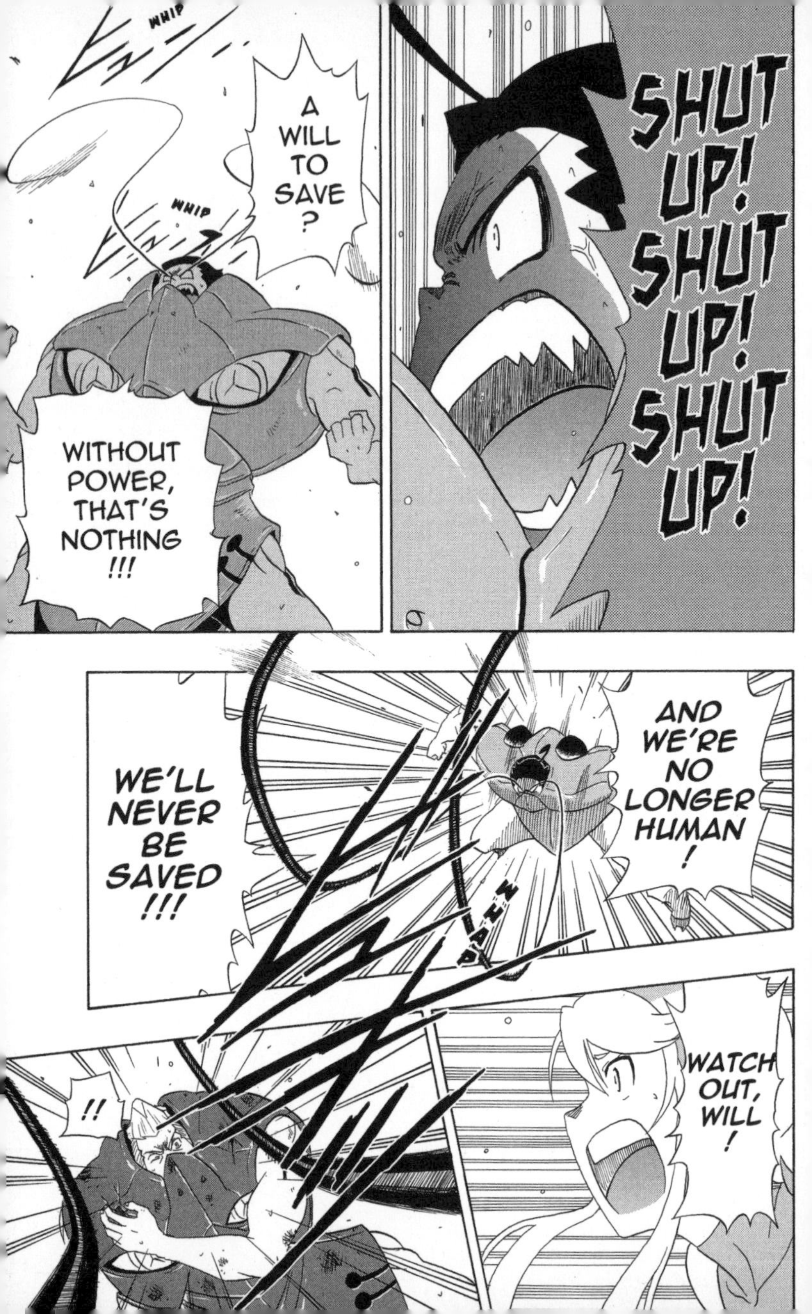
SHUT UP! SHUT UP! SHUT UP! SHUT UP!
WHIP
A WILL TO SAVE?
WHIP
WITHOUT POWER, THAT'S NOTHING!!!
AND WE'RE NO LONGER HUMAN!
WE'LL NEVER BE SAVED!!!
WHAP
WATCH OUT, WILL!
!!

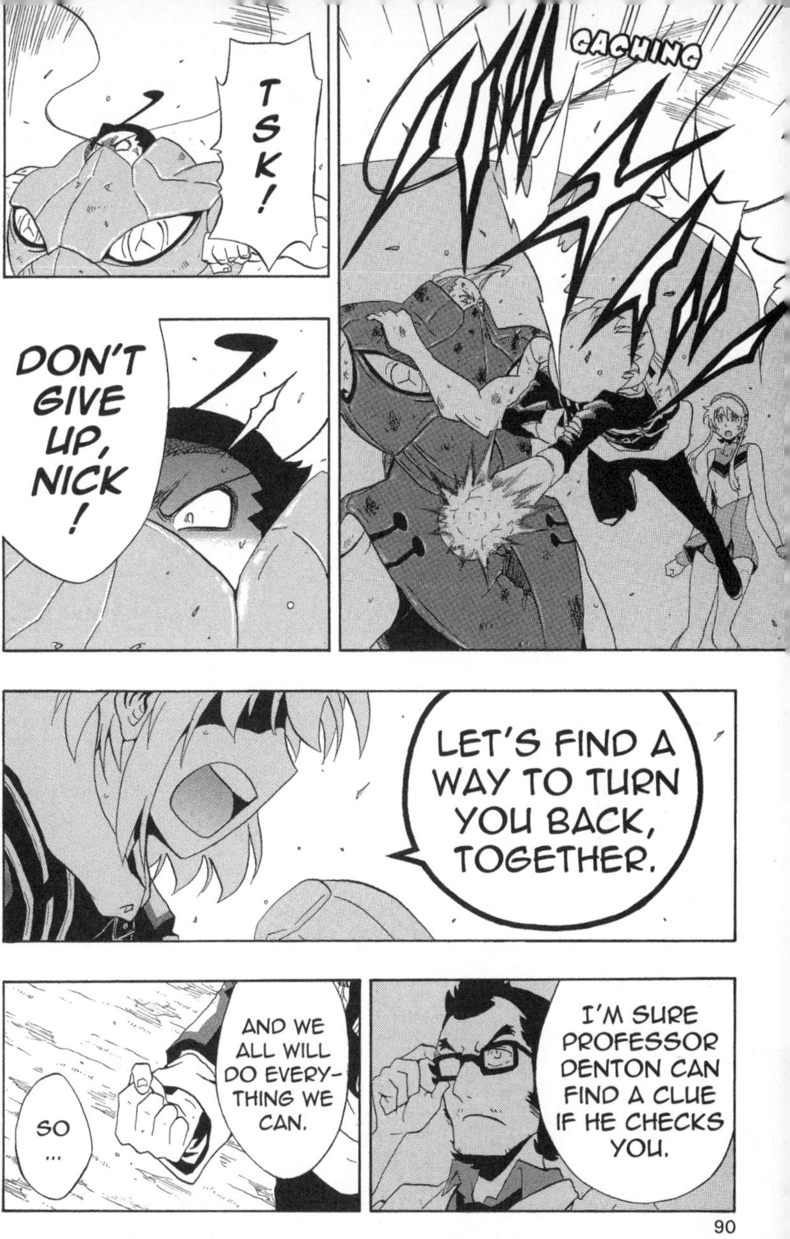
GACHING
TSK!
DON'T GIVE UP, NICK!
LET'S FIND A WAY TO TURN YOU BACK, TOGETHER.
I'M SURE PROFESSOR DENTON CAN FIND A CLUE IF HE CHECKS YOU.
AND WE ALL WILL DO EVERY-THING WE CAN.
SO ...

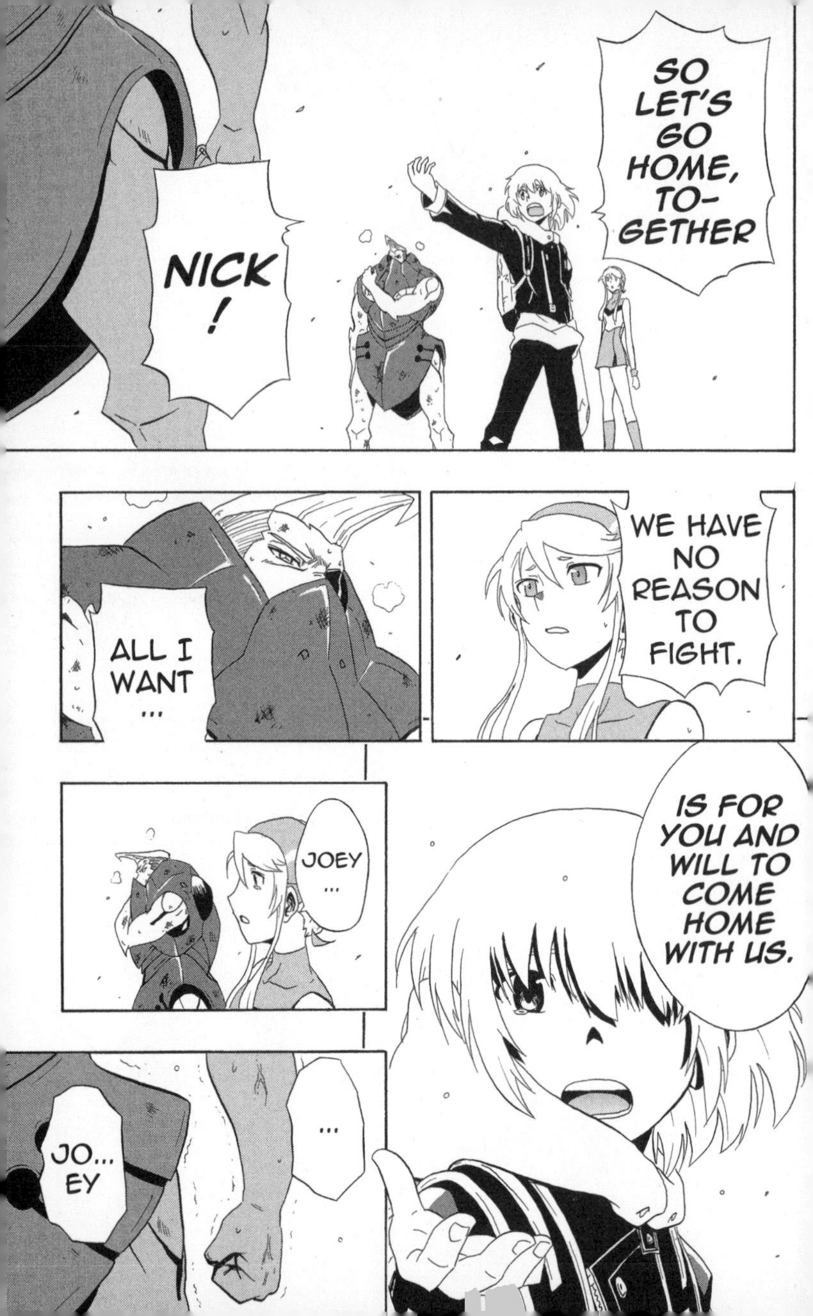
SO LET'S GO HOME, TO-GETHER
NICK!
WE HAVE NO REASON TO FIGHT.
ALL I WANT...
IS FOR YOU AND WILL TO COME HOME WITH US.
JOEY...
...
JO... EY

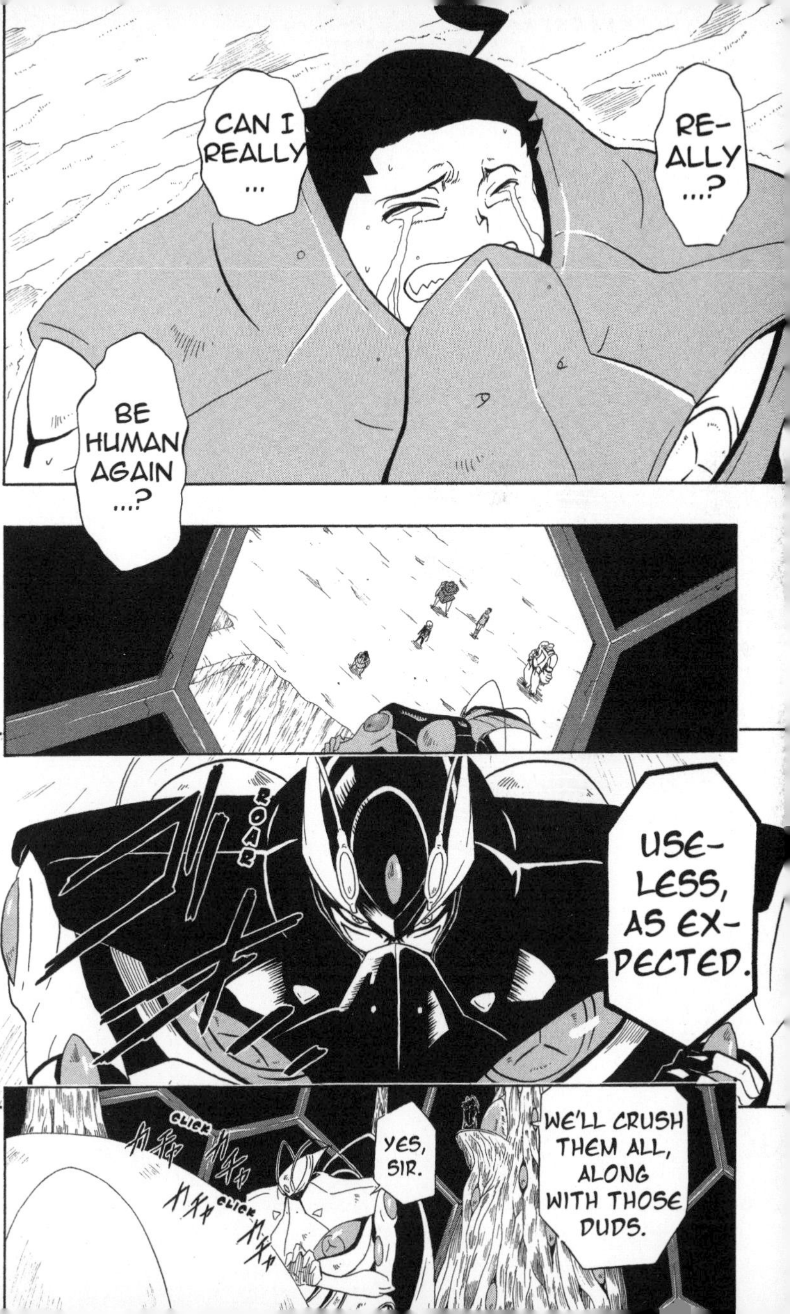
RE-ALLY ...?
CAN I REALLY ...
BE HUMAN AGAIN ...?
USE-LESS, AS EX-PECTED.
ROAR
WE'LL CRUSH THEM ALL, ALONG WITH THOSE DUDS.
YES, SIR.
CLICK
CLICK

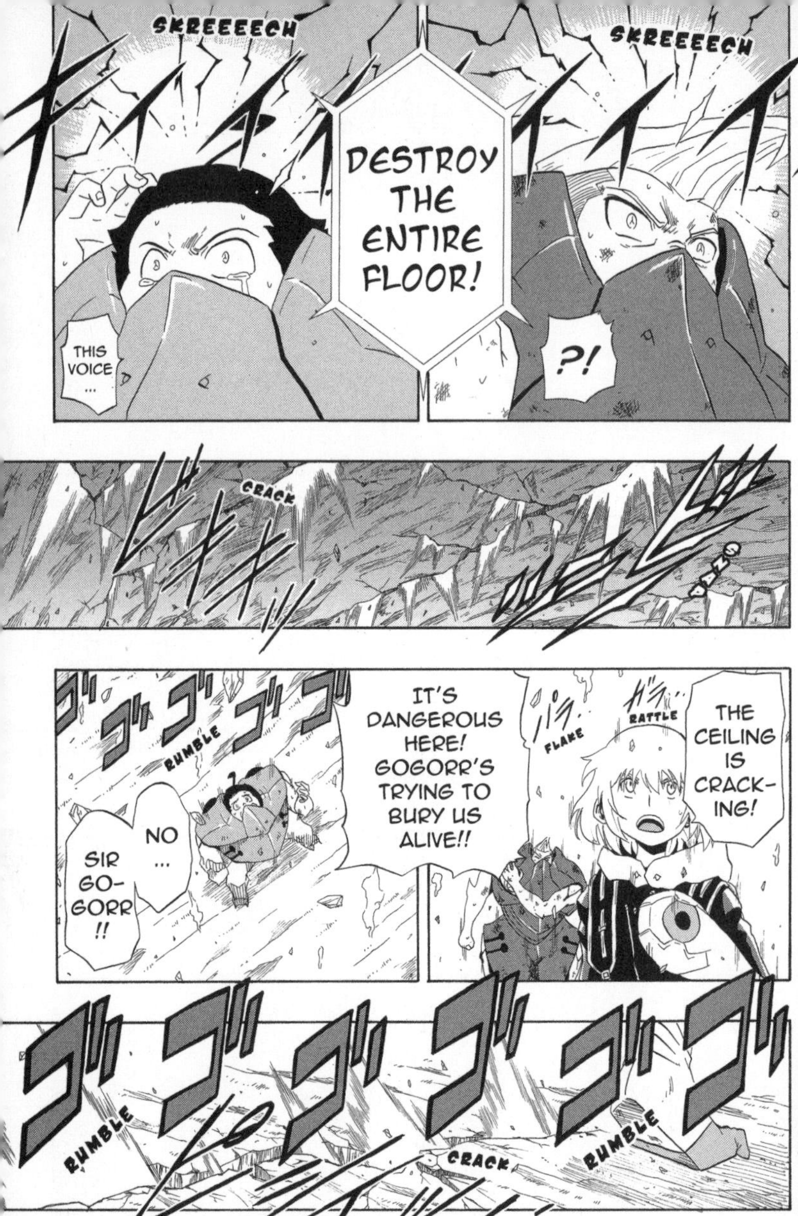
SKREEEECH
DESTROY THE ENTIRE FLOOR!
?!
SKREEEECH
THIS VOICE ...
CRACK
THE CEILING IS CRACK-ING!
RATTLE
FLAKE
IT'S DANGEROUS HERE! GOGORR'S TRYING TO BURY US ALIVE!!
RUMBLE
NO ...
SIR GO-GORR !!
RUMBLE
CRACK
RUMBLE

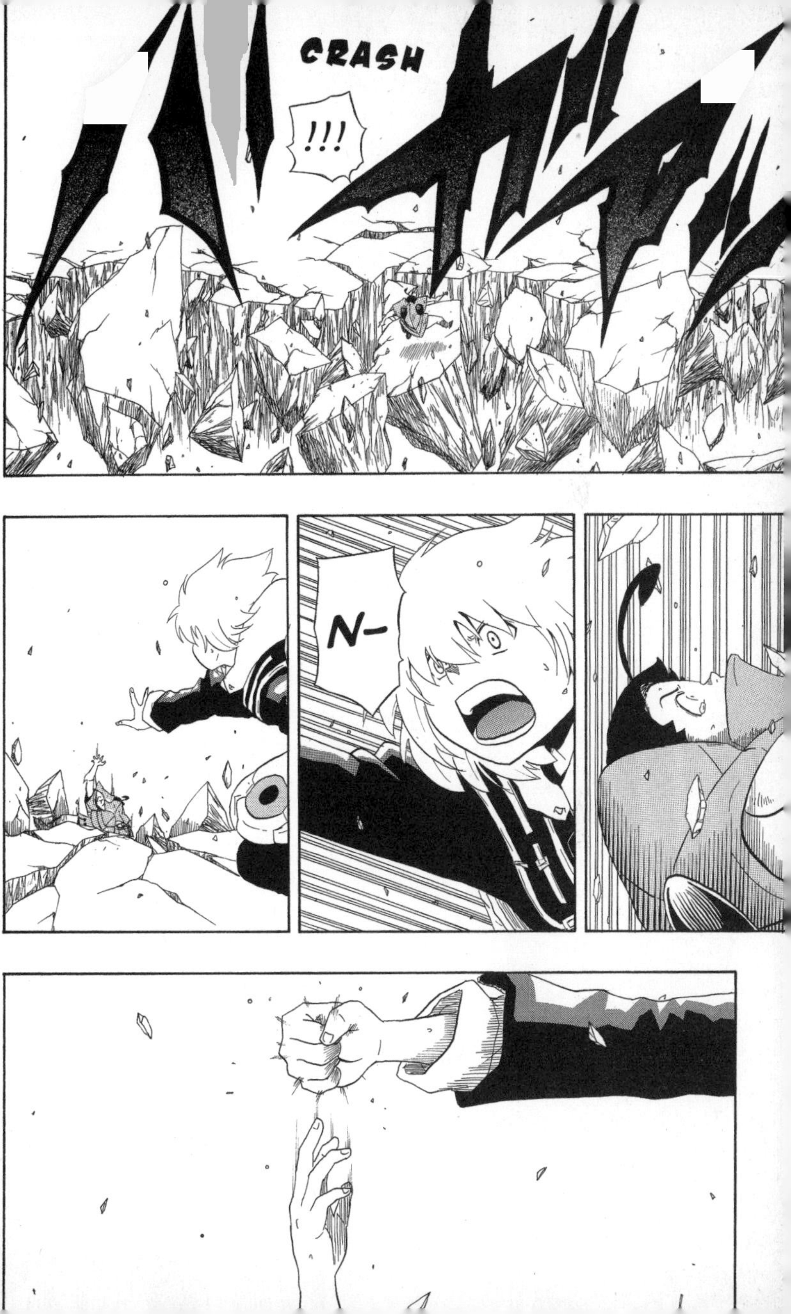
CRASH
!!!
N-

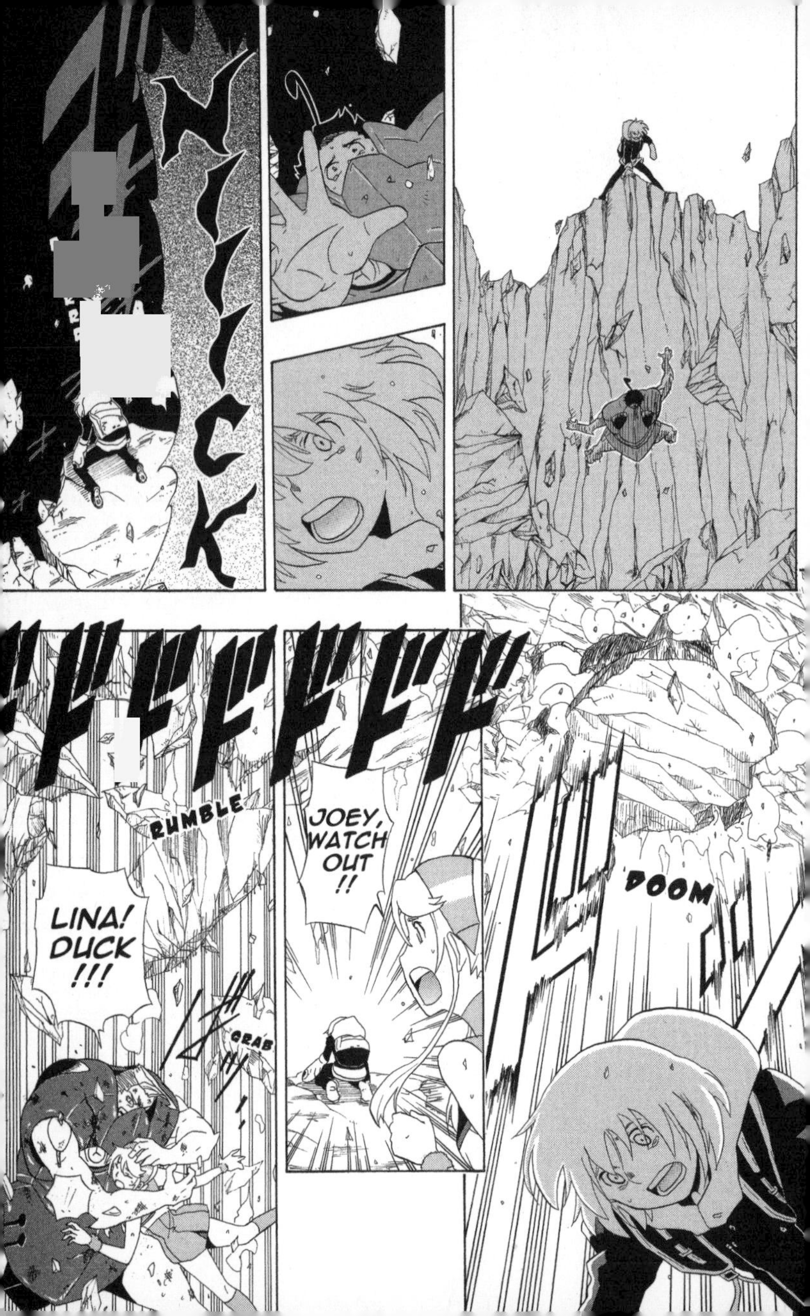
DOOM
JOEY, WATCH OUT!!
RUMBLE
LINA! DUCK!!!
GRAB

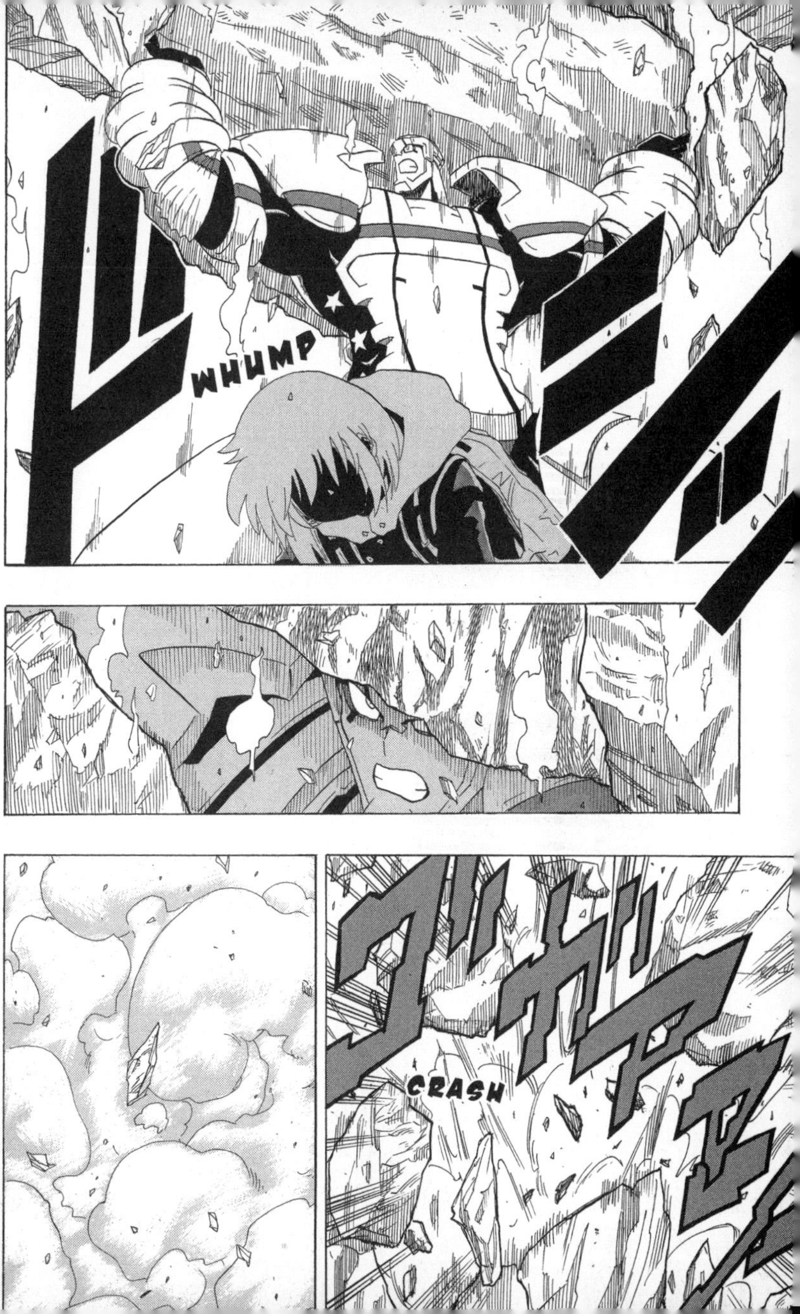
WHUMP
CRASH

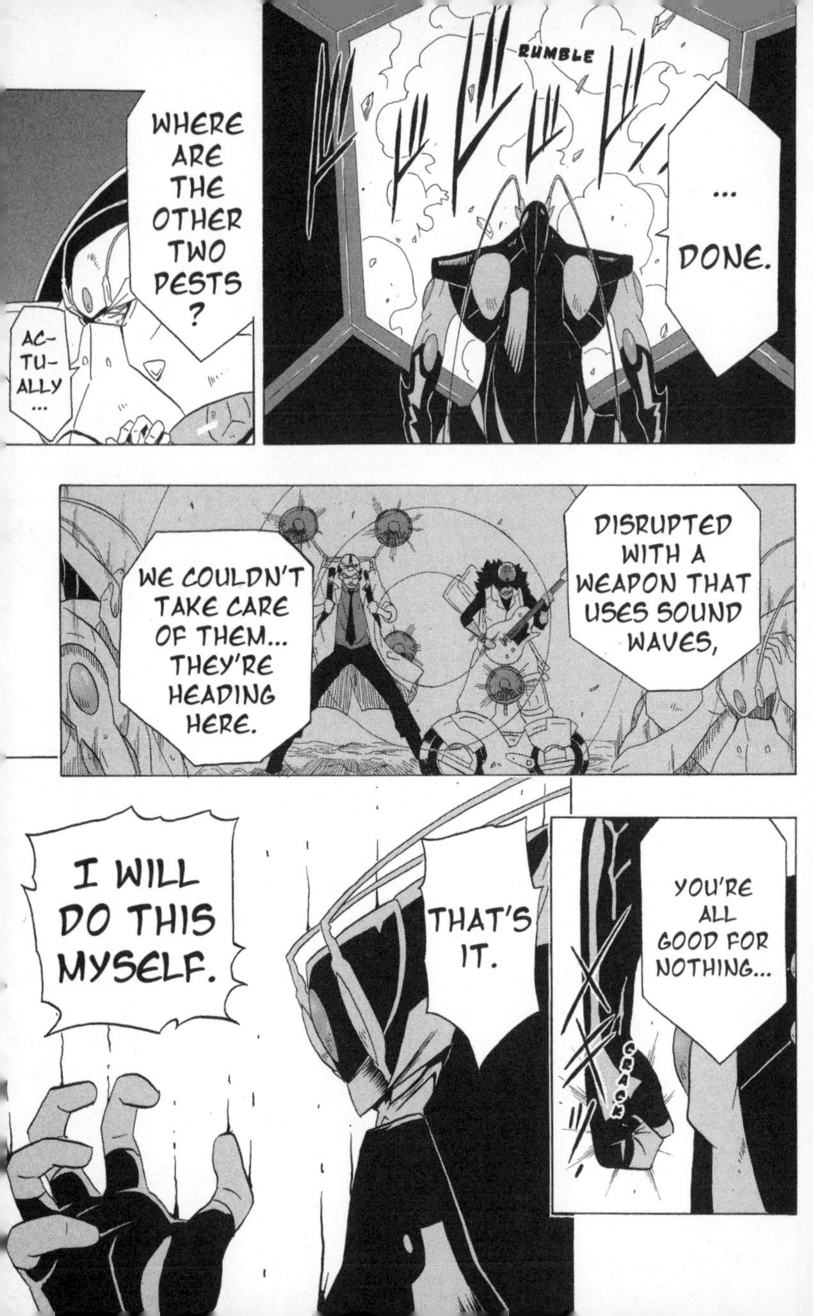
RUMBLE
... DONE.
WHERE ARE THE OTHER TWO PESTS?
AC-TU-ALLY ...
DISRUPTED WITH A WEAPON THAT USES SOUND WAVES,
WE COULDN'T TAKE CARE OF THEM... THEY'RE HEADING HERE.
YOU'RE ALL GOOD FOR NOTHING...
CRACK
THAT'S IT.
I WILL DO THIS MYSELF.

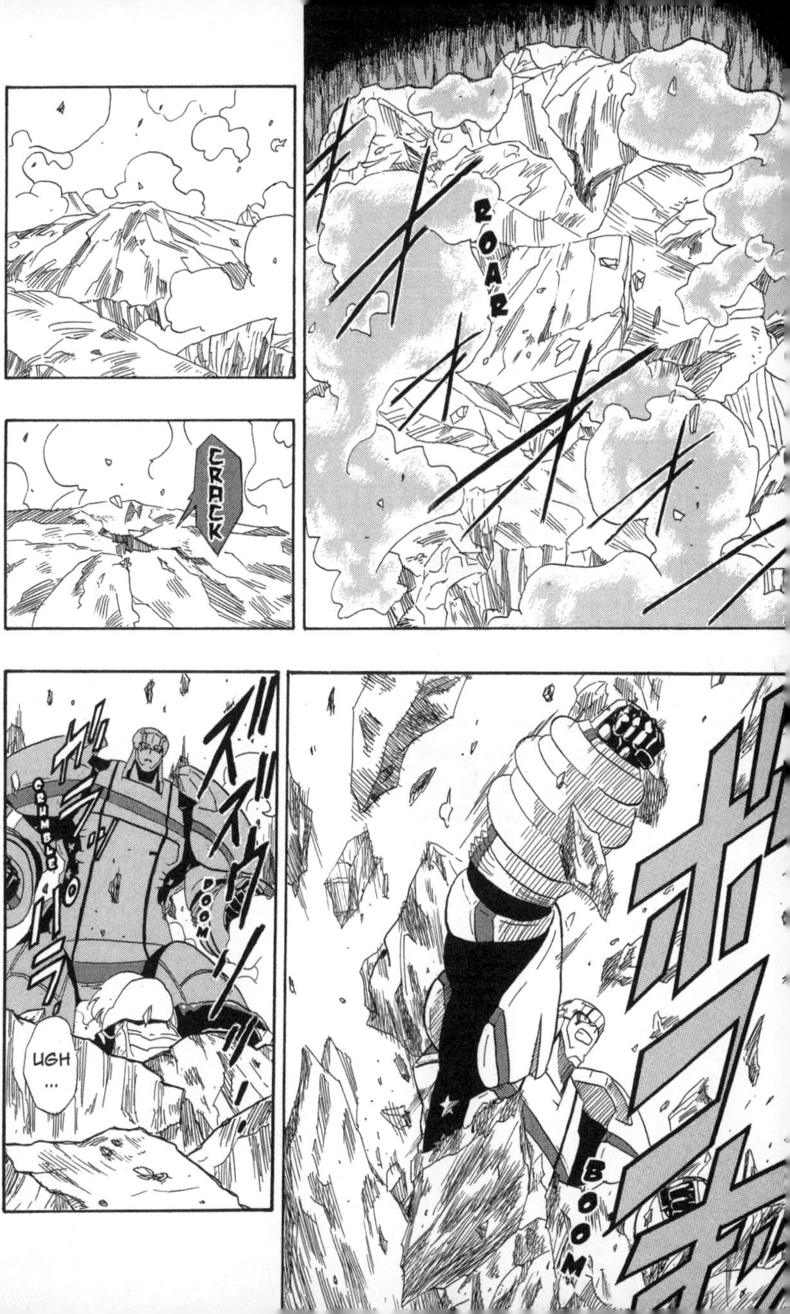
ROAR
CRACK
BOOM BOOM
CRUMBLE
BOOM
UGH ...

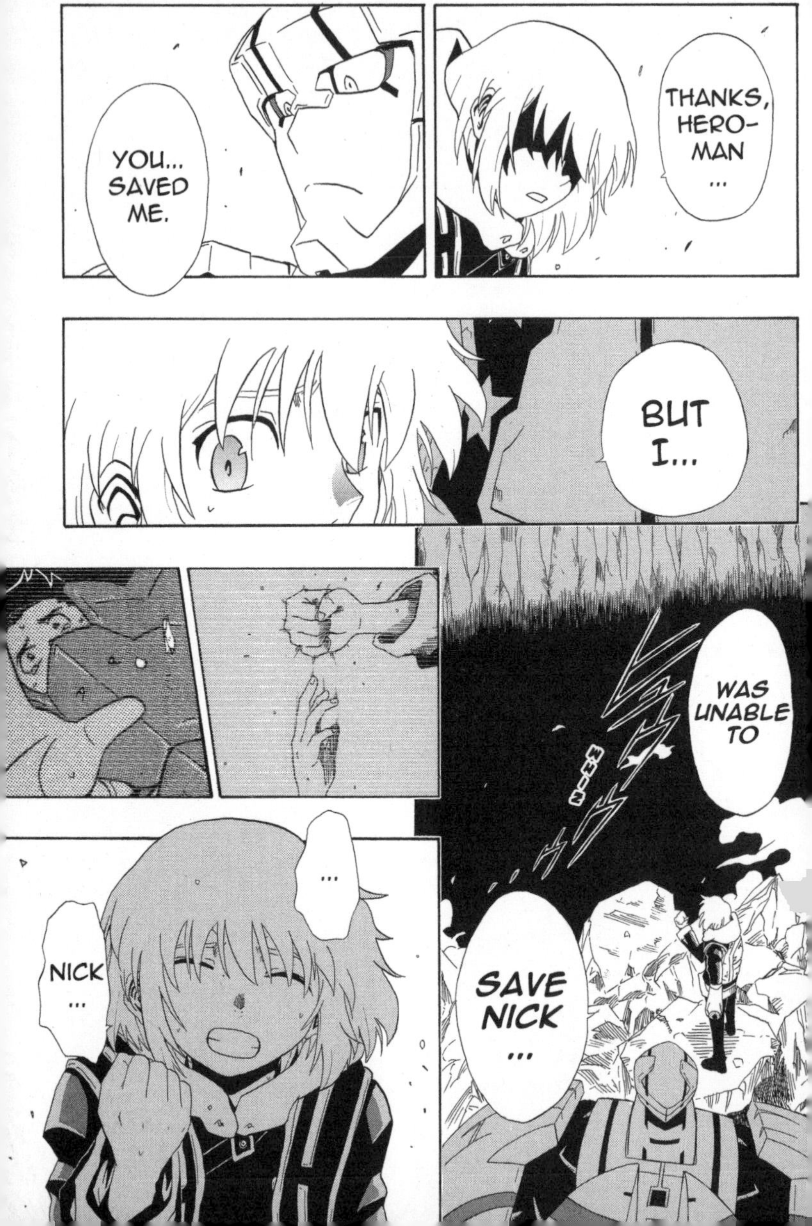
THANKS, HERO-MAN ...
YOU... SAVED ME.
BUT I...
WAS UNABLE TO
SAVE NICK ...
...
NICK ...

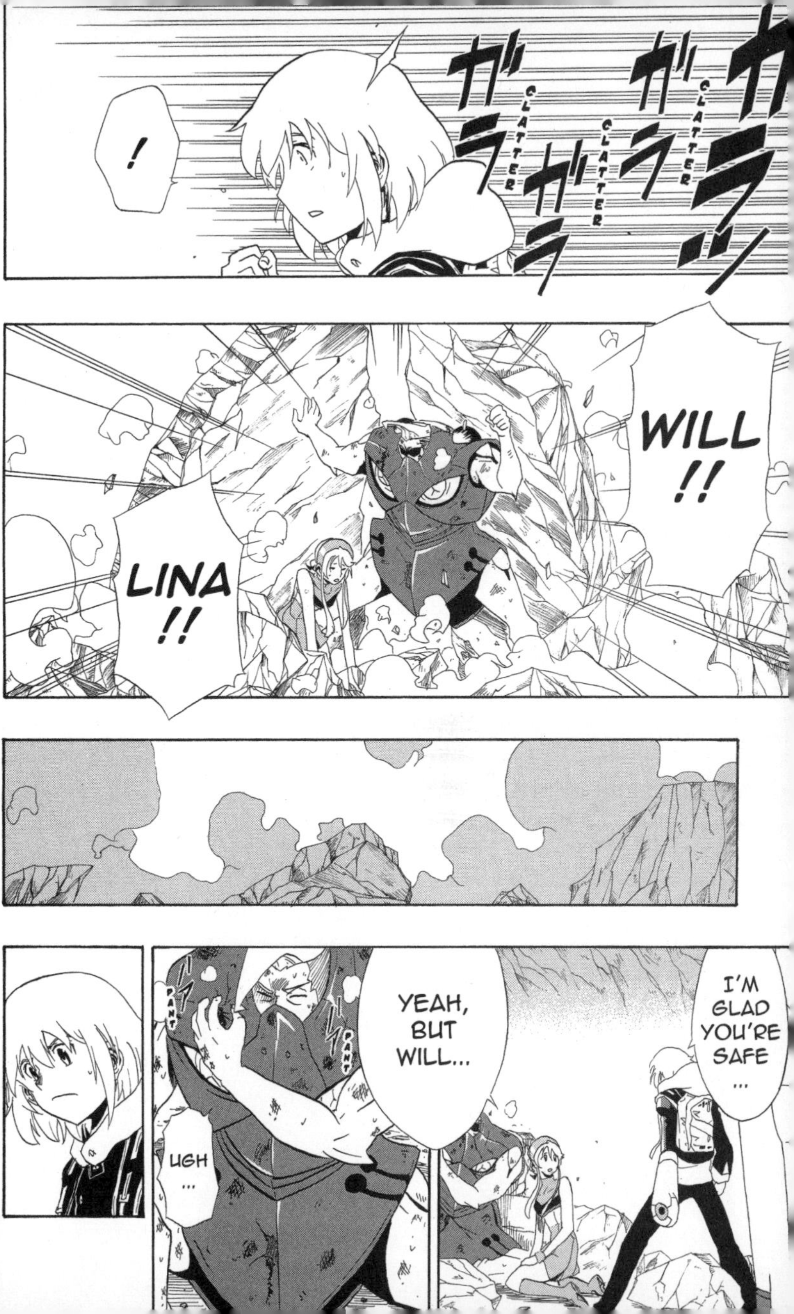
カラッ
CLATTER
ガラ ガラ
CLATTER
ガラ
CLATTER
!
WILL !!
LINA !!
I'M GLAD YOU'RE SAFE ...
YEAH, BUT WILL...
PANT
PANT
UGH ...

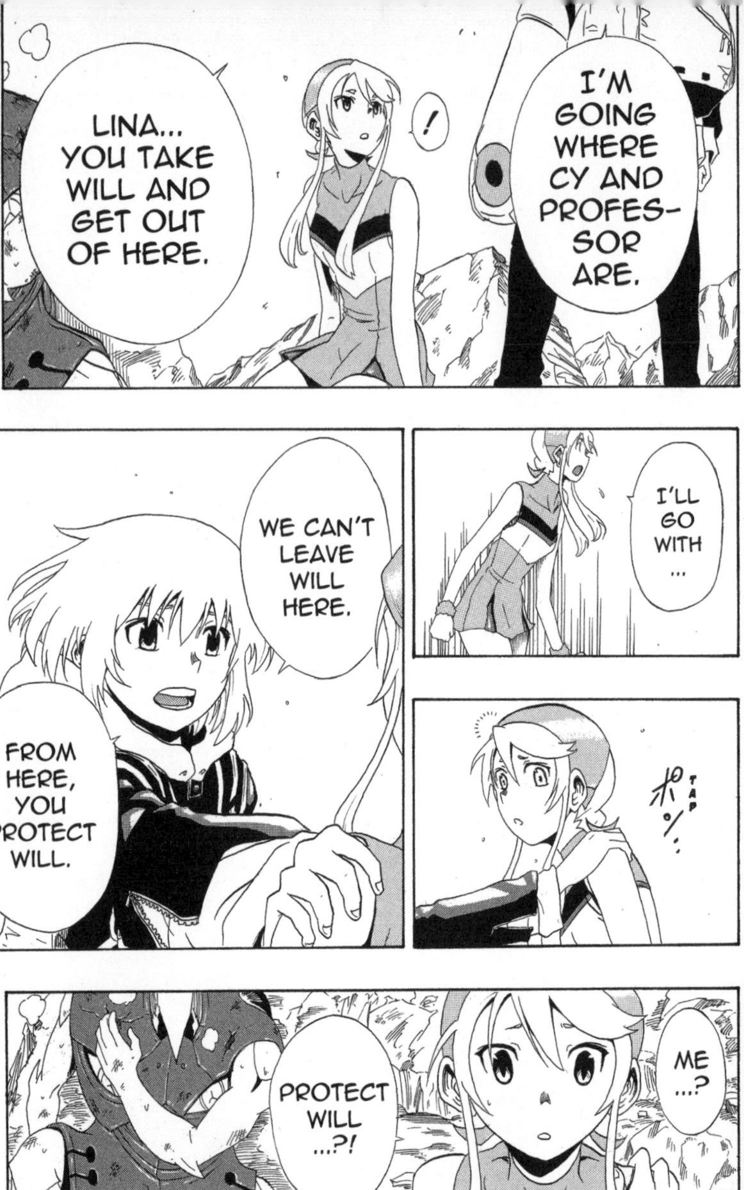
I'M GOING WHERE CY AND PROFESSOR ARE.
!
LINA... YOU TAKE WILL AND GET OUT OF HERE.
I'LL GO WITH ...
TAP
WE CAN'T LEAVE WILL HERE.
FROM HERE, YOU PROTECT WILL.
ME ...?
PROTECT WILL ...?!

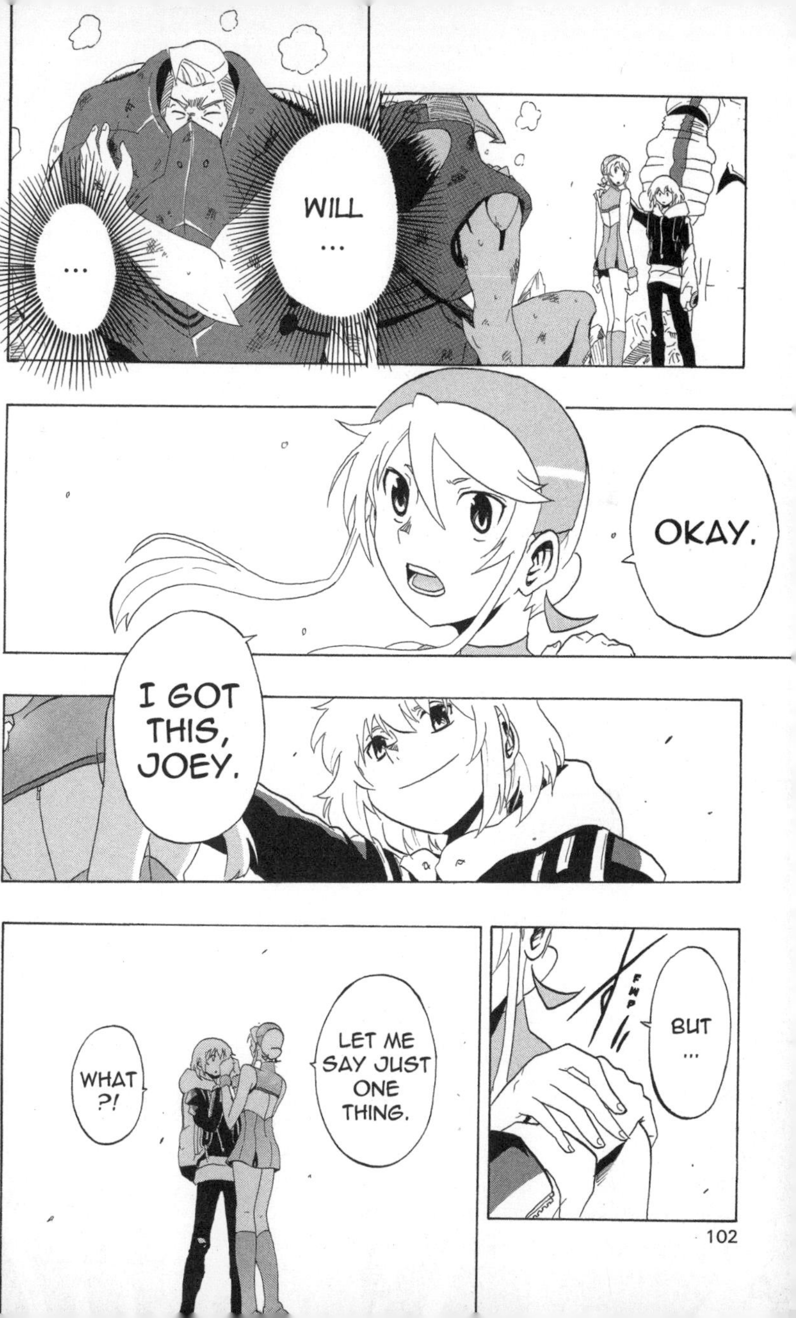
WILL ...
...
OKAY.
I GOT THIS, JOEY.
FWP
BUT ...
LET ME SAY JUST ONE THING.
WHAT ?!

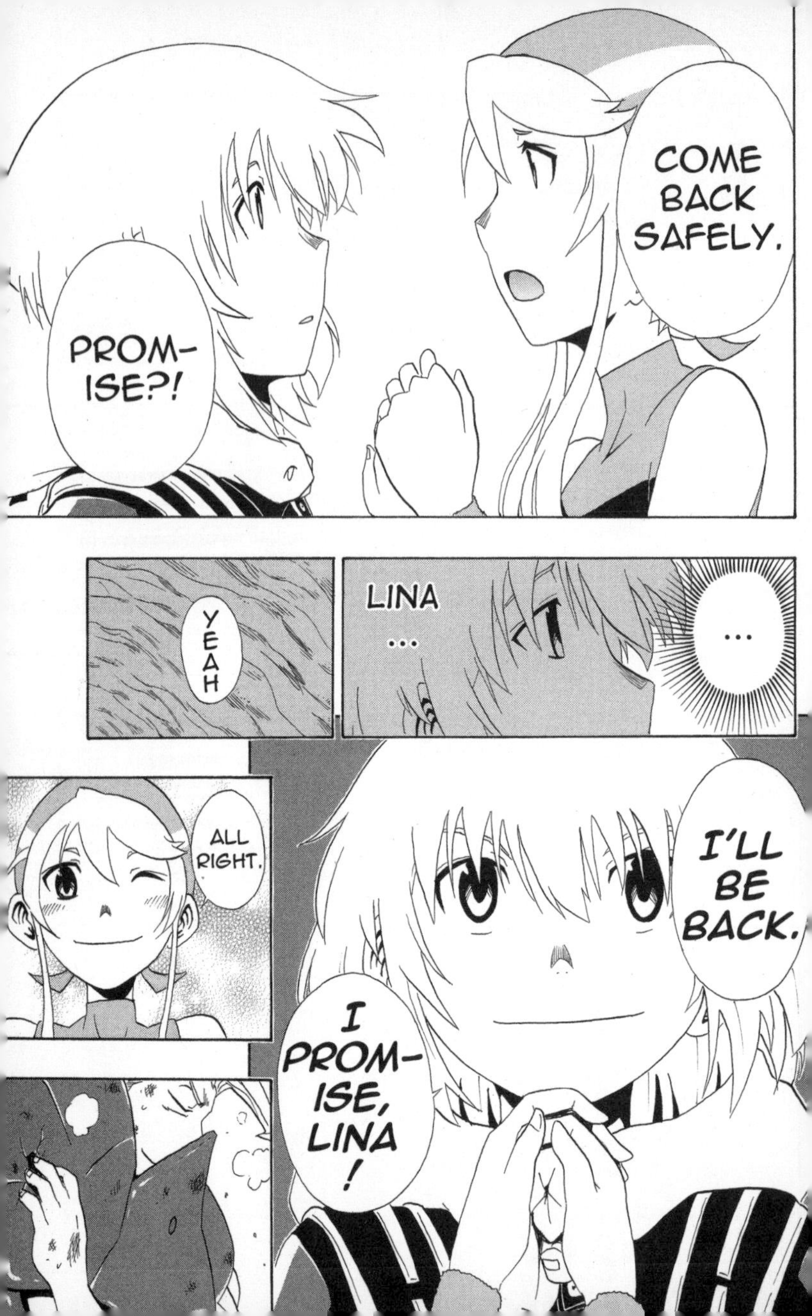
COME BACK SAFELY.
PROMISE?!
...
LINA ...
YEAH
I'LL BE BACK.
I PROMISE, LINA!
ALL RIGHT.

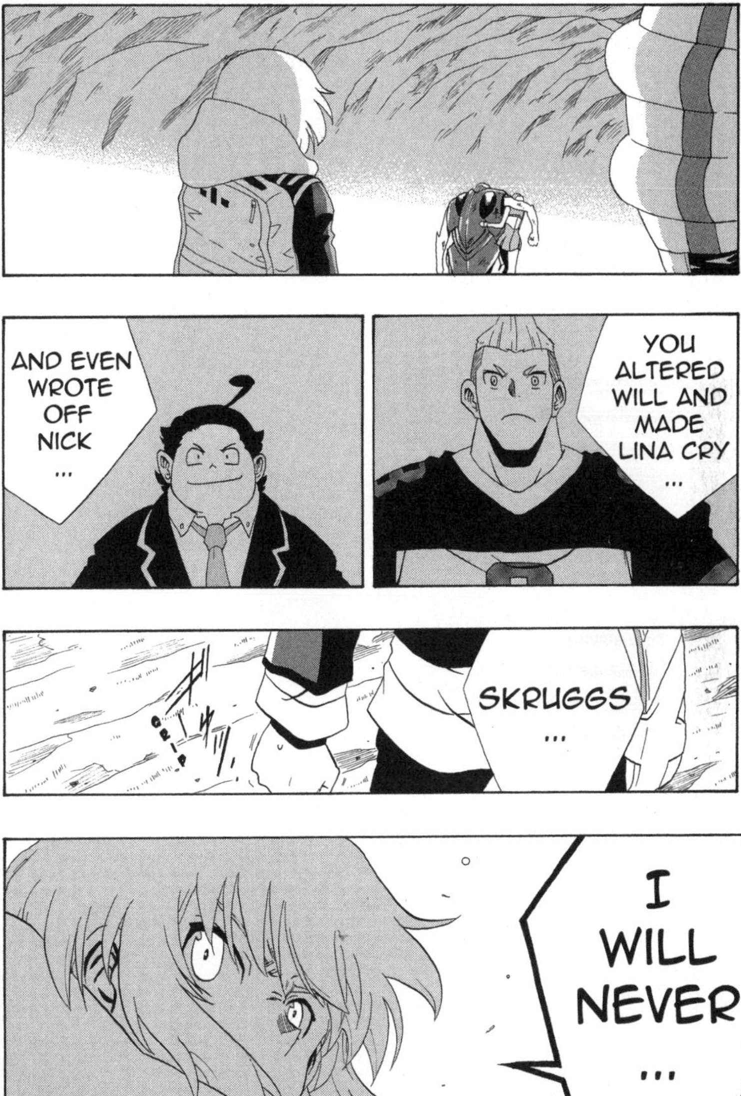
YOU ALTERED WILL AND MADE LINA CRY ...
AND EVEN WROTE OFF NICK ...
SKRUGGS ...
GRIP
I WILL NEVER ...

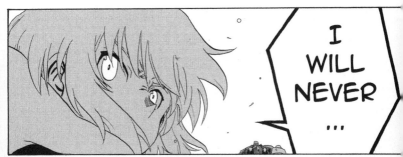

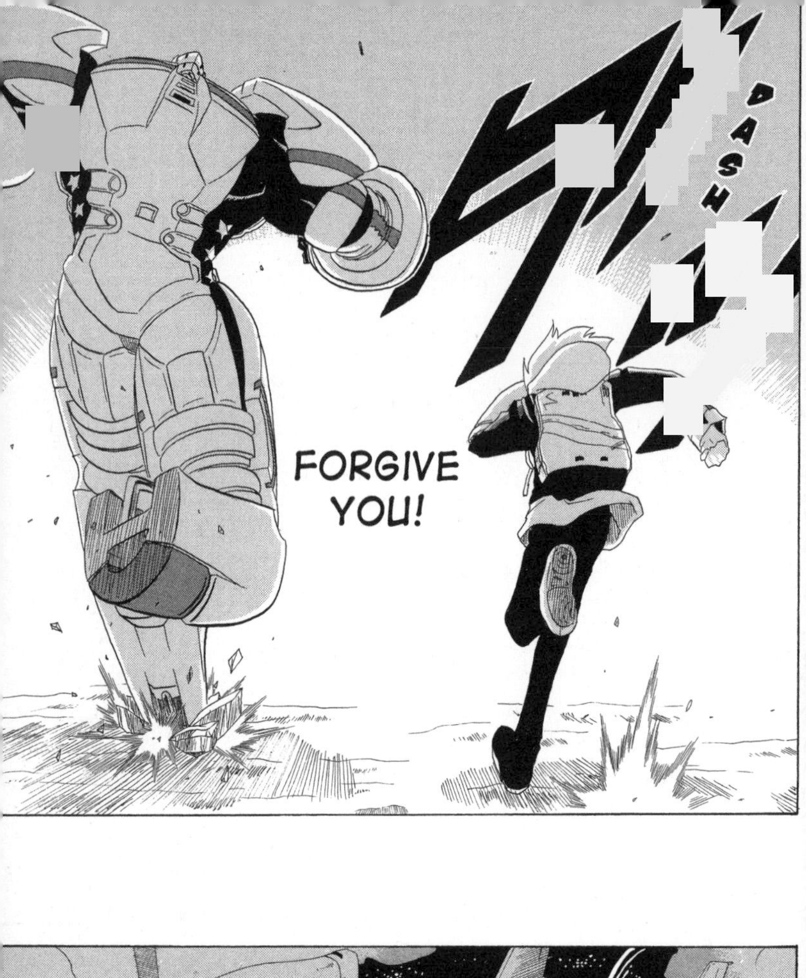
DASH
FORGIVE YOU!
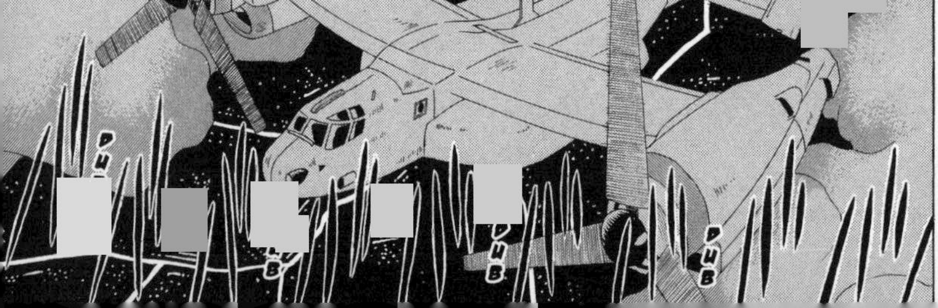
DUB
DUB

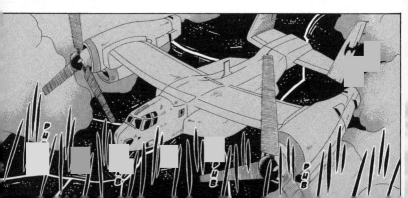

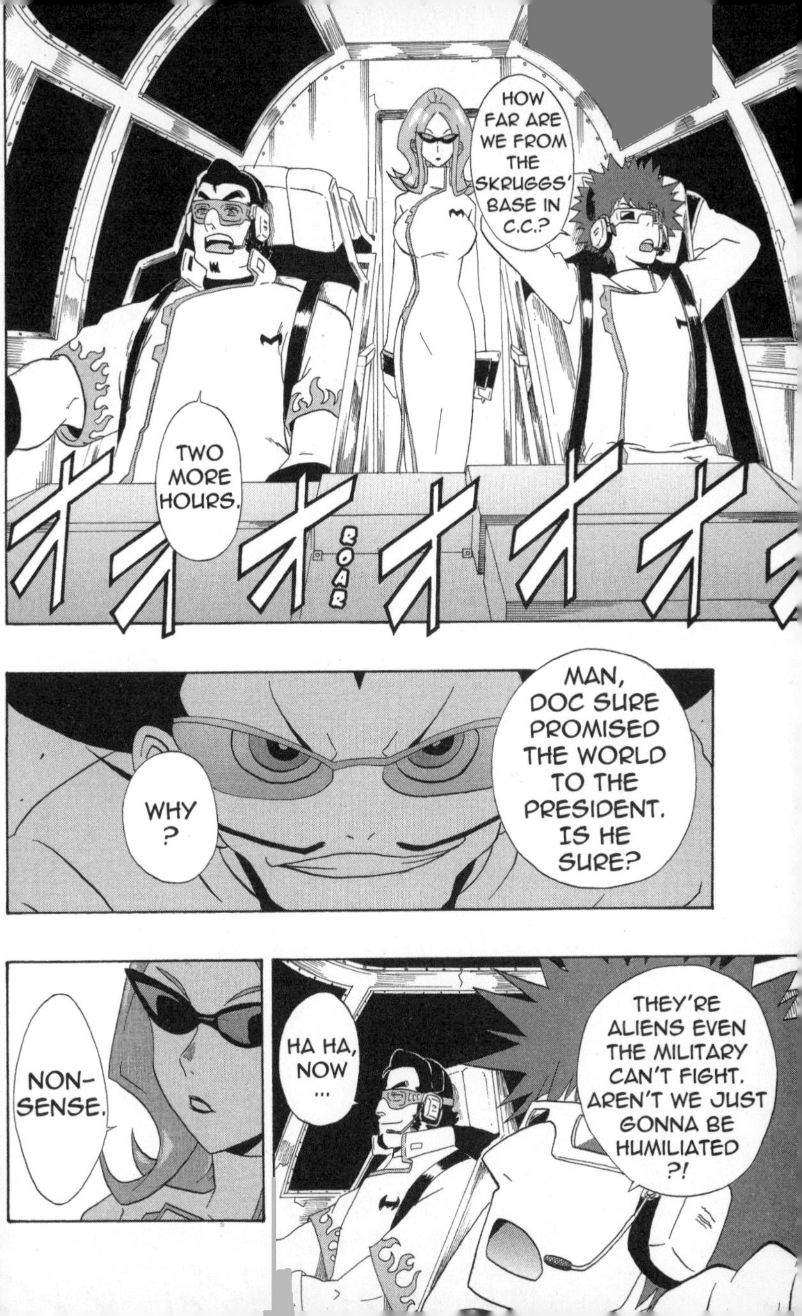
HOW FAR ARE WE FROM THE SKRUGGS' BASE IN C.C.?
TWO MORE HOURS.
ROAR
MAN, DOC SURE PROMISED THE WORLD TO THE PRESIDENT. IS HE SURE?
WHY?
THEY'RE ALIENS EVEN THE MILITARY CAN'T FIGHT. AREN'T WE JUST GONNA BE HUMILIATED?!
HA HA, NOW ...
NON-SENSE.

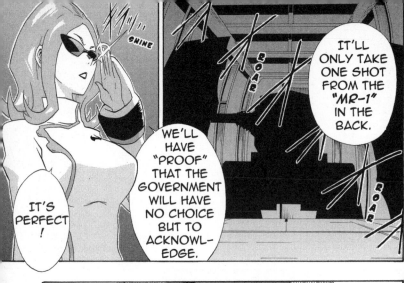

IT'LL ONLY TAKE ONE SHOT FROM THE "MR-1" IN THE BACK.

WE'LL HAVE "PROOF" THAT THE GOVERNMENT WILL HAVE NO CHOICE BUT TO ACKNOWL-EDGE.

IT'S PERFECT!

SHINE

ROAR

ROAR

NO WOR-RIES, THEN!

HA HA HA!

ALIENS SHOULD BE NO PROB-LEM ♪

PUB

PUB

ROAR

ROAR

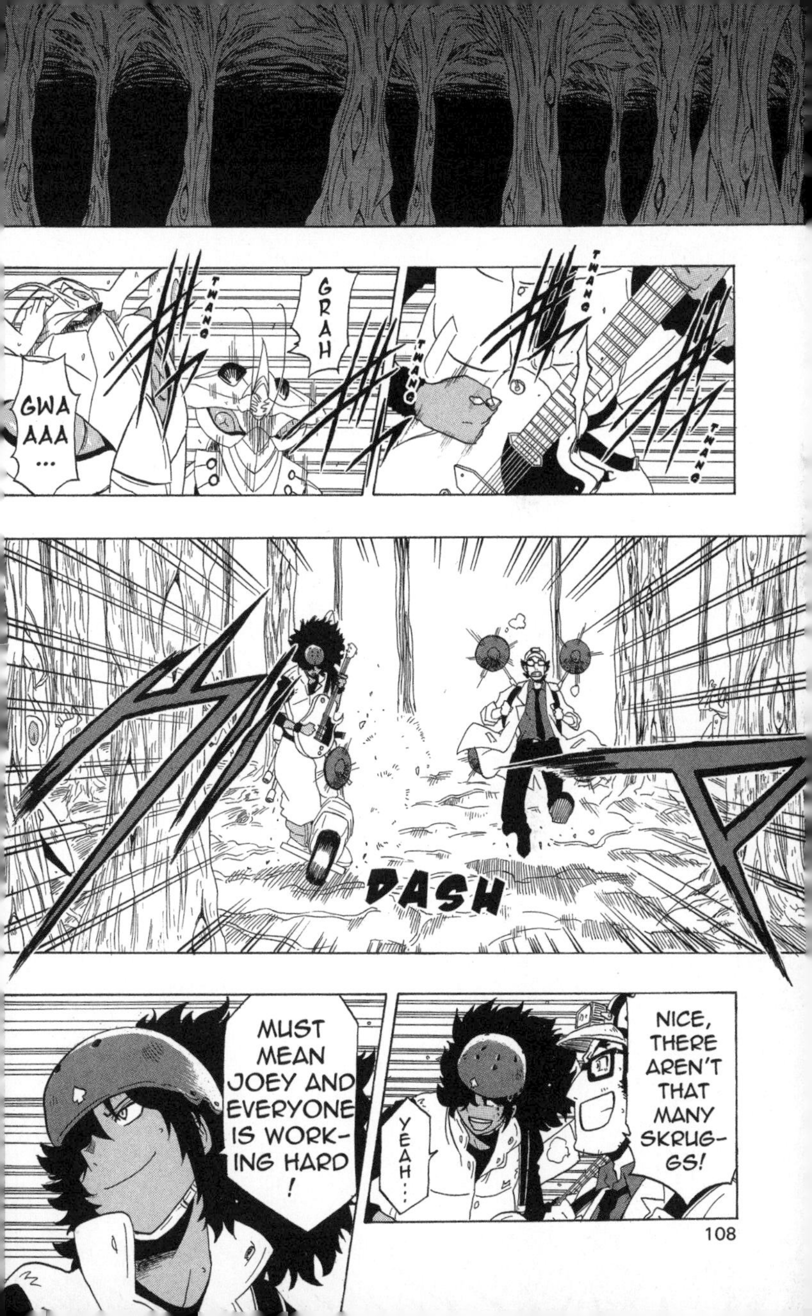
THWANG
THWANG
THWANG
GRAH
THWANG
GWAAAA...
DASH
NICE, THERE AREN'T THAT MANY SKRUGGS!
YEAH...
MUST MEAN JOEY AND EVERYONE IS WORKING HARD!

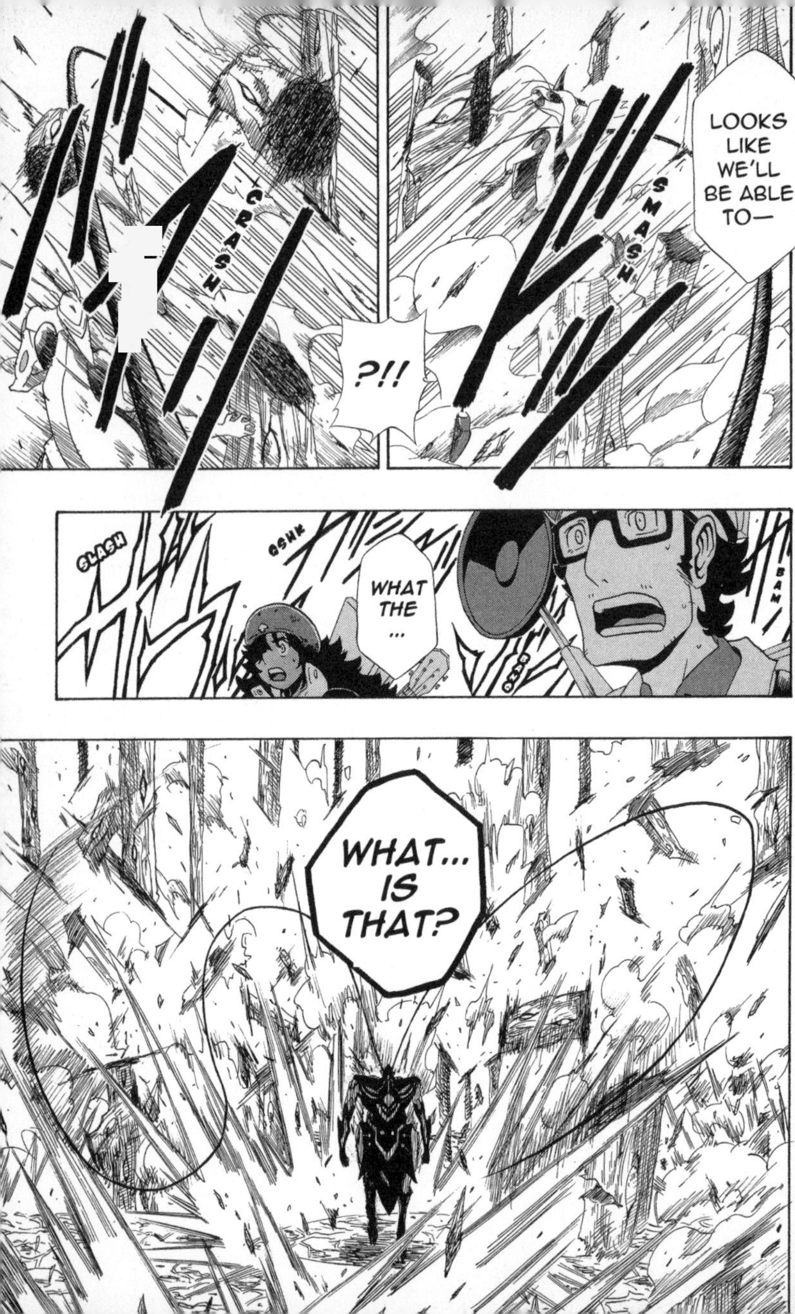
LOOKS LIKE WE'LL BE ABLE TO—
SMASH
?!!
CRASH
BAM
BANG
WHAT THE ...
GSHK
SLASH
WHAT... IS THAT?

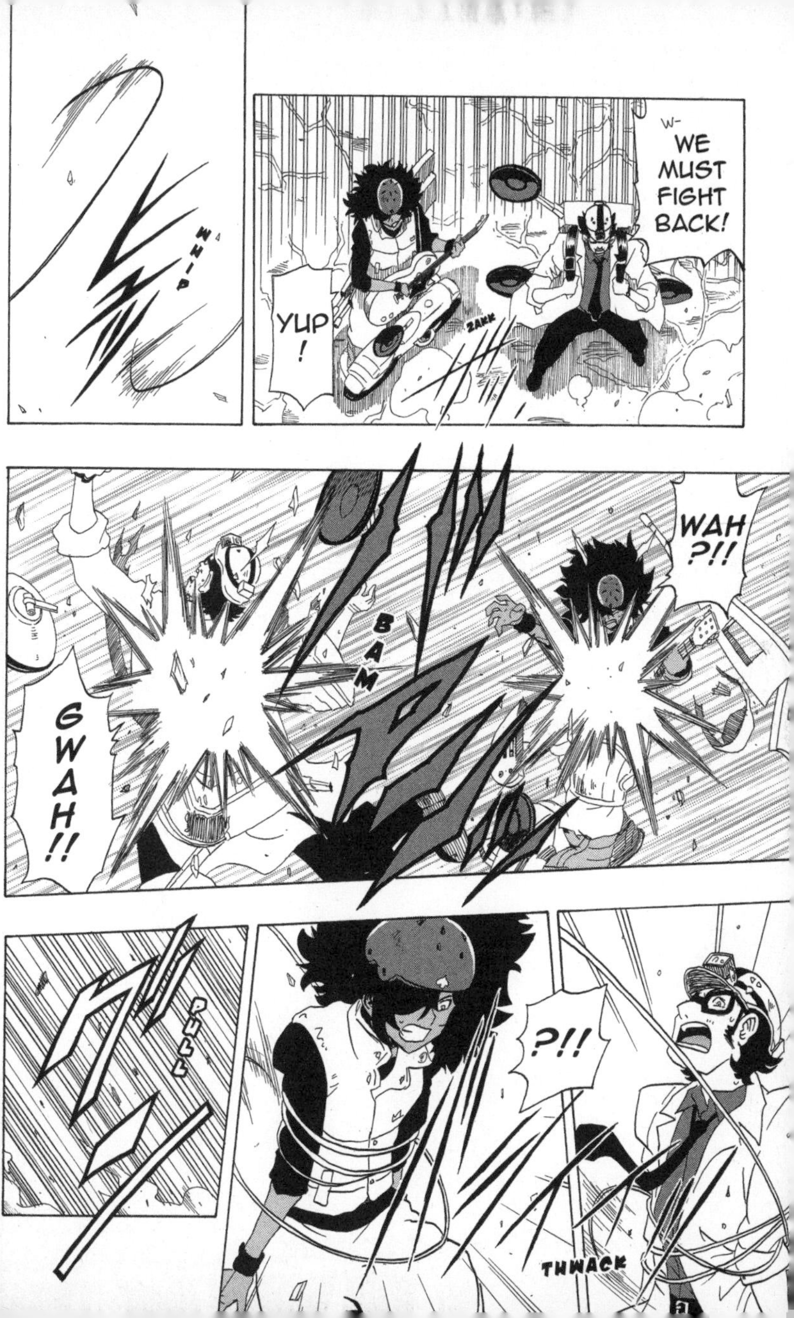
W- WE MUST FIGHT BACK!
YUP!
ZAKK
WHIP
WAH?!!
BAM
GWAH!!
?!!
THWACK
PULL

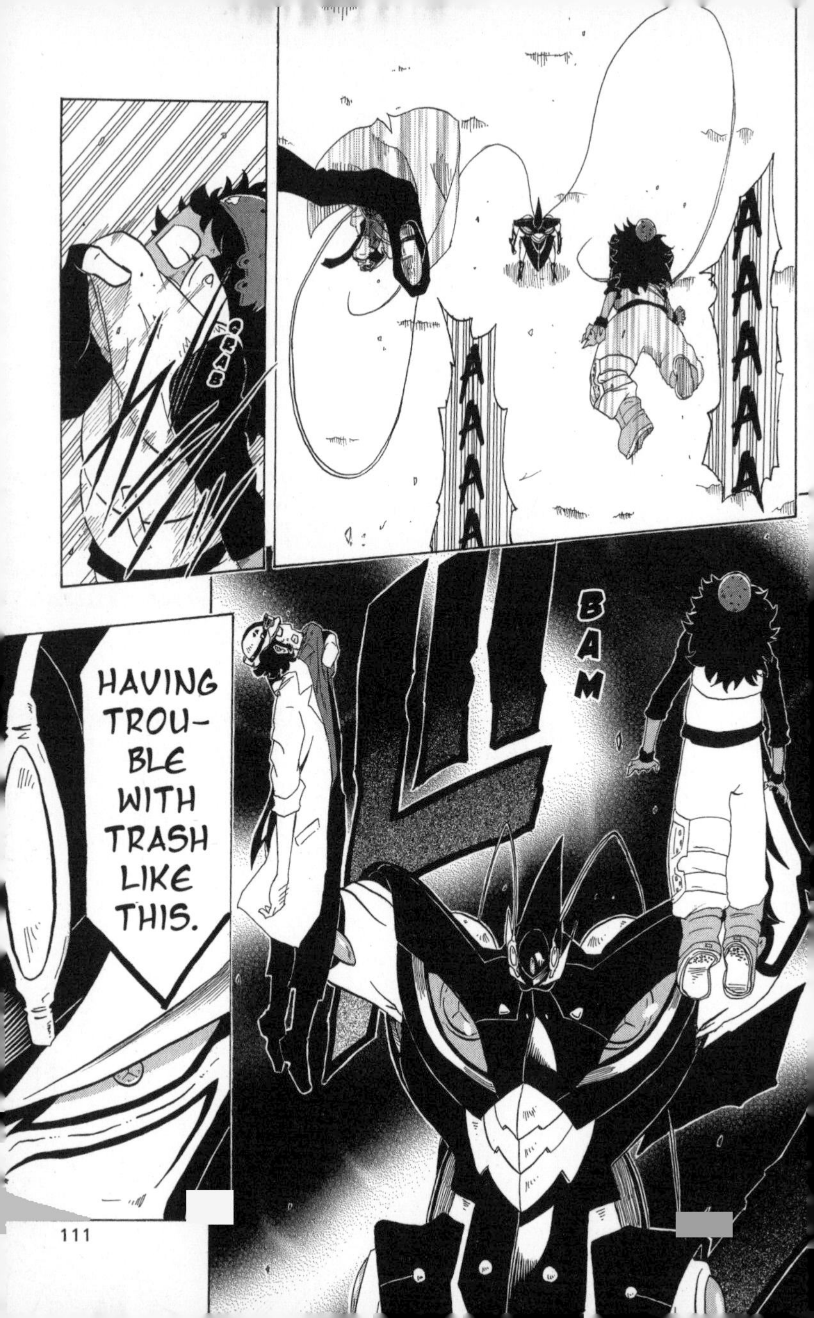
AAAAAAA
AAAAAA
GRAB
BAM
HAVING TROU-BLE WITH TRASH LIKE THIS.

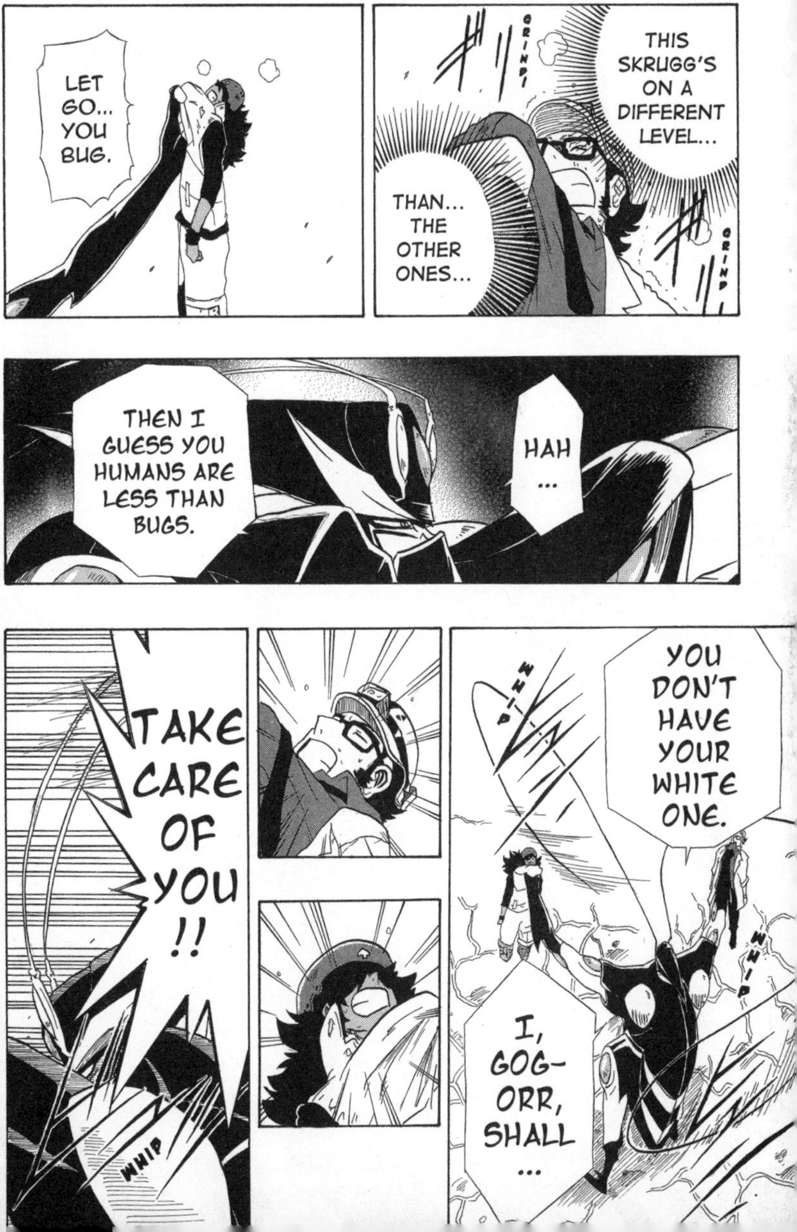
GRIND
THIS SKRUGG'S ON A DIFFERENT LEVEL...
THAN... THE OTHER ONES...
GRIND
LET GO... YOU BUG.
HAH ...
THEN I GUESS YOU HUMANS ARE LESS THAN BUGS.
WHIP
YOU DON'T HAVE YOUR WHITE ONE.
WHIP
I, GOG-ORR, SHALL ...
TAKE CARE OF YOU !!
WHIP

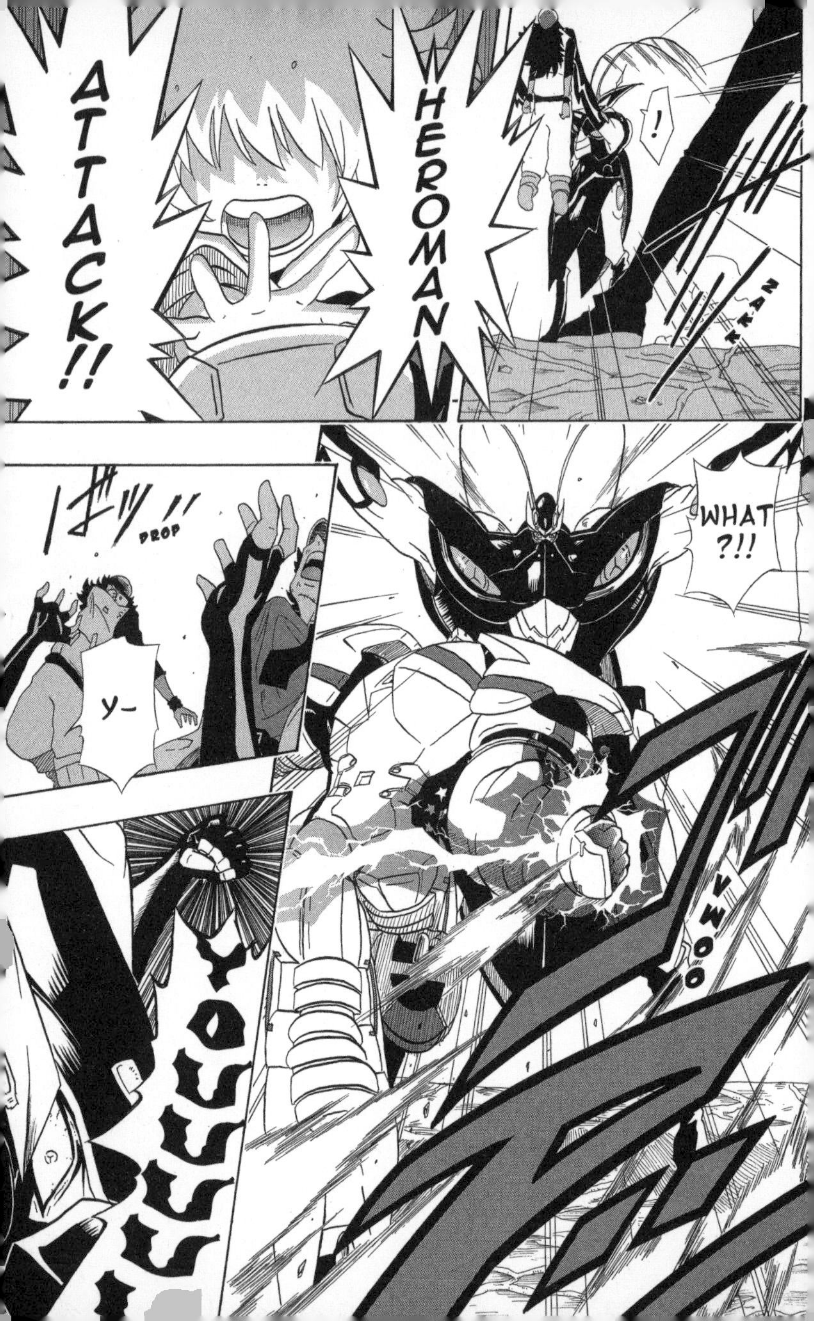

!
ZAKK
HEROMAN
ATTACK!!
WHAT?!!
VWOOO
ばッ!!
DROP
Y-
YOUUUU

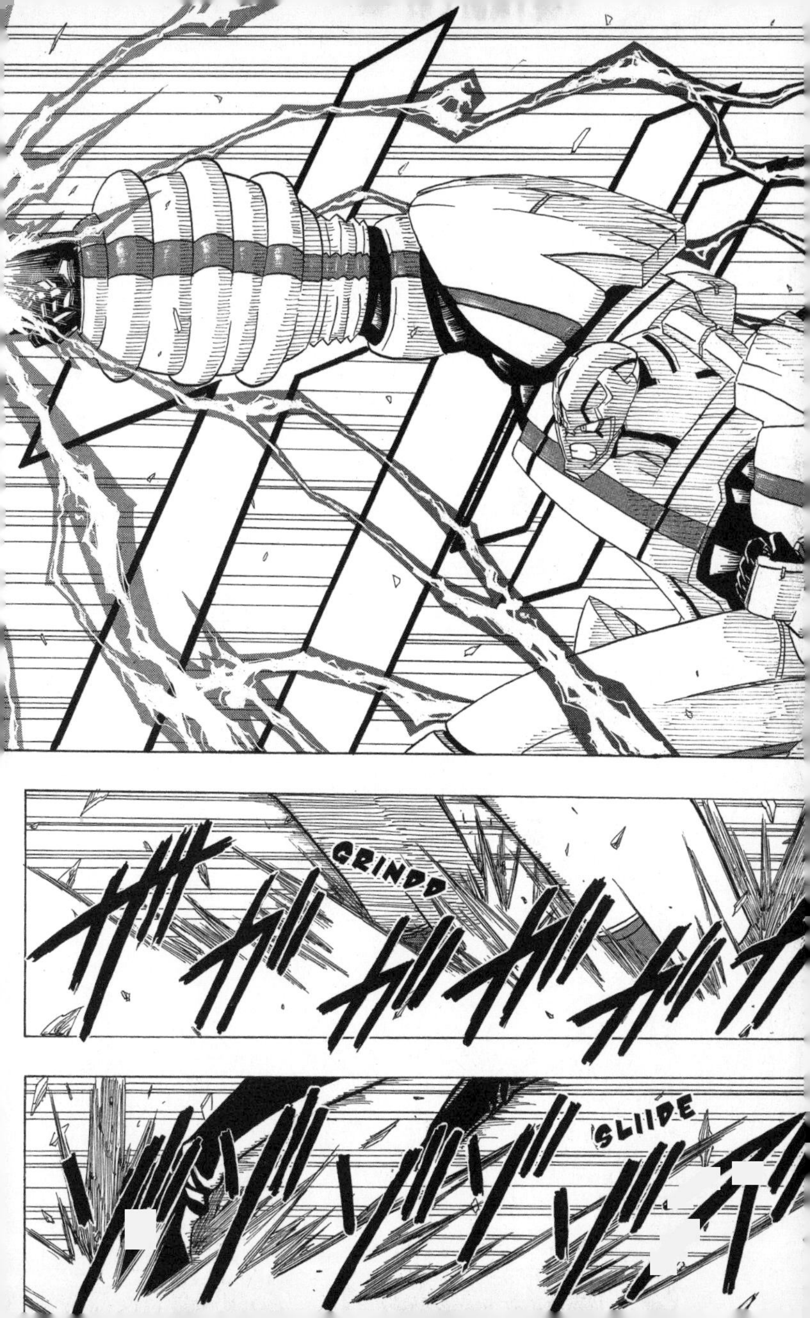
GRINDD
SLIIDE

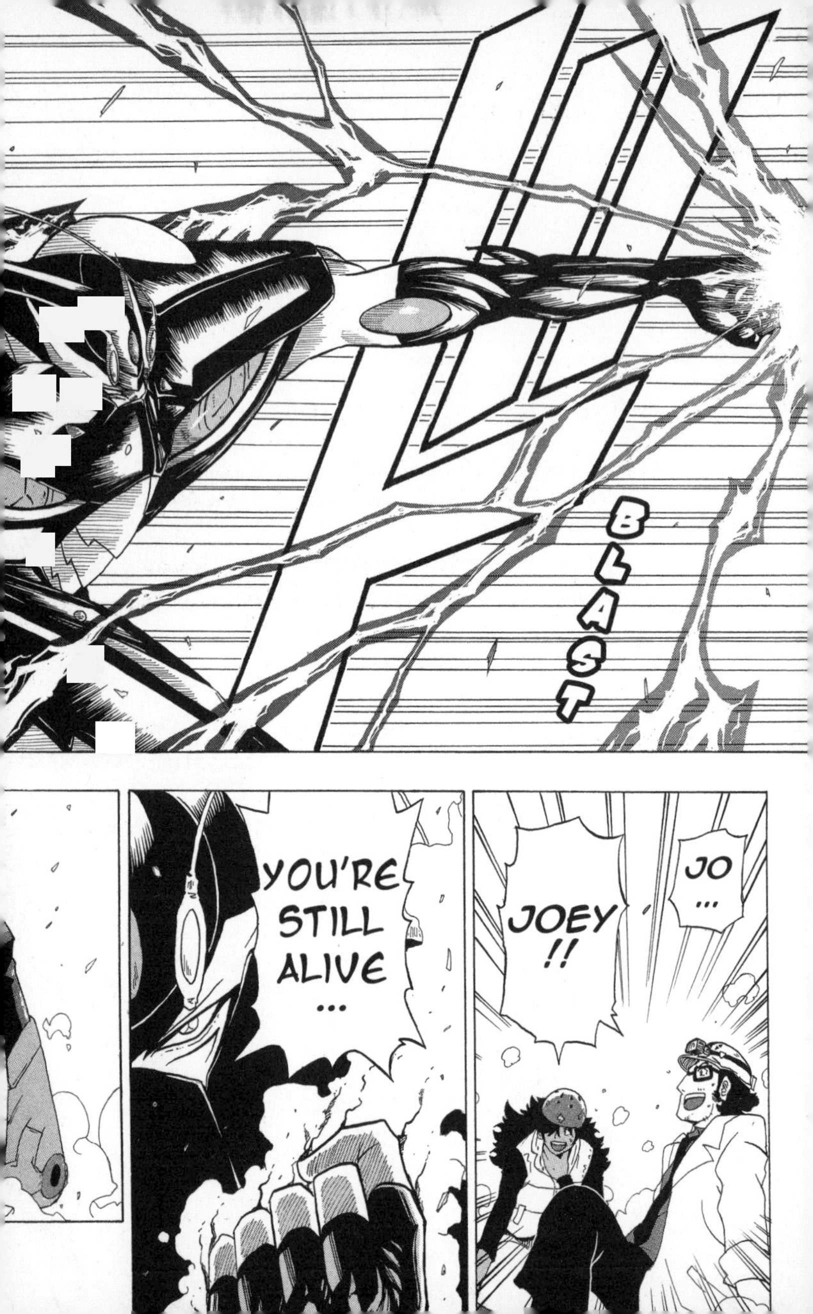
BLAST
JO ...
JOEY !!
YOU'RE STILL ALIVE ...

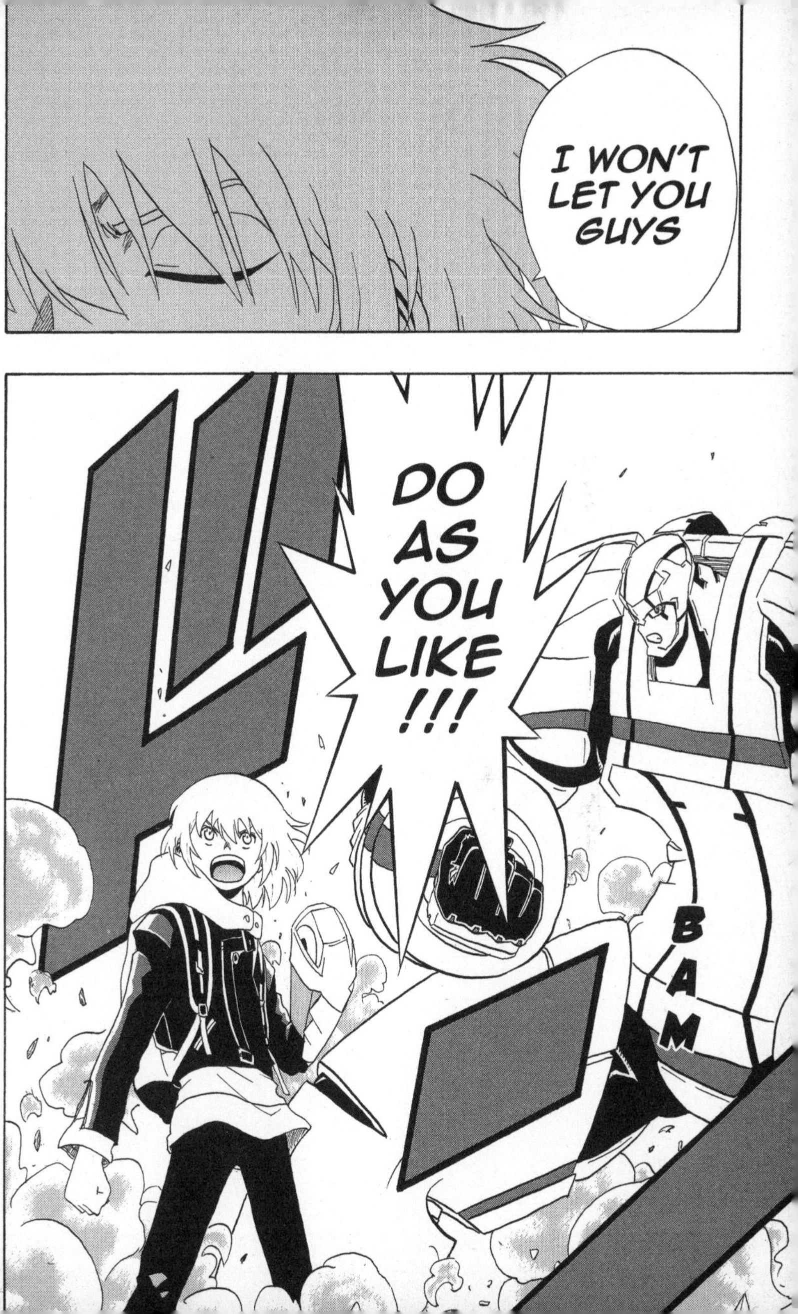
I WON'T LET YOU GUYS
DO AS YOU LIKE !!!
BAM

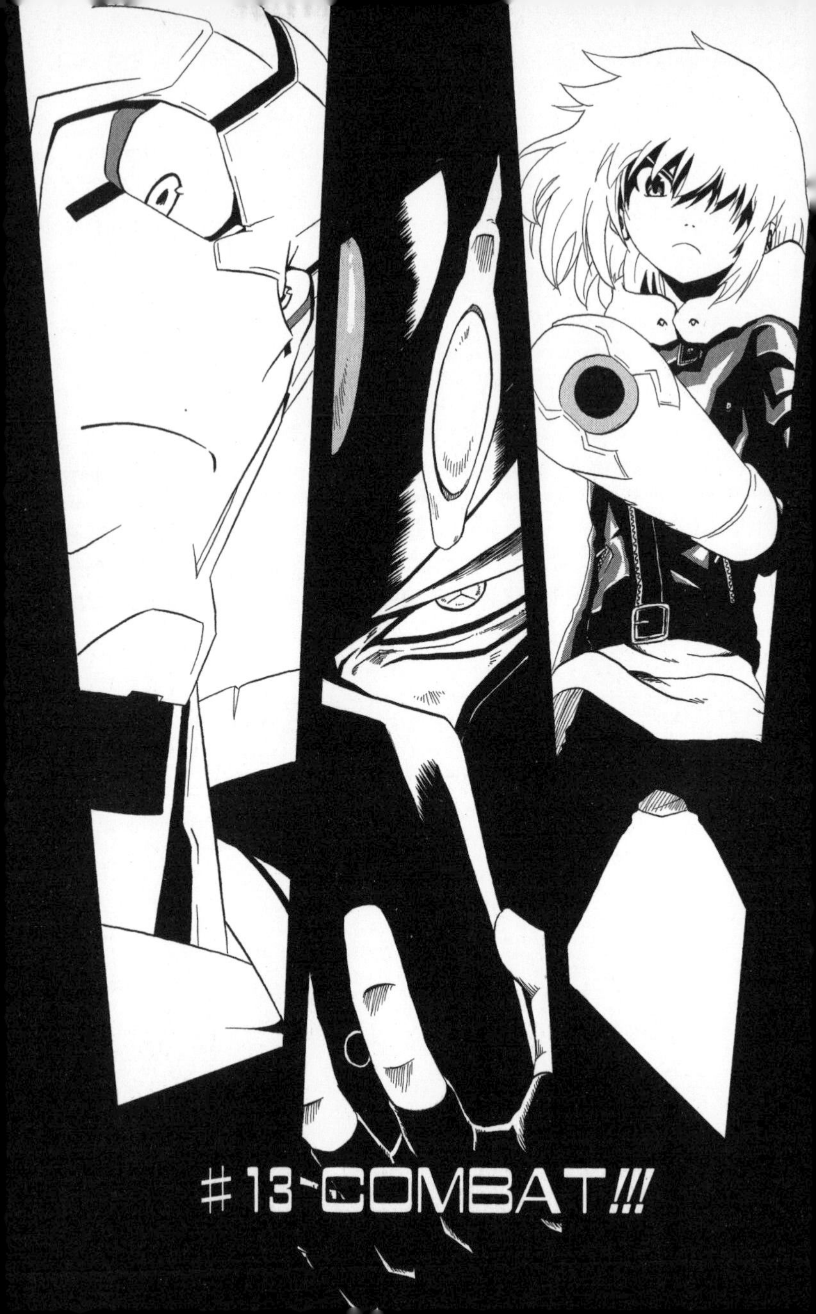
#13-COMBAT!!!

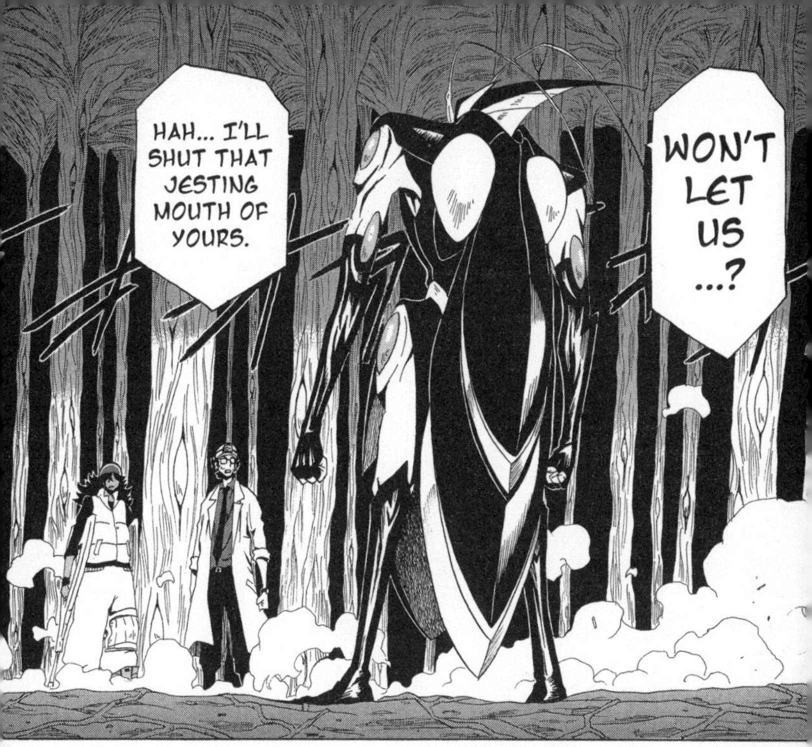
WON'T LET US ...?
HAH... I'LL SHUT THAT JESTING MOUTH OF YOURS.
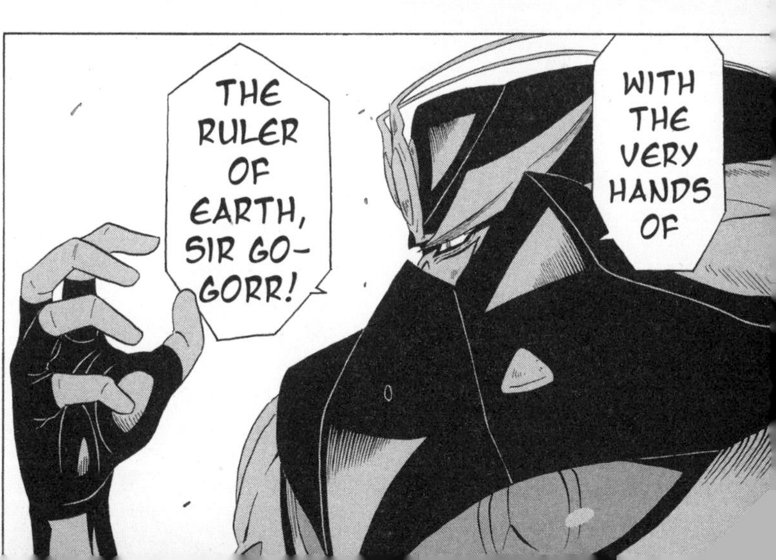
WITH THE VERY HANDS OF
THE RULER OF EARTH, SIR GO-GORR!

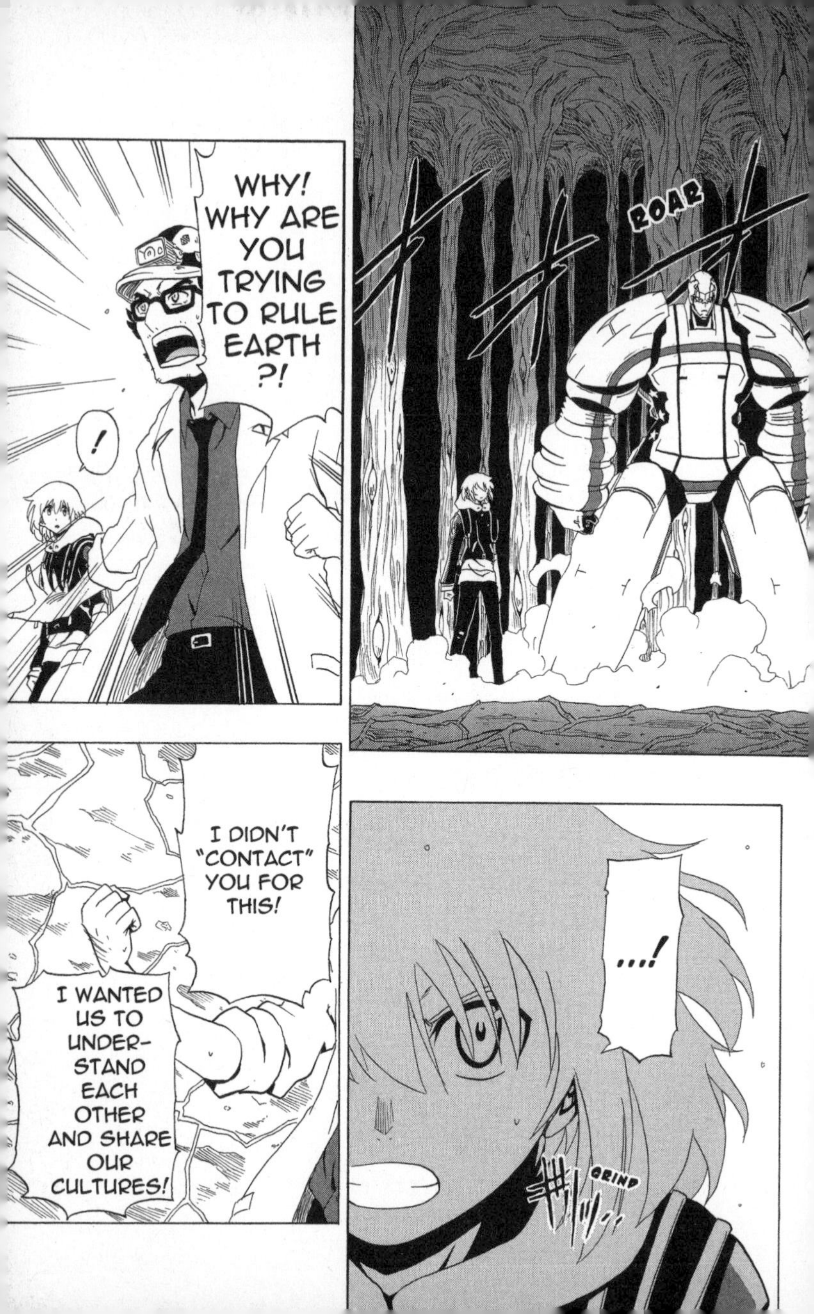
ROAR
WHY! WHY ARE YOU TRYING TO RULE EARTH ?!
!
...!
GRIND
I DIDN'T "CONTACT" YOU FOR THIS!
I WANTED US TO UNDER-STAND EACH OTHER AND SHARE OUR CULTURES!

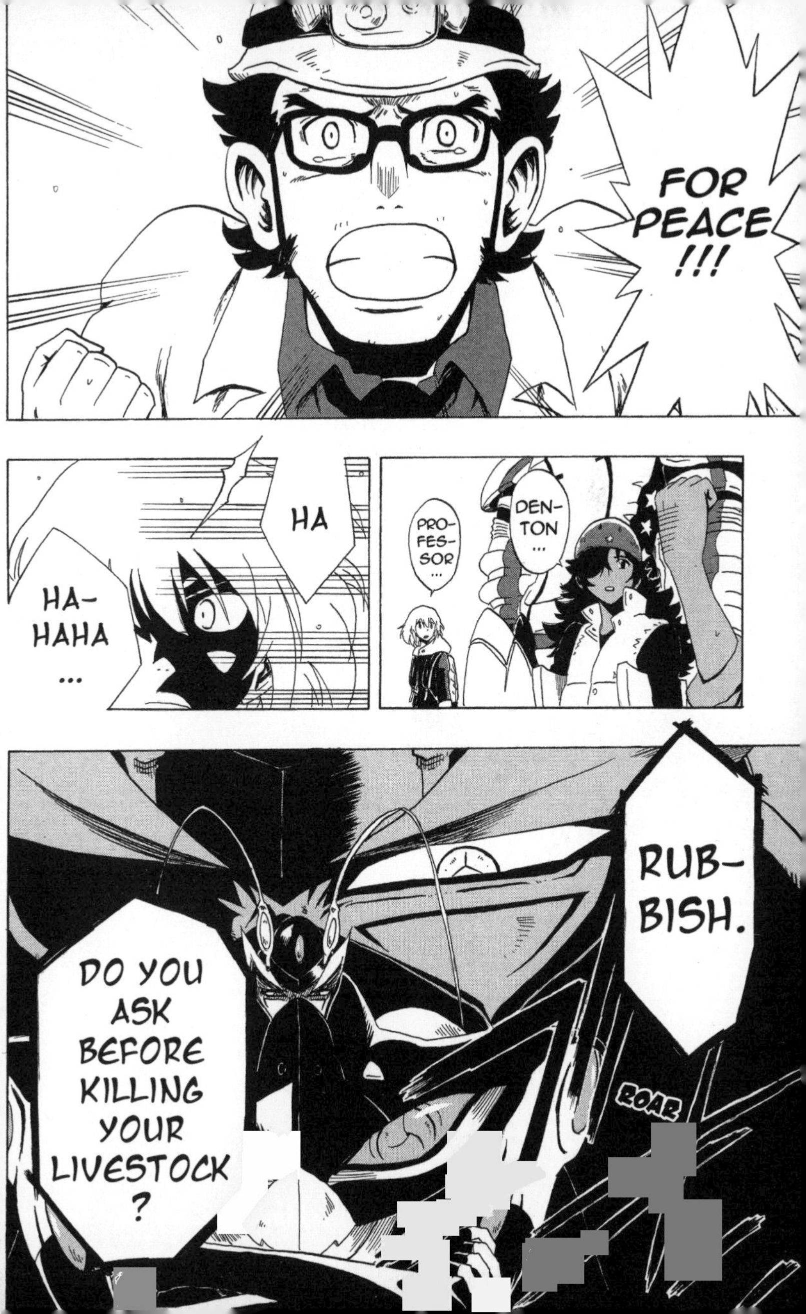
FOR PEACE!!!
DEN-TON...
PRO-FES-SOR...
HA
HA-HAHA...
RUB-BISH.
DO YOU ASK BEFORE KILLING YOUR LIVESTOCK?
ROAR

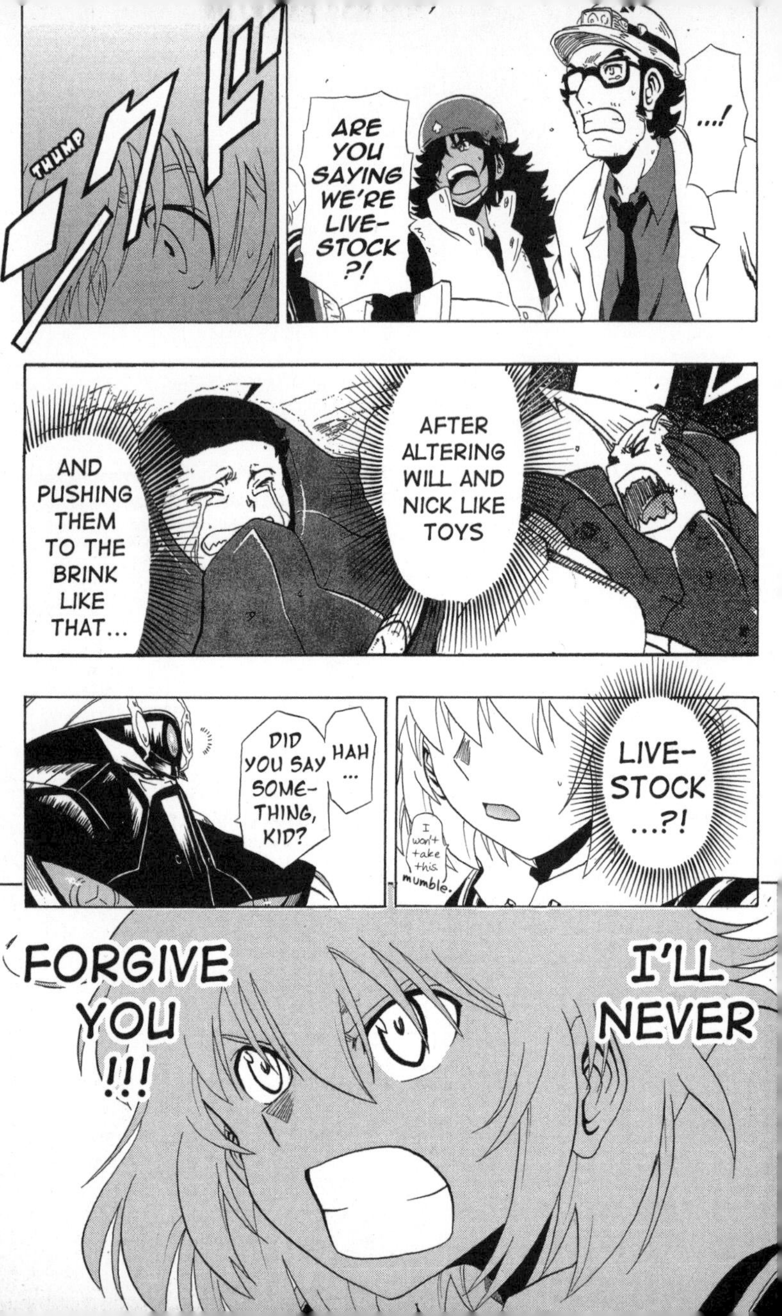
...!
ARE YOU SAYING WE'RE LIVE-STOCK?!
THUMP
AFTER ALTERING WILL AND NICK LIKE TOYS
AND PUSHING THEM TO THE BRINK LIKE THAT...
LIVE-STOCK...?!
I won't take this mumble.
HAH...
DID YOU SAY SOME-THING, KID?
I'LL NEVER
FORGIVE YOU!!!

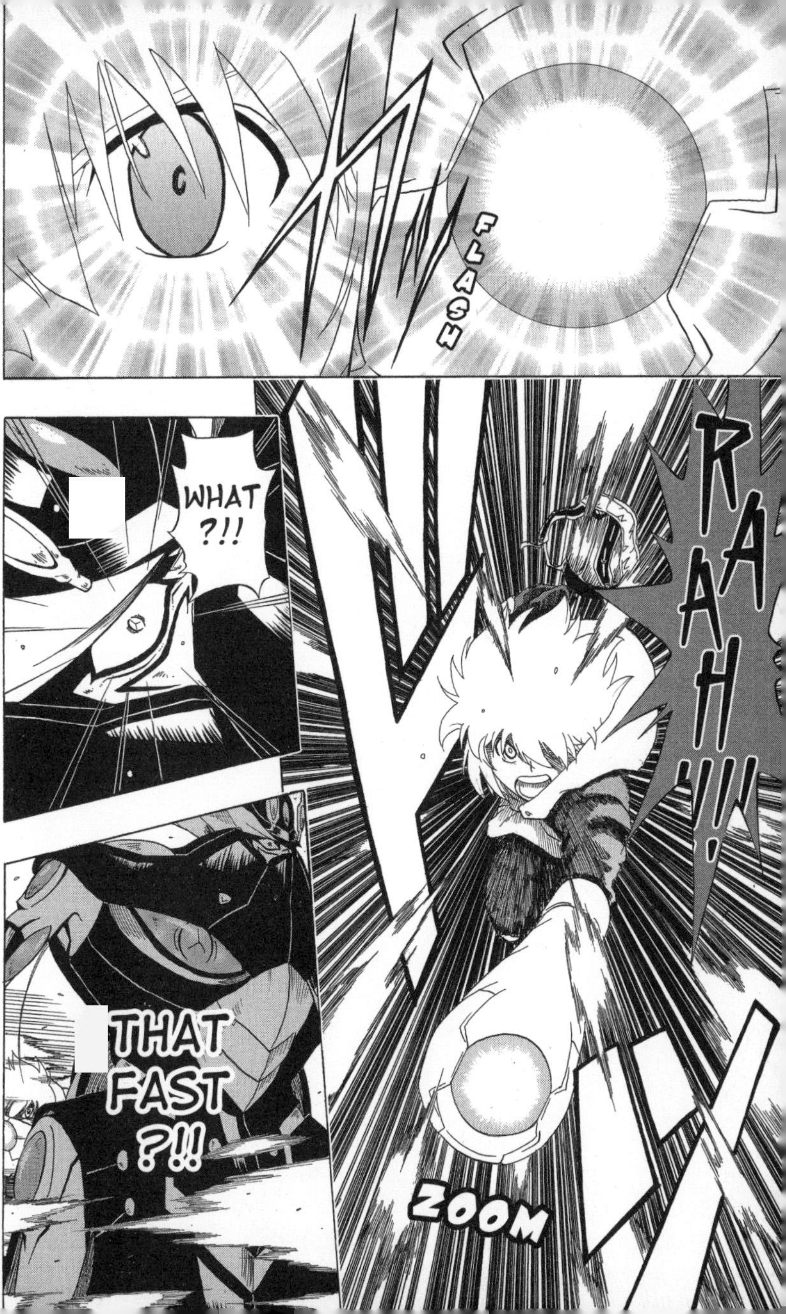
FLASH
RAAH!!!
ZOOM
WHAT ?!!
THAT FAST ?!!

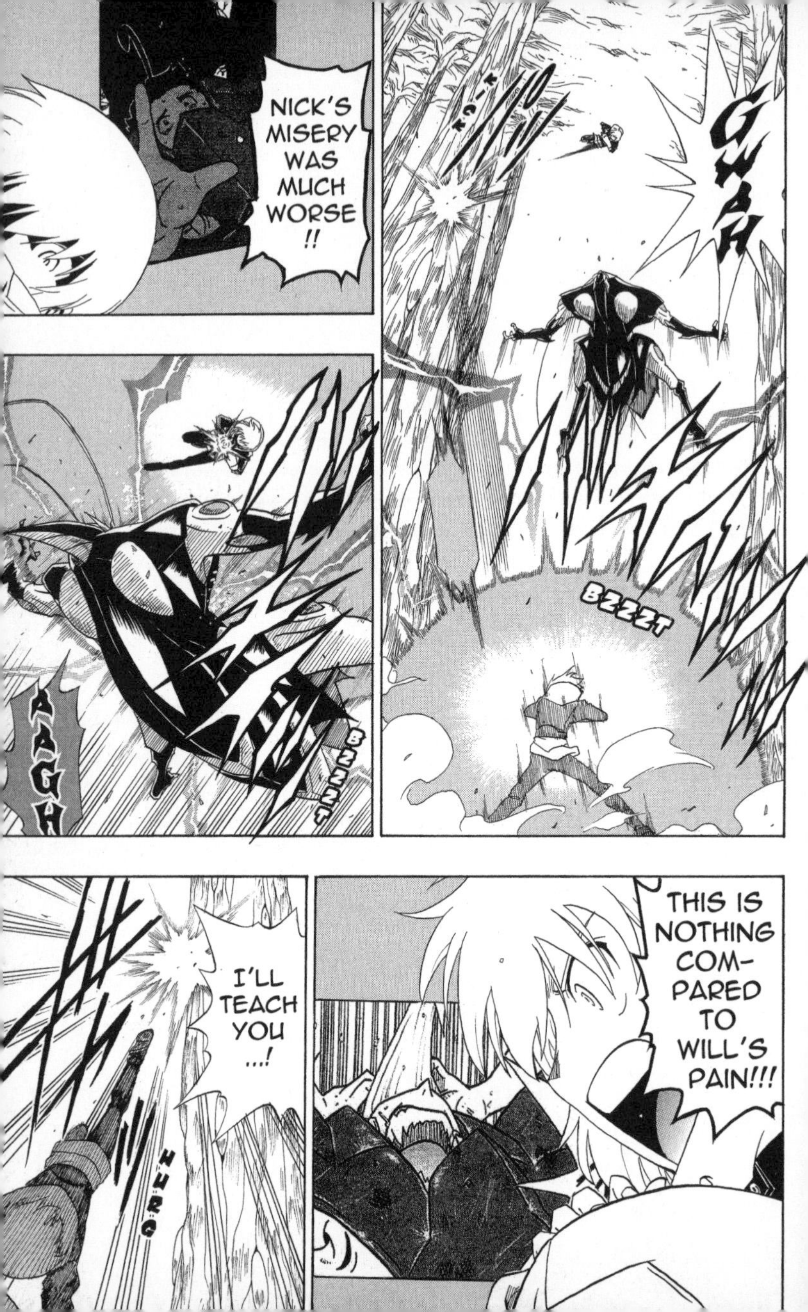
K-I-C-K
GWAH
BZZZT
NICK'S MISERY WAS MUCH WORSE !!
AAGH
BZZZZT
THIS IS NOTHING COM-PARED TO WILL'S PAIN!!!
I'LL TEACH YOU ...!
HÜRRG

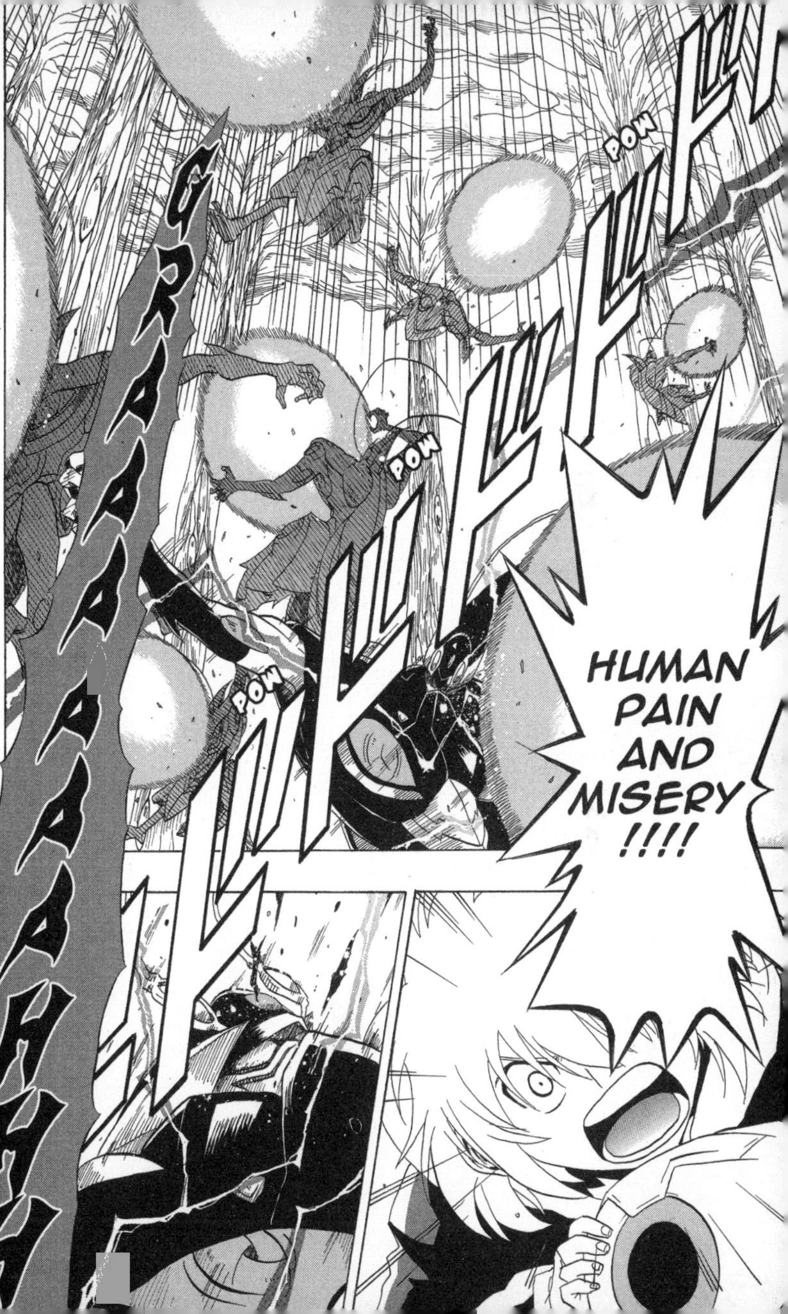
POW
HUMAN PAIN AND MISERY !!!!
POW
POW

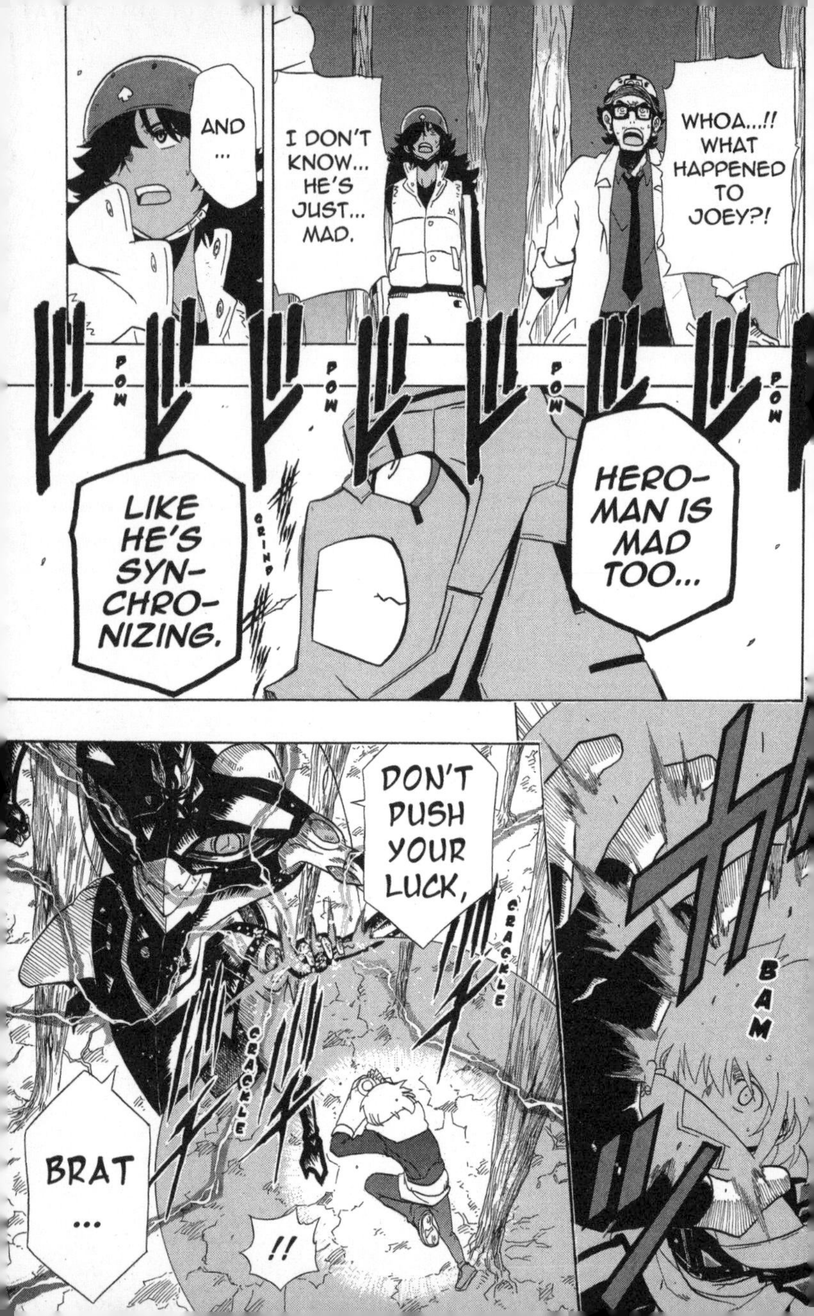
WHOA...!! WHAT HAPPENED TO JOEY?!
I DON'T KNOW... HE'S JUST... MAD.
AND ...
POW
POW
HERO-MAN IS MAD TOO...
POW
POW
GRIND
LIKE HE'S SYN-CHRO-NIZING.
BAM
DON'T PUSH YOUR LUCK,
CRACKLE
CRACKLE
BRAT ...
!!

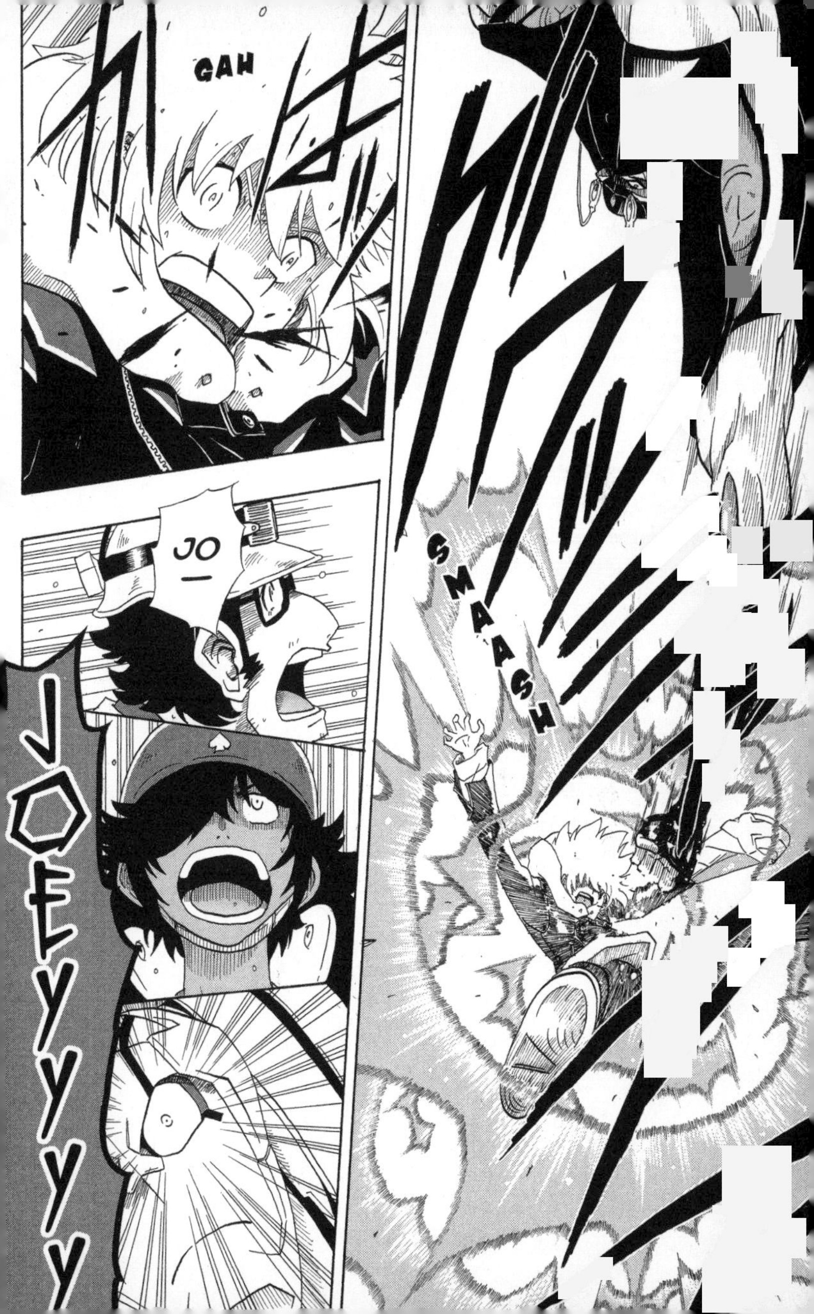
SMAAASH
GAH
JO—
JOEYYYY

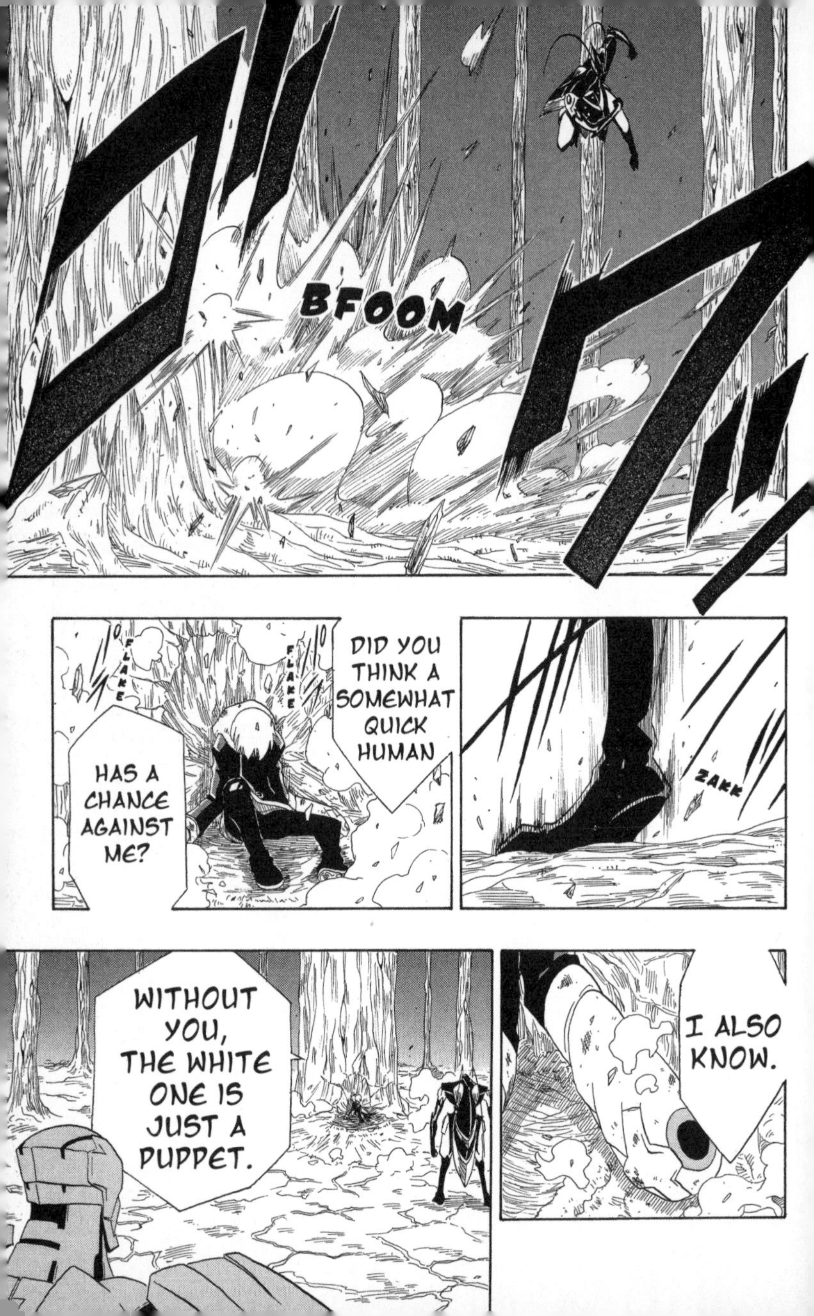
BFOOM
ZAKK
FLAKE
FLAKE
DID YOU THINK A SOMEWHAT QUICK HUMAN
HAS A CHANCE AGAINST ME?
I ALSO KNOW.
WITHOUT YOU, THE WHITE ONE IS JUST A PUPPET.

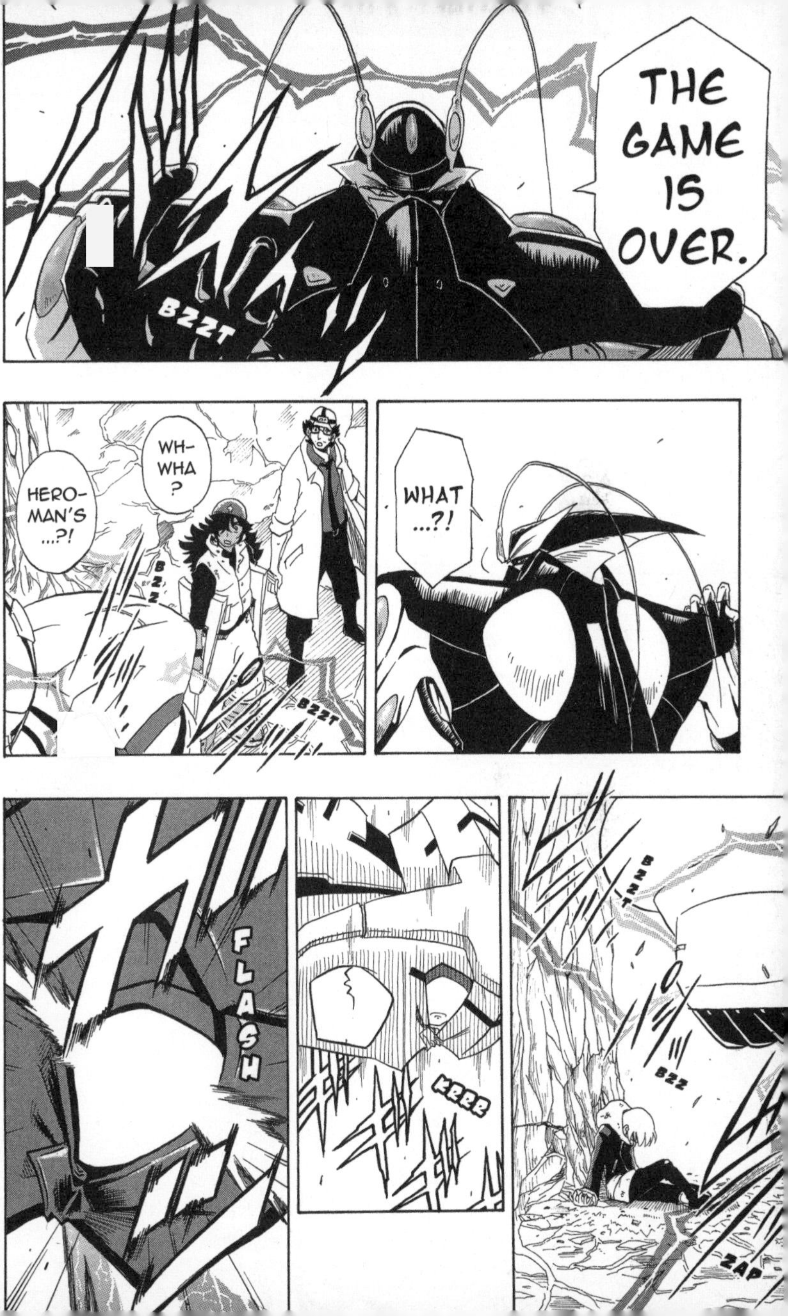
THE GAME IS OVER.
BZZT
WHAT ...?!
WH-WHA ?
HERO-MAN'S ...?!
BZZ
BZZT
BZZT
BZZ
ZAP
KRRR
FLASH

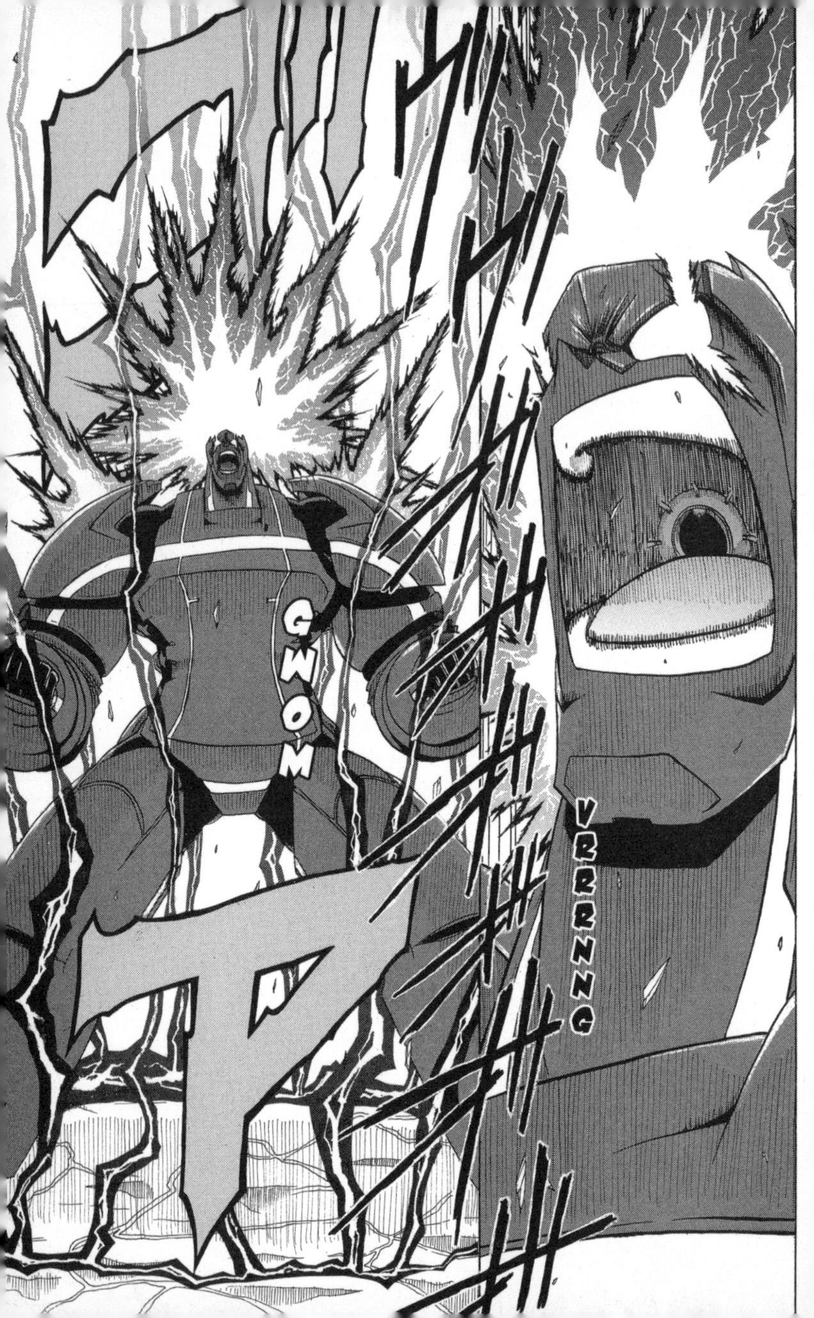
VRRRNNG
GWOM

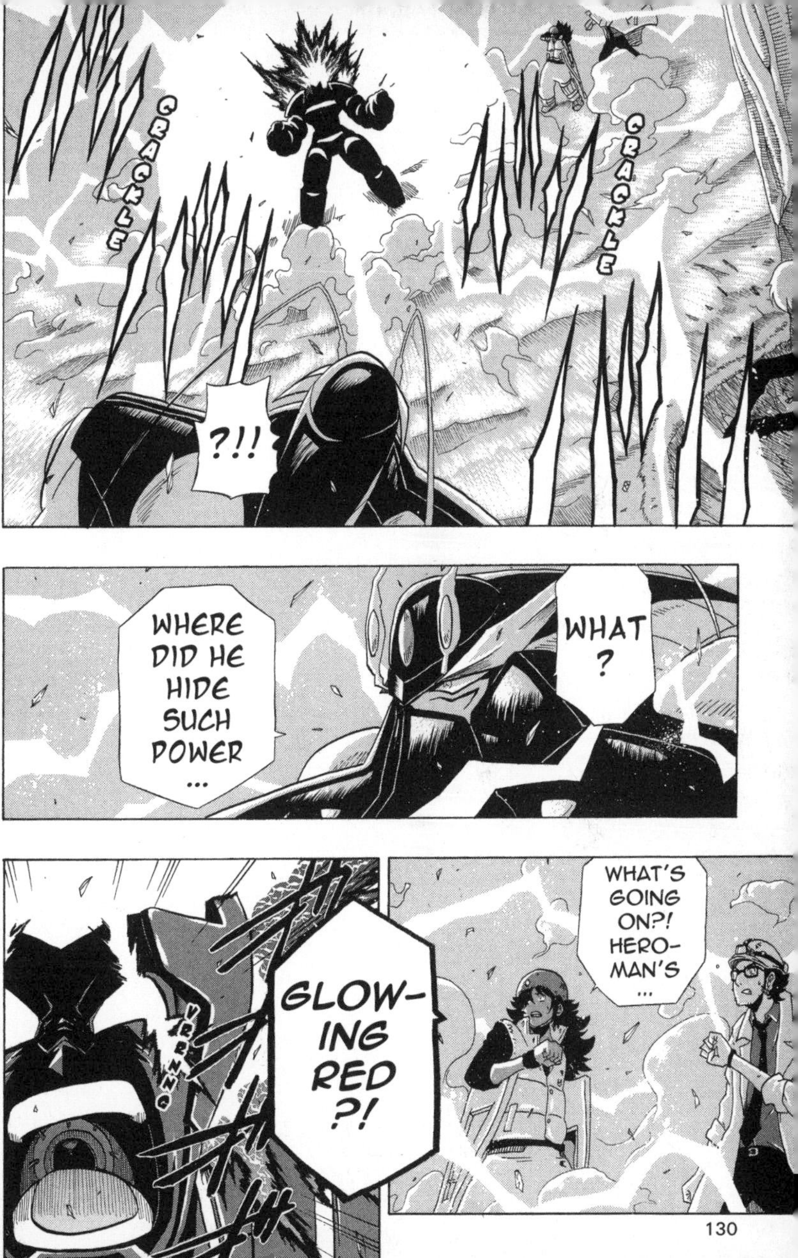
CRACKLE
CRACKLE
?!!
WHAT?
WHERE DID HE HIDE SUCH POWER...
WHAT'S GOING ON?! HERO-MAN'S...
GLOWING RED?!
VRRNNG

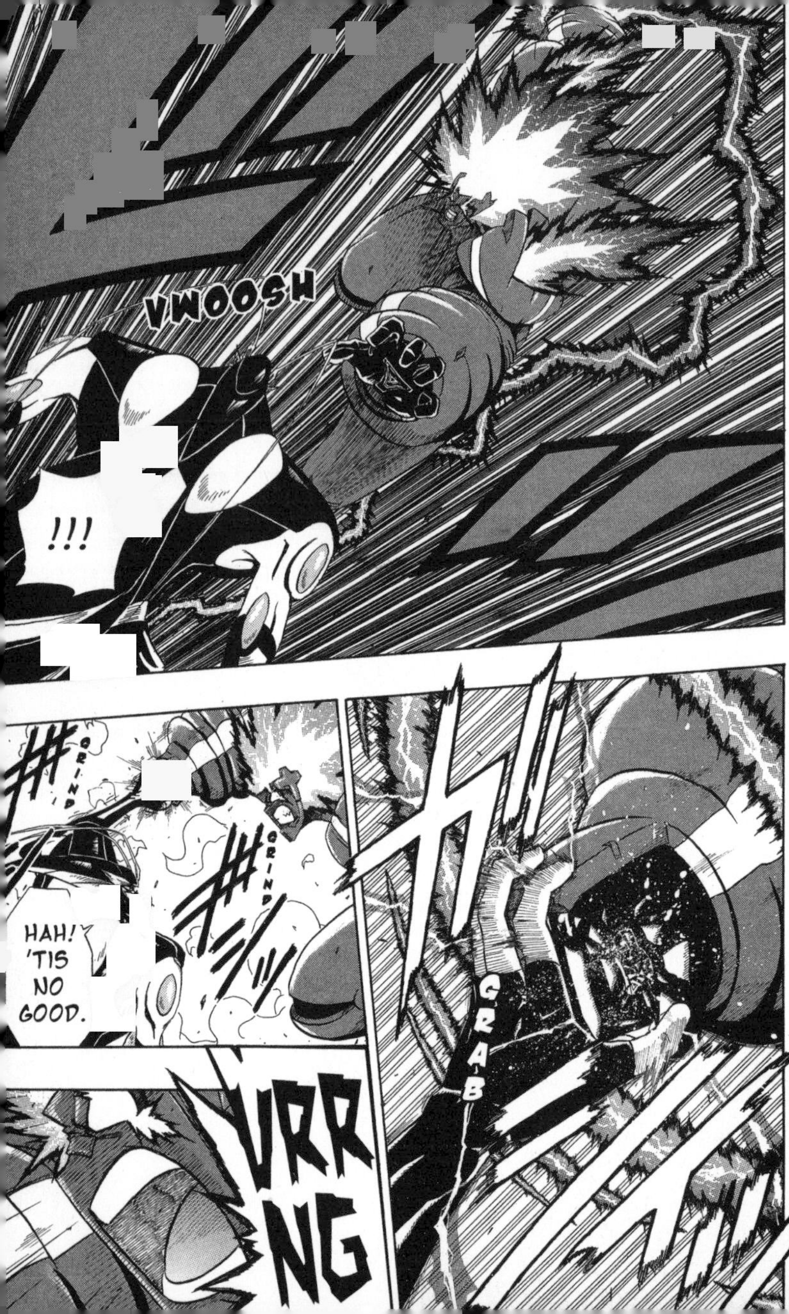
VWOOSH
!!!
GRAB
GRIND
GRIND
HAH! 'TIS NO GOOD.
VRRNG

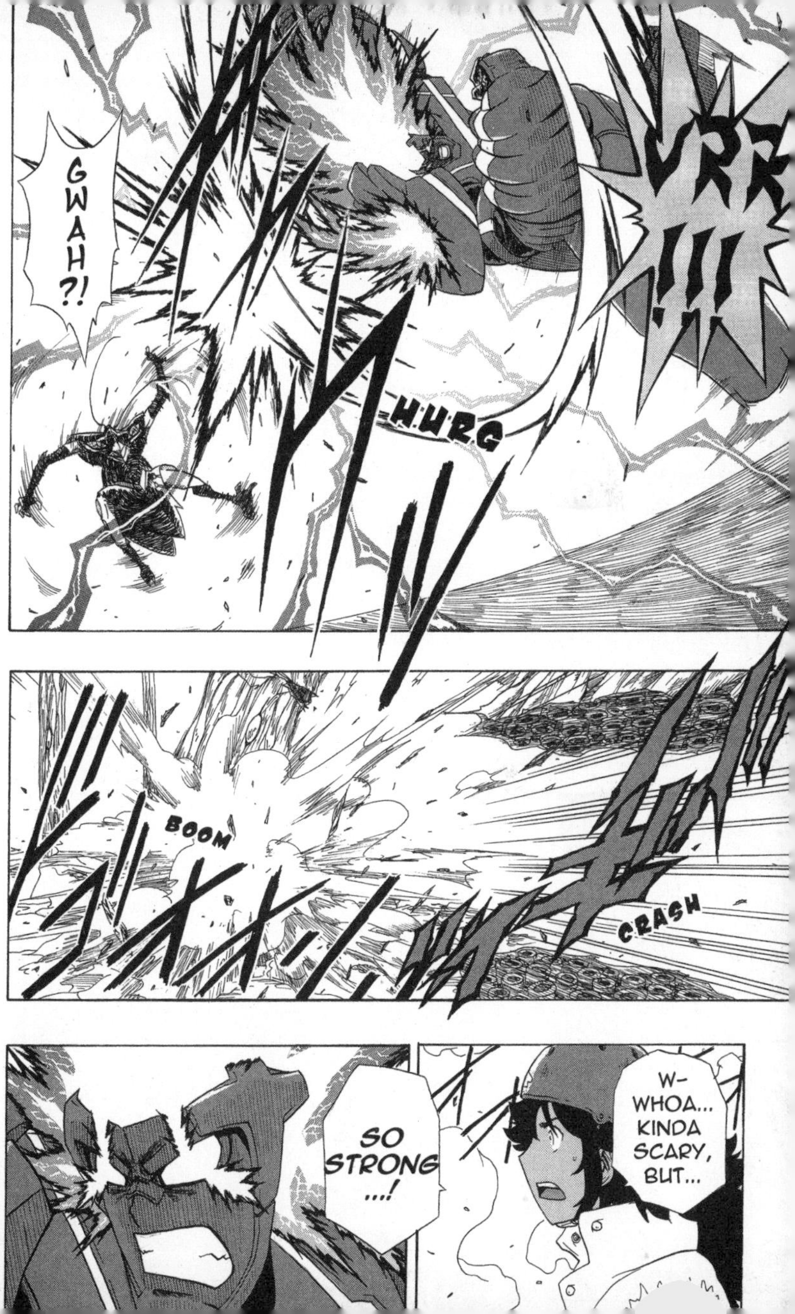
URR!!!
GWAH?!
HURG
CRASH
BOOM
W-WHOA... KINDA SCARY, BUT...
SO STRONG...!

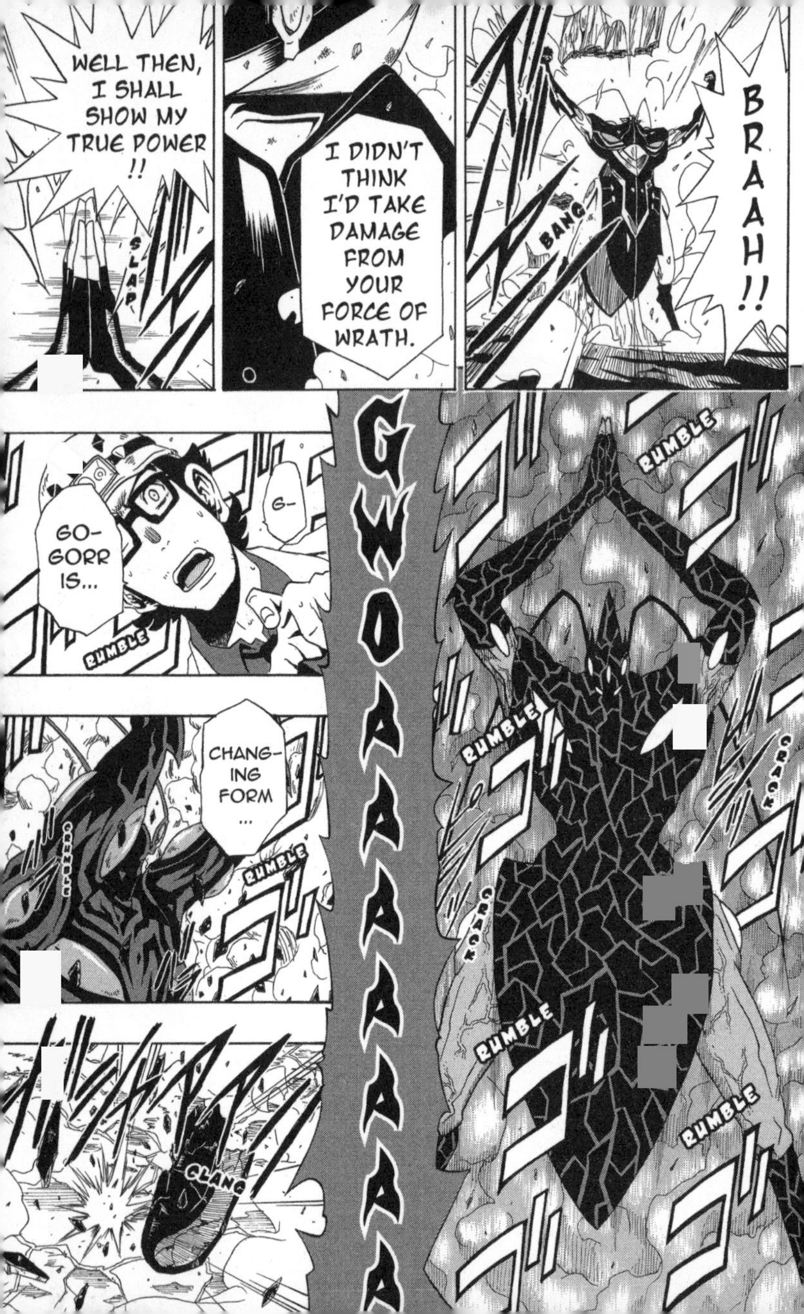
BRAAH!!
BANG
I DIDN'T THINK I'D TAKE DAMAGE FROM YOUR FORCE OF WRATH.
WELL THEN, I SHALL SHOW MY TRUE POWER!!
SLAP
GWOAAAAAAAA
RUMBLE
RUMBLE
CRACK
CRACK
RUMBLE
RUMBLE
G-
GO-GORR IS...
RUMBLE
CHANGING FORM...
CRUMBLE
RUMBLE
CLANG

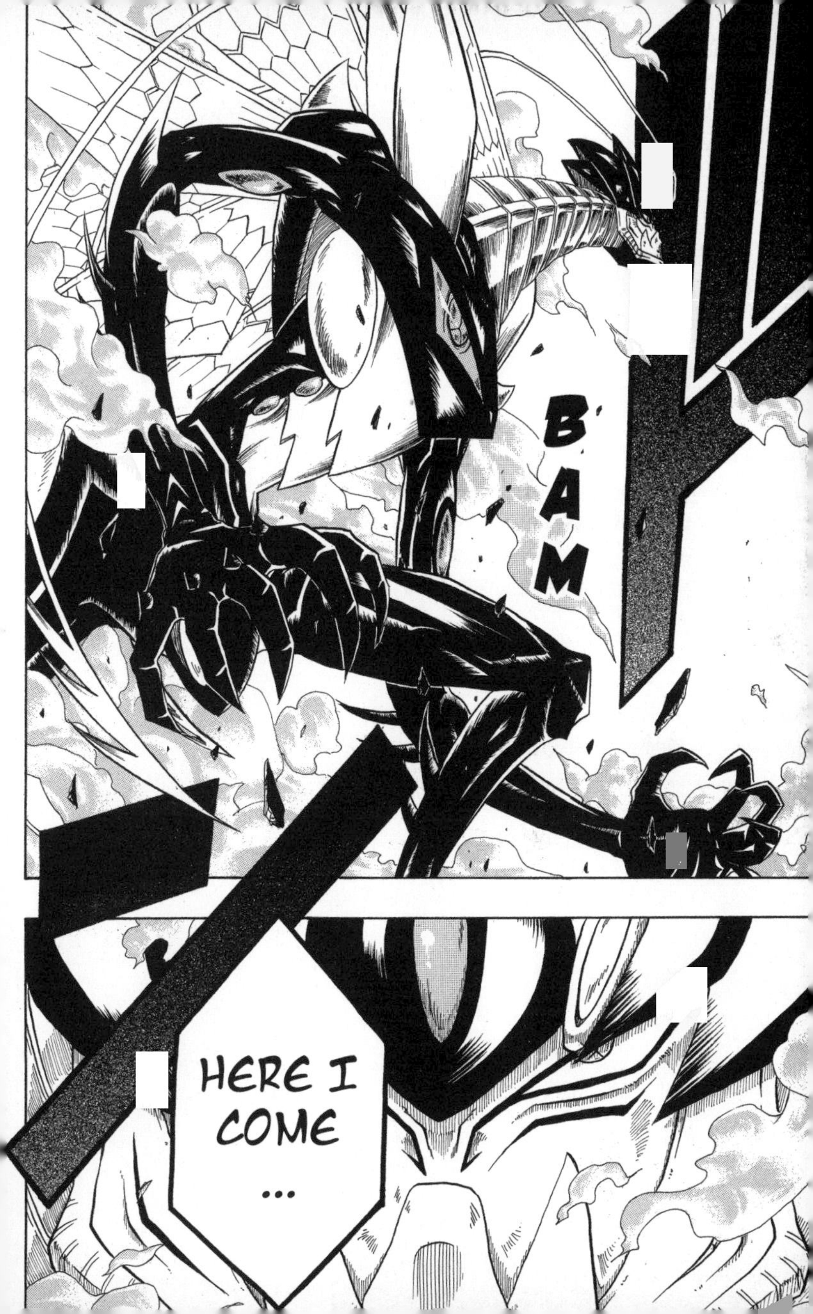
BAM
HERE I COME ...

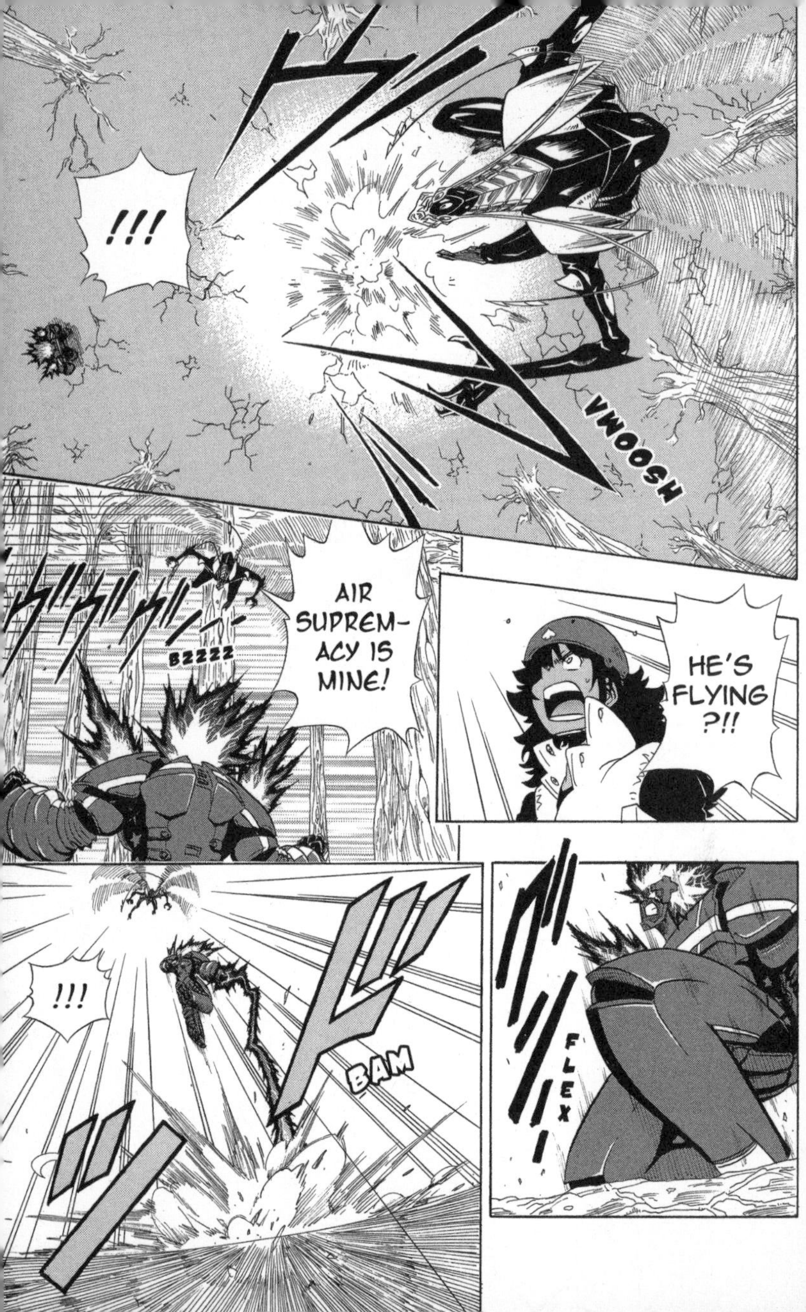
!!!
VWOOSH
HE'S FLYING ?!!
AIR SUPREM-ACY IS MINE!
BZZZZ
FLEX
!!!
BAM

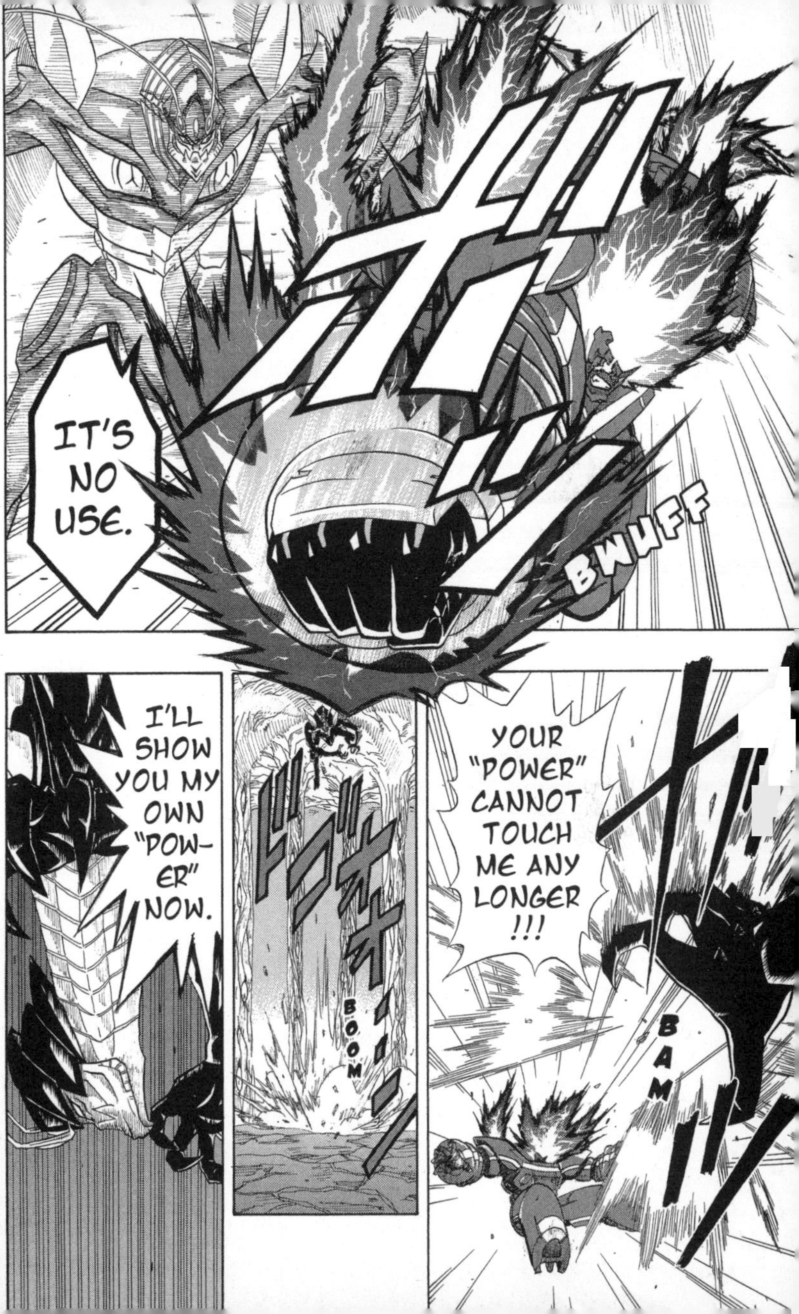
IT'S NO USE.
BWUFF
YOUR "POWER" CANNOT TOUCH ME ANY LONGER!!!
BAM
BOOM
I'LL SHOW YOU MY OWN "POW-ER" NOW.

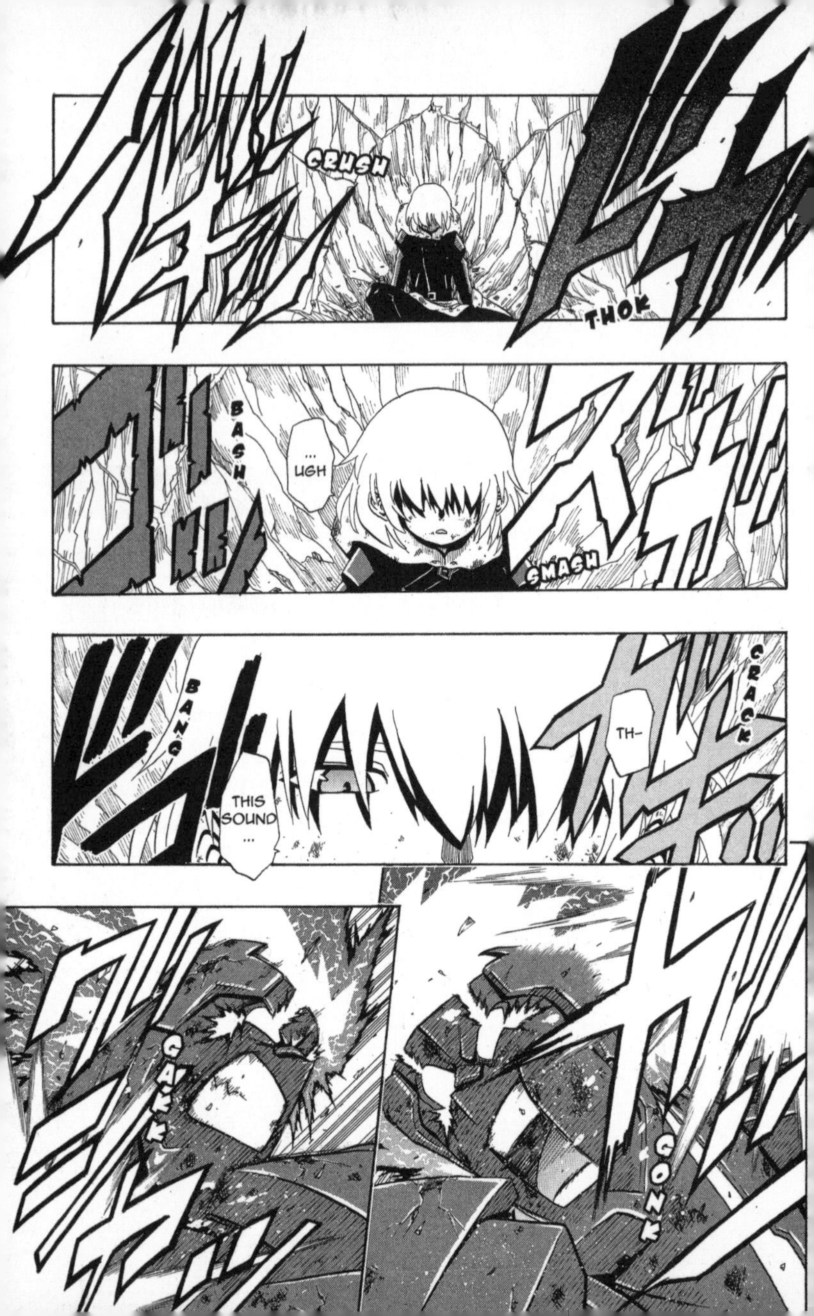
THOK
CRUSH
SMASH
... UGH
BASH
CRACK
TH-
THIS SOUND ...
BANG
GONK
GAKK

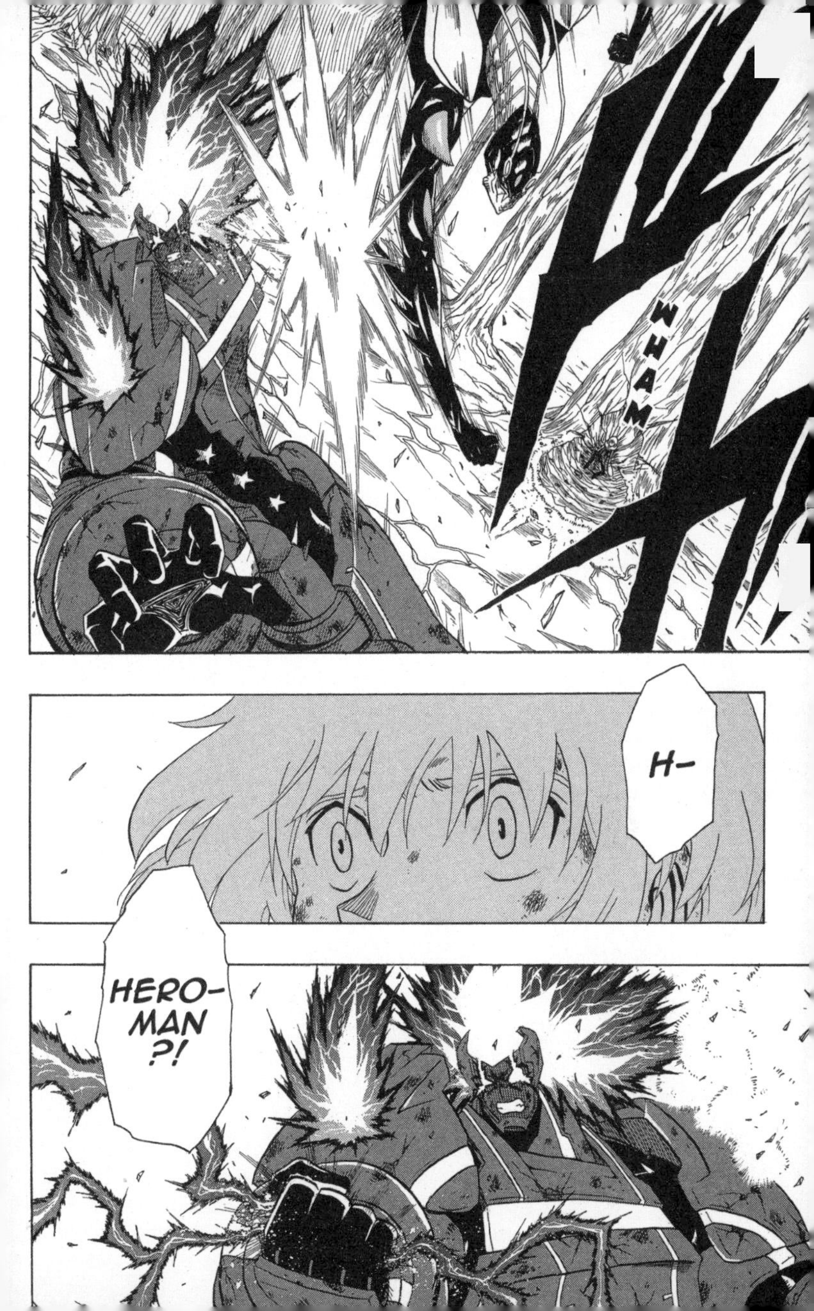
WHAM
H-
HERO-MAN?!

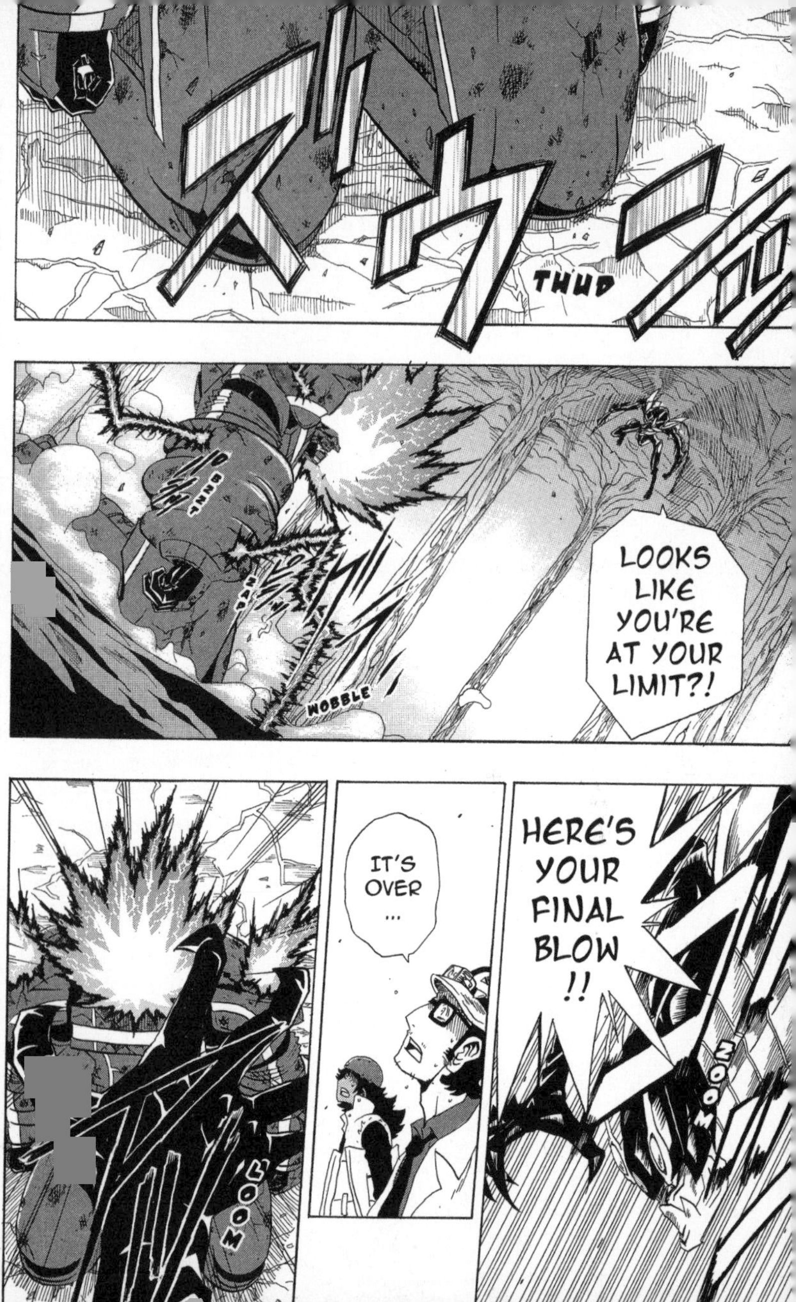
THUD
LOOKS LIKE YOU'RE AT YOUR LIMIT?!
BZZT
ZAP
WOBBLE
HERE'S YOUR FINAL BLOW!!
ZOOM
IT'S OVER...
LOOM

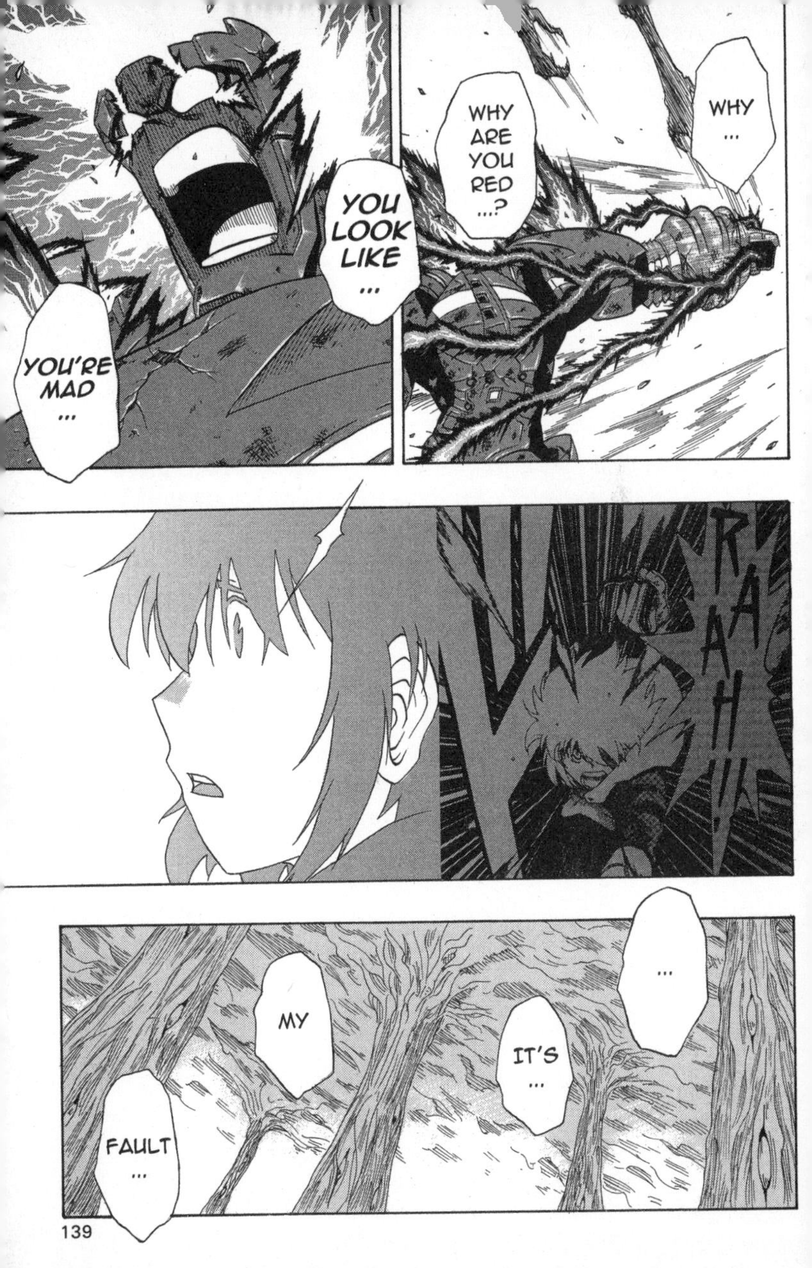
WHY ...
WHY ARE YOU RED ...?
YOU LOOK LIKE ...
YOU'RE MAD ...
RAAHH!!
...
IT'S ...
MY
FAULT ...

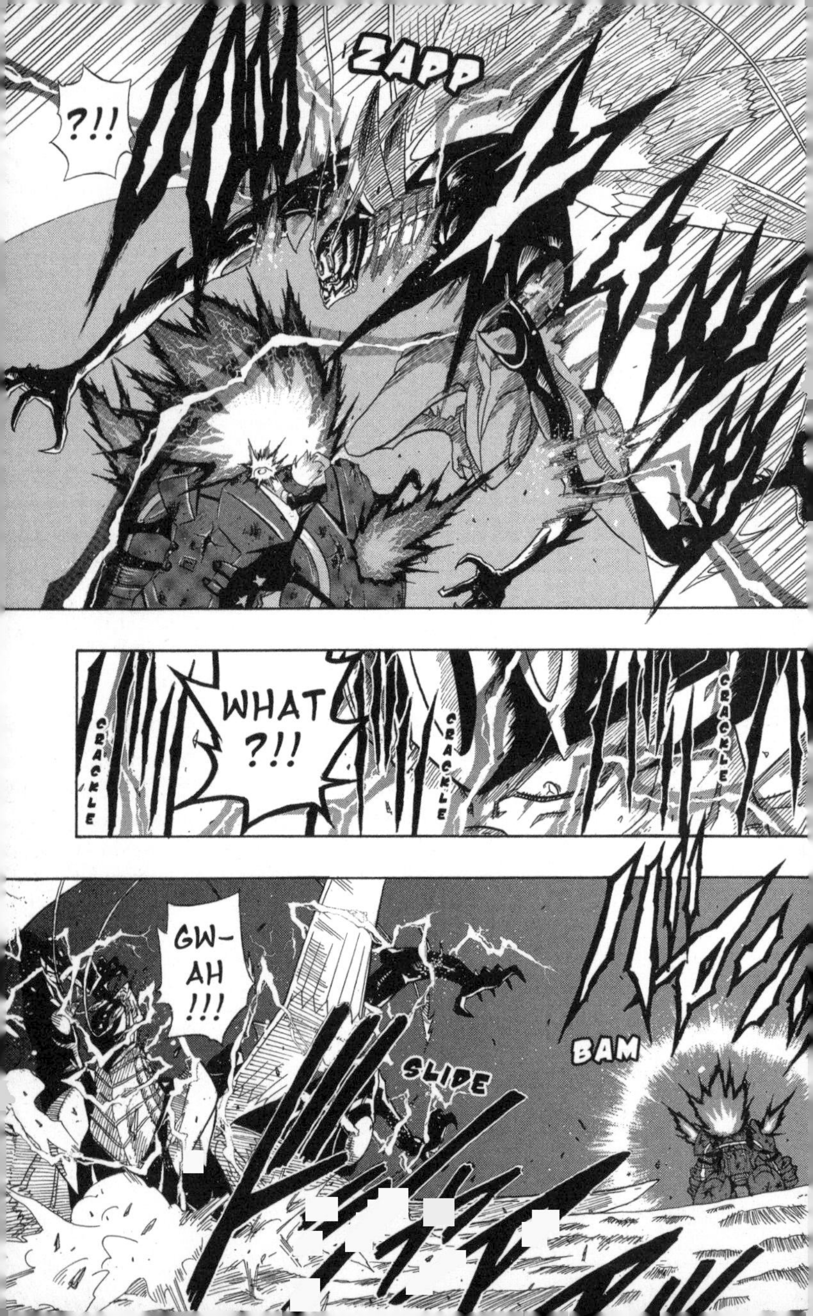
ZAPP
?!!
CRACKLE
CRACKLE
WHAT ?!!
CRACKLE
BAM
SLIDE
GW-AH !!!

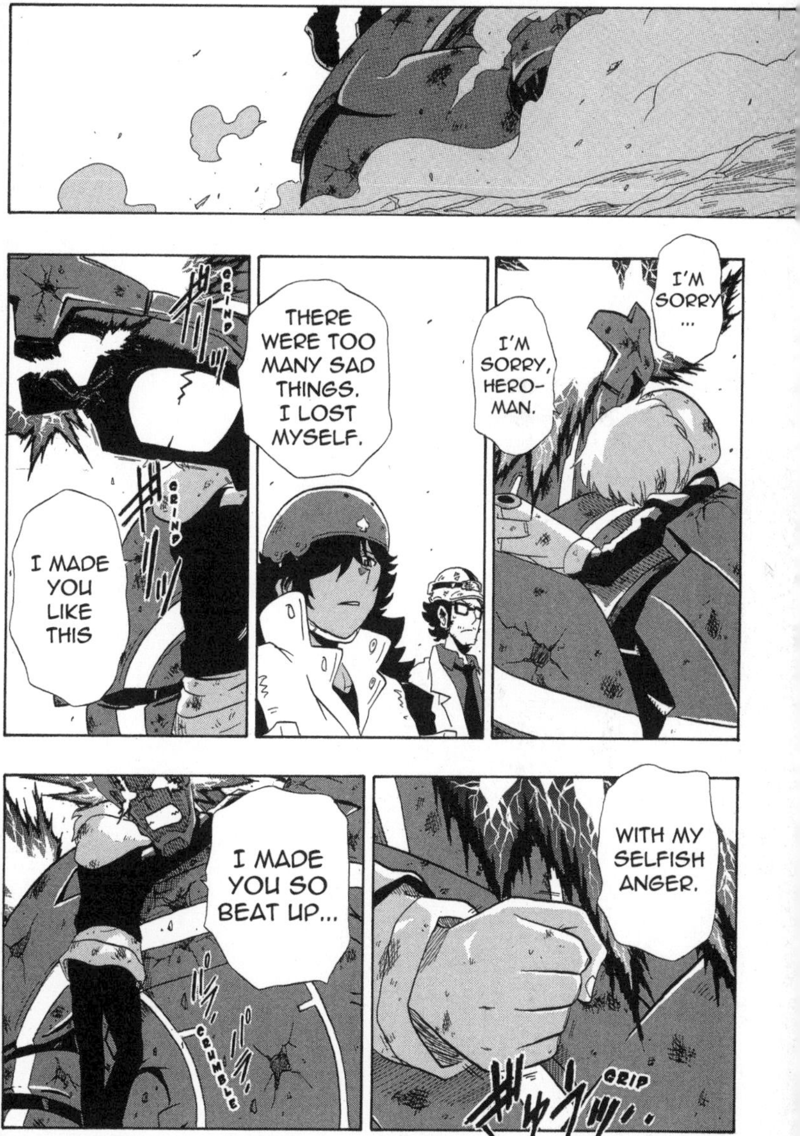
I'M SORRY...
I'M SORRY, HERO-MAN.
THERE WERE TOO MANY SAD THINGS. I LOST MYSELF.
GRIND
GRIND
I MADE YOU LIKE THIS
WITH MY SELFISH ANGER.
GRIP
I MADE YOU SO BEAT UP...
CRUMBLE

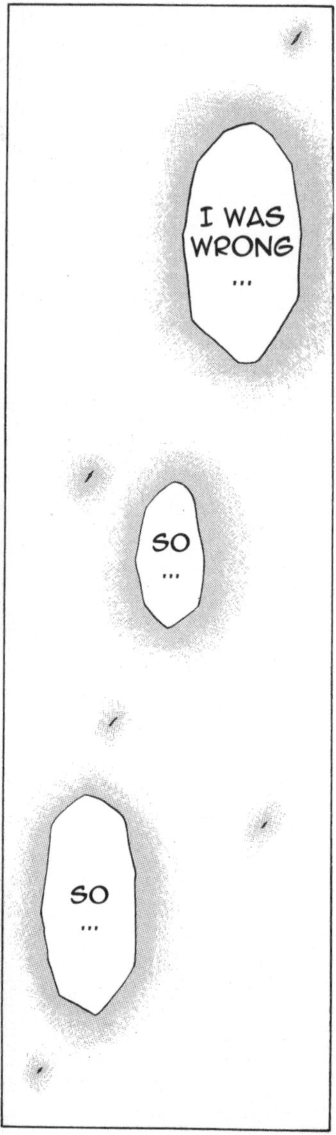
I WAS WRONG ...
SO ...
SO ...

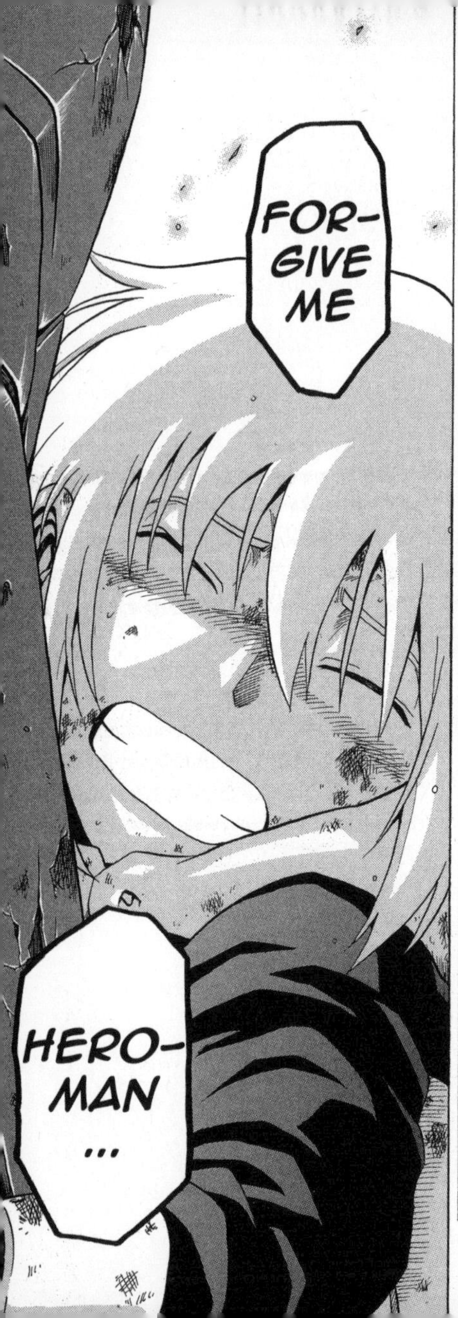
FOR-GIVE ME
HERO-MAN ...

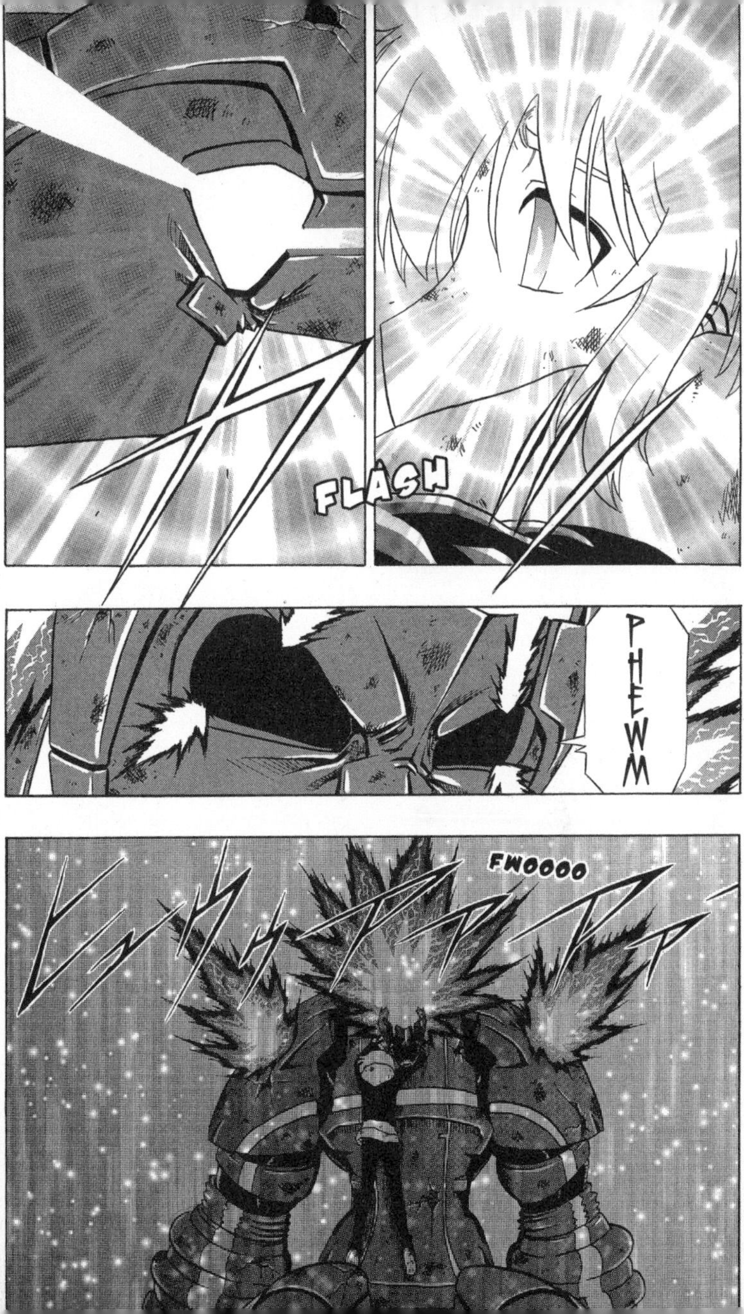
FLASH
PHEWM
FWOOOO

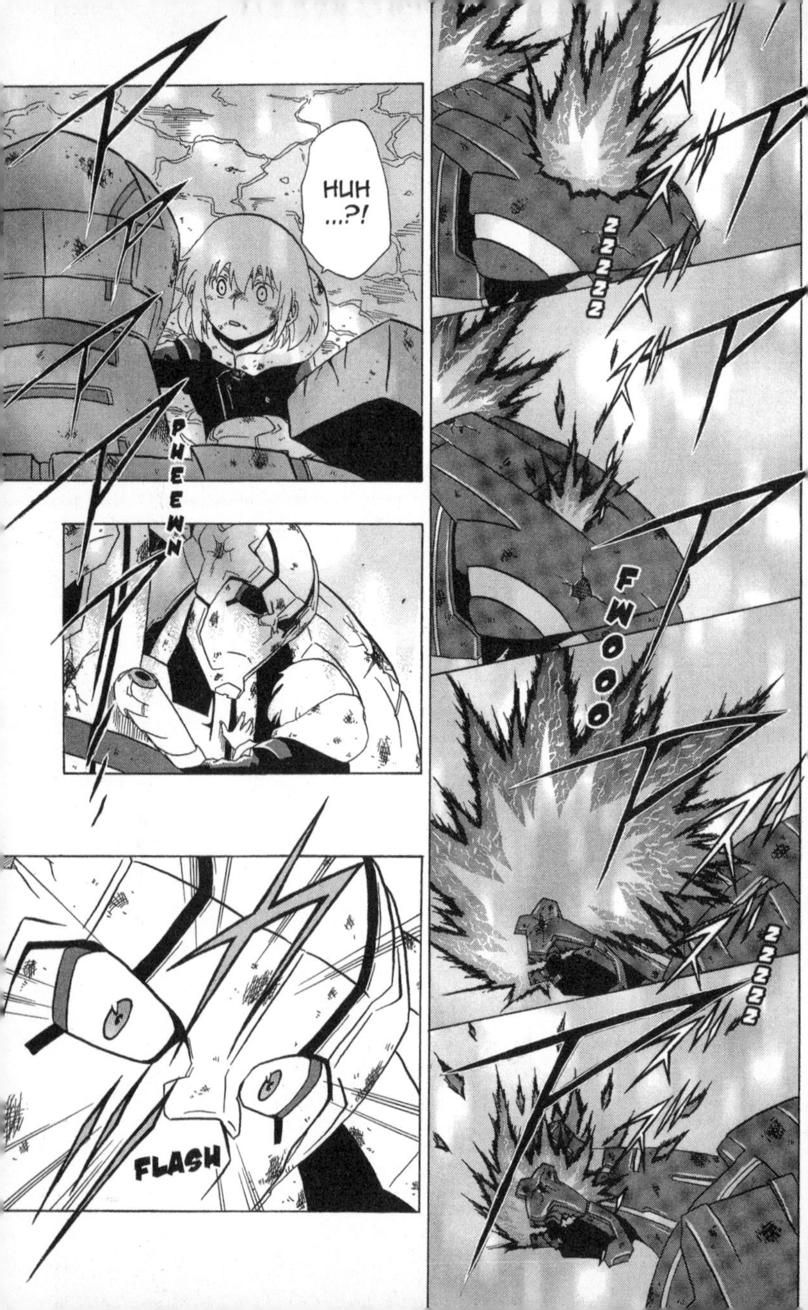
ZZZZZ
FWOOOO
ZZZZZ
HUH ...?!
PHEEWN
FLASH

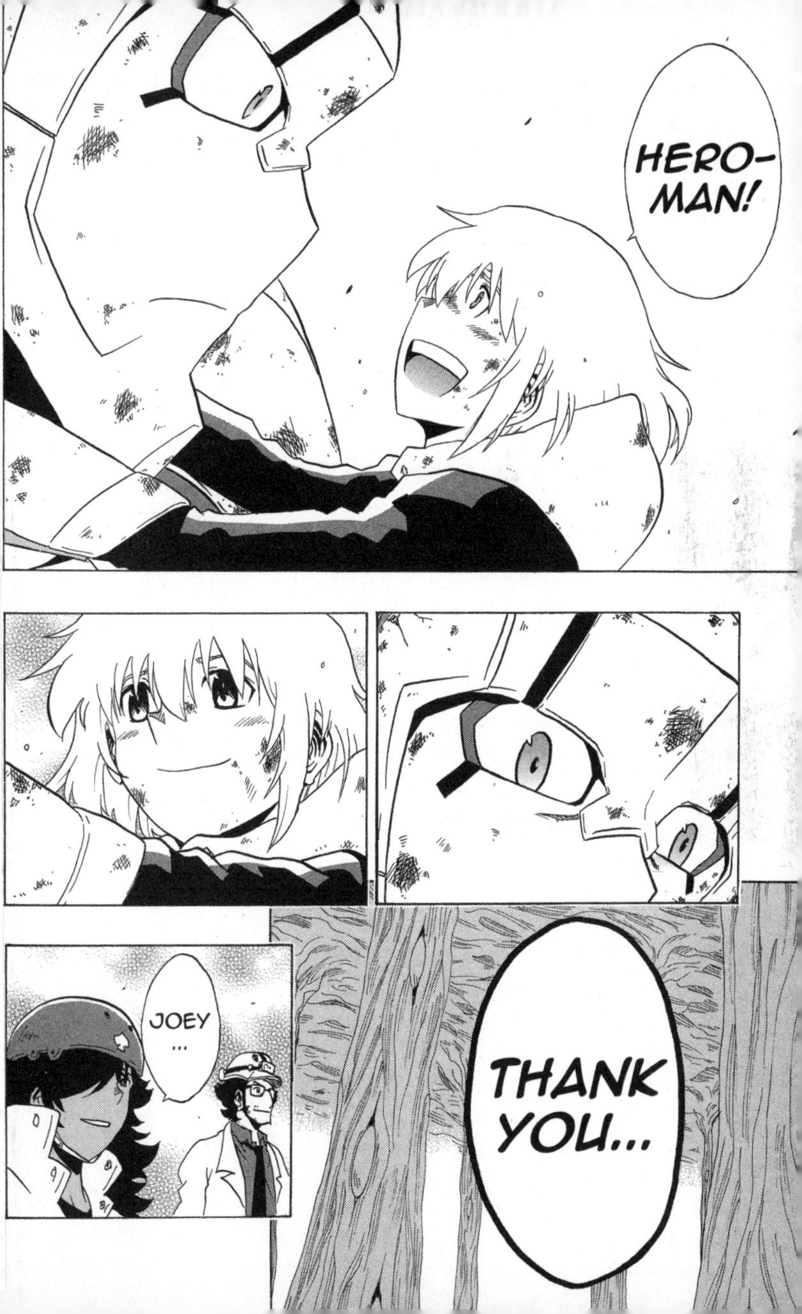
HERO-MAN!
THANK YOU...
JOEY ...

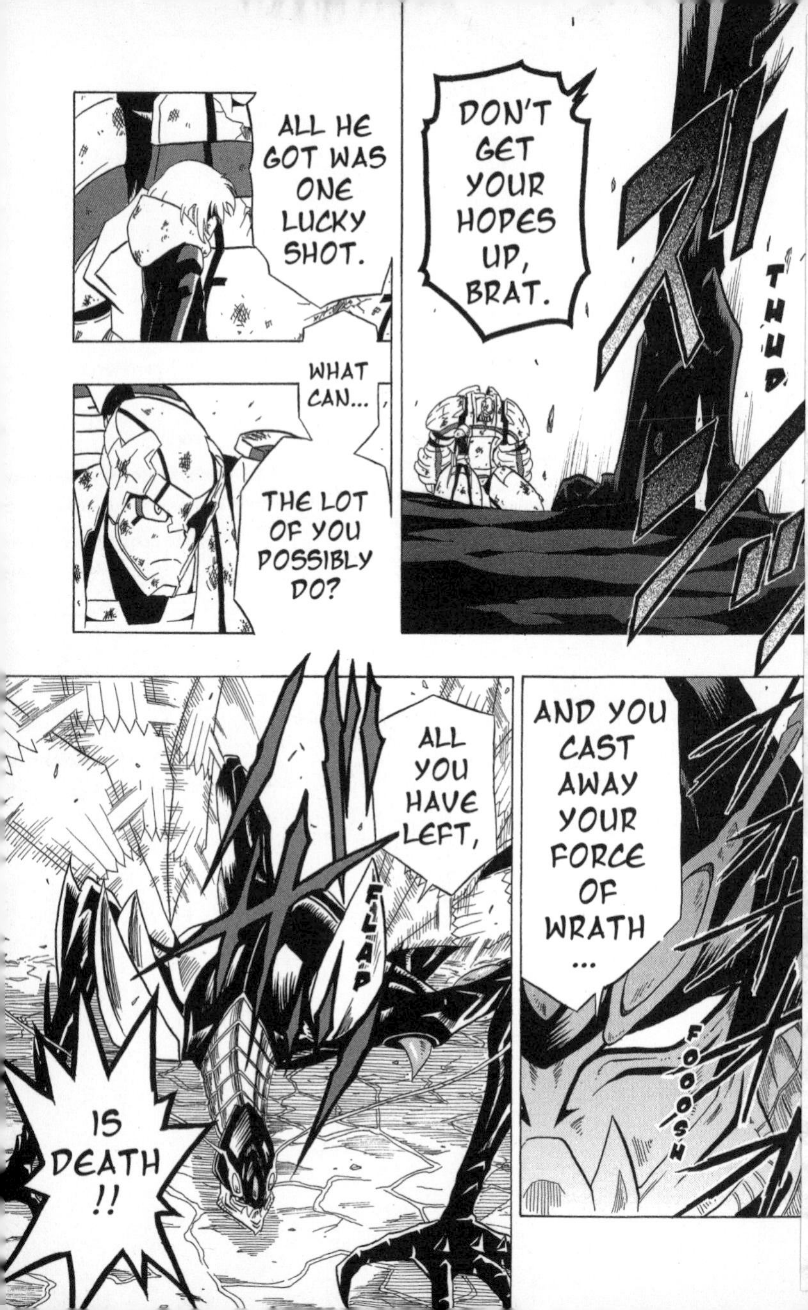
DON'T GET YOUR HOPES UP, BRAT.
THUD
ALL HE GOT WAS ONE LUCKY SHOT.
WHAT CAN...
THE LOT OF YOU POSSIBLY DO?
AND YOU CAST AWAY YOUR FORCE OF WRATH ...
FOOOOSH
ALL YOU HAVE LEFT,
FLAP
IS DEATH !!

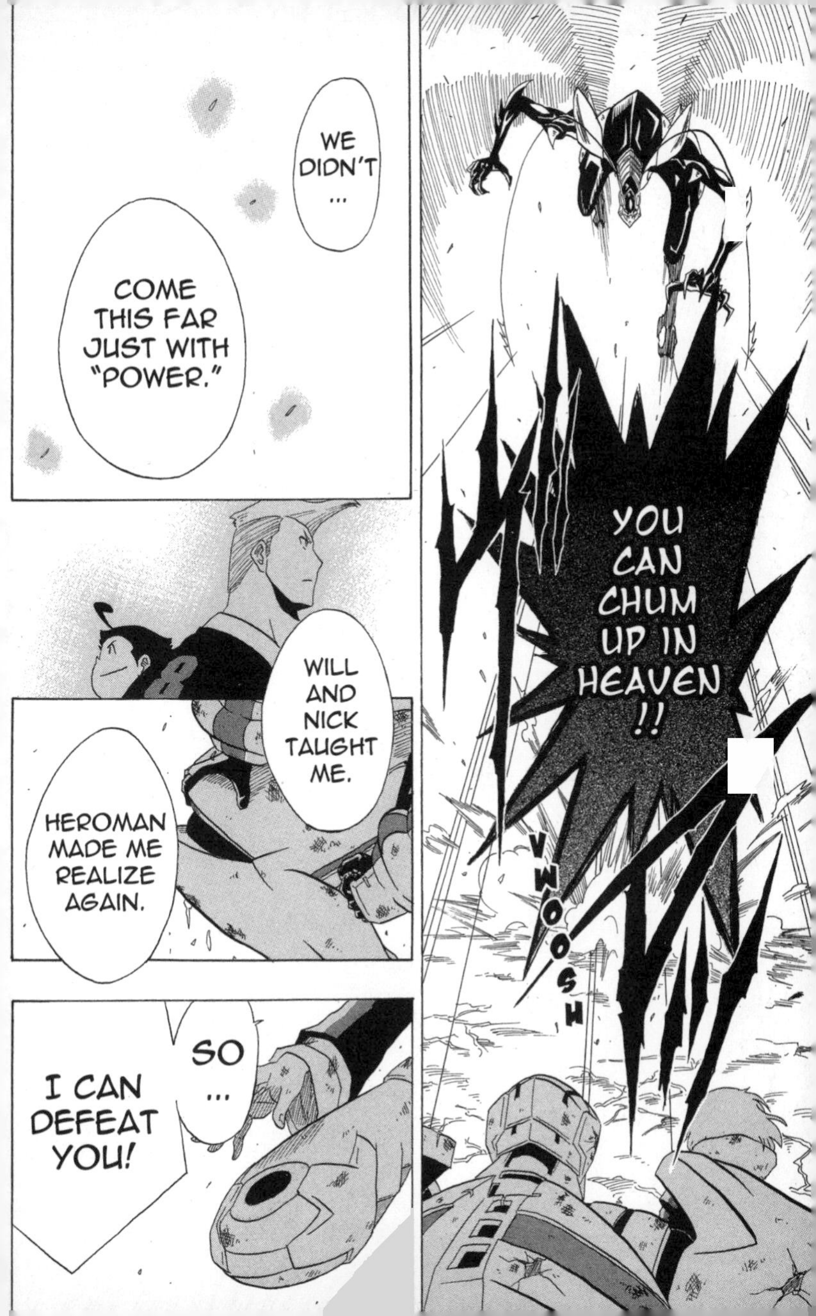
YOU CAN CHUM UP IN HEAVEN!!
VWOOOSH
WE DIDN'T ...
COME THIS FAR JUST WITH "POWER."
WILL AND NICK TAUGHT ME.
HEROMAN MADE ME REALIZE AGAIN.
SO ...
I CAN DEFEAT YOU!

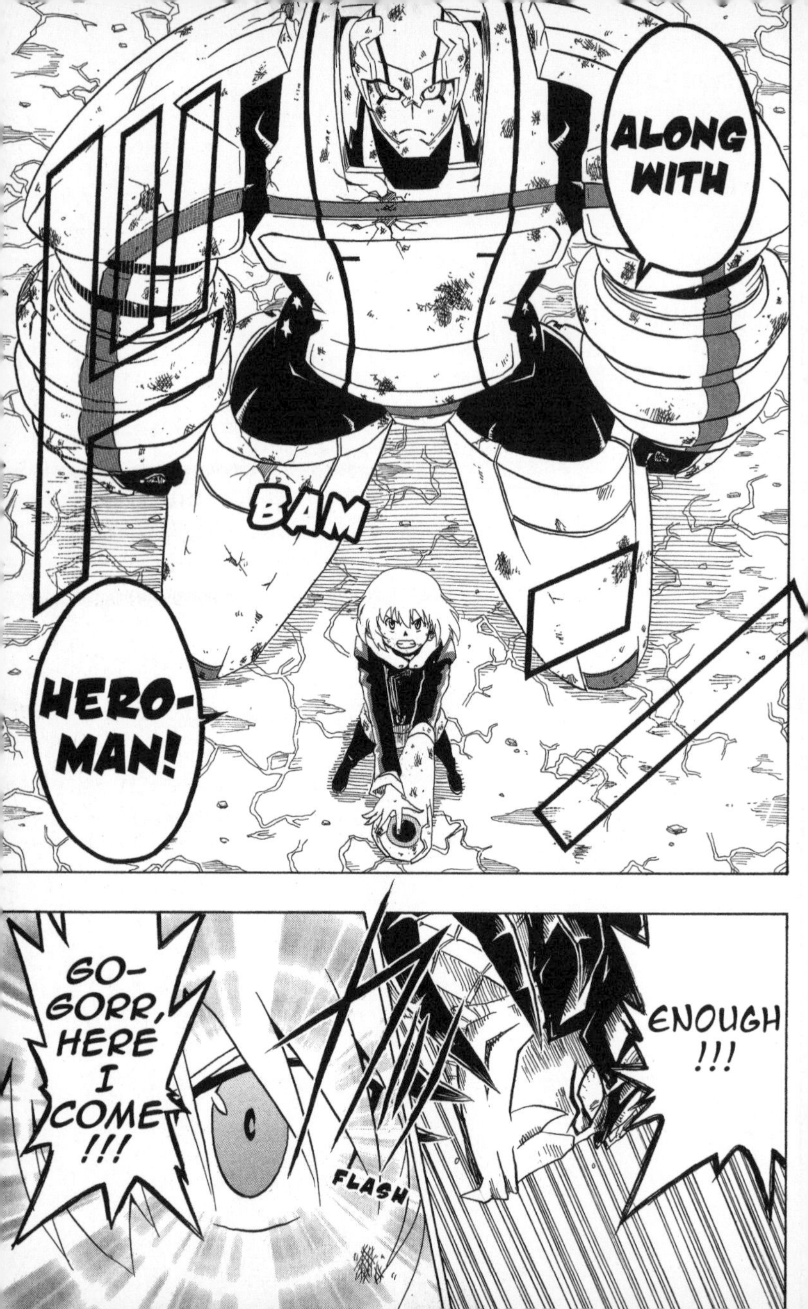
ALONG WITH
BAM
HERO-MAN!
ENOUGH!!!
FLASH
GO-GORR, HERE I COME!!!

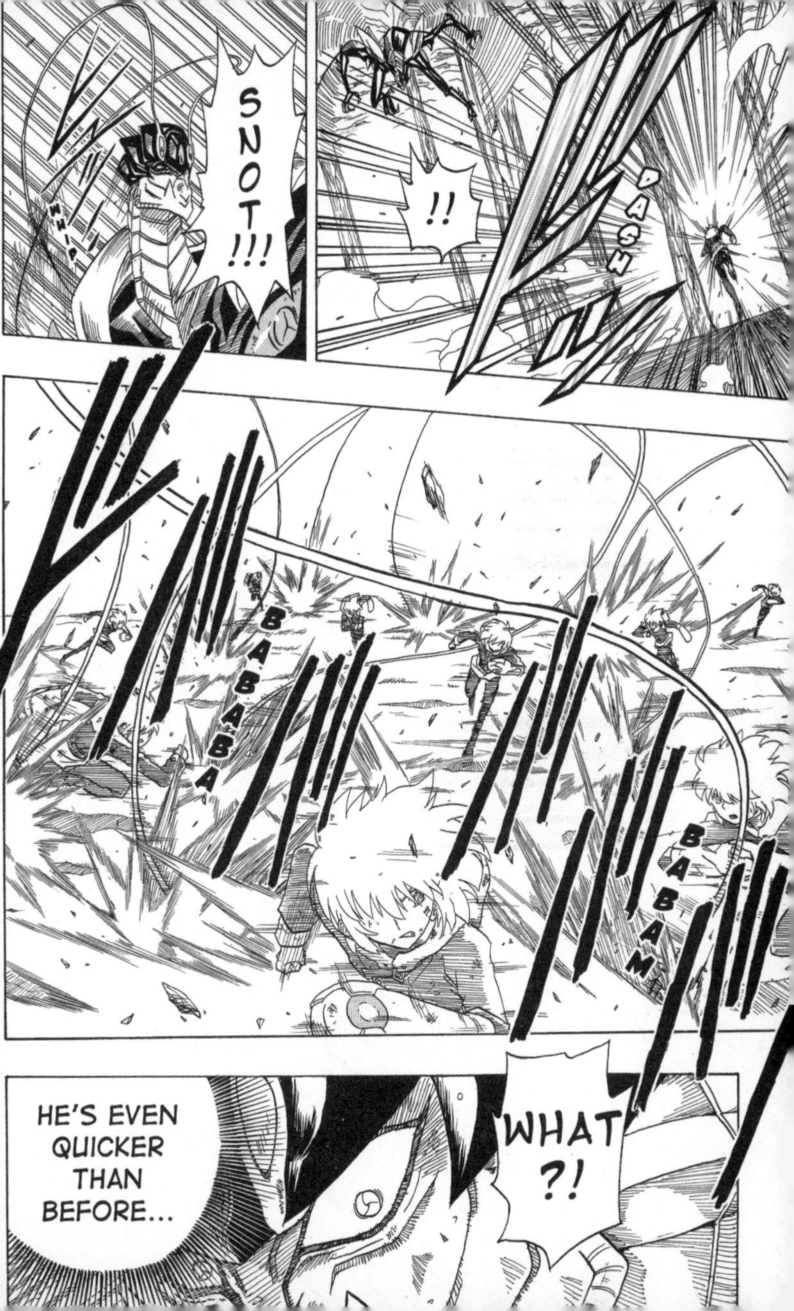
DASH
!!
SNOT!!!
WHIP
BABAM
BABABABA
WHAT?!
HE'S EVEN QUICKER THAN BEFORE...

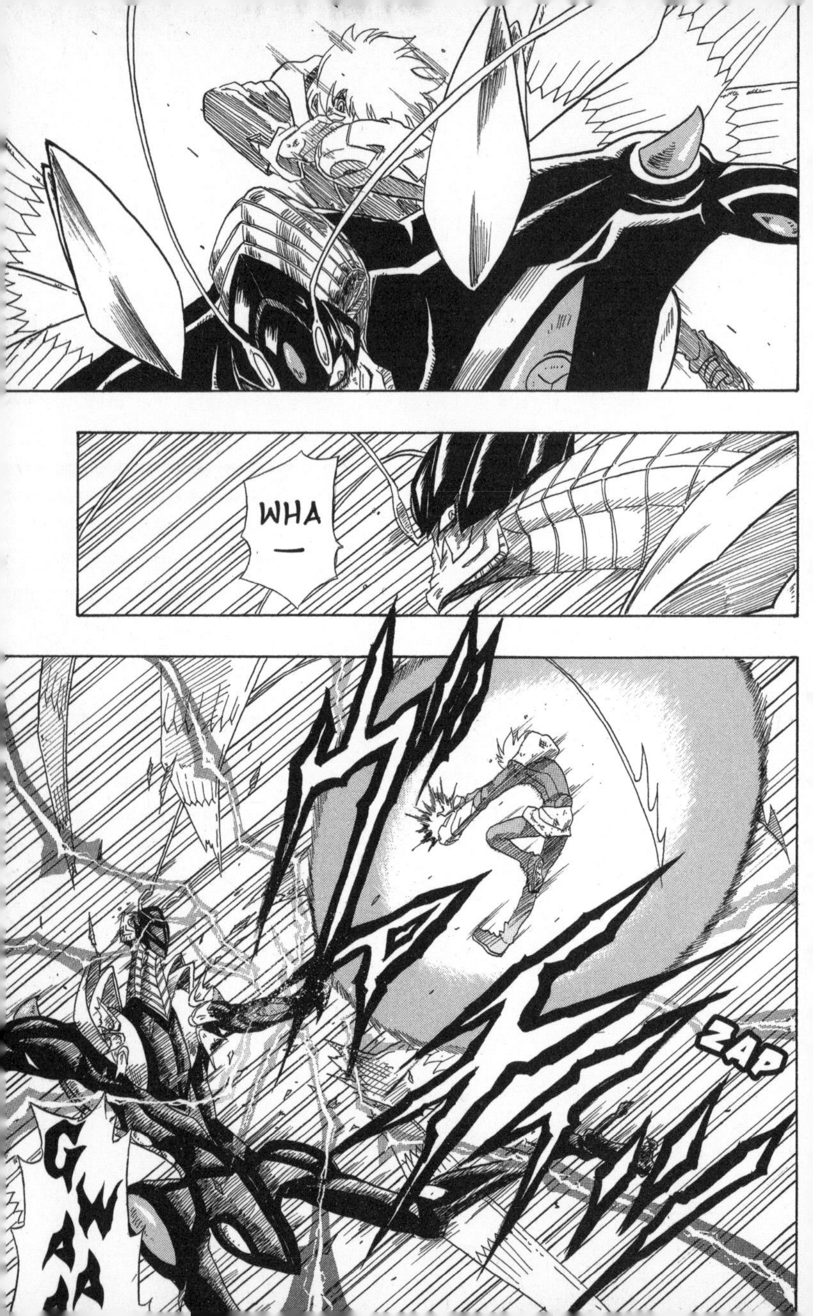
WHA —
ZAP
GWAAAA

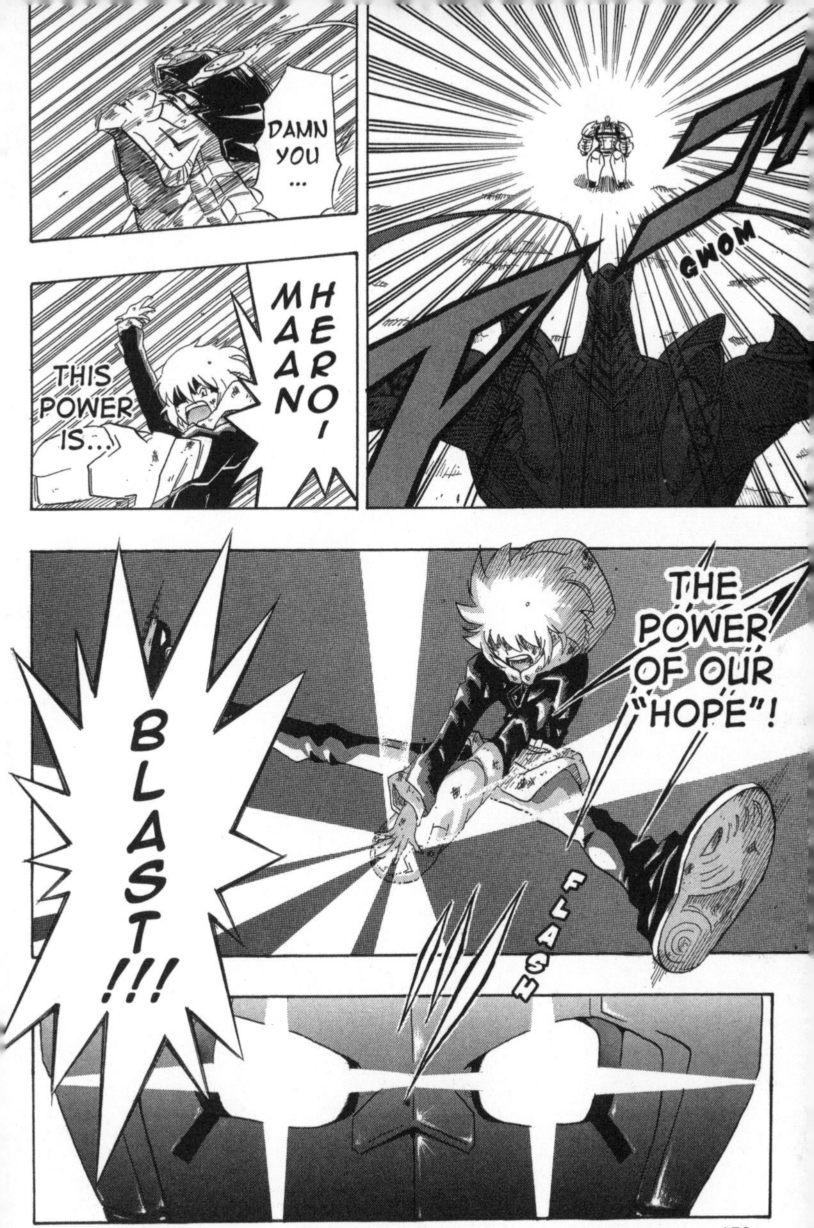
GWOM
DAMN YOU ...
HERO, MAAN
THIS POWER IS...
THE POWER OF OUR "HOPE"!
BLAST!!!
FLASH

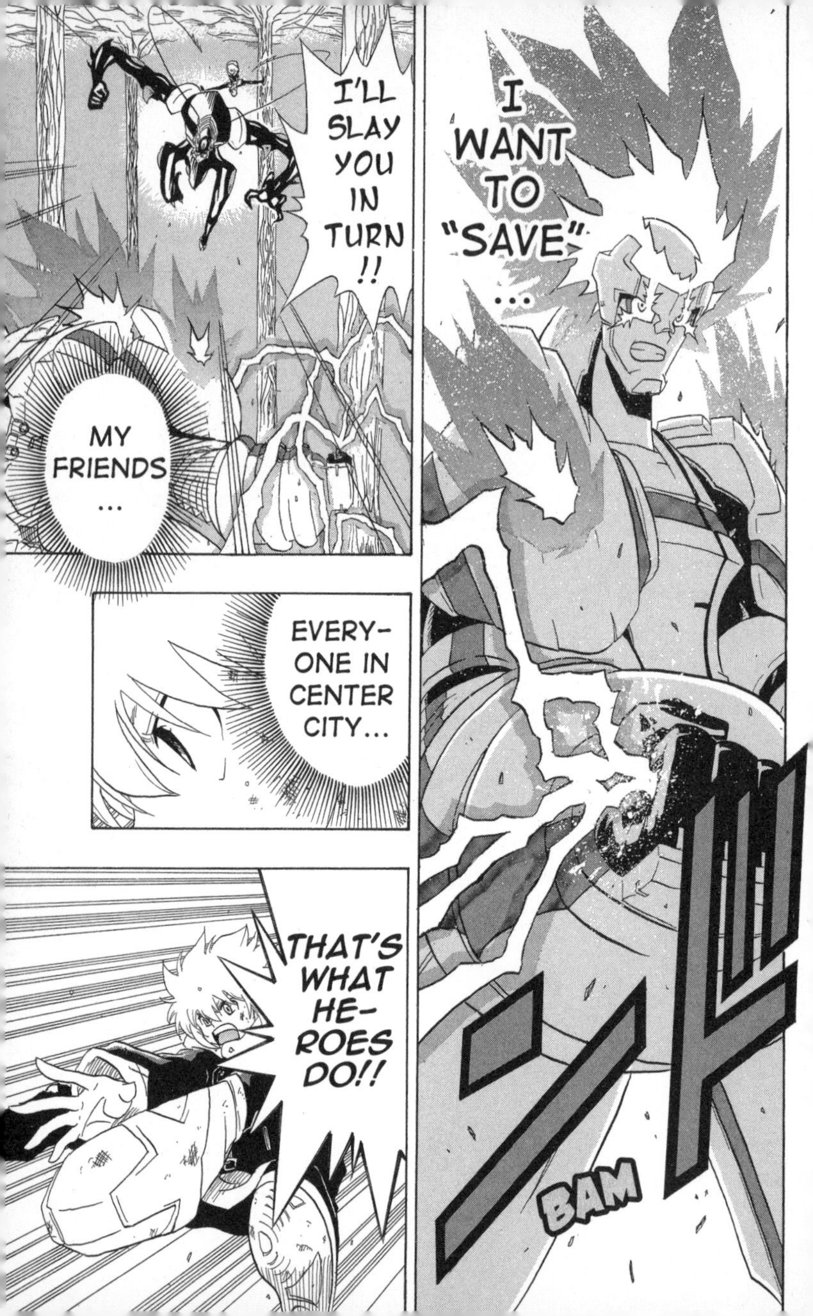

I WANT TO "SAVE"...
BAM
I'LL SLAY YOU IN TURN!!
MY FRIENDS...
EVERY-ONE IN CENTER CITY...
THAT'S WHAT HE-ROES DO!!

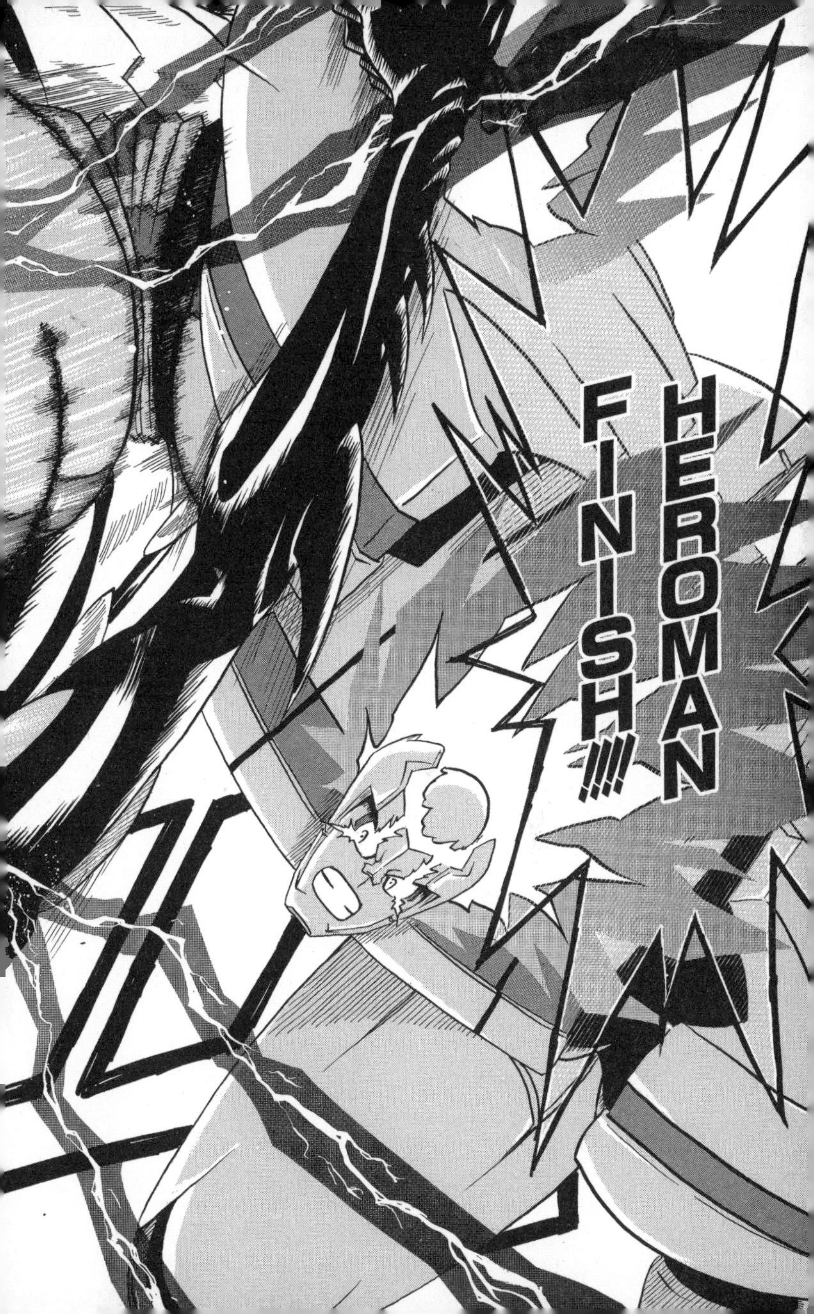
HEROMAN
FINISH!!!!

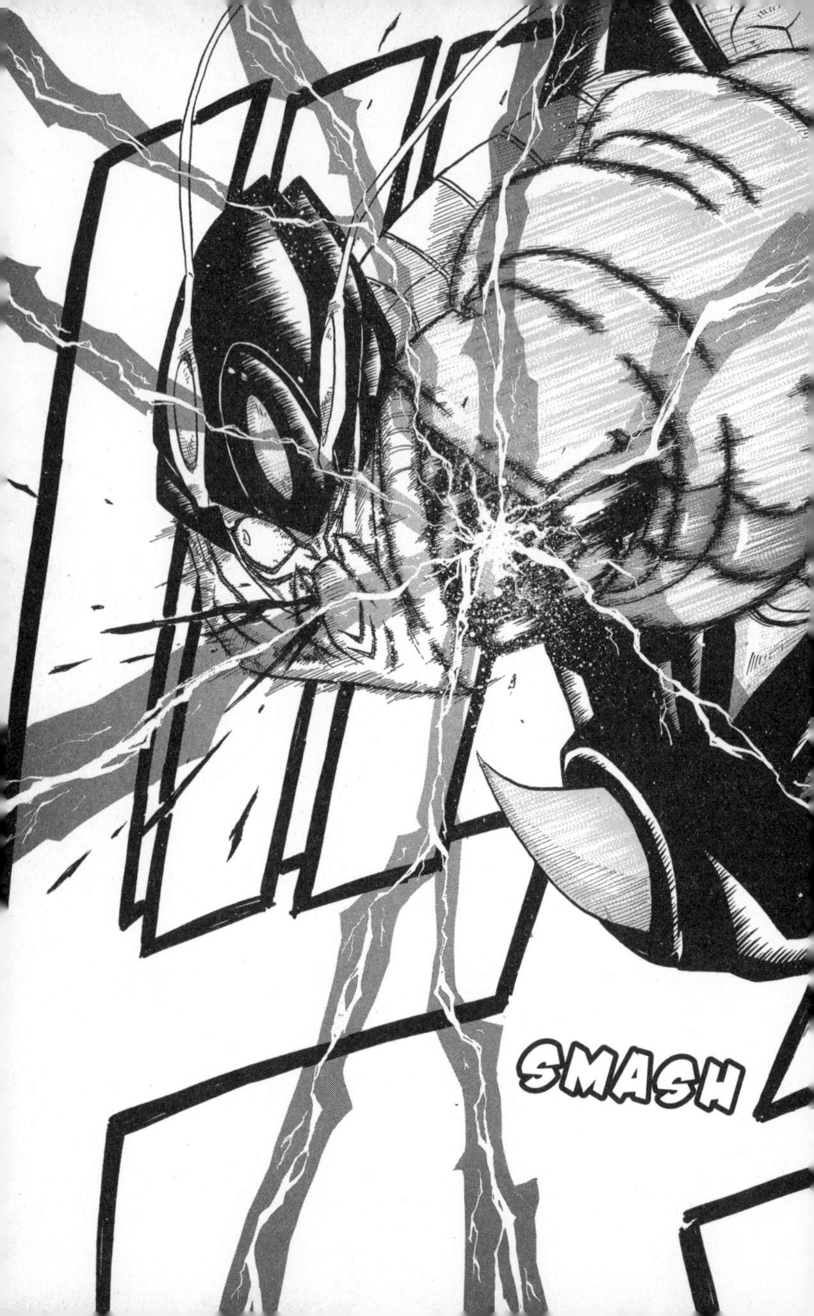
SMASH

HEROMAN

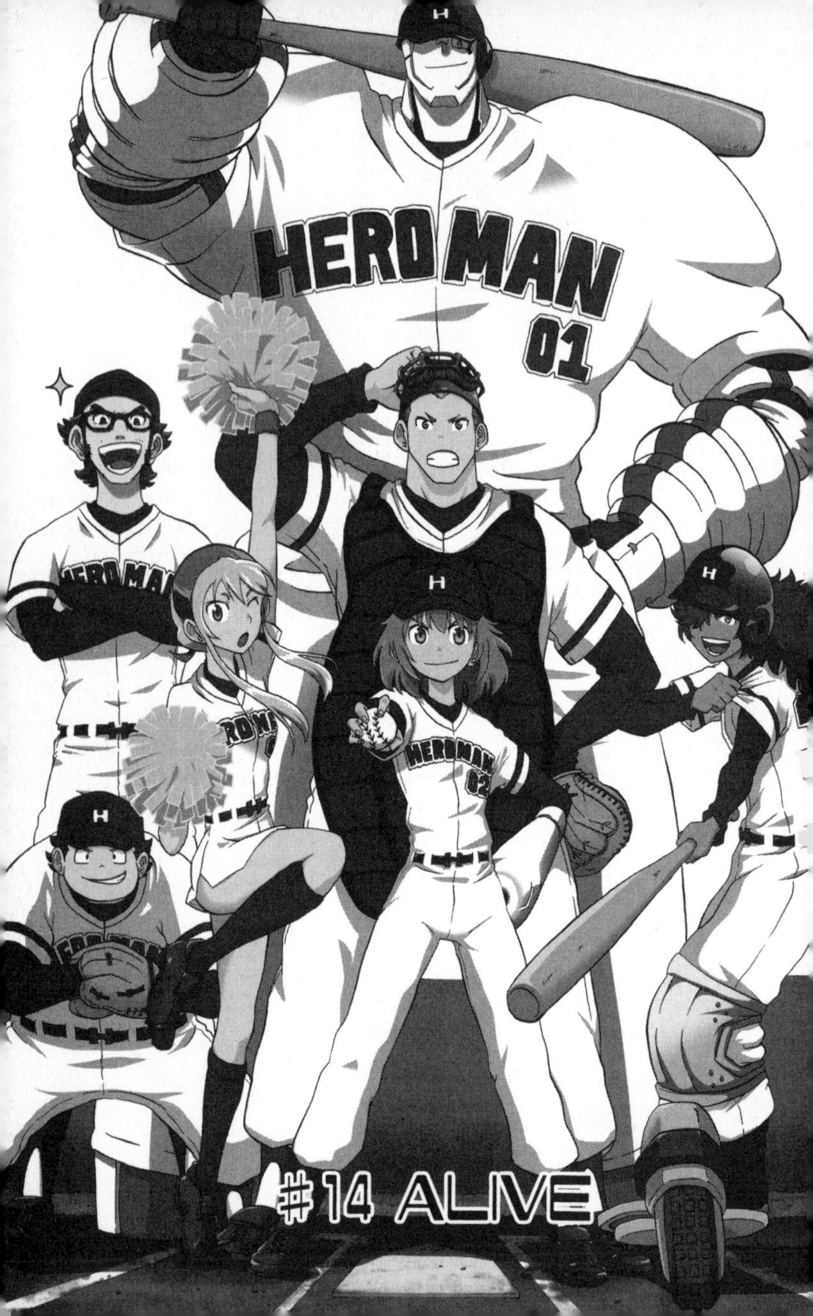
HEROMAN 01
HEROMAN 02
#14 ALIVE

—HEROMAN・3—

〈STAFF〉

YUKI SUZUKI
MASATO YOSHIOKA
CHITOSHI AOKI
NOBUYUKI YAMAMORI
HIROSHI IWASAKI

〈SPECIAL THANKS〉

HITOSHI NANBA
SHIGETO KOYAMA
SHINGO TAKEBA
NAOKI AMANO

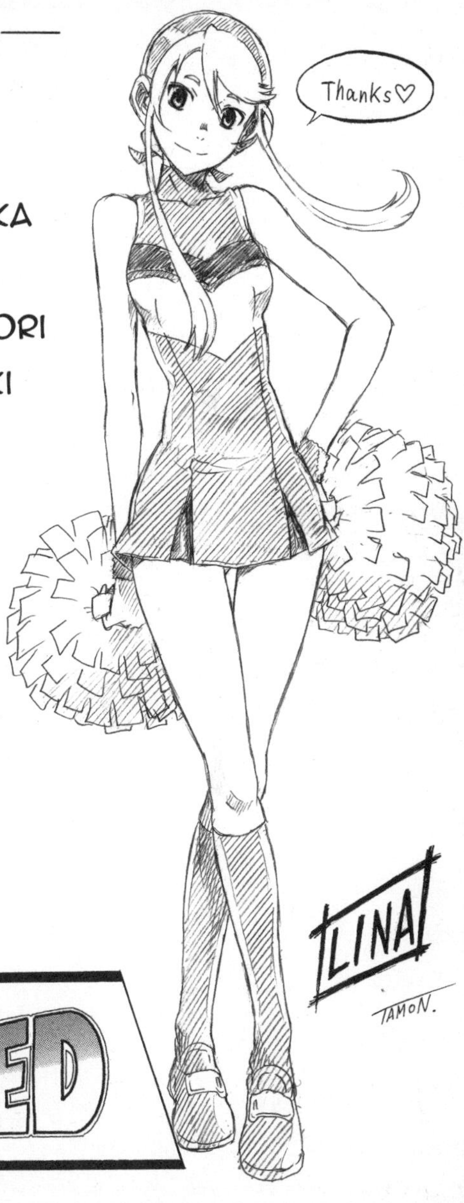
Thanks♡
LINA
TAMON.

TO BE CONTINUED

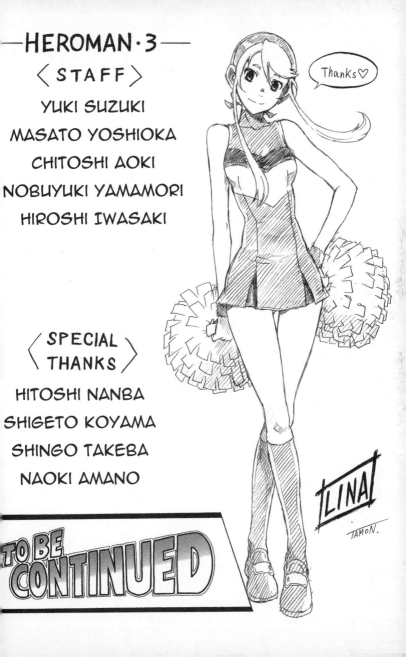

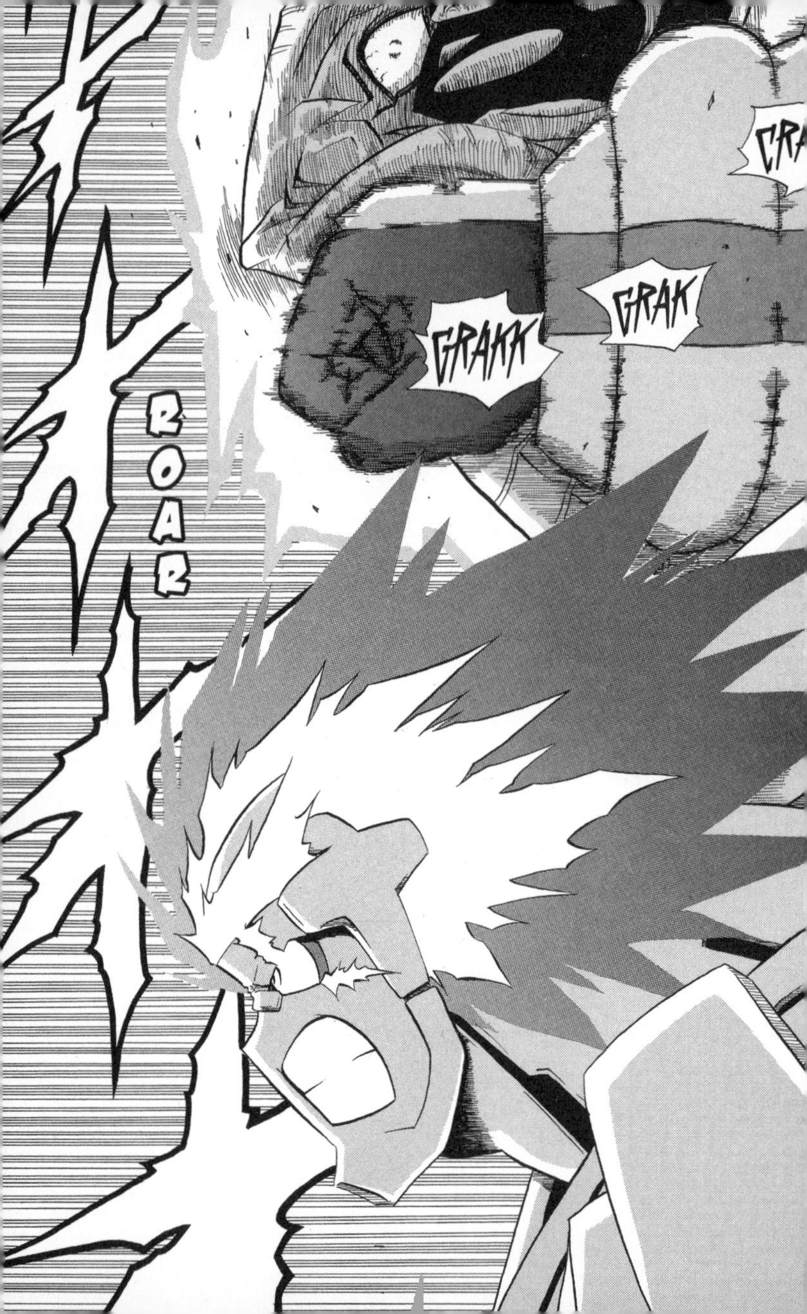
CRA
GRAK
GRAKK
ROAR

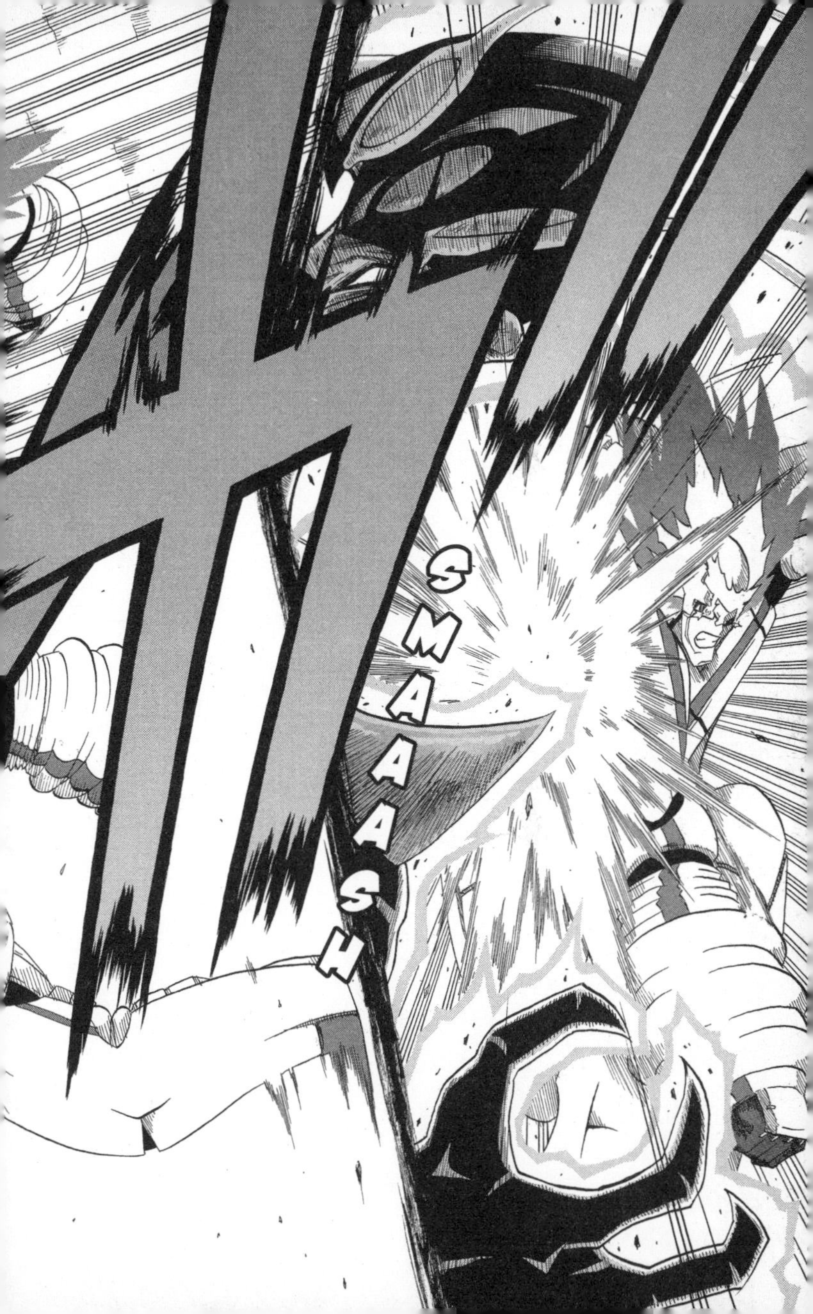
SMAAAASH

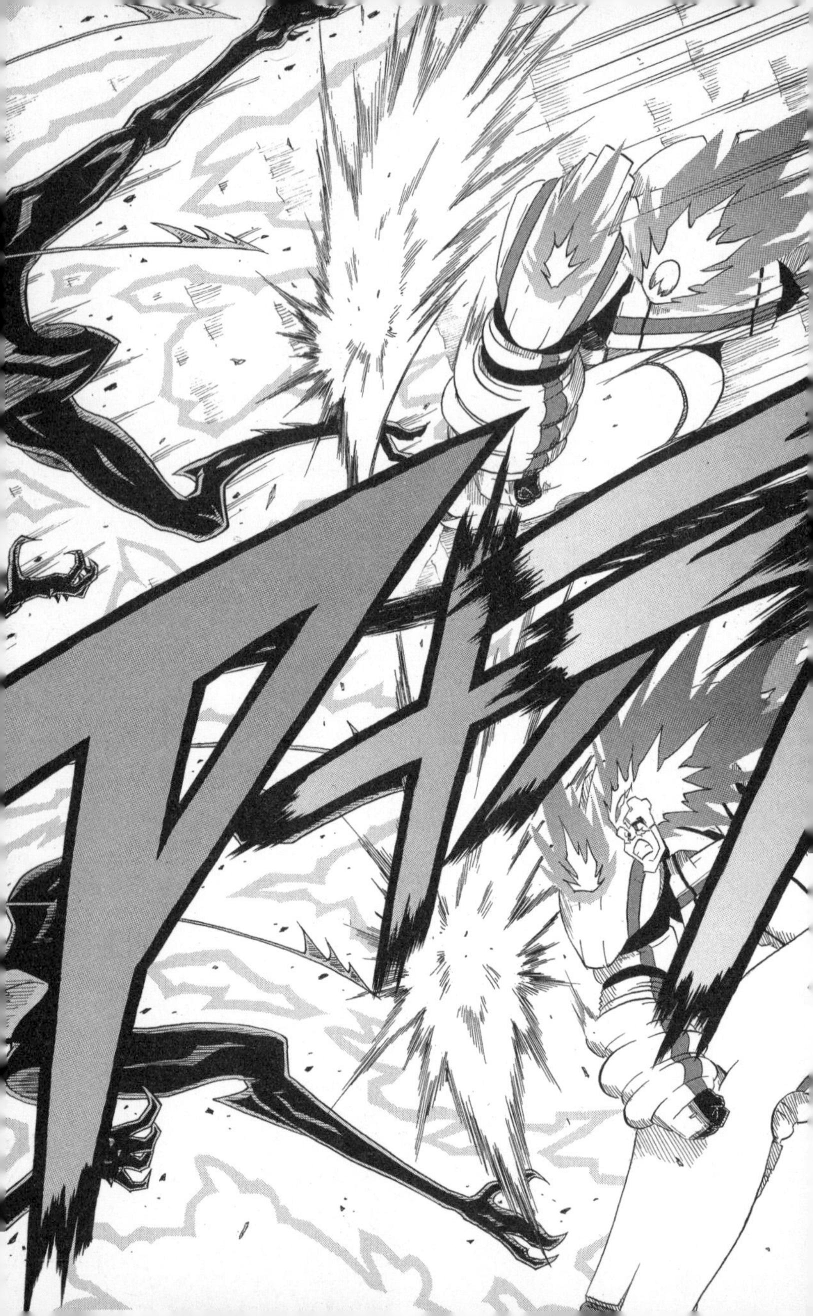

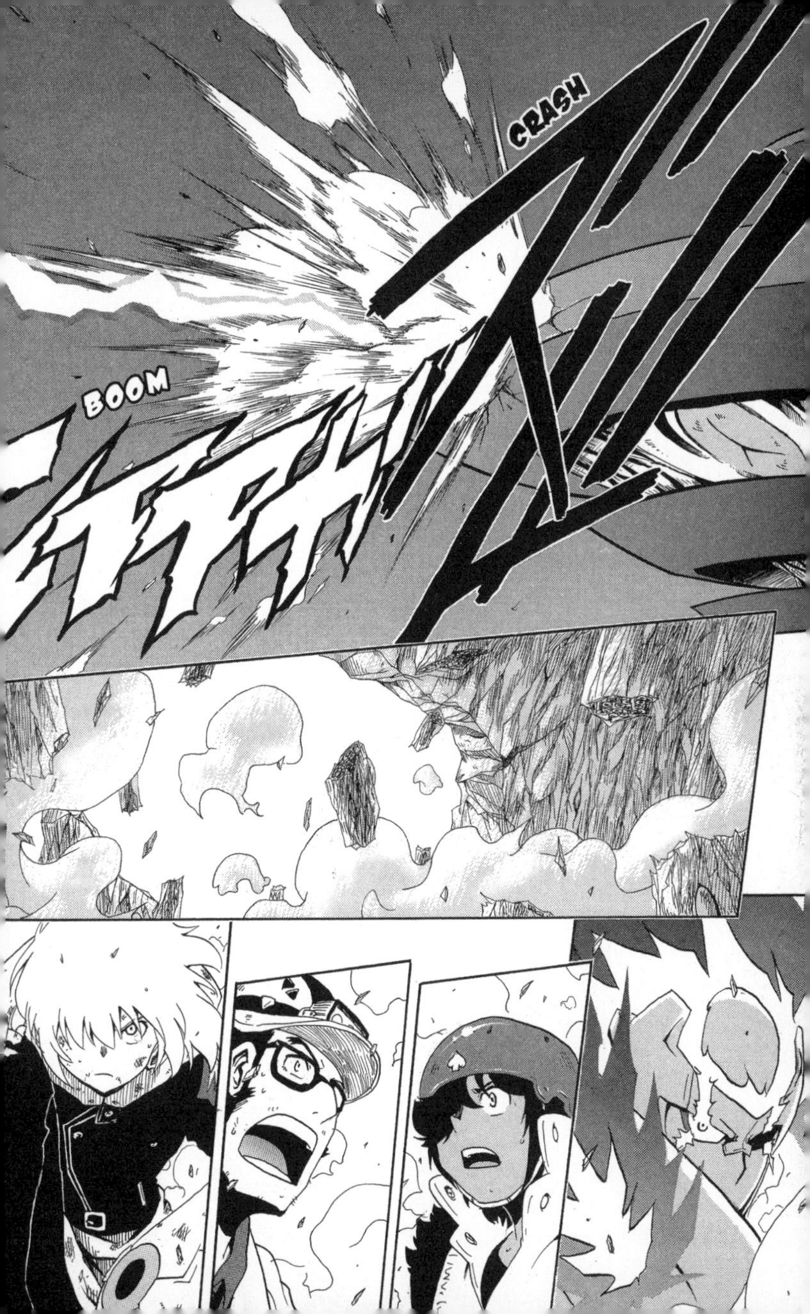
CRASH
BOOM

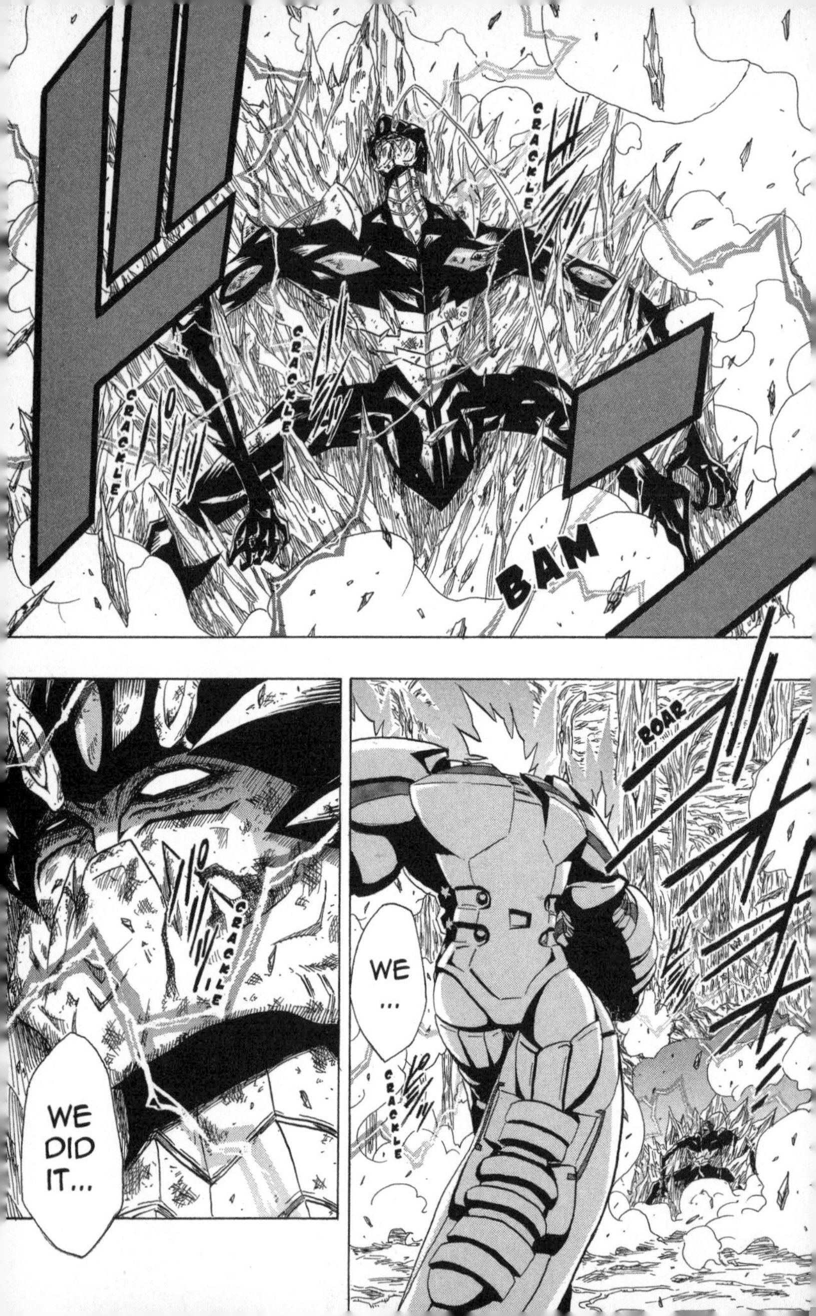
CRACKLE
CRACKLE
CRACKLE
BAM
ROAR
WE ...
CRACKLE
CRACKLE
WE DID IT...

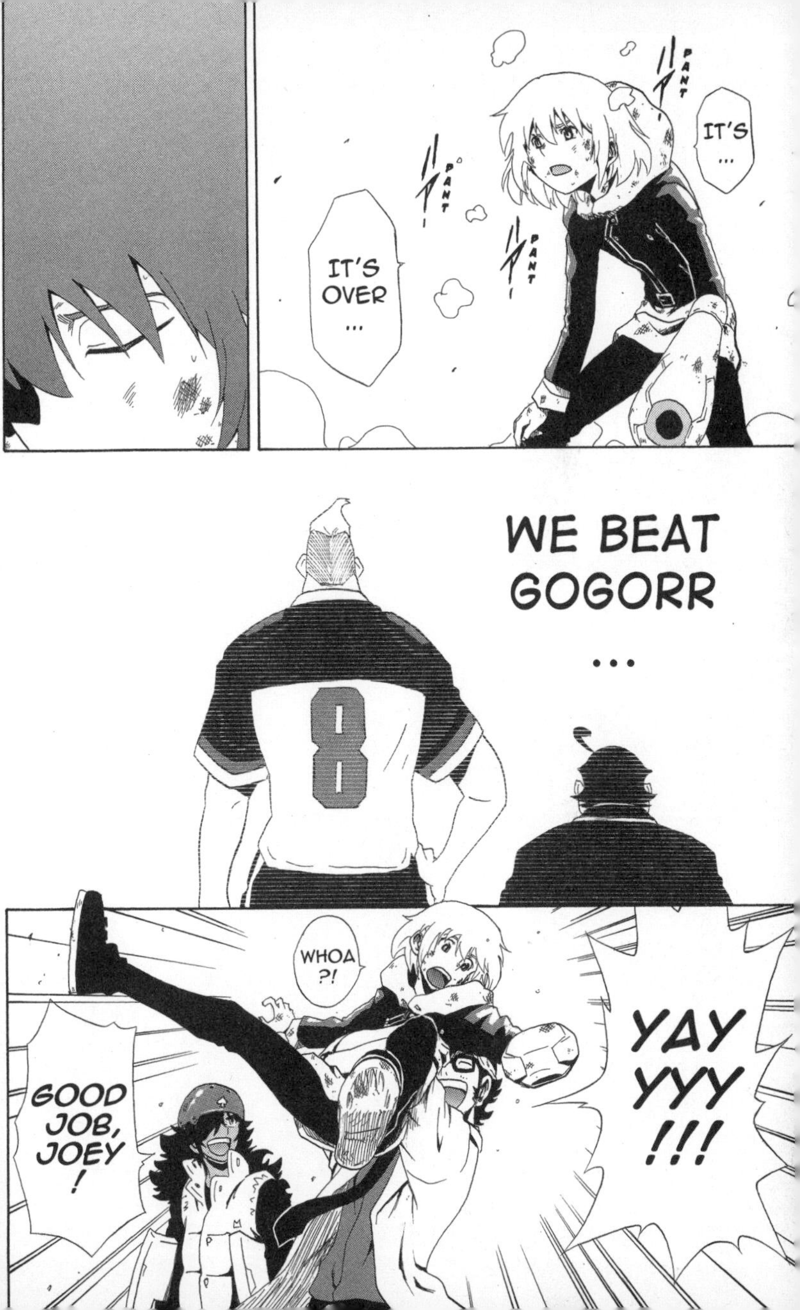
IT'S ...
PANT
PANT
IT'S OVER ...
PANT
WE BEAT GOGORR ...
YAY YYY !!!
WHOA ?!
GOOD JOB, JOEY !

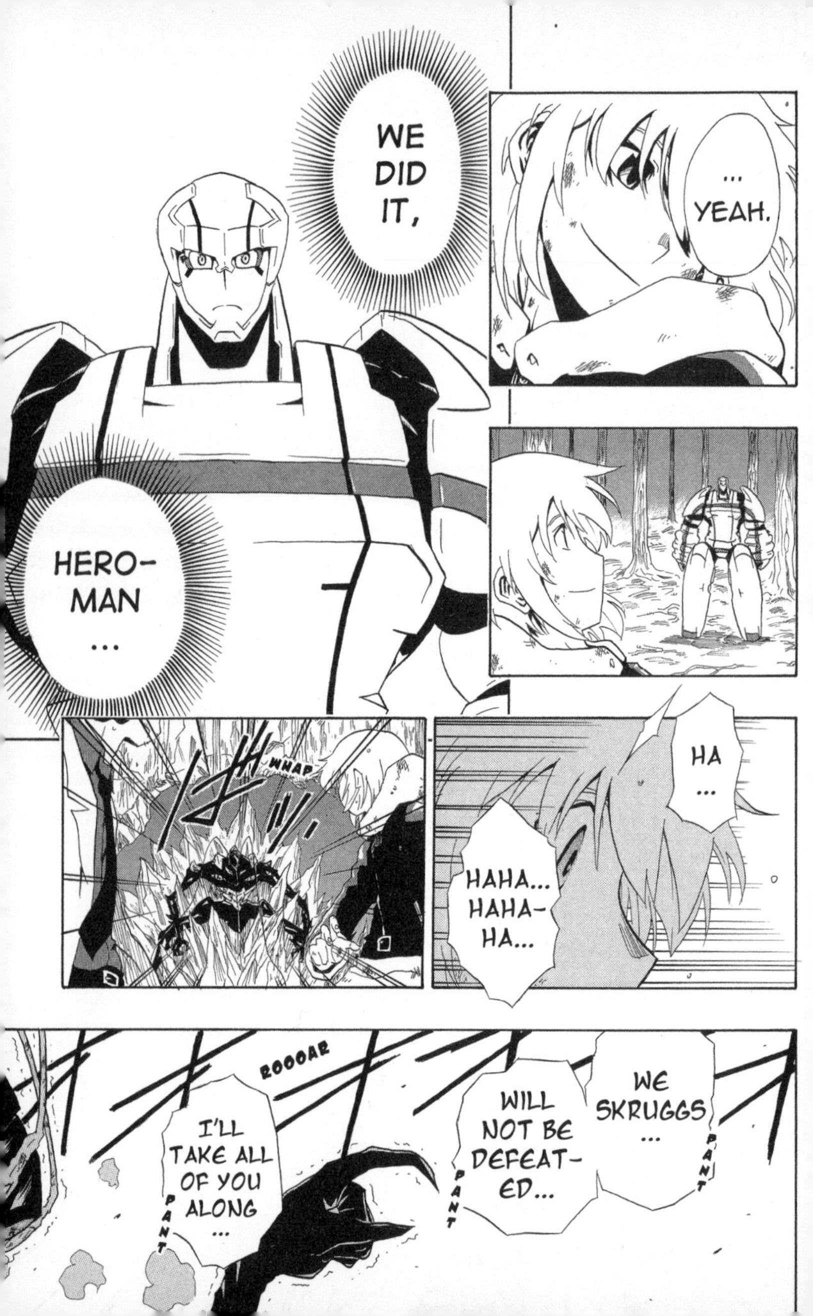
... YEAH.
WE DID IT,
HERO-MAN ...
HA ...
HAHA... HAHA-HA...
WHAP
WE SKRUGGS ...
PANT
WILL NOT BE DEFEAT-ED...
PANT
ROOOAR
I'LL TAKE ALL OF YOU ALONG ...
PANT

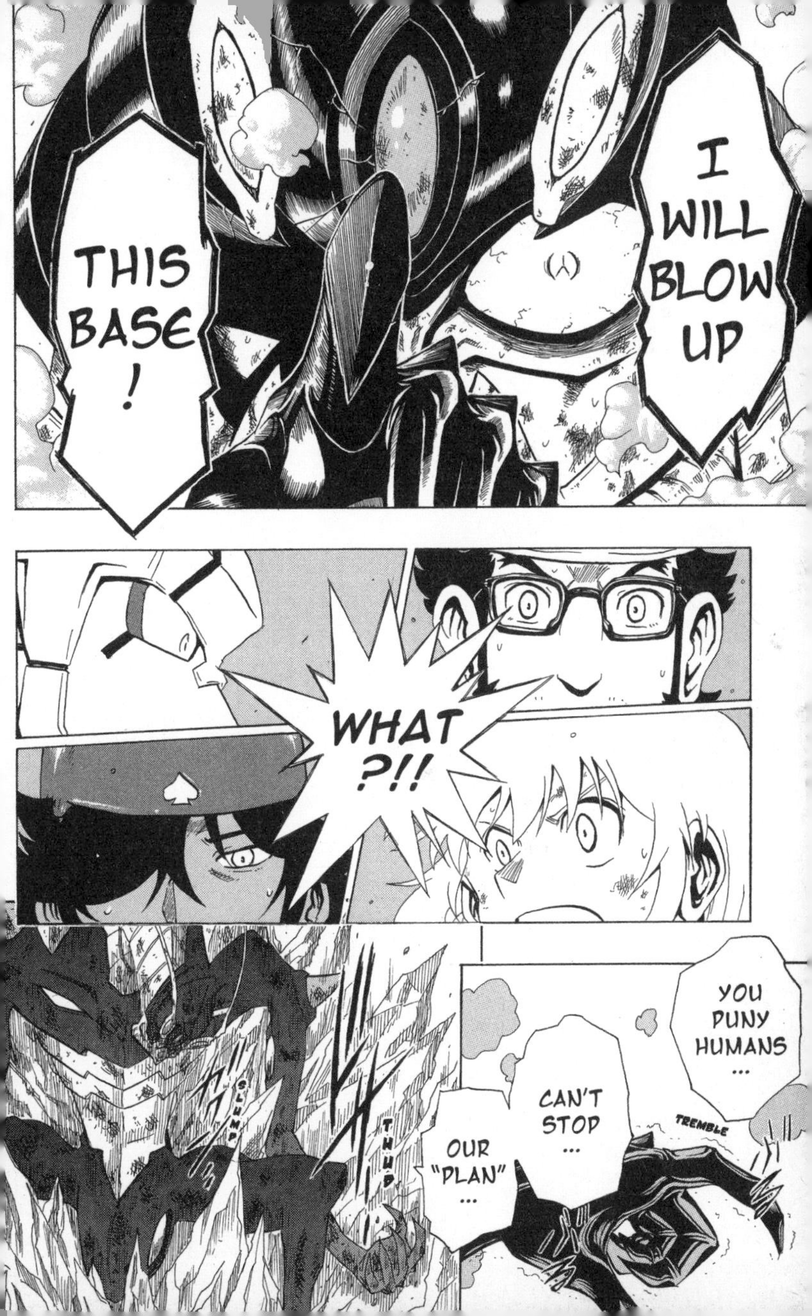
I WILL BLOW UP
THIS BASE!
WHAT?!!
YOU PUNY HUMANS ...
CAN'T STOP ...
OUR "PLAN" ...
TREMBLE
THUD
SLUMP

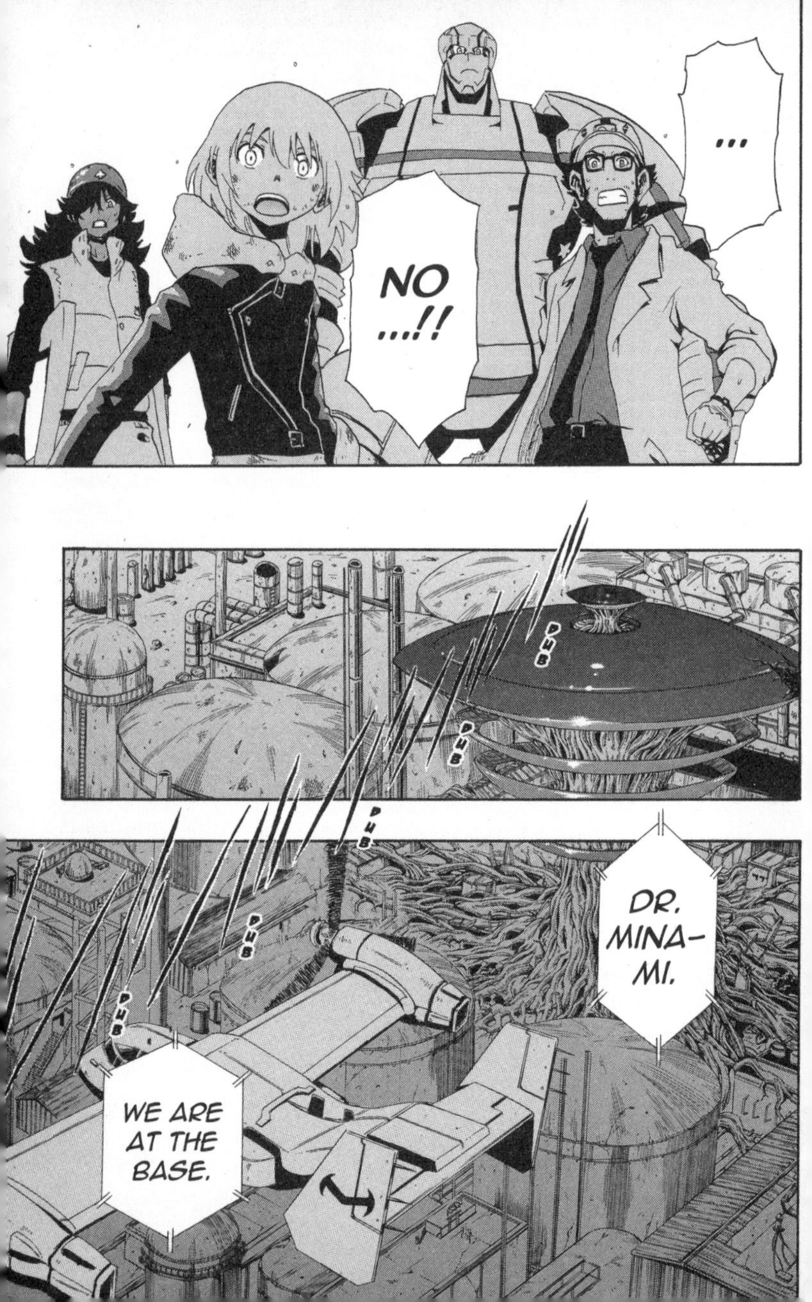
...
NO ...!!
DUB
DUB
DUB
DUB
DR. MINA-MI.
WE ARE AT THE BASE.
DUB

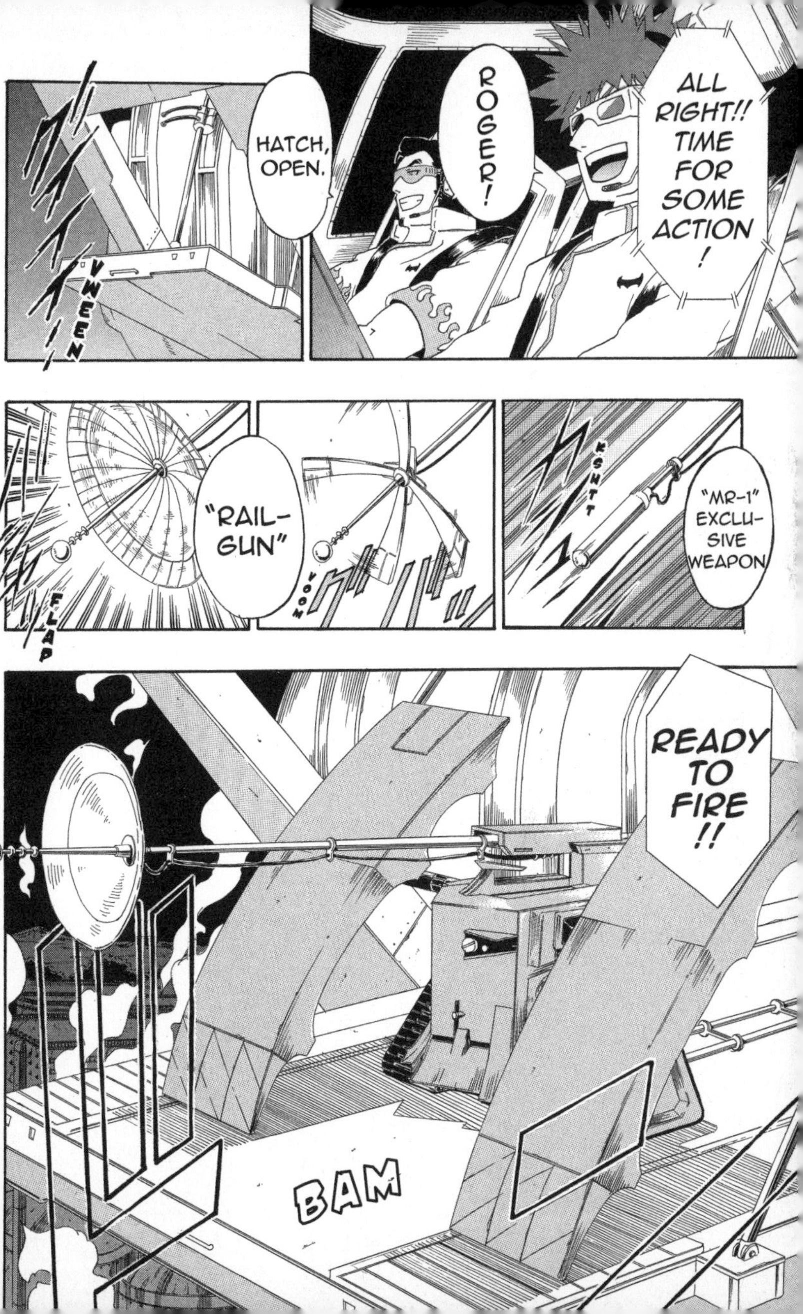
ALL RIGHT!! TIME FOR SOME ACTION!
ROGER!
HATCH, OPEN.
VWEEN
KSHTT
"MR-1" EXCLUSIVE WEAPON
"RAIL-GUN"
VOOM
FLAP
READY TO FIRE!!
BAM

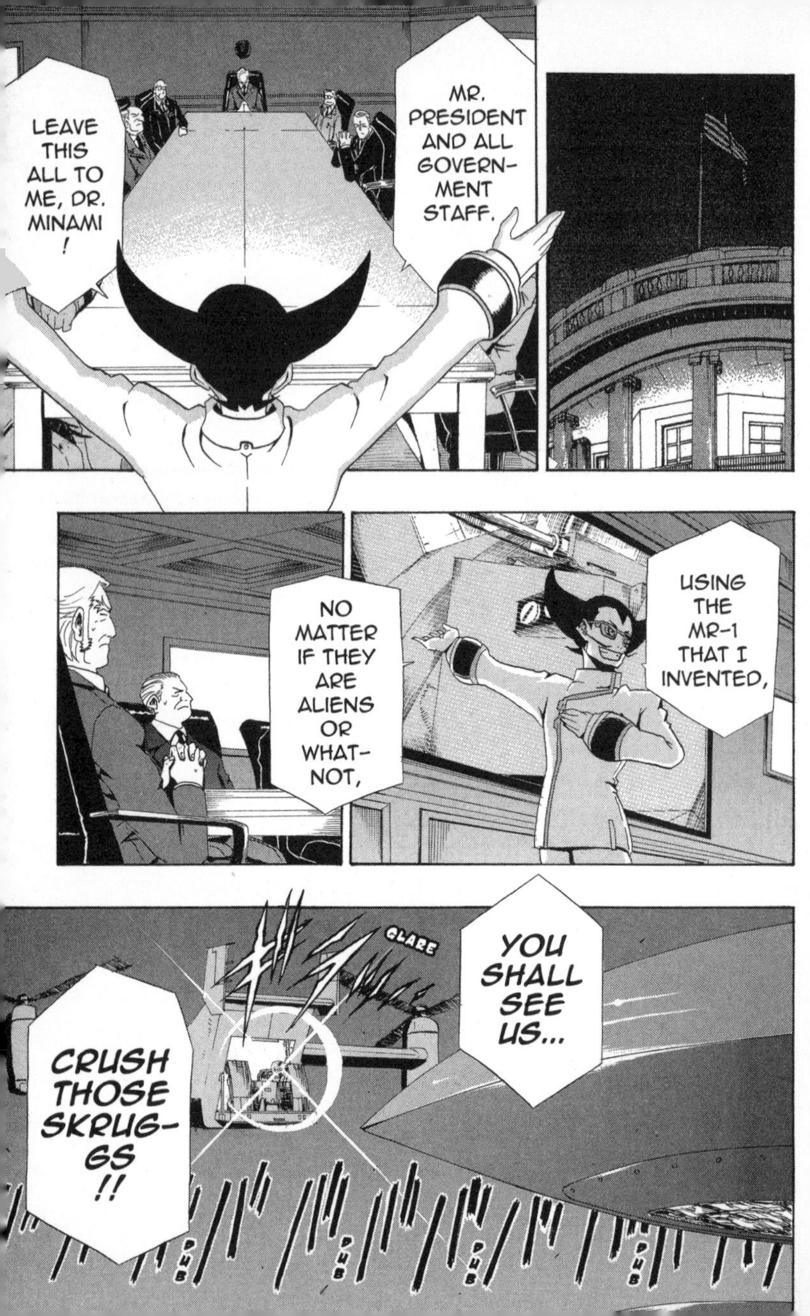
MR. PRESIDENT AND ALL GOVERN-MENT STAFF.
LEAVE THIS ALL TO ME, DR. MINAMI!
USING THE MR-1 THAT I INVENTED,
NO MATTER IF THEY ARE ALIENS OR WHAT-NOT,
GLARE
YOU SHALL SEE US...
CRUSH THOSE SKRUG-GS!!
DUB
DUB
DUB
DUB

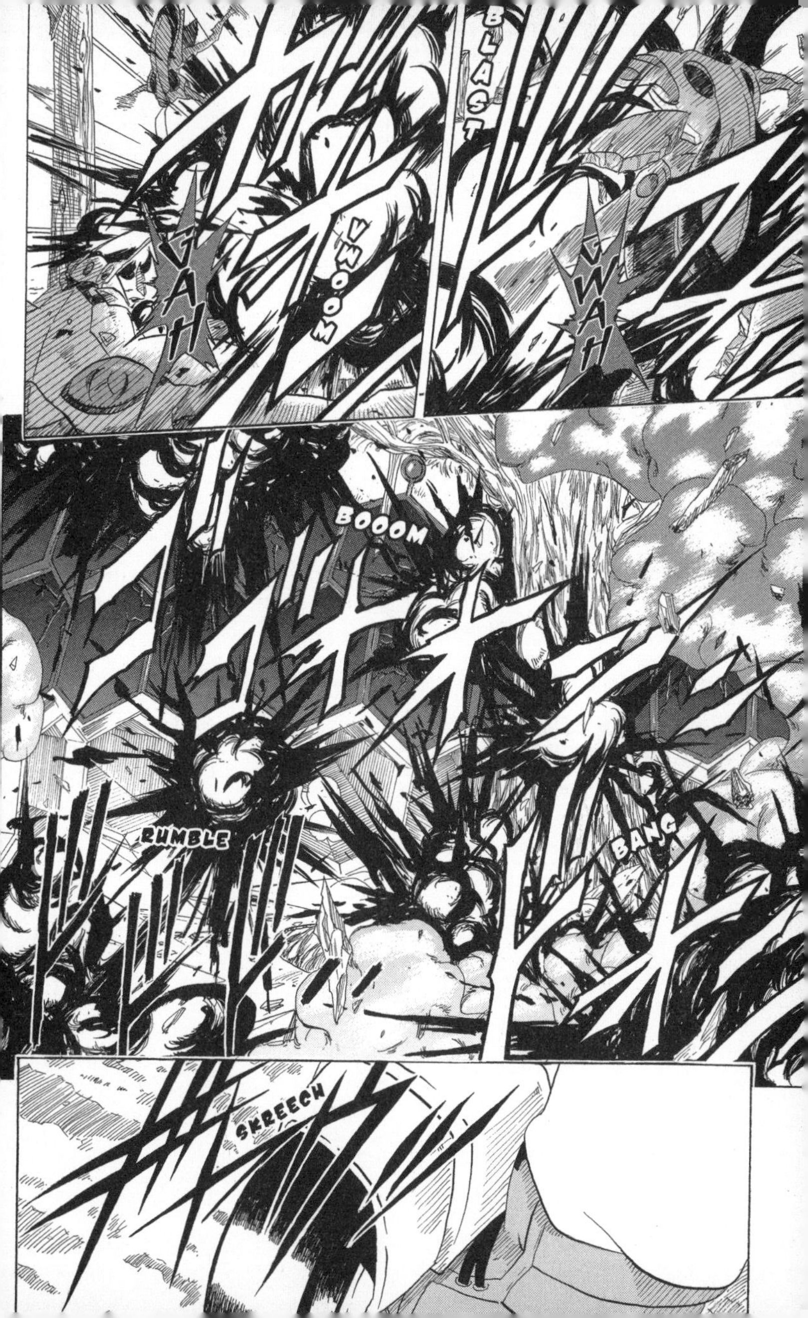
BLAST
GWAH
VWOOOM
GWAH
BOOOM
BANG
RUMBLE
SKREECH

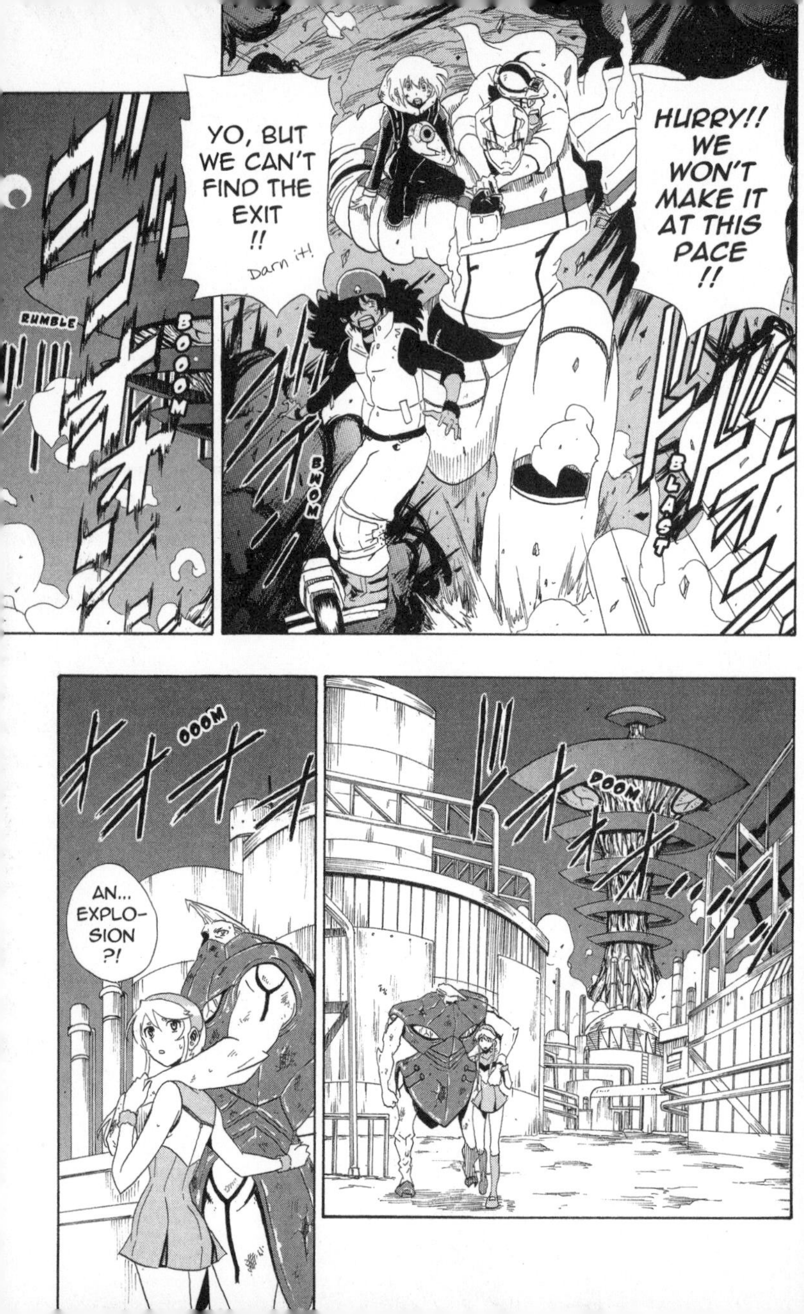
HURRY!! WE WON'T MAKE IT AT THIS PACE!!
YO, BUT WE CAN'T FIND THE EXIT!!
Darn it!
BLAST
BWOM
BOOOM
RUMBLE
DOOM
OOOM
AN... EXPLOSION?!

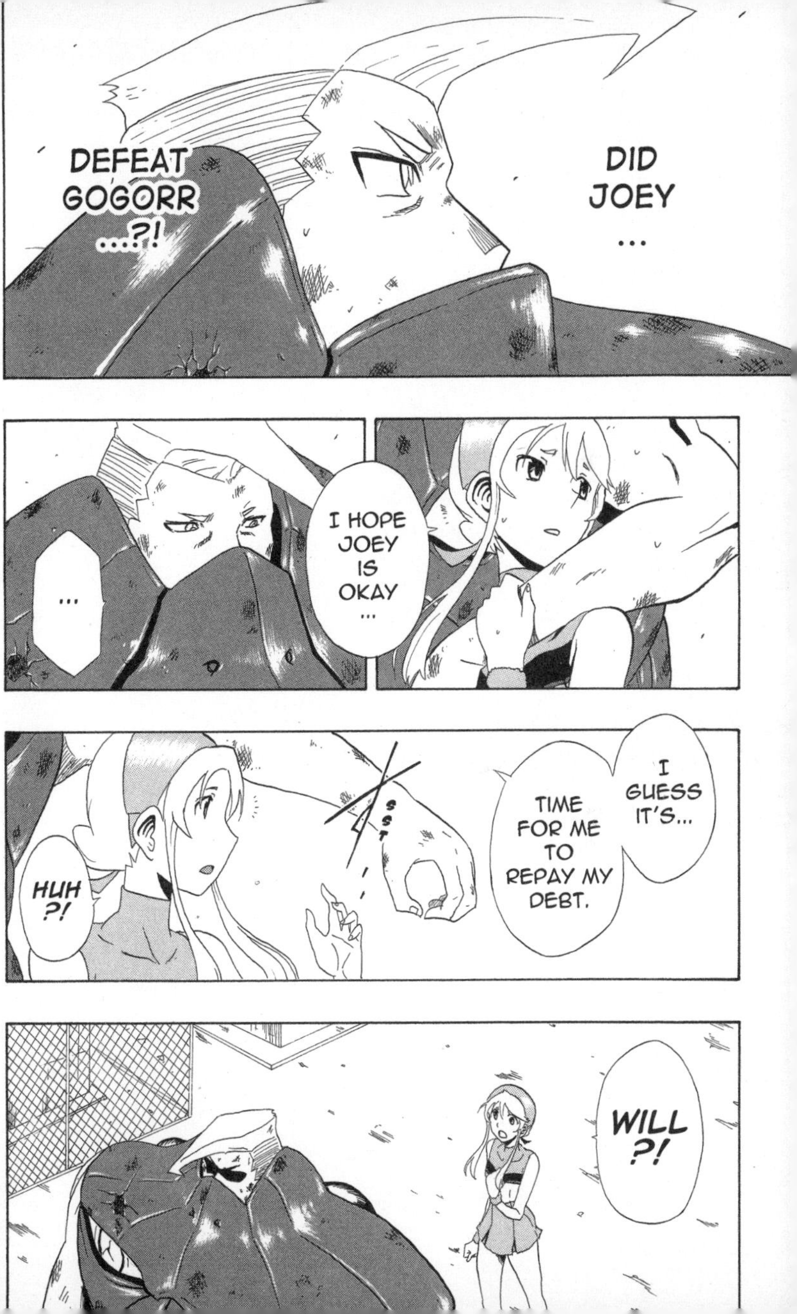
DID JOEY ...
DEFEAT GOGORR ...?!
I HOPE JOEY IS OKAY ...
...
I GUESS IT'S...
TIME FOR ME TO REPAY MY DEBT.
SST
HUH ?!
WILL ?!

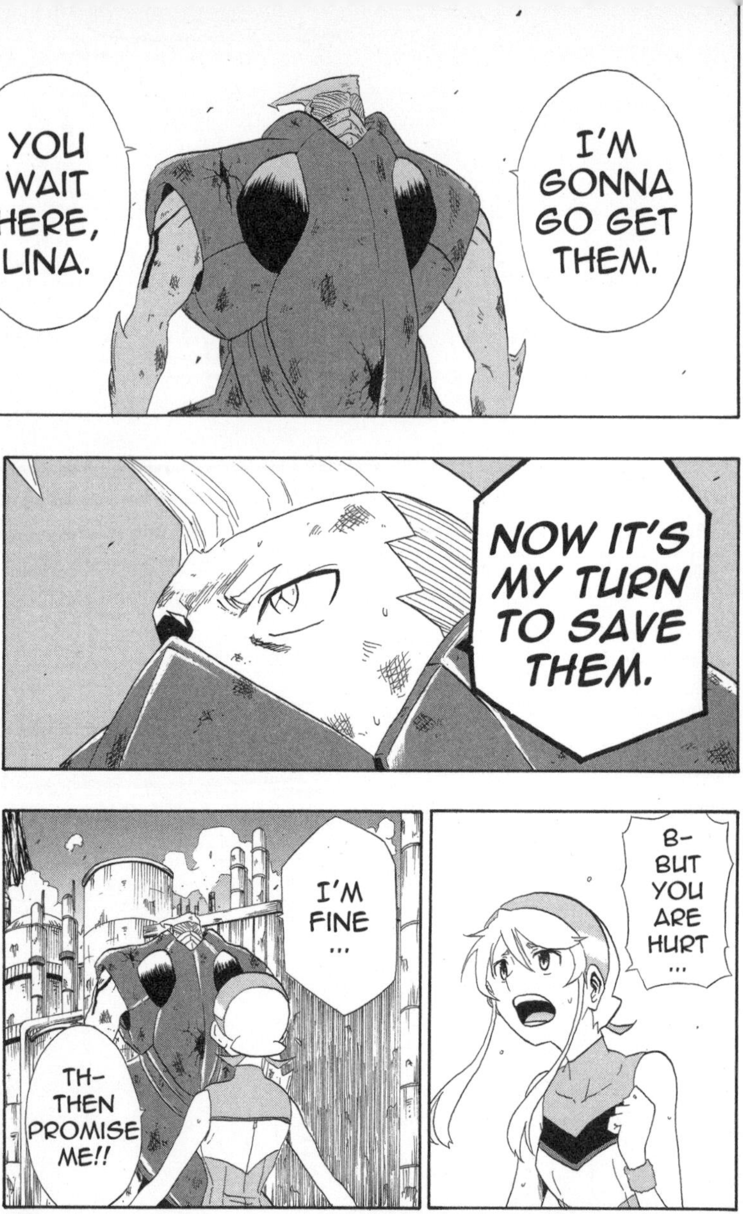
I'M GONNA GO GET THEM.
YOU WAIT HERE, LINA.
NOW IT'S MY TURN TO SAVE THEM.
B-BUT YOU ARE HURT...
I'M FINE...
TH-THEN PROMISE ME!!

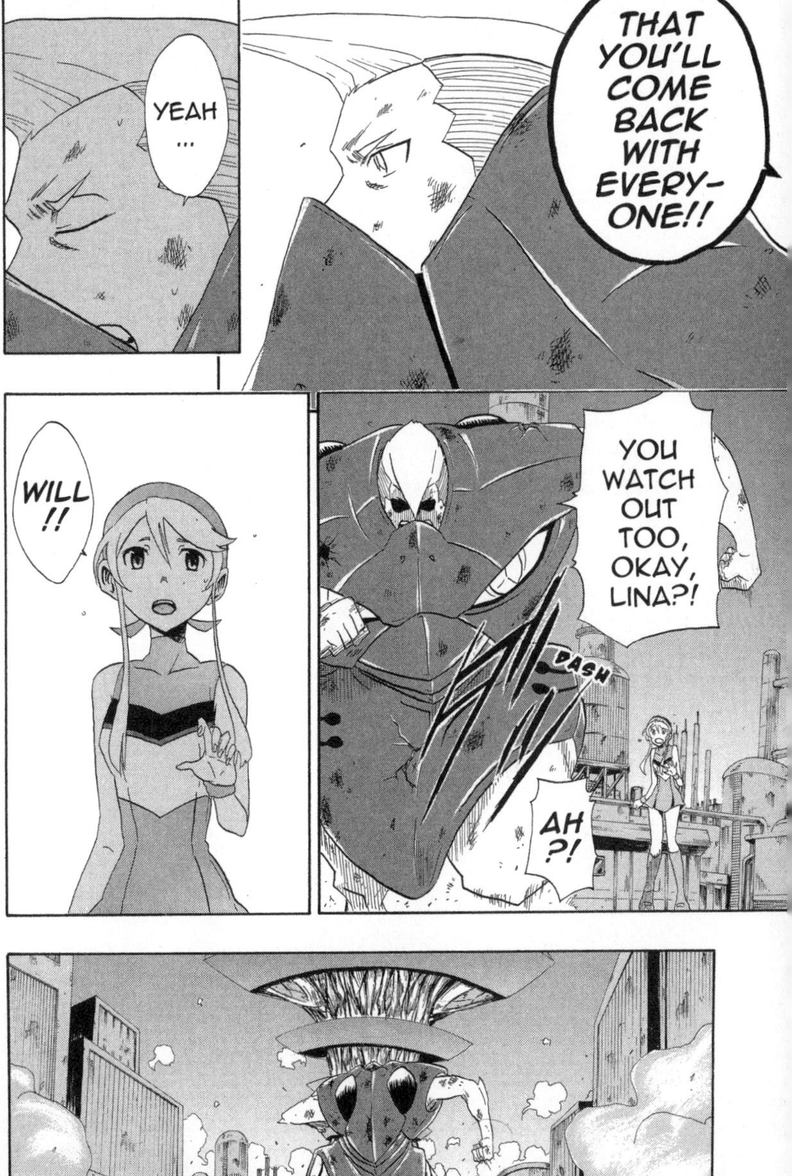
THAT YOU'LL COME BACK WITH EVERY-ONE!!
YEAH ...
YOU WATCH OUT TOO, OKAY, LINA?!
DASH
AH ?!
WILL !!

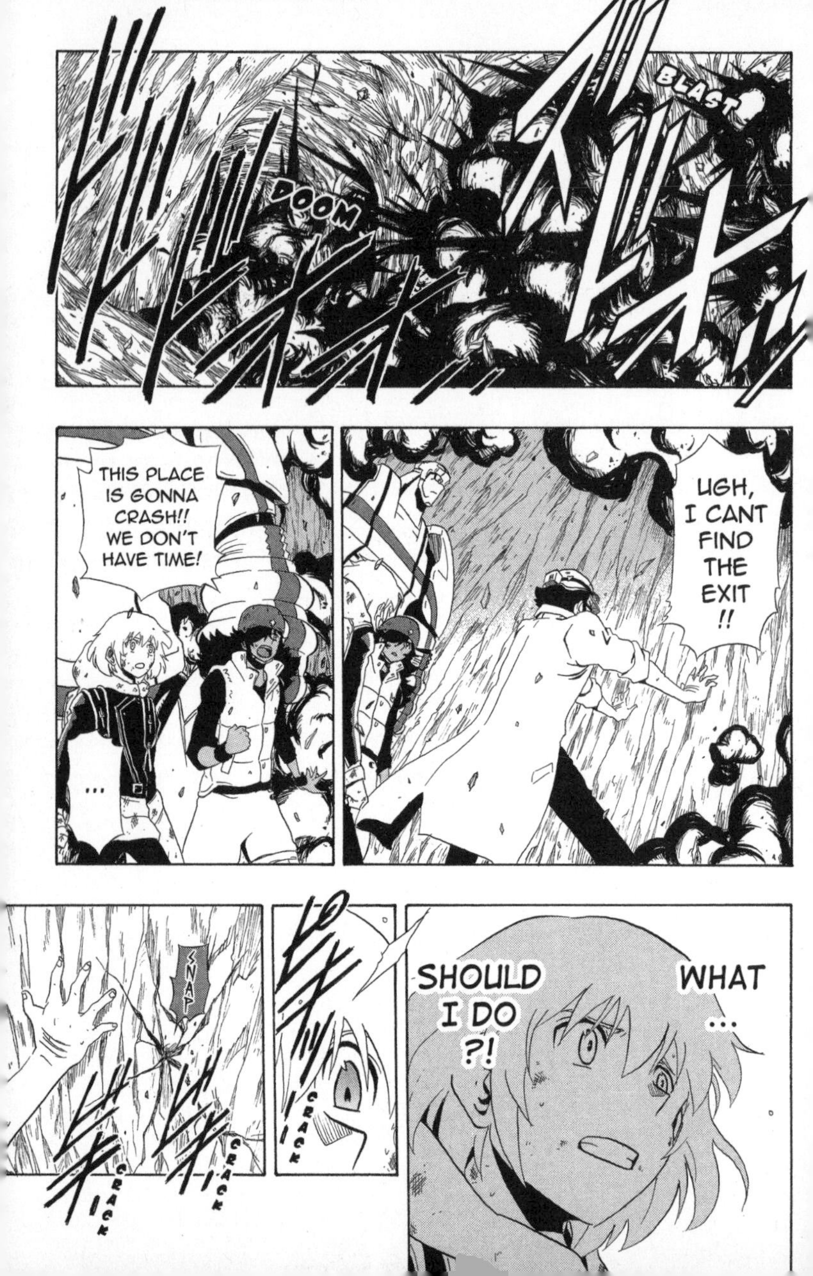
BLAST
DOOM
UGH, I CANT FIND THE EXIT !!
THIS PLACE IS GONNA CRASH!! WE DON'T HAVE TIME!
...
WHAT ...
SHOULD I DO ?!
CRACK
SNAP
CRACK
CRACK

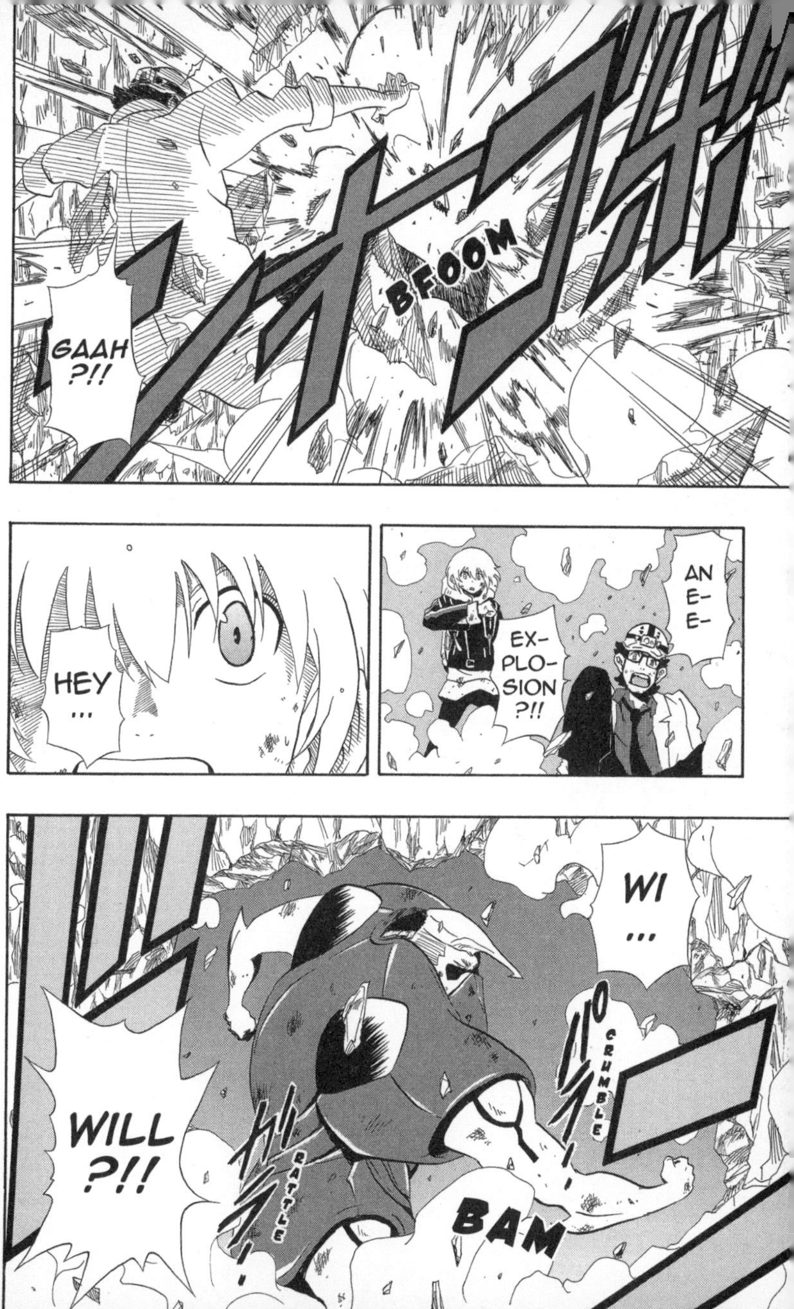
BFOOM
GAAH?!!
AN E-E-
EXPLOSION?!!
HEY...
WI...
CRUMBLE
RATTLE
BAM
WILL?!!

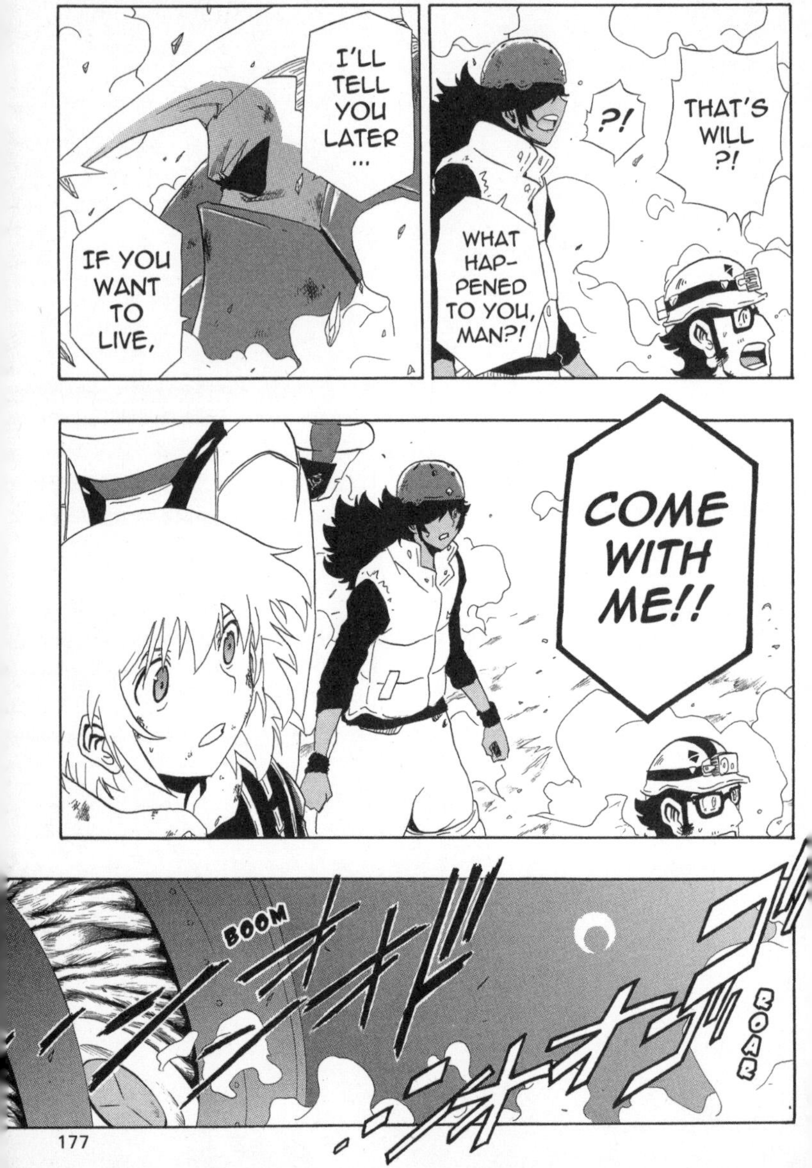
THAT'S WILL?!
?!
WHAT HAPPENED TO YOU, MAN?!
I'LL TELL YOU LATER...
IF YOU WANT TO LIVE,
COME WITH ME!!
ROAR
BOOM

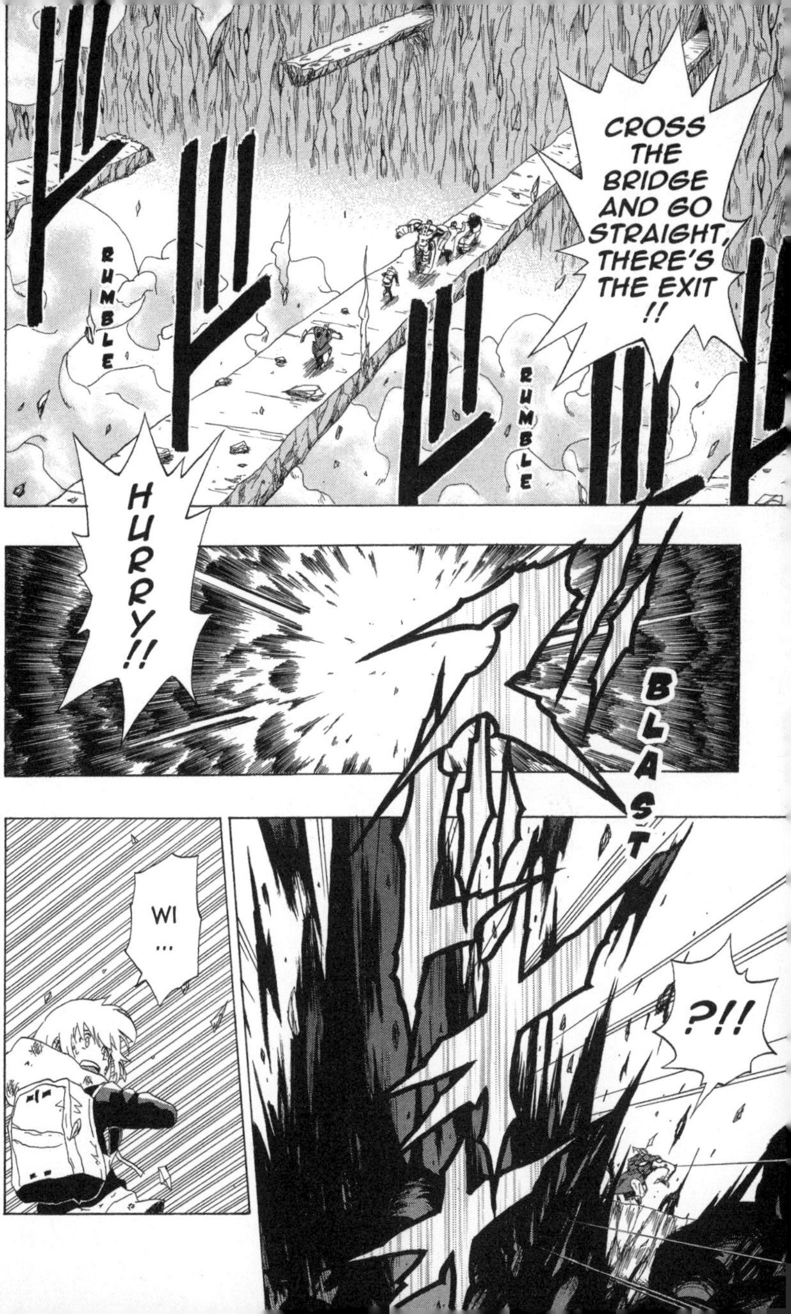
CROSS THE BRIDGE AND GO STRAIGHT, THERE'S THE EXIT!!
RUMBLE
RUMBLE
HURRY!!
BLAST
?!!
WI...

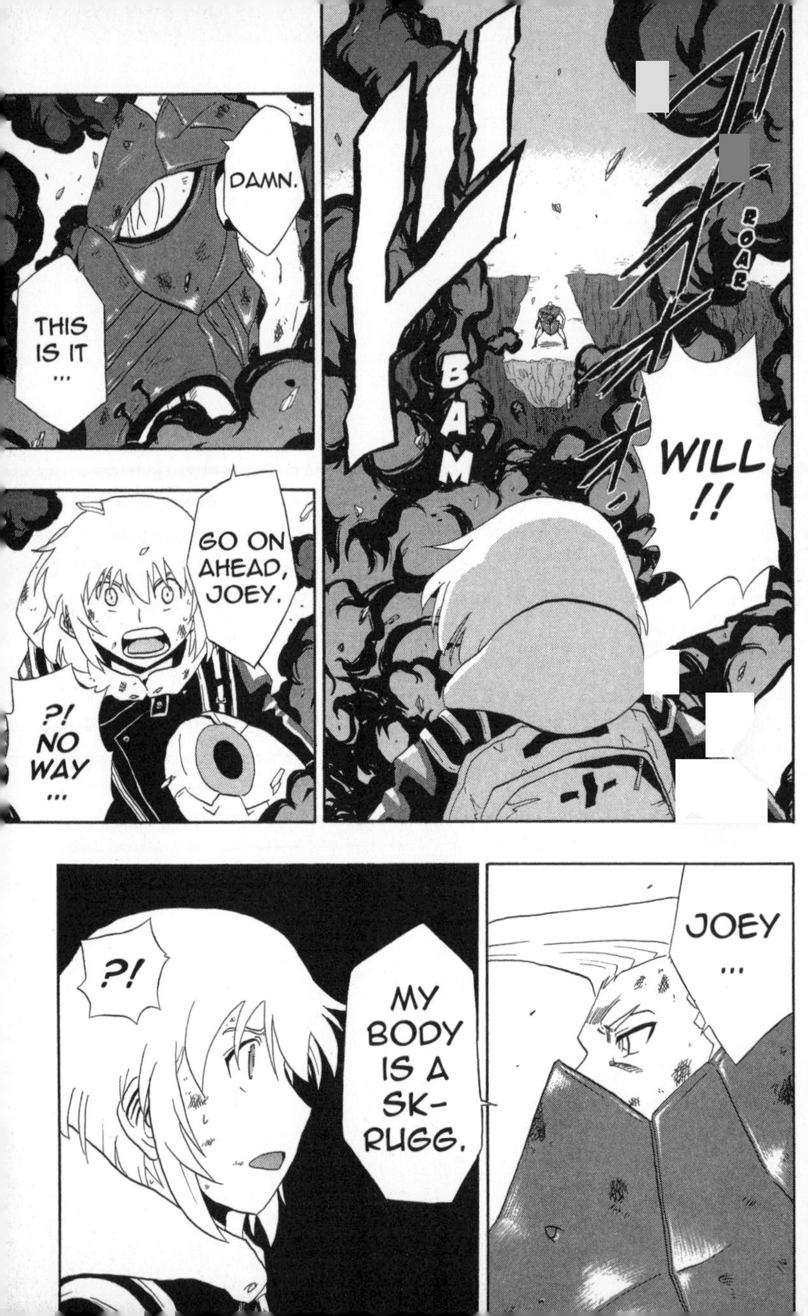
ROAR
WILL !!
BAM
DAMN.
THIS IS IT ...
GO ON AHEAD, JOEY.
?! NO WAY ...
JOEY ...
MY BODY IS A SK-RUGG.
?!

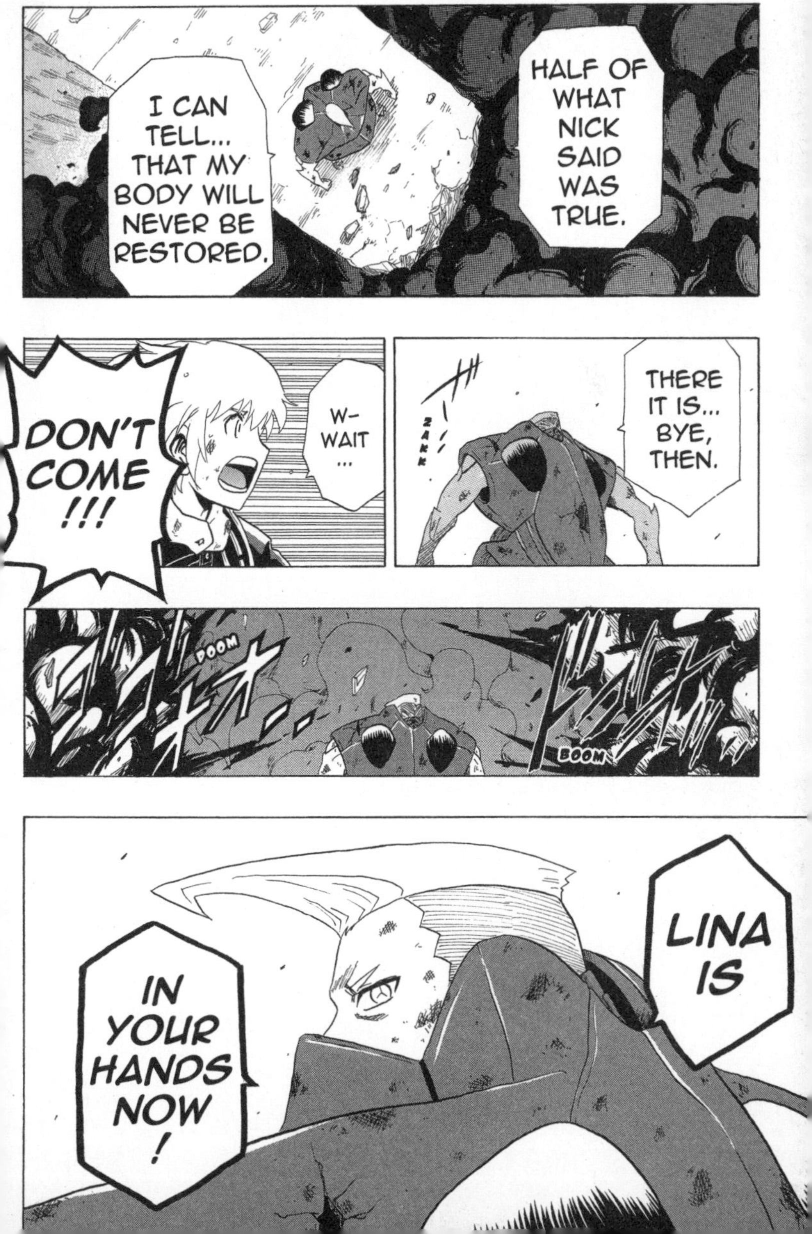
HALF OF WHAT NICK SAID WAS TRUE.
I CAN TELL... THAT MY BODY WILL NEVER BE RESTORED.
THERE IT IS... BYE, THEN.
ZAKK
W-WAIT...
DON'T COME!!!
BOOM
DOOM
LINA IS
IN YOUR HANDS NOW!

BOOOM

WILLLLL

NO, JOEY!!

WILL...

BZZZT

BZZZT

BZOOM

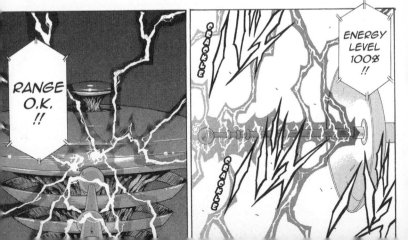

RANGE O.K.!!

ENERGY LEVEL 100%!!

CRACKLE

CRACKLE

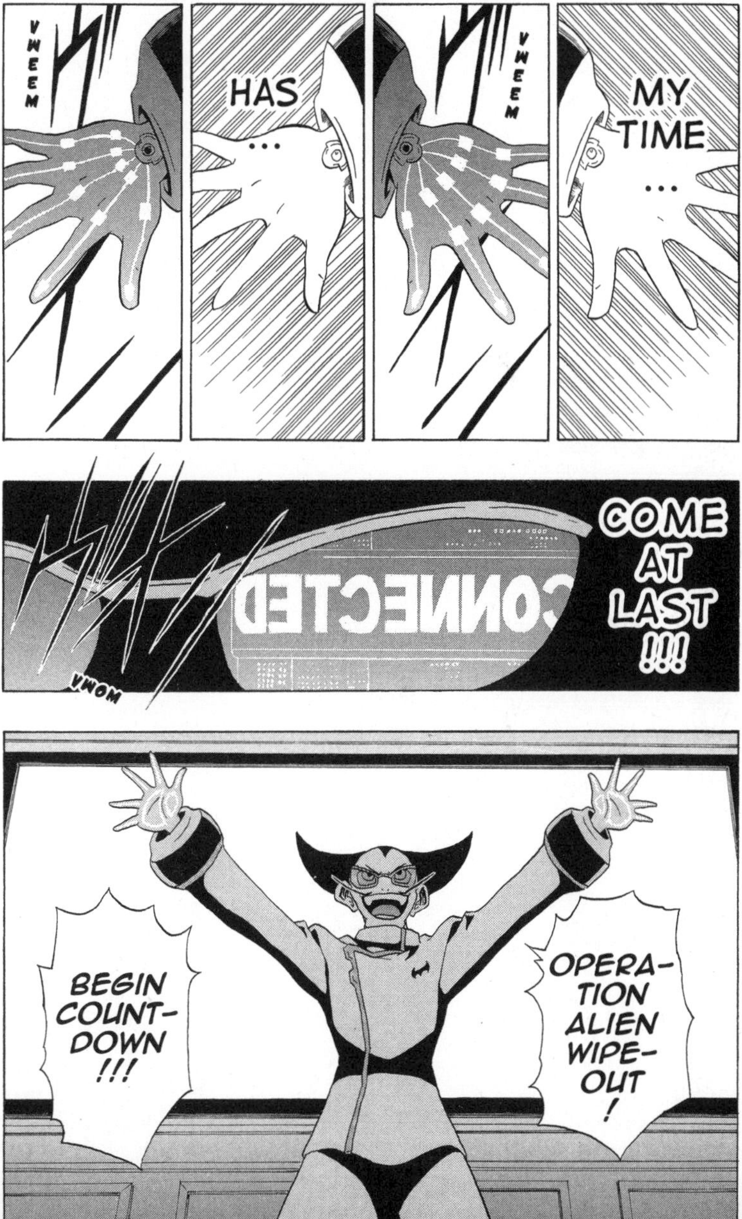
MY TIME ...
VWEEM
HAS ...
VWEEM
COME AT LAST !!!!
CONNECTED
VWOM
OPERA-TION ALIEN WIPE-OUT !
BEGIN COUNT-DOWN !!!

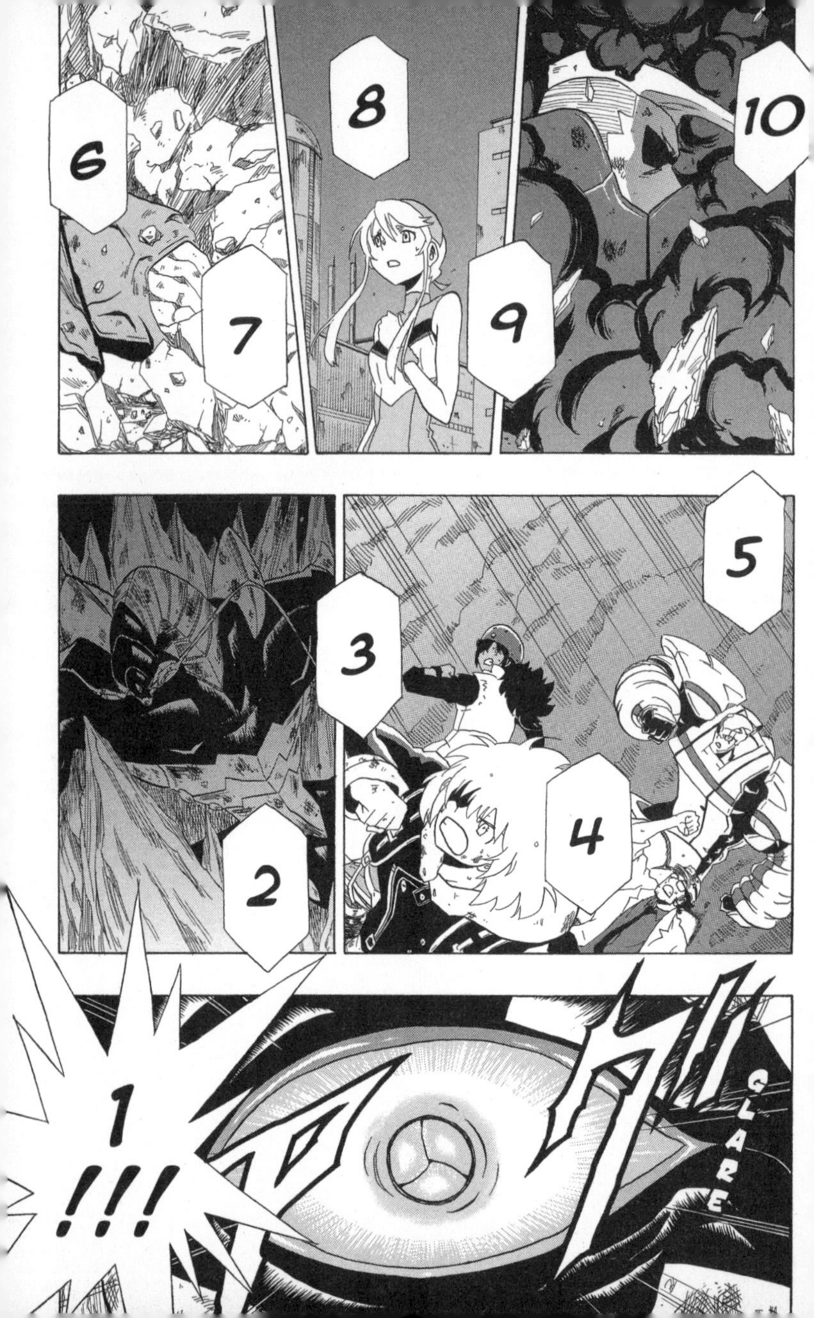
1
!!!
GLARE
2
3
4
5
6
7
8
9
10

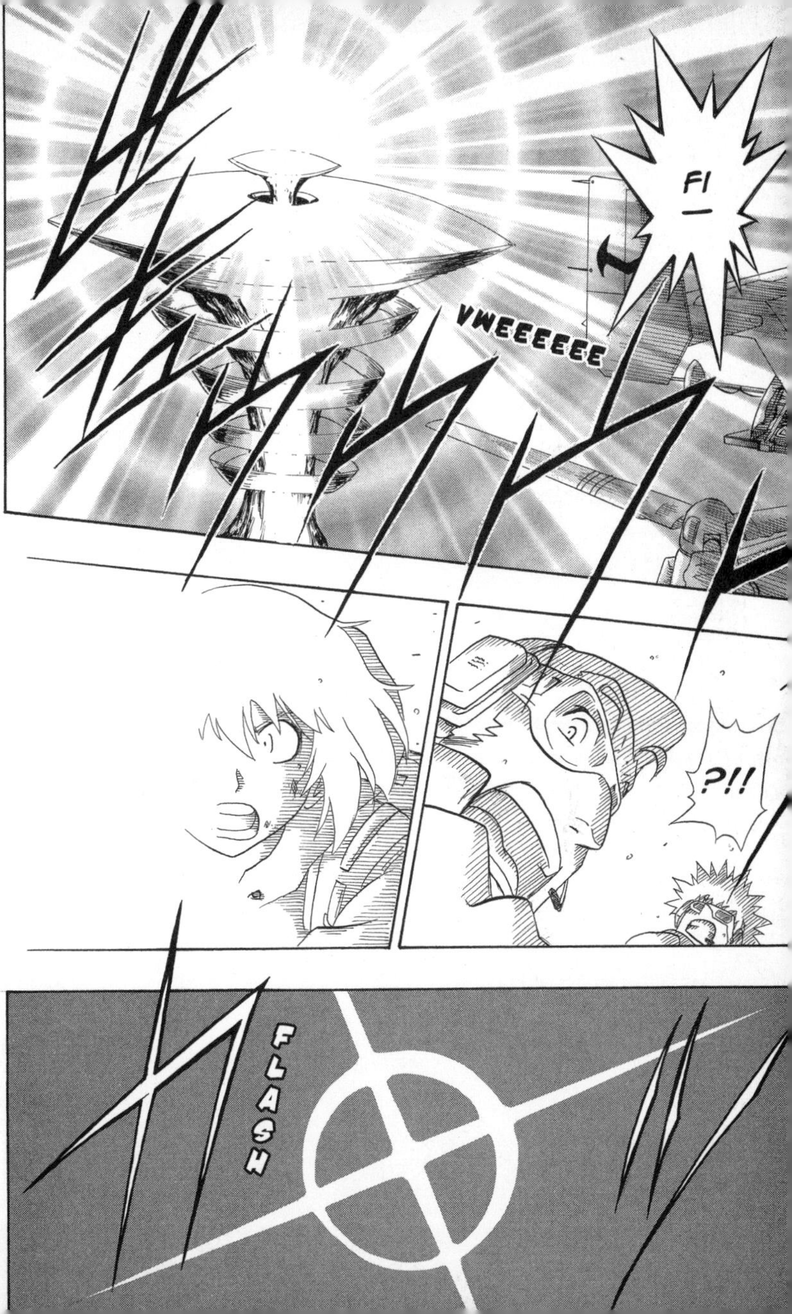
FI—
VWEEEEEEE
?!!
FLASH

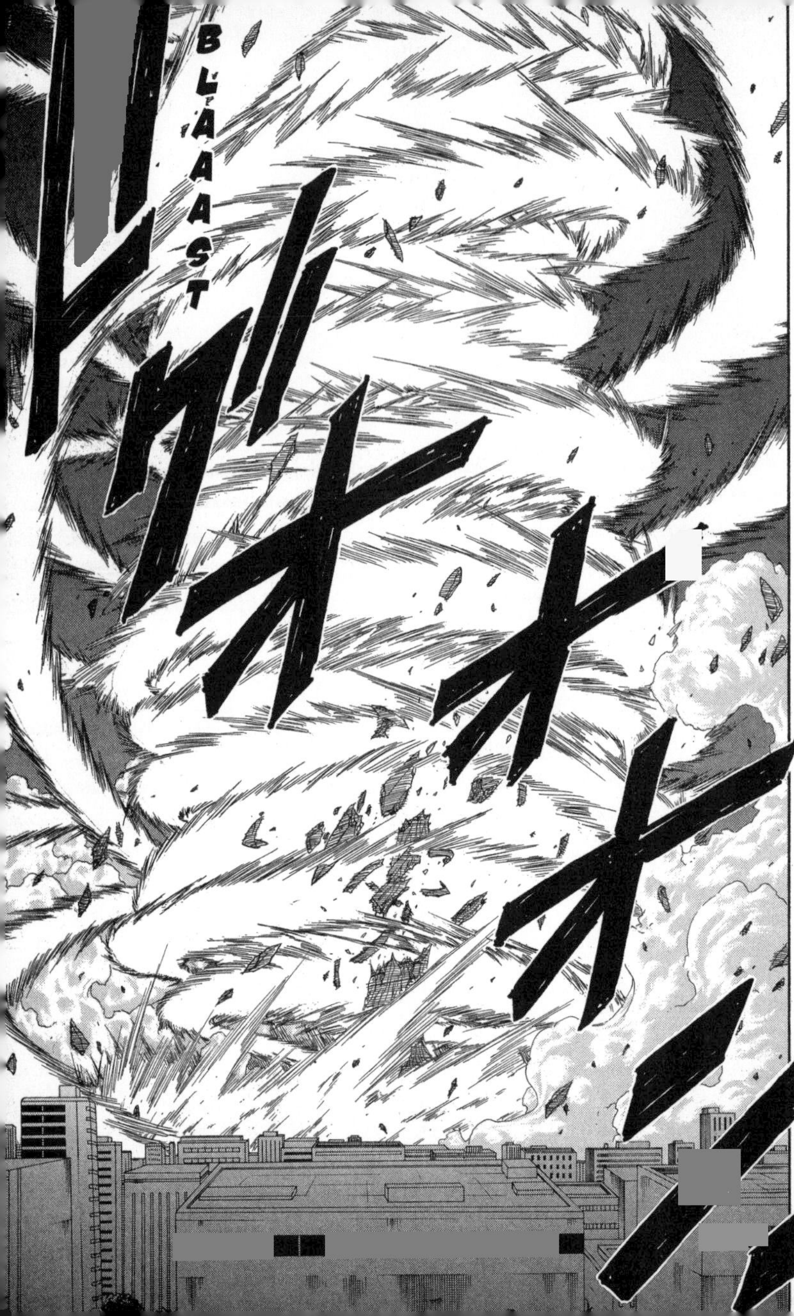
BLAAAST

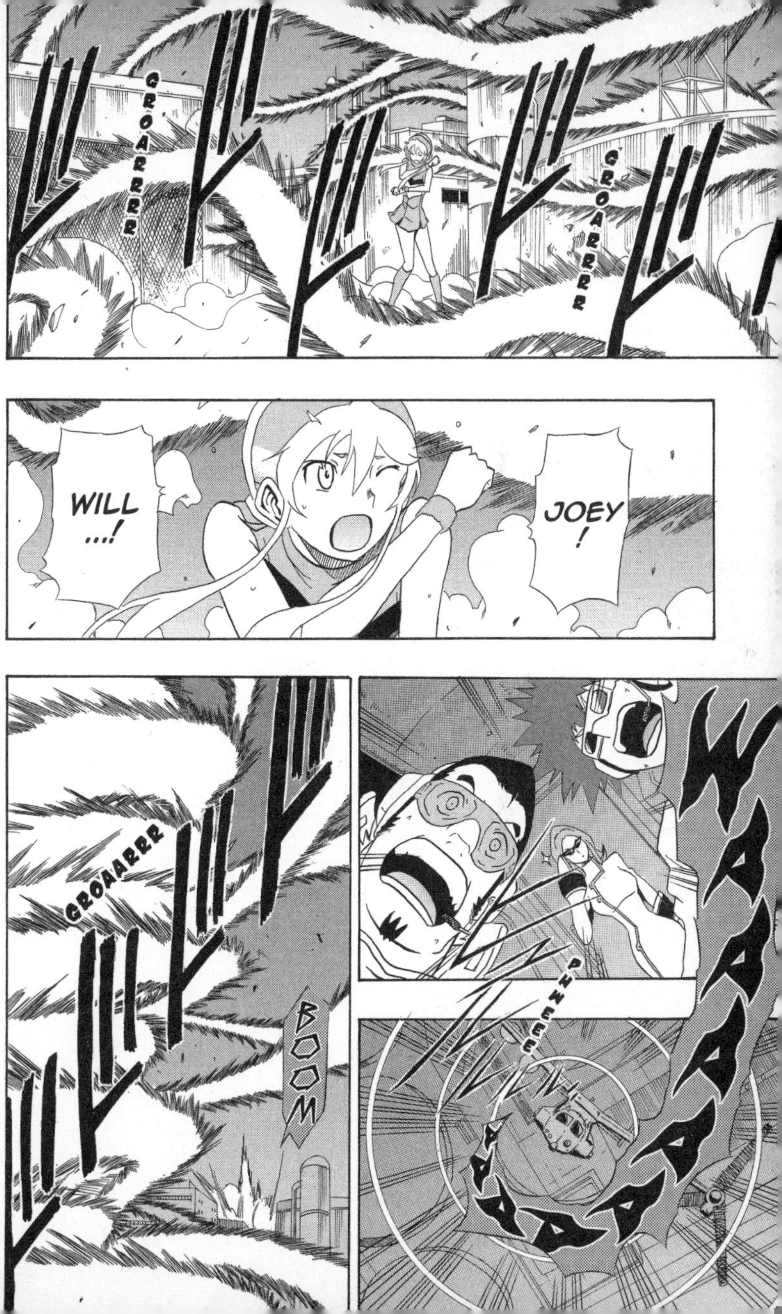
GROARRRR
GROARRRR
JOEY!
WILL...!
WAAAAAAAA
PWHEEE
BOOM
GROAARRR

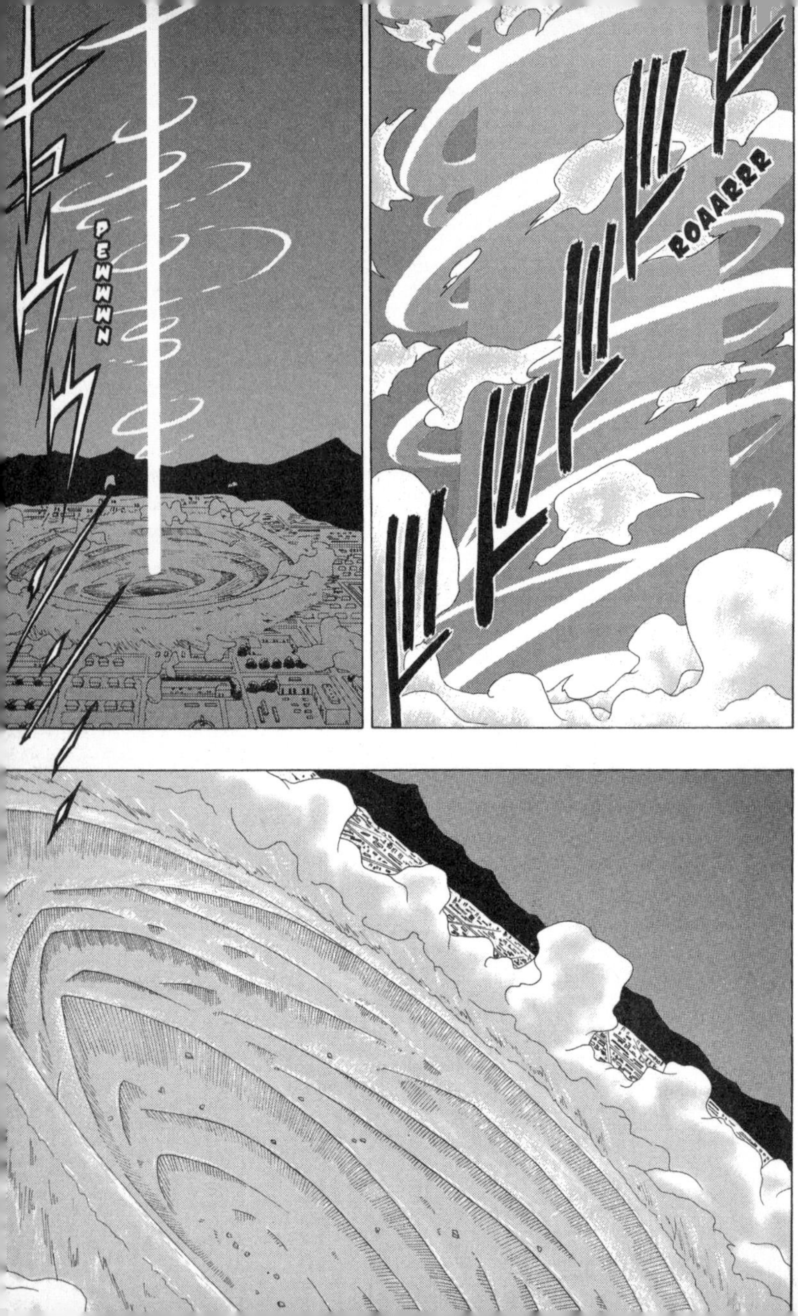
ROAAARRR
PEWWWN

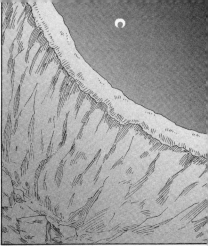

PHEW
...

I
THINK...
WE'RE
ALIVE.
Haha~

YEAH
...

VNOOSH

DOOM

188

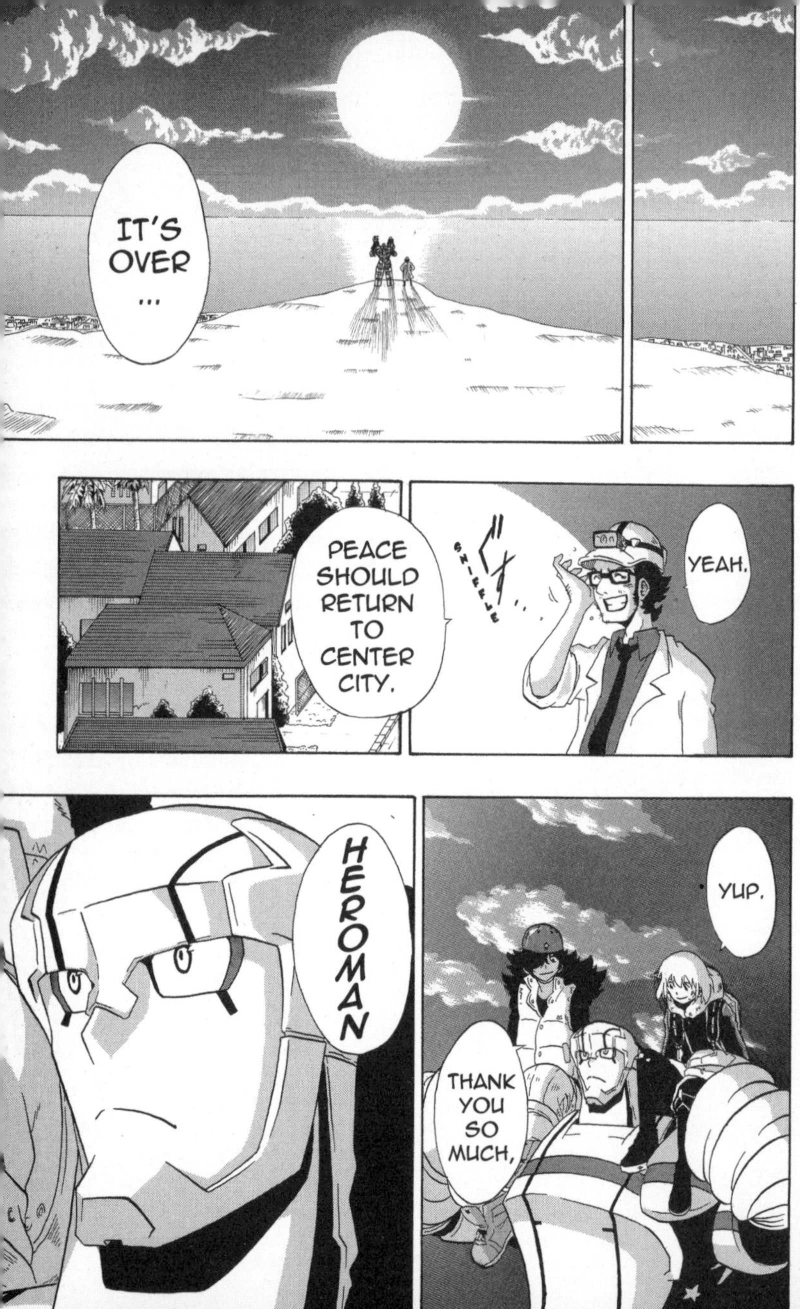
IT'S OVER ...
YEAH.
SNIFFLE
PEACE SHOULD RETURN TO CENTER CITY.
YUP.
THANK YOU SO MUCH,
HEROMAN

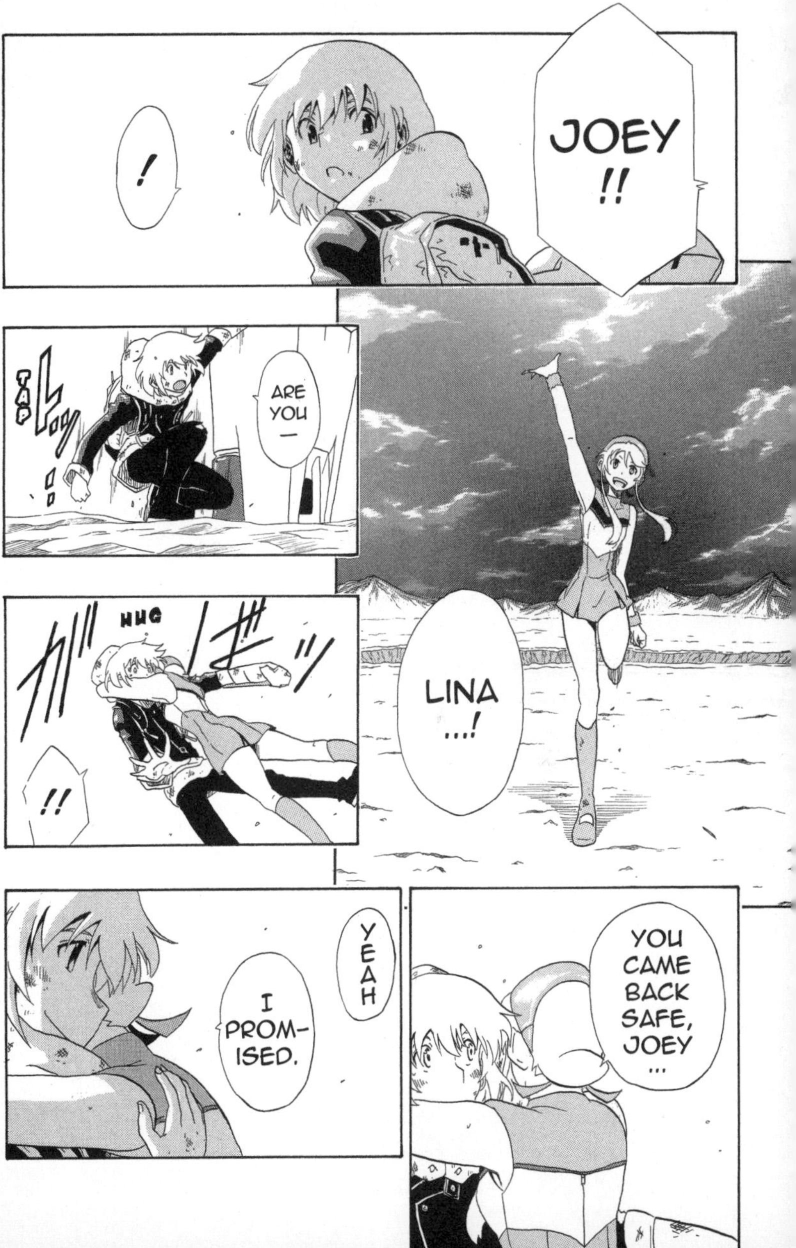

JOEY !!
!
LINA ...!
TAP
ARE YOU —
HUG
!!
YOU CAME BACK SAFE, JOEY ...
YEAH
I PROM-ISED.

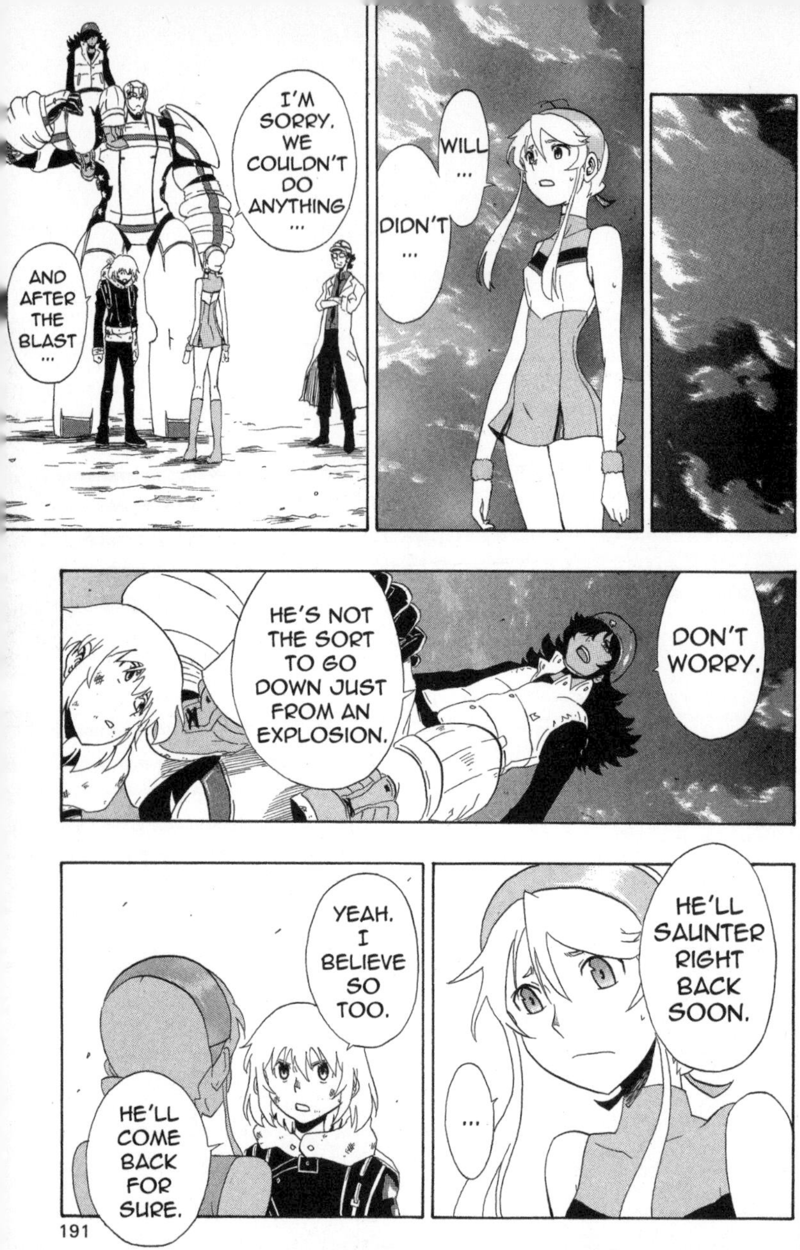
WILL ...
DIDN'T ...
I'M SORRY. WE COULDN'T DO ANYTHING ...
AND AFTER THE BLAST ...
DON'T WORRY.
HE'S NOT THE SORT TO GO DOWN JUST FROM AN EXPLOSION.
HE'LL SAUNTER RIGHT BACK SOON.
...
YEAH. I BELIEVE SO TOO.
HE'LL COME BACK FOR SURE.

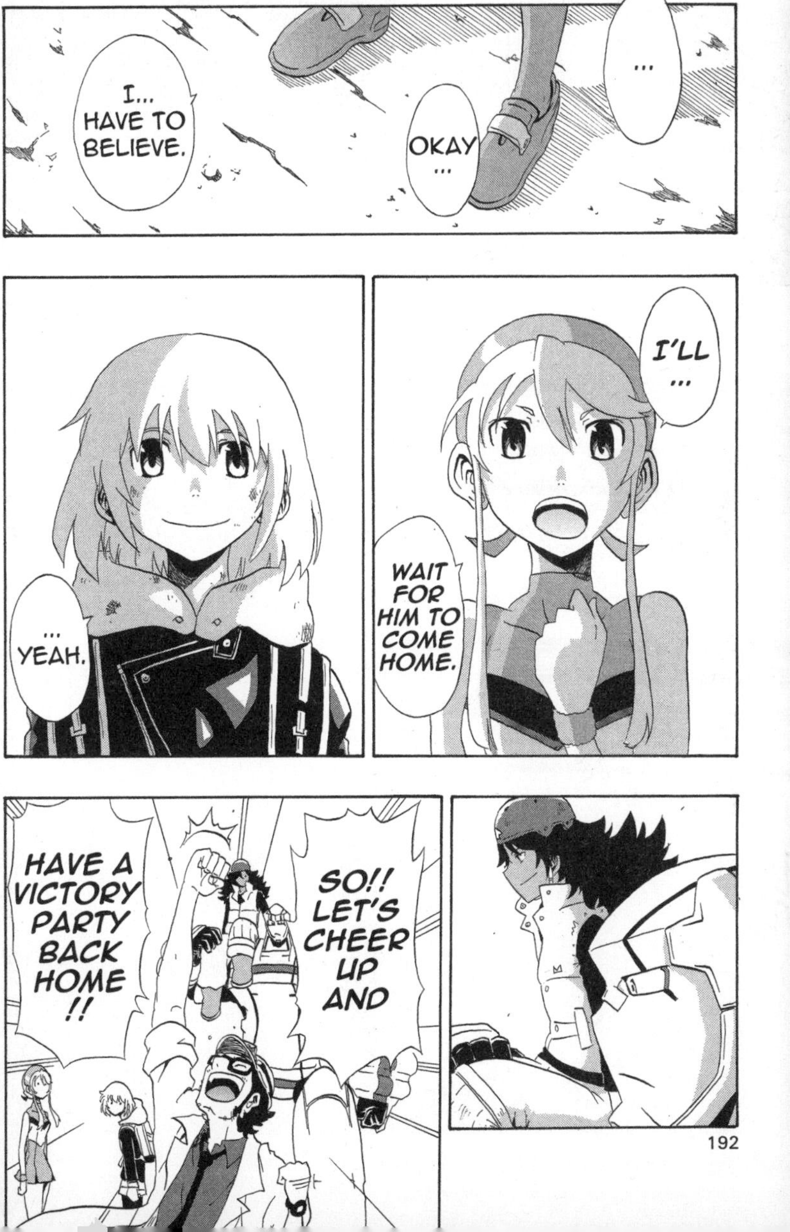
...
OKAY ...
I... HAVE TO BELIEVE.
I'LL ...
WAIT FOR HIM TO COME HOME.
... YEAH.
SO!! LET'S CHEER UP AND
HAVE A VICTORY PARTY BACK HOME !!

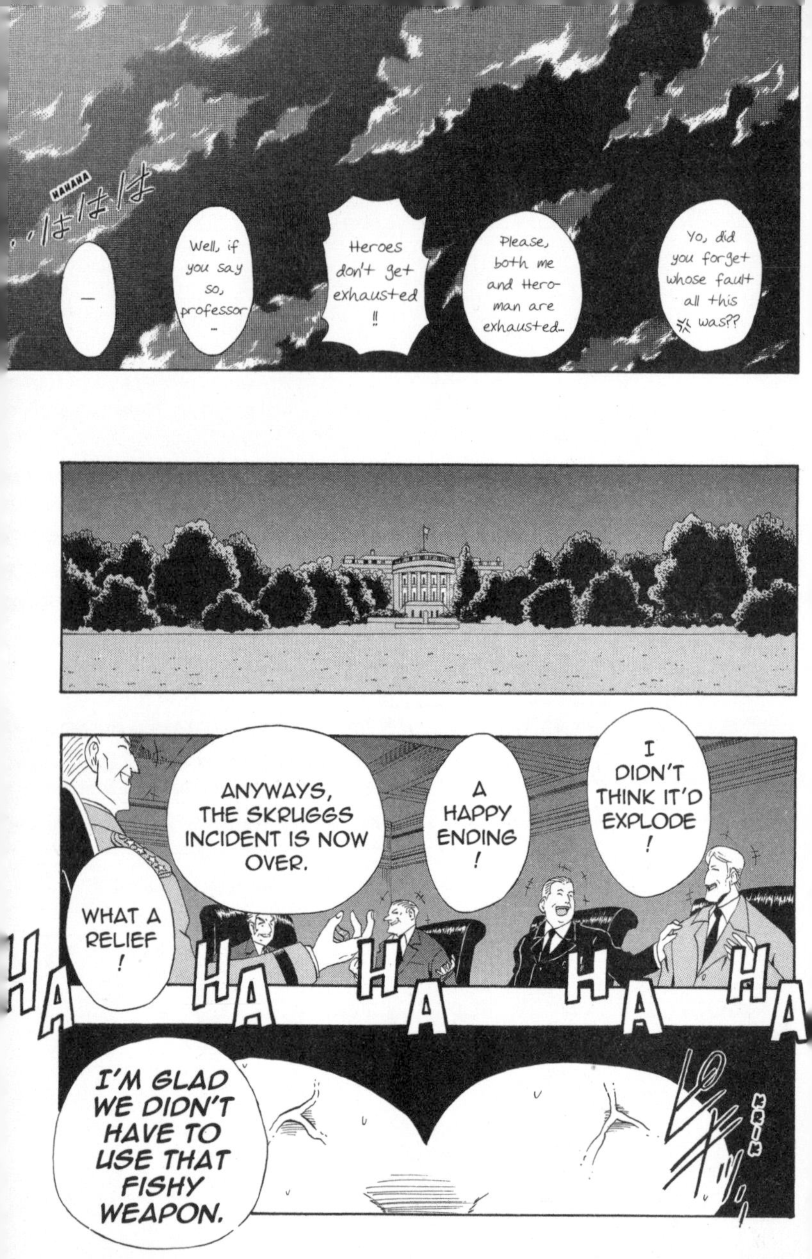
Yo, did you forget whose fault all this was??
Please, both me and Hero-man are exhausted...
Heroes don't get exhausted!!
Well, if you say so, professor...
—
HAHAHA
..ははは
I DIDN'T THINK IT'D EXPLODE!
A HAPPY ENDING!
ANYWAYS, THE SKRUGGS INCIDENT IS NOW OVER.
WHAT A RELIEF!
HA HA HA HA HA
KRIK
I'M GLAD WE DIDN'T HAVE TO USE THAT FISHY WEAPON.

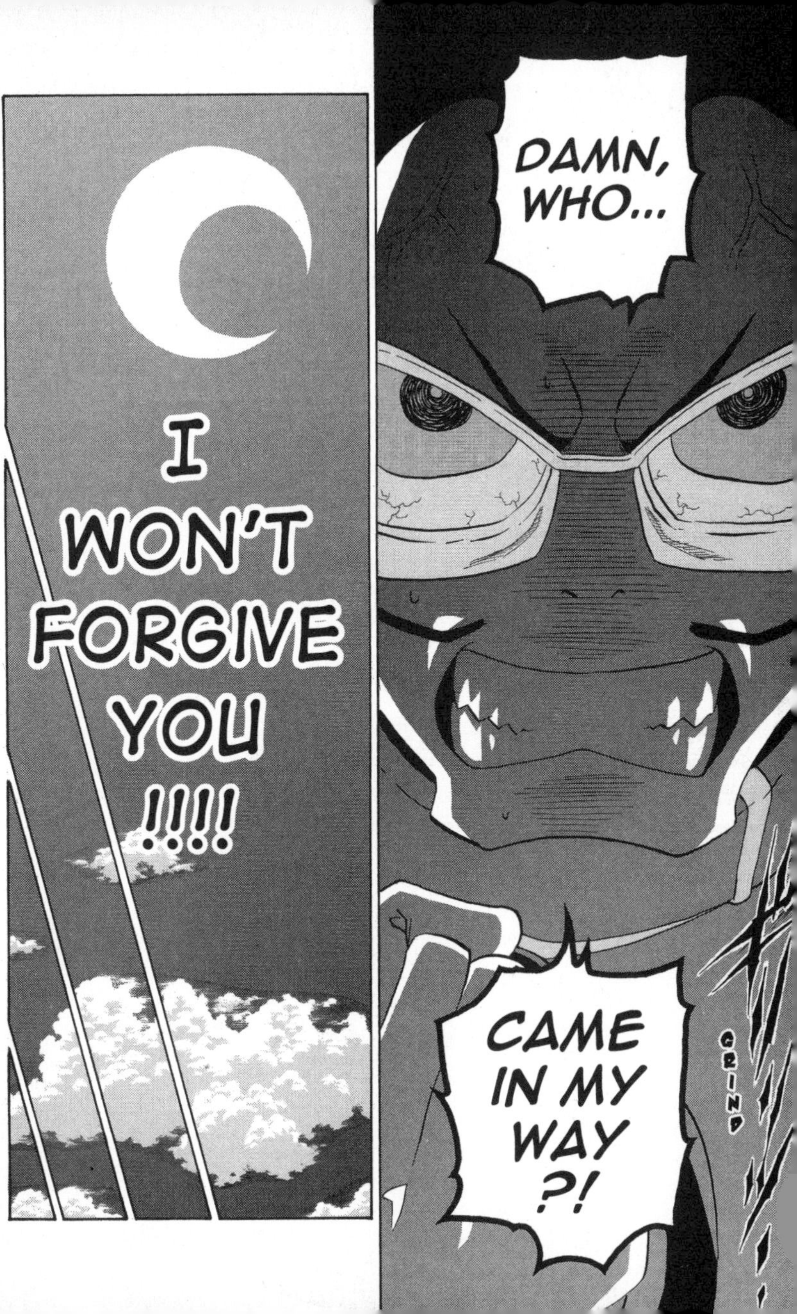
DAMN, WHO...
CAME IN MY WAY?!
GRIND
I WON'T FORGIVE YOU!!!!

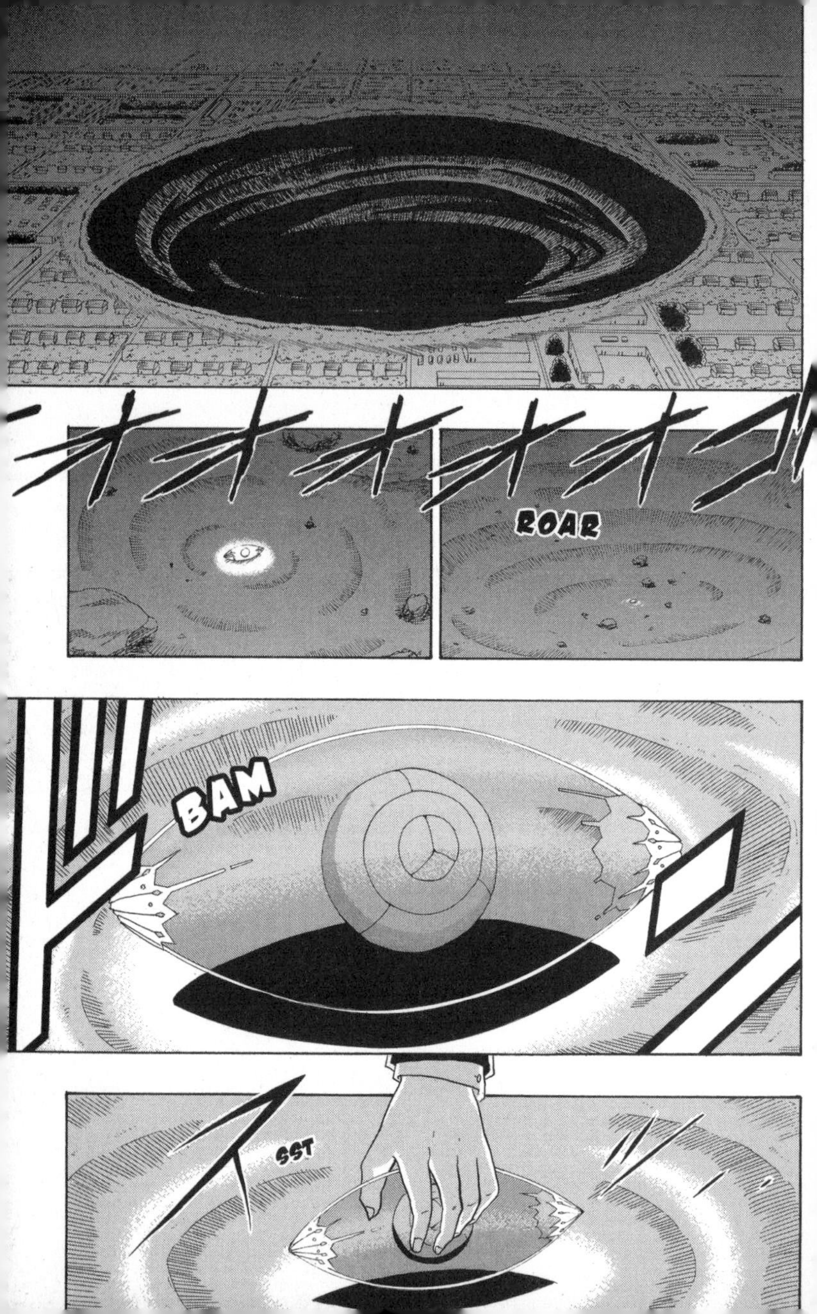
ROAR
BAM
SST

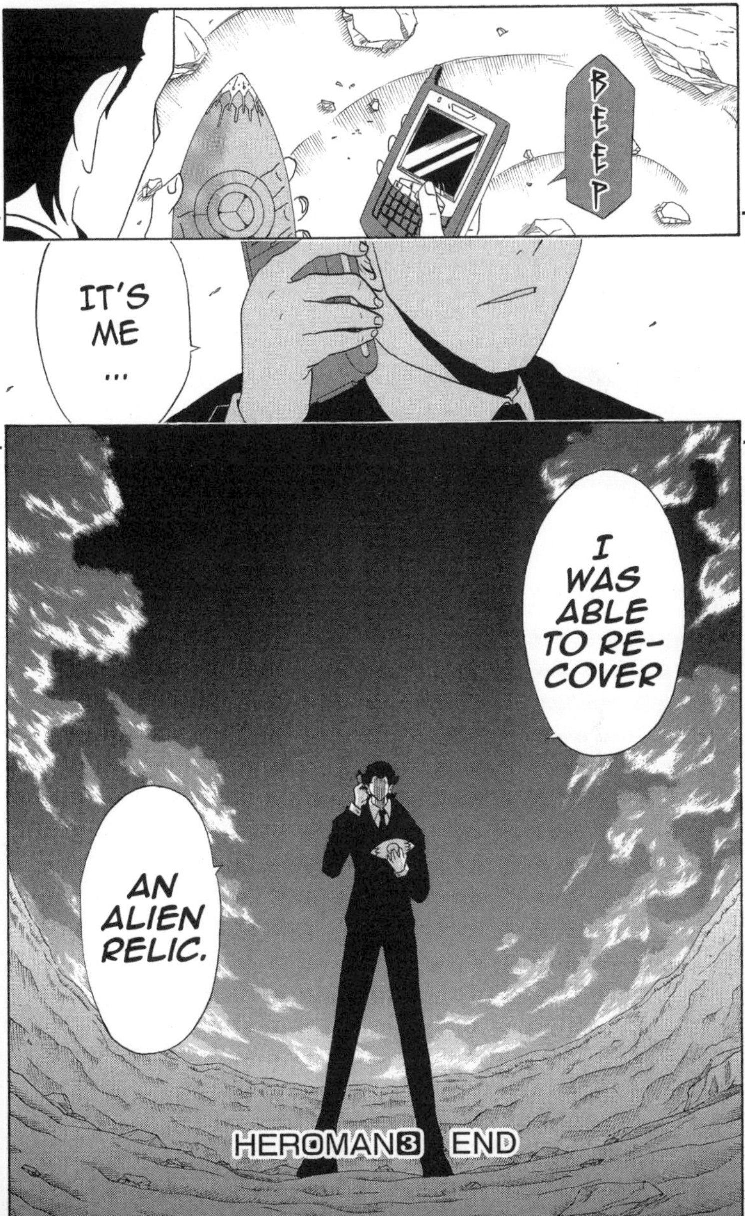
BEEP
IT'S ME ...
I WAS ABLE TO RE-COVER
AN ALIEN RELIC.
HEROMAN 3 END

VOLUME 4
COMING THIS
SPRING!

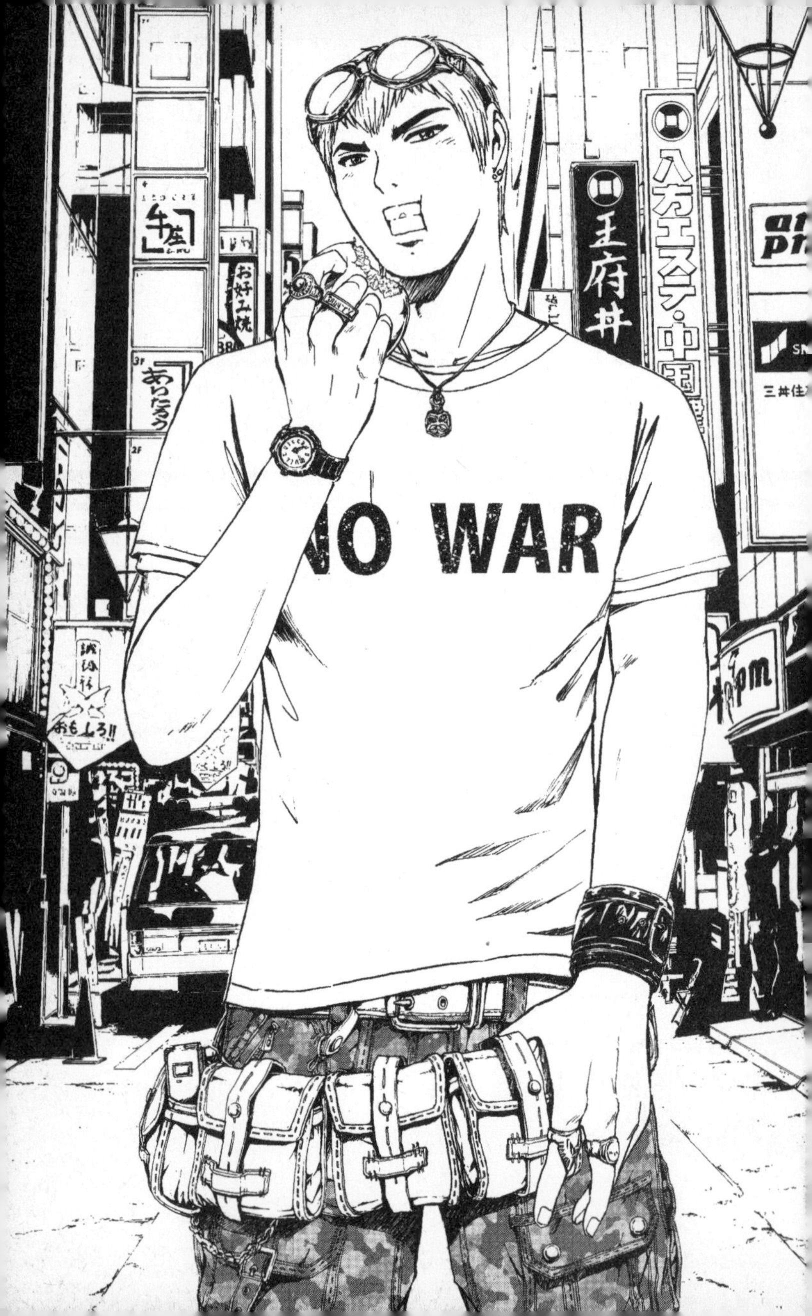
NO WAR
お好み焼
王府井
おもしろ!!

Heroman, volume 3

Translation: Yoshito Hinton
Production: Hiroko Mizuno
            Nicole Dochych
            Daniela Yamada
            Jeremy Kahn

Copyright © 2010 Tamon Ohta / SQUARE ENIX Co., Ltd.
© B.P.W. / HEROMAN PRODUCTION COMMITTEE / TV TOKYO
All Rights Reserved.

First published in Japan in 2010 by SQUARE ENIX CO., LTD.
English translation rights arranged with SQUARE ENIX CO., LTD. and Vertical, Inc.
through Tuttle-Mori Agency, Inc.

Translation provided by Vertical, Inc., 2013
Published by Vertical, Inc., New York

Originally published in Japanese as *HEROMAN 3* by Square Enix Co., Ltd.
First serialized in *Gekkan Shounen GanGan*, 2009-2011

This is a work of fiction.

ISBN: 978-1-935654-66-7

Manufactured in Canada

First Edition

Vertical, Inc.
451 Park Avenue South
7th Floor
New York, NY 10016
www.vertical-inc.com

D0003836